Unlikely Radicals

Irish Post-Primary Teachers and the ASTI

1909–2009

Unlikely Radicals

Irish Post-Primary Teachers and the ASTI

1909–2009

John Cunningham

CORK
CUP
UNIVERSITY
PRESS

First published in 2009 by
Cork University Press
Youngline Industrial Estate
Pouladuff Road
Togher
Cork
Ireland

© John Cunningham, 2009

British Library Cataloguing in Publication Data
A CIP catalogue record for this book is available from the British Library

Hardback ISBN 978-185918-460-8
Paperback ISBN 978-185918-470-7

Printed by Gutenberg Press, Malta

Contents

Foreword

In this year marking the centenary of the foundation of the ASTI, we celebrate the work of ASTI members who served their communities and served the ASTI: the thousands of teachers who gave of their time, energy, ideas and talents to serve their fellow teachers and to promote education.

The ASTI has a noble and, of course, an occasionally turbulent history. Because education is so intimately linked with human and, indeed, social developments, its history is interwoven with the major movements in our broader social history. Thus in this history we find the ASTI featuring not only in the great struggle for improvement in the terms and conditions of employment of trade union members but also in the contestation between Church and state for control of education, in the great move for economic expansion assisted by the introduction of free second-level education in 1968 and in the development of Ireland as a modern European state. Seen from this perspective, *Unlikely Radicals: Irish Post-Primary Teachers and the ASTI, 1909–2009* is at one and the same time a history of teaching, a history of education and a social history.

But amidst all of this turbulent history, leavened with some victories, the occasional setback, and robust engagement both internally and externally, we must remember the centrality of the teacher in his or her classroom and the quality of the engagement with his or her pupils. And there is a proud tradition in our schools that this engagement is founded not on a mechanical transmission of knowledge (though this has its place) but on a respect for the dignity of each pupil that we teach and a desire to open their minds to the world and to better their lives.

I remember as a pupil in Callan CBS in Kilkenny being taught *Mo Scéal Féin*, written by An tAthair Peadar Ó Laoghaire. I recall the section in which he describes the delights of a teacher and pupils working together in harmony and how I felt that that was exactly what was happening at that moment in the classroom I was in. We must always endeavour to foster this engagement and to support it in all our negotiations on terms and conditions of employment.

As teachers, we are always optimistic. Our founding members, who first sowed the seeds of the ASTI in the College of Commerce in Cork and then founded the ASTI at a meeting in the Mansion House, Dublin, 100 years ago, were people who believed in service to their community and in solidarity with their fellow teachers. That is what we do as teachers and as members of the ASTI: we serve our communities in solidarity with our colleagues. And what a proud tradition this is – the tradition of P.J. Kennedy, our first president, Thomas Mac-

Donagh, Hanna Sheehy-Skeffington, and taoiseach and president of Ireland, Éamon de Valera.

In this time of recession, we have good reason to be concerned about the well-being of our education system but I have no doubt that the ASTI will face the challenge and continue to work for education. The value of a history such as this is that it allows us to see our present issues in the light of past endeavours. Inspired by the struggles of our forebears, the ASTI will continue to serve education and serve our teachers.

JOHN WHITE
General Secretary
ASTI

Acknowledgements

This work was commissioned in 2006 to mark the centenary of the ASTI, and it could not have been completed on time without the efforts of a great number of people.

I am indebted to the custodians, past and present, of the extensive ASTI archives, and also to the many who have written previously about the Association and about post-primary education. That secondary teachers are very interested in the history of their Association is indicated, in the first instance, by the fact that this is the second volume on the subject in a relatively short period – John Coolahan's fine study having appeared as recently as 1984. It is further indicated by the remarkable number of ASTI presidents and other leading members who have produced scholarly work which illuminates its history, including in recent decades David Barry, Louis O'Flaherty, Michael McCann, Sheila Parsons, Pierce Purcell and Padraig Ó Riordáin.

I wish to express my gratitude to the members of the Central Executive Council of the ASTI, who entrusted me with their centenary history, and to the staff and officers of the Association who were welcoming during my visits to head office and convention, who were extremely accommodating in facilitating my research, and who were always prompt in responding to my queries. I thank especially those with whom I had most contact: John White, general secretary; Moira Leydon, assistant general secretary; Gemma Tuffy, communications officer; Brigid Fitzgerald; and Sheila Parsons, president 2005–06.

I would also like to express my profound gratitude to Paul Michael Garrett and to Gearóid Ó Tuathaigh, colleagues at NUI Galway and good friends, who read drafts and offered welcome guidance. Also generous with their time and perceptive in their comments were Mary Cunningham (as always), Brian Hanney and Ciarán Ó Murchadha. Other friends, colleagues and family members who helped in various ways include Fergus Campbell, Caitríona Clear, Katie Cunningham, Liam Cunningham, Jim Donnelly, Steve Ellis, Alison Forrestal, Gerry Glynn, Phil Glynn, Alf MacLochlainn, Gerry Moran, Dáibhí Ó Cróinín, Brendan O'Mahony, Vera Orschel and Tony Varley.

The following ASTI members generously lent material that was in their possession: Michael Corley, Tommy Francis, Carmel Heneghan, John Mulcahy, Louis O'Flaherty, Pierce Purcell, Kathleen Ryder, and Michael Waddell. I am grateful also to those who agreed to be interviewed for the project, whose names are listed separately in the bibliography at the back of the book.

I thank Brendan Byrne, Ed Penrose and my other colleagues on the committee of the Irish Labour History Society who were most accommodating in facilitating my research on the records of the ASTI which are held in the Labour History Archive in the Beggars Bush Barracks. I am grateful too to the staff of the James Hardiman Library at NUI Galway – I particularly thank Marie Boran for her generous assistance. My gratitude also to those whose help I sought at the National Archives of Ireland, the National Library of Ireland, the St Jarlath's College archive, the UCD archives, the Galway County Libraries, the Dublin Diocesan Archives, and the Tuam Diocesan Archives.

At Cork University Press, I thank Maria O'Donovan, as well as that publisher's anonymous internal readers.

JOHN CUNNINGHAM
NUI Galway
21 September 2009

Acronyms

AIUT	Association of Intermediate and University Teachers
CBS	Christian Brothers' School
CCSS	Conference of Convent Secondary Schools
CEB	Curriculum and Examination Board
CEC	Central Executive Council
CEU	Council of Education Unions
CHA	Catholic Headmasters' Association
CIU	Congress of Irish Unions
CMC	Catholic Managerial (Consultative) Committee
CMCSS	Catholic Managerial Committee, Secondary Schools
CSSPA	Catholic Secondary School Parents' Association
CSW	Commission on the Status of Women
CTU	Council of Teachers' Unions
EI	Education International
ESRI	Economic and Social Research Institute
FIPESCO	International Federation of Secondary Teachers
FIRE	*Future Involvement of Religious in Education*
FWUI	Federated Workers' Union of Ireland
HDip	Higher Diploma in Education
IAAM	Incorporated Association of Assistant Masters
IBEC	Irish Business and Employers' Confederation
ICPSA	Irish Conference of Professional and Service Associations
ICTU	Irish Congress of Trade Unions
IFA	Irish Farmers' Association
IFUT	Irish Federation of University Teachers
INTO	Irish National Teachers' Organisation
IWWU	Irish Women Workers' Union
IRA	Irish Republican Army
ISA	Irish Schoolmasters' Association
ISSC	Interim Secondary Students' Council
ITGWU	Irish Transport and General Worker's Union
ITUC	Irish Trades Union Congress
IUSS	Irish Union of School Students
IWWU	Irish Women Workers' Union
JCCM	Joint Committee of Catholic Managers

JMB	Joint Managerial Body
LRC	Labour Relations Commission
NATFHE	National Association of Teachers in Further and Higher Education
NCCA	National Council for Curriculum and Assessment
NPCPP	National Parents' Council, Post Primary
NUJ	National Union of Journalists
OECD	Organisation for Economic Co-operation and Development
PCW	Programme for Competitiveness and Work
PESP	Programme for Economic and Social Progress
PPF	Programme for Prosperity and Fairness
RTÉ	Radio Telefís Éireann
SC	Senior Counsel
TBA	Teaching Brothers' Association
TCD	Trinity College Dublin
TD	Teachta Dála (member of parliament)
TUI	Teachers' Union of Ireland
UCC	University College Cork
UCD	University College Dublin
UCG	University College Galway
UNESCO	United Nations Educational, Scientific, and Cultural Organisation
USI	Union of Students in Ireland
VTA	Vocational Teachers' Association
WCOTP	World Confederation of the Teaching Profession
WTA	Women Teachers' Association
WUI	Workers' Union of Ireland

Part One

1

An 'outcast pedagogue'
The secondary teacher's life, *c.*1909

During the early days of the Association of Secondary Teachers, Ireland (ASTI), the feminist campaigner and writer Hanna Sheehy Skeffington drew attention to the position of women secondary teachers in Catholic schools – in her own experience as one of them, the 'most harassed and exploited class in the whole country'.[1] Distinguishing between the categories of 'intern' and 'extern', she described the conditions of each. Those who were interns, living in their workplace on modest salaries, had challenging schedules and precarious prospects:

> In return for a fixed sum the teacher devotes practically her whole time to her pupils, teaching or supervising their studies, eating, playing, and walking with them. She keeps convent hours, and is as entirely shut off from the outer world as if she were herself a cloistered nun. Her tenure of office is usually a yearly one, but may be terminated at any time without notice. Her salary is not increased as she gains experience ... Frequently, she instructs the nuns, and, having equipped them in certain subjects, she finds her place filled by her pupils. Sometimes her pupils enter the convent and supersede her.[2]

The hourly-paid extern Catholic woman teacher had more personal freedom, but her security was no greater, and she was left unpaid during 'holidays, convent retreats, feast days, and the like'.[3] In Protestant schools, although there was little risk of being supplanted by a nun, there was nonetheless intense competition for positions.

As one experienced teacher, Elizabeth Boyd of the Raphoe Royal School, related:

> A principal of a school can get teachers for a small salary, because some of them come and take the salary just as pocket money; it is only a kind of temporary thing with them; and good teachers who are dependent upon teaching for their means of earning their living are obliged to take the work at the same rate as these other teachers. I myself was offered £40 non resident ...[4]

For many women in education, their sense of grievance was compounded by the fact that they were routinely paid less than men for doing what was essentially the same work.[5] But the position of male teachers in Catholic schools was also far from satisfactory, as was indicated by a remark from another radical commentator and educator of the period: 'We are all alive to the truth that a teacher ought to be paid better than a policeman, and to the scandal of the fact that many an able and cultured man is working in Irish secondary schools at a salary less than that of the viceroy's chauffeur.'[6] The writer was Pádraic Pearse.

Teachers' memoirs of the period support the assertions of Sheehy Skeffington, Boyd, and Pearse with regard to pay and job security, although they also reveal that the life of the early twentieth-century teacher had its compensations. In 1909, Micheál Breathnach (a future secretary of the Department of Education and a writer in Irish), having recently graduated from University College Galway, joined the staff of St Flannan's College, Ennis, where four of his five colleagues were priests. With minimal experience and no training, he struggled to devise a serviceable teaching methodology, an endeavour in which he later realised some teachers were more successful than others.[7] Having enjoyed no-holds-barred games of football and handball with his students, and having got on well with the good-humoured president of the college, who encouraged him as a teacher and introduced him to the writing of Mark Twain, he was hopeful that his post would become a permanent one. However, on an Ennis railway platform at the end of the academic year, the president gave him disappointing news. There was no criticism of his work, he was reassured, but the circum-

stances with regard to finance were so precarious that he could be
given no definite promise of employment for the following year.
Incidentally, it is probable that the platform conversation described
by Breathnach was not the first such, for the records show that he
was the twelfth short-serving lay teacher in St Flannan's during the
first decade of the twentieth century. And that financial precari-
ousness was the norm in such establishments is indicated by circumstances at around that time in another diocesan college with
which Breathnach had a personal association, St Jarlath's of Tuam.
At that institution, debts were serviced and expenses met from a
number of not-consistently-dependable sources: the fees of students, results fees from the Intermediate Board, grants from other
state and public bodies, an annual levy on diocesan clergy, and
'burses' created by the wills of priests and other pious Catholics.
The detail would have been of no particular interest to young
Breathnach, and by the time a job offer did arrive from Ennis in
September, he had found apparently more remunerative employment in a grinding establishment that prepared young men for examinations. There, however, he encountered another occupational
hazard when he was fired for insisting that he be paid the contracted
amount.[8] Breathnach's mixed feelings about his experience were
echoed in the memoir of Joe O'Connor, a near contemporary at St
Brendan's College, Killarney:

> Though I had no hope of promotion from the ranks and was
> often put to the pin of my collar to make ends meet, I was al-
> ways as happy as Larry when at work. The priests on the staff
> were a band of brothers, and the successive headmasters real
> foster fathers to me ... The only easement they did not give me
> was a living wage.[9]

The casual character of employment arrangements meant that
secondary teachers were regularly on the move. As one of their
number put it: 'No degree of efficiency ... no amount of devotion
to his work, no conduct, however satisfactory, guarantees him security of tenure.' During summer holidays, even established teachers were inclined to 'start at the postman's knock, lest it be the
herald of the fatal missive' notifying them that their services were
no longer required.[10] And insecurity brought with it the challenge

of having to settle regularly in unfamiliar towns, far from friends and family. Gregarious men like O'Connor and Breathnach would probably have adapted easily anywhere, but loneliness and isolation was the lot of many, especially of women, who were subject to more social restrictions than men. One young teacher, Eileen Gould, wrote from a temporary abode, according to the account of her future husband, Sean O'Faolain, 'with a brilliant and hideous vividness, born of a terror that she might never escape from it, or if she did, it would be to another, identical Ballinasloe'. In different circumstances, the wide street, the surrounding bog, the seemingly immovable blanket of cloud would not have seemed so oppressive, but there were few distractions in the midland town. Her digs were in a lodging house, which was otherwise patronised by male bank clerks, members of another peripatetic profession, and she did not feel at ease beside the small parlour fireplace, so each evening after tea, she withdrew to her room to spend cold lonely hours by herself. For every Breathnach hoping to have a contract extended, there must have been a sensitive soul like Gould – discomfited by the banter of bank clerks; dismayed when a landlady displayed the flowers sent by her fiancé in a jamjar – looking forward to the end of the academic year, and to the possibility of finding a position in a more congenial place.[11]

'Stipend, fee, honorarium'

The well-attested poverty of teachers was relative, though no less severely felt for that. They were generally well-educated, with about 40 per cent of them being drawn from the small cohort of university graduates, and they had expectations of professional status. Many had the title of 'professor' and felt obliged, not least to the institutions that employed them, to keep up middle-class appearances. But the signifiers of middle-class status – respectable dress, an acceptable address, support for local causes, maintaining a servant – were not easily afforded on salaries that were totally at the discretion of the employer and that, while varying considerably, averaged £48 a year for women and £82 for men in the early twentieth century. In the circumstances, according to an ASTI founder, it was inevitable that rosy expectations yielded to an 'ignominious acceptance of one's self as the outcast pedagogue, who had no social rating among the solid citizens of the town'.[12]

A comparison with the earnings of other occupations will place secondary teachers' salaries in context, although bald figures give an approximate picture only, since perquisites, which also varied from one occupation to another, might have a considerable effect on standards of living. With the analogous group in the primary schools – who were by no means satisfied with their own lot – the key differences lay in the existence of official salary scales and a clear career path. In the early years of the twentieth century, male salaries in the national school sector ran from £56 to £175, and female from £44 to £141, and although only a minority working in larger schools could ever reach the top of the scale, average earnings were probably at least a quarter higher than those of secondary teachers until an increase in 1907–08 widened the gap further.[13] In the Royal Irish Constabulary at this time, rank-and-file 'peelers' earned between £39 and £72, and sergeants up to £78, indicating that Pearse was accurate only to the extent that some policemen earned more than some secondary teachers. In domestic service, the major employer of women, average annual earnings varied between £11 a year for housemaids and £40 for cook/housekeepers. Among males, a regularly employed Dublin building tradesman might earn up to £100 a year, while a Dublin building labourer, in the admittedly unlikely event that he had constant work, might earn as much as £50.[14]

As a 'respectable working man', the typical tradesman had social aspirations higher than those of the labourer, but the standards that society set for him were less expensive to maintain than those it set for the secondary teacher. And in budgeting to keep up appearances, the tradesman had the benefit of weekly pay, which was not usually the case for the 'professor'. In his first teaching position with the Christian Brothers in Sullivan's Quay in Cork, Joe O'Connor's wage of fifteen shillings a week was paid at noon every Saturday, just as a building worker's might have been. Unlike a building worker's, however, his pay came in the unusual shape of a long white cylinder – contrived from a plain sheet of paper wrapped around sixty of the 3d. coins known as 'thrupenny bits' that his pupils paid each week for their tuition. All but eight of these small coins were required for the rent of the room over a back-street pub that was recommended by his employer. When, after a few months in Cork, O'Connor was recruited by his alma mater, St Brendan's, Killarney, he looked forward to the comforts he might enjoy on a salary of £80 a year. But when he arrived at the college, he discovered that he was to be paid quarterly – an arrangement intended to demonstrate, he observed, 'that the august staff of the diocesan college were not teachers earning a weekly wage but professors enjoying a quarterly stipend, fee, honararium, or whatever you like to call the remuneration given to professional gentlemen in the upper strata of society'.[15]

As a single man, O'Connor was able to get by, supplementing his income by selling the cups and medals he won at summertime village sports to an acquaintant jeweller and, on his marriage, he was informed by the president that the bishop had given permission for his salary to be raised to £100. 'Could you ever pay me weekly?' was his response to the news. The president could not, but he did agree to pay him at the end of each month. Finding, as time went on, that the monthly £8 and some shillings was inadequate, he made several unsuccessful requests for a raise and, eventually, when he threatened to resign, the president offered to schedule his classes to finish at 1.30 p.m. each day, so that he might have an opportunity to supplement his income. In his colourful way, the multi-talented O'Connor described his subsequent fortunes:

> From that onwards, I was like the Gobadawn that worked double tides on the strand. In the morning I was the Professor; in the evening, I was Jack-of-all-Trades. I valued farms for the land court, designed shop fronts for expanding drapers, made illustrations for magazine stories, and prepared elaborate maps of estates under the Land Purchase acts. But it was all in vain. The fees were small and the jobs infrequent.[16]

It was sheer necessity that compelled O'Connor to turn his hand to such diverse endeavours – and not every teacher would have had the chutzpah or the skills to do the same – but the range of experience he described must have made for an interesting life (and probably for an interesting teacher). And on the face of it, there are echoes of O'Connor's account of his 'Gobadawn' existence in Karl Marx's description of life in an ideal society, 'where nobody has one exclusive sphere of activity, but each can become accomplished in any branch he wishes', where it would be possible 'to do one thing today and another tomorrow, to hunt in the morning, fish in the afternoon, rear cattle in the evening, criticise after dinner ... without ever becoming hunter, fisherman, herdsman or critic'.[17]

If it was difficult to make ends meet on a St Brendan's salary, salaries at more prestigious Dublin schools were not much better. The maximum at Castleknock College, which considered itself 'generous' to its lay teachers, was £120 a year in 1915 and greater caution, apparently, was required of those seeking to improve their situation there than was required in Killarney. That a simple request from one Castleknock teacher for an increase to £110 from £90 was not well-received is indicated by the record of the response: 'It was thought that it would be better to give him a month's notice and look for a high-class teacher.'[18]

Intermediate Education

So why was it that the earnings of secondary teachers in 1909 compared poorly with those of tradesmen and chauffeurs? And, more significantly, why were these teachers worse off in most respects than their colleagues in the national schools? To answer these questions, indeed to understand why secondary teachers had been unable successfully to assert themselves collectively up to that point, it is necessary to examine the origins and development of the secondary education system in Ireland.

During most of the nineteenth century, education was a matter of contention between the state and the increasingly-assertive post-penal law Catholic Church. Long-running controversies surrounding primary and university sectors were rooted in the state's desire to exercise some control over what it paid for on the one hand, and the Catholic hierarchy's insistence on its right to oversee the education of members of its flock on the other. The major Protestant denominations, also, were alert to infringements on their educational liberties. As a result of relentless whittling on the part of the churches, the system of national education that was instituted on non-denominational lines in 1831 had been moulded into a decidedly denominational shape by the end of the century.[19]

That secondary education remained relatively uncontroversial for most of the century was due to the fact that it was not, by and large, in the public sphere. Protestant-endowed schools enjoyed a form of public funding, but most of the colleges, schools, academies, and seminaries, offering what was sometimes described as a 'superior' education, depended on the fees paid by their students and they set their own examinations and their own standards. It was a patchy and deficient network that developed, however, and most interested parties came to accept that it was in need of reform, or at least of investment.[20]

The significant legislation that shaped secondary education was the Intermediate Education (Ireland) Act, 1878, a product of the ongoing struggle for hegemony between the Catholic Church and the British state. Government sought some form of accountability before it could agree to publicly fund schools, but, for the Irish bishops, notwithstanding their anxiety to secure a fresh source of funding for their schools, the conventional form of accountability, which was school inspection, represented unacceptable state 'interference' in Catholic education. A compromise was found in the model operating on the predominantly Catholic British colony of Trinidad, where state support rewarded performance in public examinations. The French Holy Ghost Fathers, who ran elite second-level colleges in both British-controlled jurisdictions, were influential advocates of a similar system for Ireland.[21]

Under the provisions of the 1878 legislation for Ireland, accordingly, state funding for schools came in the form of premiums based on students' performance in the intermediate examinations. (There were premiums also for successful students, but, it was often remarked, none for teachers.) Against the wishes of the Catholic bishops, girls were allowed to compete. A fiercely competitive system evolved in the decades following the legislation, with exams at preparatory, junior, middle and senior grades, and with growing numbers of boys and girls competing against one another and against the Intermediate Board, which was obliged by its declining budget to relentlessly raise standards.[22] The maximum value of the 'exhibitions' that could be earned by a student was reduced early in the twentieth century, from £40 to £30, although this was still a relatively generous amount, as an anonymous 'Intermediate Teacher' complained in 1911, by comparison with the average annual salary of £48 earned by women teachers.[23]

From 1890, the board's principal source of income was the so-called 'whiskey money', proceeds of an excise tax on spirits, but because Irish drinkers were switching to beer, this generated in 1909 only two-thirds of what it had generated in 1900.[24]

By the new century, intermediate schooling had become the emblematic element of an education system described by Pearse as a 'murder machine' – an oppressive regime, he wrote, where 'the programme bulks so large that there is no room for education'.[25] Pearse was by no means the only critic. Indeed, people at all levels of the system expressed reservations, from secondary teachers and those who trained them, to members of the Intermediate Board itself. For W.J.M. Starkie, Catholic ex-president of Queen's College Galway and a noted writer on Irish education, who would be appointed chairman of the Intermediate Board in 1911, the principal defect of the system was that it served to discourage the development of a secondary teaching profession offering 'an attractive and remunerative career to able and energetic laymen'.[26]

In the opinion of ex-Irish Nationalist MP Frank Hugh O'Donnell (known as 'Crank Hugh'), the system gave too much control to the unworldly religious:

> Goody-goodyness, and superficiality and helplessness, trumpery accomplishments, and total unfitness for home and wifehood, these appear to be the darling objects of the saintly and incompetent sisterhoods, who, having foresworn the knowledge and use of the world, devote themselves, for a modest remuneration, to the misinformation and depreparation of the future wives and mothers of the country.[27]

There were other critics of convent second-level schools who, like O'Donnell, lamented their emphasis on 'accomplishment' rather than solid academic achievement.[28] A rather different view of intermediate education was held by some of those involved in the education of girls. For Alice Oldham, sometime secretary of the Central Association of Irish Schoolmistresses, the system – flawed as it was – had 'revolutionised girls' schools by giving them a wide and valuable programme of studies, a high standard of efficiency, and sorely-needed endowment'.[29] In intermediate education at least, females were not as disadvantaged as they were in other fields of public endeavour.

And, as regards comments like O'Donnell's, they were exceptional in the early twentieth century, for nationalists, even the few Protestants among them, were rarely as outspokenly critical of

11

Catholic institutions as he was. That saintly sisterhoods, and brotherhoods for that matter, had a role in education was taken for granted, although the nature of Catholic ambition in education was not always fully appreciated.

Direct state involvement in education had been vigorously opposed by Cardinal Cullen, archbishop of Dublin between 1852 and 1878 and widely regarded as the most influential Irish churchman of the nineteenth century. As Emmet Larkin has authoritatively argued, Cullen was opposed 'not just to state control over education, but any form of lay control over education, whether English or Irish'.[30] The attitude of his successors was to be the same. Given the circumstances during Cullen's ascendancy, it was possible to regard his efforts to assert the independence from the state of Catholic education as serving to promote home rule in the educational sphere, so they had broad support in the nationalist community.

Cullen and those in his circle were distrustful of the political home rulers of their day, but in the post-Cullen era the hierarchy reached an accommodation with Parnell and his party, amounting to a 'clerical-Nationalist alliance' in Larkin's phrase. There were political advantages for the party in securing a benevolent recognition of its bona fides from the bishops, but part of the price was to guarantee to support the Catholic view on education in parliament.[31] After Parnell's fall, nationalist MPs continued to support the hierarchy on education, and public dissent in the matter was infrequent within the nationalist constituency, even from those adhering to the ostensibly secular republican tradition. Due to another element of Cullen's legacy – his imposition of a rigid discipline within the Church – there was rarely any ambiguity about the Catholic perspective. The bishops determined that position, and, in all essential matters, the responsibility of subordinate agencies, such as those representing school authorities, was to support it. With regard to non-essential matters, authority was widely diffused, something which was to prove frustrating for teachers' union representatives and others involved in negotiations with Catholic agencies.[32]

Towards the intermediate system itself, the impression is of continuing relative satisfaction as far as the Catholic authorities were concerned. Cardinal Logue stated as much in 1898: 'With regards to Intermediate Education, very little fault can be found with it as a general system. I think it is one instance in which they try to give us what we want.'[33] From time to time, it will be seen that the bishops did join with other critics, but their principal focus was on the undeniable under-funding of Irish secondary education rather than on anything structural. It has been argued by Brian Titley that the Irish bishops in fact took a certain pride in the system, regarding it as substantially their own creation, and they certainly took some pleasure from the fact that the original seed capital came from funds freed up by the disestablishment of the Church of Ireland in 1870. Whether or not the bishops felt that they had a proprietorial duty to protect intermediate education is a moot point, but they were certainly wary of attempts to reform it. Reform in the early twentieth century meant giving more power to others – to the state, and perhaps to teachers – power that would be lost to the Church. The bishops' resistance to the claims of the state with regard to education was fully consistent with the policy of the Vatican in opposition to the advance of the secular state, but there was a distinctively Irish dimension to the bishops' case against reform in the early twentieth century. For, much as Cardinal Cullen had discovered half a century earlier, arguments stressing the 'foreign' and the 'Protestant' character of the alternatives continued to have more resonance among the mass of Irish Catholics than those grumbling about their 'secular' character.[34]

Post-1878, therefore, Irish secondary education was denominationally segregated as before, with schools that were funded in most cases, although in varying proportions from one to the next, by results fees from the Intermediate Board and by tuition fees from parents. It was a system which served a relatively small part of the population – less than 10 per cent of national school pupils in 1900 proceeded to second-level – and which employed about 2,000 teachers. If it is surprising that there were more Protestant (399 men; 425 women) than Catholic lay teachers (298 men; 84 women), this was partly because of the high number of Catholic religious (428 men; 344 women) who exercised their vocation in secondary schools, and partly because there was a somewhat higher demand among Protestants for post-primary education. This was a gap that was narrowing, however.[35]

In Protestant-run schools, generally, there were opportunities for advancement, but this was rarely the case in Catholic schools where all senior posts were held by diocesan clergy or members of religious orders. With religious in most of the ordinary teaching positions also, lay teachers had little leverage, which was why conditions became so unattractive and staff turnover was so high. The observation of one chairman of the Intermediate Board that 'no layman wilfully takes up teaching as a permanent career'[36] is supported by impressionistic evidence, and there are indications that a high proportion of those working as secondary teachers were doing so either because they were disqualified from, or not yet qualified for, other professions. Micheál Breathnach's colleagues in one academy, according to his memoir, were a Trinity theology graduate who had last-minute qualms about taking orders, a former civil servant sacked for drunkenness, and a man who had failed his medical exams. Among the 223 undergraduates who were employed in secondary schools in 1905, there were undoubtedly some whose studies were intended to better equip them as teachers, but an enquiry team formed the impression that many of them had 'no intention of adopting the profession permanently'. These were the 'briefless barristers, living at home … while waiting to come in for their own at the Bar' and the university students 'helping to pay for their keep by earning ten shillings a week' that Hanna Sheehy Skeffington condemned for 'keeping the professional out of a living wage'.[37]

The schools

If it is accepted that pay and prospects were poor for secondary teachers, what about the condition of their workplaces, the schools? It became possible to answer this question after a temporary system of inspection was introduced in 1902. Messrs Dale and Stephens, who were commissioned two years later to enquire into post-primary education, drew on the information gathered by the first inspectors in order to provide a description of the schools. They divided them into three categories.

Though the surroundings might be grim, Dale and Stephens found facilities to be satisfactory in the first of their categories, that of 'larger school'. There were more than a hundred of these, and their combined enrolment accounted for a majority of intermediate students. Since very large schools were few – perhaps twenty on the island had 200 on the rolls – the category comprised all schools with fifty or more students, including diocesan colleges, convent schools and larger Protestant schools. They were generally boarding schools, situated in their own grounds, and most of them had sports facilities as well as commodious classrooms that were adequately equipped and ventilated. They had libraries and laboratories, though they did not have facilities for manual instruction (woodwork/metalwork), which was more disappointing to contemporary educationists, and to 'advanced' nationalists concerned about Irish economic underdevelopment, than to the generality of parents of students at these schools.[38] If such schools represented a single category for Dale and Stephens, there were several social gradations within that category. According to one who was acquainted with the particulars of Dublin's Catholic middle-class society, places like Clongowes Wood (for boys) and Mount Anville (for girls) occupied the top tier socially, Belvedere College and the Dominican Convent, Eccles Street, were on the second level, with the various diocesan colleges and convent boarding schools being below these.[39]

The commissioners' second category, with fewer than fifty students, comprised most of the schools of the Christian Brothers and the smaller endowed Protestant schools. These were mainly day schools, which were attached to national schools, with the secondary class occupying one or two classrooms. Few had libraries, though a majority had some laboratory facilities for science, and many had taken advantage of the funding that had recently become available for the provision of manual instruction. In the third category, there were some schools that Dale and Stephens considered satisfactory, but most of them they did not. Moreover, as if to demonstrate that Catholics had no monopoly on misery in early twentieth-century Ireland, the utterly inadequate small private schools, of which a disproportionate number were located in Ulster, were patronised overwhelmingly by Protestants. Lacking playgrounds and cloakrooms, even sufficient ventilation, lighting and sanitary accommodation, these schools occupied 'such places as a single room over a shop, or behind a chapel, in a dilapidated farm house, in a low wooden shed attached to a dwelling house'. In most of them, 'walls were dirty and bare except for one or two worn maps, and the desks were of the most antiquated kind'.[40]

For Dale and Stephens, it was a flaw in the system that those responsible for it had 'not the power to refuse any grant of public money' to a school, however dilapidated or mismanaged, if some of its pupils managed to perform satisfactorily in intermediate examinations. Furthermore, as was so much else, the organisation of classes was entirely at the discretion of the individual school head. Staffs were small, so each teacher had responsibility for a range of subjects, and it was not only in the smallest schools that an individual might have to teach the full intermediate programme. In Killarney, young Joe O'Connor found himself 'in complete charge of the Juniors in every subject from Greek to Geometry', while in Roscrea, Micheál Breathnach taught English, Irish, History, Geography, and Accounting.[41]

To teach successfully, order was important, and order in the early twentieth century was synonymous with punishment. There were enlightened educationists who were opposed to the use of corporal punishment – among them Pádraic Pearse – but in most boys' schools, punishment was severe and exemplary, even if the precise means employed varied from one to the other. In St Jarlath's of Tuam, there were public floggings and canings, while at St Columba's in Dublin, there were 'penal drills' conducted by an in-house 'drill sergeant'.[42] (Former army drill sergeants were employed as physical trainers in many schools – the Laurel Hill Convent in Limerick and the St Louis Convent in Monaghan, for example – but they did not necessarily have 'penal' functions.[43]) Discipline generally was a responsibility of school authorities, but clearly lay teachers were expected to maintain order in their own classrooms. At the Cistercian College, Roscrea, Micheál Breathnach was not permitted to chastise his pupils, rather he was obliged to despatch wrongdoers with an explanatory note to the headmaster.[44] It was otherwise at St Brendan's, Killarney, and Joe O'Connor, who went on to become an inspector of schools, evidently felt no embarrassment at the end of his career in recounting how he had devised his own successful approach. Angered, during his early teaching days, that a student defied him in the classroom, he caught the offender 'by the slack of the pants and the back of the neck, swung him out of his seat, and out the large window behind him in one mad sweep'. Finding that the pupil was a considerably meeker fellow afterwards, and that his classmates became more co-operative, he was satisfied that he had accidentally discovered a 'trick of discipline'. That he consciously applied it thereafter is indicated by his shocking denouement:

Self-willed lads came to St Brendan's as to every college in the land ... I watched out for these ebullient newcomers and provoked the brashest of them to rebel when he was obviously in the wrong. Then I took him in hand and gave him the father of an all-in thrashing as an example to the rest. I never had cause to raise a hand in that class again and it came to pass that, at last, I could dispense with the premonitory thrashings altogether. A lick of my tongue was sufficient.[45]

In girls' schools, physical chastisement was unusual and discipline was maintained by the levying of fines and the issuing of severe public scoldings – terrifying to many students.[46] And staff did not always have immunity, as one young teacher at Dublin's Alexandra College discovered:

In those days, there was a fashion for wearing a velvet band to keep one's hair tidy, which I found a great help. To my horror and shame, I was stopped by [the headmistress] on the corridor and told to remove it ... Her tongue was sharp, and she was liable to walk into one's class and rebuke a girl for some fault in very harsh terms, reducing the poor girl to tears in front of her friends.[47]

Those of Alexandra College's staff who 'stood up' to the headmistress gained her respect, according to this teacher, but she emphasised that she herself was 'not one of that number'. Indeed, due to schools' recruitment policies, it was a normal occurrence that a young teacher had been a relatively recent student of the same school, making it awkward for the individuals concerned to assert themselves.

As one of subordinate status, who became accustomed to having her professional competence undermined and who was wary of the consequences of standing up for herself, the situation of Miss X in Alexandra College might be regarded as paradigmatic of that of the lay secondary teacher in early twentieth-century Ireland. To bring about improvement would require time and effort, but most of all it would require a sense of collective purpose among the 'outcast pedagogues' themselves. The next chapter will trace the gradual awakening of secondary teachers to this reality in the decades before the Anglo-Irish Treaty of 1921.

2

'Dissatisfaction with the present condition of things'

Foundation and early years of the ASTI

The genesis of the ASTI may be traced to a meeting in Cork during January 1907, which was chaired by science teacher W.D. Horgan, then of St Joseph's College, Ballinasloe, and later of Belvedere College.[1] The meeting, which was 'largely attended', according to a subsequent press statement, passed a resolution expressing dissatisfaction with the organisation purporting to represent secondary teachers, the Association of Intermediate and University Teachers (AIUT), dismissing it as a 'Dublin organisation', and demanding that it alter its constitution 'so that it shall consist of four provincial branches and a central committee consisting of members of each provincial branch'. If the Dublin body's response was to prove to be 'of an unfavourable kind', the resolution continued, the unrepresented teachers of the rest of Ireland would make their own arrangements, and 'hold meetings both at Mallow and Galway for the purpose of founding a new organisation, to be known in future as the Irish Secondary Teachers Association, a central committee to be elected at Dublin during the teachers' courses next July'.[2]

Whether the AIUT attempted to accommodate the alienated southern teachers is not known, though it can be stated that nothing substantial came immediately of the Cork ultimatum. Efforts continued, however, and letters from secondary teachers to the editors of national papers expressed frustration that no organisation existed to represent their grievances adequately .[3] The efforts culminated in Cork's College of Commerce on St Patrick's Day 1909,

18

when secondary teachers from Tipperary, Limerick, Kerry and Cork responded to an invitation issued by lay teachers at St Colman's College, Fermoy, to establish 'an association similar to the INTO'.[4]

Contacts were made with the AIUT – one presumes that the tone was more tactful than it was in 1907 – and, at its Easter 1909 meeting in Dublin, that body agreed to co-operate with the Munster initiative. The co-operation led to a meeting in the Mansion House on 10 July. If the date was chosen to facilitate teachers of art and science who were attending summer courses in Dublin, efforts had also been made to circularise every secondary teacher on the island. It was a successful meeting, and, in the words of one activist, 'a memorable one for all who were there, the crowd was so great and the atmosphere so charged with enthusiasm and derring do'.[5] Thus was founded the Association of Secondary Teachers, Ireland. Before proceeding with its story, however, it is essential to look backwards, and to briefly trace the history of the ASTI's forerunner, the AIUT.

Forerunner: the AIUT, 1897–1909
During the early years of the intermediate era, relatively few of the small number of Irish secondary teachers were members of professional or representative bodies, and those that were worked mainly in the Protestant sector. The British-based Incorporated Association of Assistant Masters (1892) had Irish members, as had the Teachers' Guild of Great Britain and Ireland (1884). Educational employers, it should be noted, were far quicker off the mark, and both a Catholic Headmasters' Association (CHA) and an Irish Schoolmasters' Association (ISA) were in existence before the first intermediate examinations were held in 1879. These were followed in 1882 by the Central Association of Irish Schoolmistresses and Other Ladies Interested in Irish Education.[6]

'Dissatisfaction with the present condition of things' provided the motivation for a group of teachers that came together in Cork's Municipal Buildings on 18 September 1897 to establish the AIUT. To 'embrace the assistant masters of the various Intermediate and University establishments in an organisation of their mutual interests' was the ambitious objective arrived at.[7] According to an earlier historian of the ASTI, John Coolahan, the 'University establishments' concerned were the 'special intermediate schools', which had limited status as university colleges prior to the Irish Universities Act, 1908. The limited information available, however, does suggest that some junior staff at Trinity College also became members.[8]

At the AIUT's first annual conference, which was held in Dublin during the following Christmas vacation, representatives from the major cities were among the one hundred or so delegates. The guests included the distinguished scientist, Professor George FitzGerald of Trinity College (known to physicists for the 'FitzGerald contraction hypothesis'), and it was he who delivered the main address. For FitzGerald, the 'want of money' was the cause of most of the defects in secondary education, though he did acknowledge that the universities bore some responsibility for the way that the system privileged the needs of the tiny minority who would proceed to third level.[9]

That the 'want of money' was the nub of the matter was not news to anyone involved in secondary education, but for the AIUT the urgent question was the introduction of a system of registration of teachers, along the lines of the system which was just then being introduced in Britain. Registration would prevent the conditions of career teachers being undermined by 'birds of passage' in the contemporary phrase. However, James Comerton, AIUT president, was taken to task by the *Freeman's Journal* for advocating that teachers be 'certificated':

> The teaching profession can never be made a 'close' one in Ireland ... Our higher teachers must be judged by their work not by government qualification. The attempts to force them on the nuns in the primary schools failed, and we should say fortunately failed in the interests of Irish education. The registration craze was born of the secularisation craze on the continent where in some countries a 'bureau' must rule everything from the manufacture of ships and cigarettes to that of scholarship and character.[10]

Reduced to its essentials, the argument was that qualifications were superfluous for teachers.

The AIUT had an early opportunity to represent the views of its members at an official level, when Comerton was called during 1898 to give evidence before the Commission on Intermediate

Education. Arguably, the very establishment of this body was indicative of some state interest in the reform of the sector. In his testimony, Comerton drew attention to the grievances of teachers regarding their conditions of employment and to their views on how the quality of education might be improved. More direct involvement on the part of the commissioners of intermediate education he regarded as essential – in teacher registration, in direct payments to teachers, in school inspections. Support for the AIUT position came, significantly, from another witness, Patrick Foley, Catholic bishop of Kildare and Leighlin and a former president of St Patrick's, Carlow College.[11]

The views expressed by Foley before the commissioners, while perhaps sincerely held, were not the best guide to the Catholic attitude, however. That attitude, more candidly articulated in the *Freeman's Journal* leader quoted above, might be characterised as being averse to accountability before public authority, disdainful of any right to consultation for lay teachers, and authoritarian in general tendency. Towards trade unionism or similar manifestations there was suspicion, even hostility, as the Irish National Teachers' Organisation (INTO) had discovered in 1899 when it tried to assert the security of tenure of its members. The organisation was placed under an ecclesiastical ban in the provinces of Tuam and Armagh, and a pastoral letter issued by the hierarchy advised its members in the other two provinces to resign from it.[12]

In the event, neither the arguments of James Comerton nor the emollient words of Bishop Foley were reflected in the final report of the commission, which recommended no radical changes. With regard to registration, there was the difficulty that only a small minority of the teachers in the Catholic sector would have met any minimum criteria that might be set – largely because, due to the long-standing Catholic disapproval of the secular character of Irish university education, there were few Catholic graduates. This difficulty was acknowledged by Comerton, when he stated that no acceptable form of registration could 'interfere with those at present engaged in secondary work'.[13] As it turned out, the Intermediate Education Amendment Act (1900) that resulted from the commission's work did very little to satisfy teachers or anyone else advocating reform in secondary education.

Probably the most important service for Irish secondary teachers performed by the AIUT was the publication in 1904 of a short pamphlet entitled *Secondary Education in Ireland: A Plea for Reform*. According to *The Irish Times*, it expressed the teachers' case 'in very simple and moderate language'. Arguing that the greatest need within secondary education was for 'efficient teachers to carry it out', it went on to define the characteristics of the 'efficient teacher' in the following (rather masculine) terms: '(i) he must thoroughly know the subject he is to teach; (ii) he must be a man of good general culture; (iii) he must know how to impart to others the knowledge he possesses'. Education, training, and supervision were necessary to create such creatures, and they were in extremely short supply. If 'one of the noblest of professions' was to attract the necessary numbers, the arguments went on, the rewards had to be adequate.

The minimum requirements of teachers, according to the pamphlet, were the following: 'registration, adequate salaries, security of tenure, good service pensions'. As John Coolahan has shown, the realisation of these goals would preoccupy AIUT for the remaining few years of its existence, and ASTI for several decades also.[14]

The AIUT pamphlet was available for the benefit of Messrs F.H. Dale and T.A. Stephens, appointed by Chief Secretary Wyndham to investigate Irish secondary education during 1904–05, appointments indicating dissatisfaction with the legislation that resulted from the recent commission report. These eminent English educationists visited eighty schools, and were disparaged for their trouble as 'the English tourists' in an Irish clericalist press suspicious of any state intervention. With the AIUT, Dale and Stephens shared the desire to 'establish a profession of secondary teaching in Ireland', but their report concluded that the conditions for this did not yet exist. To establish the conditions, they recommended an open-ended consultation process with interested parties – chief among which was the Catholic hierarchy. Wyndham's departure from his post meant that the recommendations of his appointees were not immediately pursued, and he was followed out of office in any case by his Conservative administration.[15]

The return of a new Liberal administration in 1906 caused apprehension among those concerned with Catholic education. As the more secular of the established British parties, its intervention in Irish education was expected to be more state-led, and to take less account of Catholic sensibilities.[16] The AIUT, however, might have expected a sympathetic hearing, and progress towards the alleviation of one of the ills which was rather brashly pinpointed in its 1904 pamphlet:

> In the majority of civilised countries ... schools are under state or public control. Unfortunately, in this country we are far from the scientific systems of education adopted on the continent and in America.

AIUT's Leinster branch did lobby Chief Secretary Birrell on several occasions during 1908, in pursuit of educational reform generally and, specifically, that in the appointment of schools' inspectors positions should not be given to outsiders, but to 'Irishmen and Irishwomen ... whose practical knowledge of our schools would enable them to enter the duties of inspection with the essential equipments of sympathy and experience'.[17] By then, if criticism from Munster is a guide, the AIUT was reduced to a shadow of its earlier self, even if reported activity on the part of an Ulster branch in mid-1907 indicates that it was rather more than a 'Dublin organisation', as alleged a few months earlier by the spokesperson for the alienated Munster and Connacht teachers.[18]

The precise reasons for the decline are not known, but one might speculate that the secularist approach articulated in the 1904 pamphlet was a contributory factor. Advocacy of 'public control' and of the 'systems of education adopted on the continent', coming from a body claiming to speak for lay teachers employed in their diocesan colleges, can hardly have escaped the attention of Catholic bishops ever-vigilant against contamination from the 'secularisation craze on the continent', and that had proscribed the INTO only five years previously. Did their disapproval adversely impact on the level of AIUT membership outside of Dublin and the Belfast area?

In its early years, AIUT had a Cork-based president – Comerton taught science at Christian Brothers College and, before that, at the Capuchin College in Rochestown – and it had members in many parts of the country, including Kilkenny, Carrick-on-Suir, Wexford, Lismore, Youghal, Derry, Enniskillen, Belfast and

Armagh. That it was still trying to achieve a geographical spread is indicated by the meeting it organised in July 1905 targeting Art and Science teachers from around the country attending summer courses in Dublin. Those attending acquiesced in a resolution declaring AIUT to be 'deserving of the support of all interested in Irish Intermediate education', but there are no indications of any further commitment on their part.[19] By 1909, clearly, AIUT had become unrepresentative and ineffective, and, from their response to the approach of the Munster teachers, it is apparent that its leaders recognised this.

Establishing the ASTI

The period during which the ASTI was founded and fortified was one of considerable upheaval in Irish society: during its first half decade in existence, Labour, feminist and cultural nationalist movements became firmly established, while tens of thousands mobilised into rival volunteer militias to oppose and defend home rule; during its second half decade, tens of thousands joined the rush to the trenches of the First World War, while others took advantage of Britain's distraction to try to establish an independent Irish republic; during its third half decade, there was a great post-war revolutionary ferment and the two Irish states were established.

These events formed part of the context for early ASTI activity, and, as one might expect of educated men and women concerned about social justice, members also participated in other movements of the era, some losing their lives as a result. Thomas MacDonagh, later executed for his part in the 1916 Rising, was one such. A poet and a Gaelic League activist, he began his teaching career at St Kieran's College, Kilkenny, in 1901, where he succeeded another 'short-term' assistant master, Francis (Sheehy) Skeffington. In 1903, he took a position at St Colman's College, Fermoy, where he remained until he joined Pádraic Pearse in establishing Scoil Éanna in 1908. MacDonagh maintained contact with his former colleagues – fellow Gaelic Leaguer, P.J. Kennedy, in particular – so he was an early link between the Munster and Dublin elements of the new Association.[20] Another founder and Gaelic Leaguer with a varied teaching career was Éamon de Valera, who was elected chairman of the ASTI's Leinster Provincial Council in 1910. Having taught at Blackrock, its sister Rockwell College, and Belvedere, he was appointed a lecturer in Mathematics at Carysfort in 1906. Evidently underpaid in that position, he took part-time teaching work at a number of other institutions – Dominican College, Eccles Street; Loreto College, Stephen's Green; Holy Cross College, Clonliffe; the Catholic University – as well as acting as an examiner for the Intermediate Board and for the new National University.[21] De Valera joined Thomas MacDonagh at the barricades in 1916 but survived to become taoiseach and president of Ireland. Loss of employment was a consequence of radical engagement for others, including the Cork feminist and republican activist, Mary MacSwiney, who was unsuccessfully represented by the ASTI in 1916, following her dismissal from St Angela's Convent School by Ursuline nuns embarrassed at her political profile.[22]

The foundation of any national organisation is a process, which in the case of the ASTI extended over several years. It was not entirely coincidental that these were also the years that witnessed the birth of James Larkin's Irish Transport and General Workers' Union (ITGWU). Larkin's union, which was a competitor of the National Union of Dock Labourers,[23] had acrimonious beginnings, and, given the continuing survival of the AIUT, there was likewise potential for conflict between rival groups of teachers. In the event, the ASTI's arrival was a relatively calm one. The Dublin meeting of July 1909 had its proceedings opened by P.J. Kennedy of Fermoy and recorded by T.J. Burke of Limerick, but the veterans of earlier struggles also played a part. While the dynamic element, arguably, was composed of those who had recently taken the lead in the south, the AIUT platform – registration, salary scale, job security, pensions – was embraced in full by the ASTI.

Temporary structures put in place in July saw the Dublin-based P.F. Condon become secretary, *pro tem*, and his AIUT comrade, W.S. Cooney, chairman. It was January 1910 before the first meeting of the Central Executive Committee (CEC) was held, while authoritative Provincial Councils were established, initially in Munster and Leinster, so as to prevent the new body becoming Dublin-dominated. Condon was confirmed as secretary at the first CEC. That meeting also elected as ASTI's first president P.J. Kennedy, of St Colman's, Fermoy – the diocesan college of Cloyne, and a place with a relatively large number of lay teachers.[24] Since it played an important role in the early history of ASTI, it is appropriate to quote from Thomas MacDonagh's correspondence where it records his earliest impressions of St Colman's:

> Fermoy is a good place; college splendid; up-to-date; billiards and hurling; first 'scholars and gentlemen'; the president a trump and a very clever man ... St Colman's is a very different place from St K[ieran]'s. Gaelic to the spine.[25]

The mixture of experience and enthusiasm was fortuitous, and the new Association proved effective in drawing attention to the neglect of Irish secondary education, and to the predicament of the Irish secondary teacher. These were two questions that the ASTI, following the example of the AIUT, insisted from the very beginning were inextricably linked. There could be no satisfactory education without professional conditions for teachers, because able individuals would seek their livelihoods elsewhere until there were reasonable career expectations in teaching. As P.J. Kennedy put it: 'a system of education which ignores the teacher is radically unsound'.[26]

Kennedy's remark was made in the course of an extensive interview published in the *Cork Examiner* during the period of his presidency. It was a notable interview which ranged widely, covering teachers' grievances, the defects of the system, and remedies for both. The nature of the 'shocking and iniquitous' conditions endured by his colleagues does not need restating, nor does the detail of the budgetary restrictions affecting intermediate education, but the attitudes of this key ASTI founder to the educational issues of that period are of interest. That teachers experienced the recently-introduced system of inspection as 'an additional terror to a lot already sufficiently hard to bear' is not surprising in circumstances where they had no recognised rights or status, and where there was not even a 'strict definition of [their] duties'. Kennedy did emphasise, however, that there was no objection to 'proper inspection'. With regard to the results system, his attitude was that of a progressive educationist – it was 'bad and pernicious' because it ignored 'many of the important sides of educational work'. The system of county council scholarships for the children of poor parents provided for in the universities legislation of 1908 was welcome, but the existing intermediate system represented a major obstacle. If poor children could not avail of secondary education, how could they get to university? For Kennedy, a solution lay in the provision of adequate state funding for schools employing 'properly qualified teachers supplied them by the state', linked to an obligation on all such schools to offer free places, based on results at an entrance examination, 'to the clever children whose parents could prove to the satisfaction of the Board that they would otherwise be unable to give them a secondary education'. Extra funding was urgent, and with regard to the amount required and its source, the ASTI president was in broad agreement with contemporaries, but there were differing views about how an increased allocation might be spent. 'The most grotesque of all,' said Kennedy, 'is the one which suggests the retention of the old discredited system of written examinations with larger endowments' – broadly, the Catholic position. Asked if ASTI's proposal, in expanding the role of the state, would not affect 'the religious and educational liberties of the schools', he responded as follows:

> It would leave the religious liberty of the schools exactly as it is. The denominational principle is frankly accepted by all parties in Ireland; and of course the state-paid teachers employed in each school would be of the same faith as that of the pupils attending the school. The educational liberty would be considerably enlarged; as under any proper system of inspection, each school would be allowed to adapt itself to the educational needs of the locality in which it is placed or the classes of students attending its courses.[27]

The position was not very different to that which had been articulated by the AIUT, but the points were more delicately made.

The ASTI was not long dependent on the mainstream press to communicate its views, for, no sooner were organisational structures put in place in January 1910 than the Association began to publish its own monthly periodical, the *Irish Journal of Education*, under the editorship of secretary Condon. This was an important departure – there was a precedent in Irish trade unionism in the *Draper's Assistant*, and an important near contemporary in the ITGWU's *Irish Worker* – which allowed for the articulation of a distinctive and independent teachers' viewpoint on educational problems and controversies. Arguably, the *Journal* was a necessary counterweight to the Catholic managers' *Irish Educational Review*, published between 1907 and the death in 1914 of its founding editor, Fr Andrew Murphy, long-time president of St Munchin's College, Limerick, and the high profile secretary/treasurer of the CHA. Moreover, the periodical gave isolated assistant masters and mistresses around the country a sense of belonging to a national body, with its range of articles dealing with professional as well as industrial relations and public policy issues. A synopsis of the contents of a typical sixteen-page issue will convey a flavour of the *Journal*: 'Notes of the month' (dealing with ASTI-related matters): 'Mr T.P. Gill on education for citizenship'; 'The schoolmaster in literature'; 'The teaching of mathematics in the USA'; 'A bishop on Mr Birrell and another' (dealing mainly with a pronouncement from Dr O'Dea of Galway on government proposals to supplement the wages of lay teachers); book reviews and notices; as well as advertisements for textbooks placed by Macmillan and Cambridge University Press.[28]

If the *Journal* was important, the lobbying efforts which brought the Irish teachers' grievances to the floor of the House of Commons, and the public meetings at which leading educationists and political leaders gave their support to the ASTI's policy platform were equally so. Certainly, it would appear that other interests within the system were taken by surprise at the adeptness with which the new Association pursued its objectives. The CHA found itself having to publicly support the ASTI's demands for increased funding, even while its *Review* was criticising its members for 'writing very unwise letters to the papers' in support of others of its demands.[29]

The impression is that management bodies were alarmed at the implications of the ASTI's demand for security of tenure, which they saw as interfering with their right to hire and fire as they saw fit, and some of their members may have been tempted in the circumstances to assert this right. Certainly, a rash of arbitrary dismissals was reported by the *Journal*, in a way that implied that it was part of a concerted attempt by school managers to re-impose authority over their assistant masters. This was not a matter that was pursued for long – a continuing focus on it would have discouraged recruitment. In any case, it may well have been that suspicions were unfounded, and that it was a matter of better intelligence, a result of better organisation, forcibly drawing attention to the real scale of dismissals. When one of the arbitrarily dismissed was *Journal* editor P.F. Condon, however, it was inevitable that the belief that the ASTI itself was being targeted would gain some currency. Tragically, Condon died very soon after his dismissal. An emotional tribute in the *Journal* that he had founded described him as 'one who never paraded what he was doing, but who was content to labour in spite of misrepresentation and opposition, without fee or reward for the furtherance of a cause from which he knew he would reap no personal advantage'.[30]

Organising the 'cadhain aonair' of the intermediate schools

The Dublin branch was a successor to the crumbling AIUT, and later occasional references to the 'reorganisation', 'reconstitution' and 'revival' of 1909 indicate that prominent members there considered the ASTI to be a new name for an existing body rather than a completely new organisation.[31] Dublin naturally was by far the largest branch and, given its origins, its location and the experience of its leading members, it was to be expected that its business would frequently overlap with the national business of the Association. Cork business, similarly, overlapped with that of the business of the Munster Provincial Council after that body was established early in 1910. For other early branches, rudimentary histories may be constructed from occasional branch reports in the Association's *Journal*. As well as Dublin and Cork, Kerry, Limerick, Roscrea, Fermoy, Mount Melleray, Waterford and Belfast all had branches by early 1914, and there were individual members elsewhere. This list of branches, however, may be incomplete, for some early branch officials were evidently shy about seeing their names in the *Journal*, due to fear of the consequences of being publicly identified with ASTI agitation.[32]

After Fermoy, one of the earliest branches was in Kerry, and we have a vibrant description from a leading member, Killarney-based Joe O'Connor, of the circumstances in which it was established:

> Early in January 1909 I got a letter which pierced the encircling gloom with a ray of kindly light. It bore a Fermoy postmark and was written by a Michael J. O'Shea, of whom I had never heard ... It was the opening shot in the long and heart-breaking campaign, to bring us, the *cadhain aonair* of

the Intermediate schools, together under one banner and fight our way as a brotherhood out of the ignoble slavery in which we worked. Like a trumpet call to the Legion of the Lost, it asked me to rally the isolate Kerrymen to the standard.[33]

According to a sober account in the *Journal* which does not substantially contradict O'Connor, the first meeting of the Kerry branch took place on 6 March 1909, the business being to select delegates to attend the meeting called for Cork on St Patrick's Day. Four went to Cork and, energised by the experience, they recruited 'almost every secondary teacher in Kerry' within four weeks. From the beginning, the seventeen members of the branch, drawn from as far apart as Killorglin and Listowel, looked forward to the monthly meetings as providing opportunities for 'exchanging views on educational subjects or of reading an interesting "paper" for the benefit of their confreres'. The *Journal*, it was found, 'infused new life' into the Kerry meetings, as well as strengthening the sense of being part of a national movement.[34]

T.J. Burke and Michael Larkin were the initiators of the important Limerick branch, the first meeting of which took place near the end of June 1909. Almost all of the secondary schools in Limerick were represented at a second meeting in September, which was held in the Town Hall at the invitation of the mayor. Thereafter, the branch met fortnightly and made good use of the local press to publicise teachers' grievances. M.H. Daly stepped into the breach as secretary/treasurer of the branch early in 1910, when the capable and committed T.J. Burke was called to serve in those roles on the Munster Council.[35]

The Roscrea branch was formed, according to the *Journal*'s local correspondent, soon 'after the meeting in Dublin at Easter 1909'. Mr Beggan was the founding chairperson, and Mr Getz the secretary/treasurer. The membership of the branch was 'necessarily small ... owing to the geographical situation of Roscrea, and the absence of secondary schools in the immediate vicinity'. The same might have been said of Fermoy, which continued to meet with a membership not much higher than the minimum of four required for recognition of a branch, and of Mount Melleray, which had nine members in the spring of 1912.[36] A Waterford branch was meeting by May 1913, and Ulstermen followed the example set by their female colleagues almost two years previously (see below) when they held the inaugural meeting of the Belfast Male Branch on Saturday 14 February 1914. Of the attendance, seven were from Belfast and one from each of Omagh, Newry and Letterkenny. (Evidently, a Derry branch, which was reported to have been formed in mid-1909, had not survived.) Early office holders, Messrs O'Connor, Gillespie and Ward, took a hand in establishing an Ulster Provincial Council soon afterwards.[37]

By late 1914, Connacht was the only province without any reported branch, let alone a provincial council but, arguably, this was not a serious omission since secondary education hardly existed there. With only 15 intermediate schools and 728 pupils, by the calculation of Dale and Stephens, it is unlikely that there were more than 25 men and women eligible for ASTI membership in the entire province.[38] Several of these, in fact, were early members of the Dublin branch, to which individuals from places where no branches existed were allocated. An examination of the Dublin membership records for 1912–14 shows that J.J. McKenna and J. Gaffney were keeping the flag flying in Joseph's College, Ballinasloe, one of the centres of an earlier effort to organise secondary teachers, and that there were individual members in the towns of Tuam, Castlebar, Ballinrobe and Westport. In the other provinces, there were *cadhain aonair* in Armagh, Newry and Omagh, in Ennis and Tipperary town, in Athy, Carlow, Dundalk, Kildare, Mullingar, Newbridge and Naas.[39]

The membership might have been thinly spread outside the metropolitan centres, but useful work was accomplished by rural branches. Following representations, the Kilmallock and Croom District Councils passed resolutions condemning the underfunding of secondary education. This so-called 'Limerick resolution' became a model and it was subsequently adopted by a range of public bodies, from Cavan Urban Council to Dublin Corporation.[40]

But the Limerick branch was not the only one to cultivate links with the local press and local political figures. Joe O'Connor was one of a deputation mandated by his branch to lobby Kerry MPs, and something like official recognition was achieved by the same branch when it was asked by Kerry Council Council to nominate two members to serve on a sub-committee concerned with the allocation of university scholarships. And it was through contact with

the Kerry branch that Thomas O'Donnell, MP for West Kerry, became the most outspoken advocate of the secondary teachers' cause
in the House of Commons. O'Donnell, a former national teacher
and a founder of the Intermediate School, Killorglin, did not always take account of ASTI strategy in his advocacy, but he proved
to be more independent of the Catholic hierarchy on education
than any other nationalist MP of the period.[41]

By the beginning of the First World War in August 1914 –
shortly after its fifth aniversary – the ASTI was well organised
among both sexes in Dublin, among Munster men, and among
Belfast women. There were many parts of the country, however,
where the Association had made no impact, despite circular letters
and other approaches. This caused frustration, the feeling being that
objectives were remaining unmet because of relatively low membership. The appointment as organising secretary of one P. Doody,
who had taught in Pearse's Scoil Éanna, was one of a number of
steps taken during 1915 that signalled a determination to do something about this matter. In its announcement of Doody's appointment, the *Journal* conveyed something of the frustration felt by the
dedicated few at the difficulties they had faced in expanding ASTI:

> Very many teachers have never joined the Association, and yet
> many of these discreditable persons have gathered very sub-
> stantial benefits by the work they meanly left others to do.
> Some of these persons – labour organisations have an un-
> savoury but expressive term to describe them – have always re-
> fused to join the Association … Some of them, out of the
> receipt from the Birrell grant scheme [see below], celebrated
> the occasion by a mild carouse in a Dublin house of entertain-
> ment. Mr Doody will only waste his time if he appeals to the
> decent feelings of such as these. Besides those who have always
> held out, there are others who, through indifference, have fallen
> away from the Association. Doubtless, it will be possible to do
> something with many of those, and Mr Doody will have a wide
> field for his energy. There are a few who used to be members,
> but whose membership ceased at the period when the Associ-
> ation refused to allow itself to be dragged at the tail of the head-
> masters' chariot, when they came forward to attack the Birrell
> scheme … Let Mr Doody keep clear of these.[42]

Doody approached his task in a systematic fashion – liaising with branch secretaries in targeting prospective members and identifying lacunae as regards organisation. His reports of October and November 1915 indicate the rate of progress. Fifty new members had been signed up, lapsed members had rejoined and five new branches had been formed, including one in Carlow. Significantly, almost all of the teachers of Connacht had joined, 'except those in Sligo and Tuam' (these two places, however, had 40 per cent of the province's secondary schools). An 'extra caution' was the reason given for the resistance to joining on the part of teachers in Wexford and Kilkenny, while it was noted that branches were 'wanted' also in Coleraine and Listowel. On 26 November 1915, one of these citadels fell to the ASTI, when a Kilkenny branch was formed at a meeting in Power's Hotel (an effort of 1909 having proved abortive), attended by five men including the chairman M.C. O'Connor. One of the first decisions taken was to elect the members of a deputation 'to interview teachers in the locality who have not yet joined'.[43]

Women

As they accounted for more than 40 per cent of non-clerical secondary teachers – and were a growing element in the early twentieth century – women were important to the ASTI, and some of them at least were awake to the particular disadvantages of their sex within the educational system. Women faced particular difficulties in organising themselves, but it is hardly surprising that the contemporary Irish women's suffrage movement – in which young female graduates played a considerable role – should have stirred consciousness regarding the rights of women in a field where discrimination was so blatant, with men being paid, on average, almost twice as much for doing what was indisputably the same work.[44]

And it would appear that the men who led the ASTI during its early years accepted the need to recruit and involve women – even proving sensitive to criticism from organised feminists on one occasion.[45] Of the type of anti-feminist reaction that emerged in the British National Union of Teachers in the pre-First World War period, there is no evidence in Ireland; indeed, when the Incorporated Association of Assistant Masters (IAAM), a British-based union that recruited in Ireland, tried to discredit the ASTI by drawing attention to the fact that it accepted women into membership, the response in the *Irish Journal of Education* was to ridicule the backwardness of the rival association.[46]

Some women won prominence early – Miss Cashel, who was elected onto the Munster Council when it was established in 1910 being a case in point – but it was considered necessary to take specific steps to better accommodate women through the provision of specific women's sections. Men tended to dominate meetings, business and elections where both sexes were involved, and, moreover, there was some social disapproval in the early twentieth century of single women attending gatherings where men might be expected to be present. The contemporary Gaelic League, for example, which had a policy of admitting men and women equally to educational and social events, came under pressure from Catholic clergy to segregate its classes.[47] And, with respect to secondary teachers, there was an additional social complication in that over 80 per cent of lay women in the profession were Protestant, whereas the majority of lay men were Catholic. In the case of some other workers, such factors had led to the establishment of separate unions for women – the Textile Operatives' Society of Ireland in Belfast; the Irish Women Workers' Union in Dublin. With regard to teaching, however, the INTO had managed, if unevenly, to organise and represent both men and women since its establishment in 1868.[48]

A decision to establish an ASTI women's section was taken at a meeting of the Dublin branch towards the end of 1910, but it was not until December 1911 that one was formally established. Claiming 52 members at the outset, it grew quickly to 70, a considerable portion of the fewer than 400 women lay teachers in Ireland. Caroline Tremaine, of Alexandra College (where her responsibilities lay in the training of secondary teachers), was elected secretary, and early meetings were held in the same institution. The section took the title Women Teachers' Association (WTA), and the Dublin branch soon became the Leinster branch.[49]

A Belfast branch of the WTA was formed at a meeting in Victoria College on 26 April 1912. This development, which gave the ASTI its first foothold in Ulster, was made possible, largely, by the misogyny of the IAAM, which had a considerable presence in Belfast. Elizabeth Steele (a clergyman's daughter of Drumlee, County Down, who would play an important national role in the

ASTI in the following years) took the chair at this first meeting, and a Miss Cumming was elected secretary.[50]

An examination of the published reports of meetings suggest that women's branch meetings were rather different to the men's, with a greater emphasis in the former on the education of the members, by means of invitations to guest speakers and debates, perhaps indicating that there was a greater interest in professional development than in industrial relations issues among women members. Caroline Tremaine of Dublin was an early guest in Belfast. Another was Douglas Lloyd Savory, professor of French at Queen's University, and a leading Unionist though progressive educationist, who spoke on 'The Art of Pronunciation'.[51]

These developments necessitated a review of the rules so as to open up positions for women. When this was done, there was a considerable shift in the gender balance on the executive council. To take one example: at an executive meeting which was held (significantly) in Alexandra College on 2 January 1915, four of the eleven participating were women – Elizabeth Steele represented Ulster; Miss Galbraith, Munster; Misses Scott and Reilly, Leinster. The impact of women led to a questioning of attitudes with regard to pay differentials, as it was doing in the INTO, with matters brought to a head by the distribution of the Birrell grant (see below).[52] The voice that expressed the policy was very much a male one, and the interests appealed to were also male, but the ASTI declared itself in favour of equal pay for men and women teachers in 1914, fully six decades before this would be achieved:

> As men, we may say it frankly, our main reason for desiring equality is due to a desire to protect our own interests which, even in Ireland, would be endangered if there was a supply of cheaper female labour available. Quite recently, we have had an instance of this danger in the appointment in a Dublin boys' school of two female teachers to take the place of a man – we suppose that the chief reason that operated in this case was the fact that women are willing to take smaller salaries than men.[53]

'Grecian gifts': the Birrell reforms

The ASTI's efforts to achieve recognition of what it saw as its members' reasonable demands appeared to be bearing fruit when, on 23

May 1911, Augustine Birrell, chief secretary for Ireland, responded as follows in the House of Commons to a question from John Dillon, MP:

> It is no use bolstering up any system of secondary education which has so shaky a foundation … and the first task and object, I think, of all persons either engaged in the profession themselves, or desirous to see it occupying the position of repute that it ought to do, would be to try to raise the standard of the secondary teacher in Ireland.[54]

The chief secretary's response, during which he accepted that a register of teachers would be a necessary feature of any reform, was seen as significant, especially since it came soon after a commitment to the schools' management bodies from the chancellor of the exchequer, Lloyd George, to increase expenditure on Irish secondary education. To teachers, it seemed to promise that redress was imminent, and the ASTI was stirred to point out what exactly was required if 'the standard of the secondary teacher' was to be raised. Registration, it continued to argue, was crucial, and moreover, the old objection to it, the lack of a university system acceptable to Catholics, had been nullified by the establishment of the National University in 1908, and of chairs of education in several universities.[55] To the Catholic authorities, Birrell's intervention was less welcome, for they did not agree that secondary education had 'so shaky a foundation' as others thought, though they concurred that it needed a considerable injection of cash. That much, however, they had been promised already.[56]

It took more than a year, during which widespread discussions took place, before Birrell unveiled his scheme on 31 July 1912 in the midst of the controversy that followed the introduction of the third Home Rule Bill. The central element was £40,000, described explicitly as the Teachers' Salaries Grant, which the government was to provide annually to intermediate education. So that the sum might bring about the improvements in the status and quality of lay secondary teachers that Birrell had been persuaded were necessary, the grant would be distributed according to very particular criteria. Intermediate examination results would determine the amount that each school would receive for the purpose of adequately paying its

lay teachers, but schools would also have to meet specific requirements with regard to conditions of employment in order to benefit: they would have to employ a minimum of one lay teacher for
each forty pupils in the school; they would have to pay a salary of
£120 in boys' schools, or £80 in girls' schools; they would have to
grant their teachers contractual entitlements to six months' notice
of dismissal. Calculations were to be based on registered teachers
only – with criteria for registration to be determined.[57]

For the ASTI, the scheme represented an 'honest attempt' to
address the grievances of teachers,[58] and it certainly went a considerable way towards meeting the demands set down by the AIUT in
1904, and adopted as its own by the ASTI. If there was a gap between the salary minima and the English teacher's pay scale beginning at £150, if there was an even wider gap between the scheme's
provision for six months' notice and the ASTI's demand for 'security of tenure', if there was a veritable gulf between the principle of
'good service pensions' and the verbal assurances given to examine
the matter, the 1912 package nonetheless was further-reaching than
any dealing with intermediate education since 1879. With the state
accepting a paymaster's role, with registration in prospect, with minimum pay rates fixed, there were grounds for optimism with regards
to the development of a 'regular profession' of secondary teaching,
comparable to primary teaching.

The ASTI's general disposition, therefore, was to support Birrell's scheme, although it did press for the inclusion of an appeals
mechanism in dismissal cases. Tactically, a more equivocal position
might have been wiser – perhaps drawing attention to more of the
scheme's shortcomings, and employing these as bargaining chips in
the inevitable contest with Catholic bodies opposing the scheme.
Instead, the ASTI ceded to Birrell its role as champion of Irish secondary teachers, offering occasional concessions to the school management bodies to smooth the way, and allowing more experienced
opponents to sow divisions in its own ranks. This happened even
before the unveiling of the scheme at a meeting of representative
bodies called by the Intermediate Board in January 1912, when
ASTI representatives articulated contradictory positions.[59]

The reaction of leading Catholics to Birrell's proposals was swift
and hostile. Contending that the scheme would force religious bodies to fire their own members and replace them with laymen, Fr

Andrew Murphy argued that it amounted to 'a claim to seize the schools built and maintained by the bishops and religious orders for the Catholic people of Ireland, and turn them into government schools'. Accusing Birrell of aligning himself with anti-clerical forces elsewhere, he likened the scheme to 'the claim of the governments of France and Portugal to the right of forcible confiscation'. For one bishop, the scheme represented 'a paltry bribe of £40,000 a year'; for another, it was a '"Grecian gift" which it was better to decline'.[60] The initial clerical reaction was out of all proportion to the contents of the scheme. Moreover, it was widely seen to be so, with the result that the collective response of the bishops was more measured. Registration was declared to be acceptable provided that the hierarchy had its say in the composition of the registration body, and that the 'special circumstances' of teaching religious were recognised. However, the bishops argued that confining the benefits of any scheme to lay teachers was discriminatory. It discriminated against clerical teachers, but also against Catholic education itself, for did not a majority of lay teachers work in already-advantaged Protestant schools?[61]

Some sympathy for the Catholic position manifested itself in the ASTI, and, to the consternation of the majority, Association president William Johnston expressed opposition to discrimination against the teaching religious in a letter to the press. A teacher at the Presbyterian St Andrew's College since 1895, 'Johnny' Johnston had a 'frightening reputation' for 'withering sarcasm' both in the classroom and in the staffroom, according to that institution's history, but he was out of his depth in complex negotiations. That the public breaking of ranks was very damaging was indicated by the denunciation of the president in the ASTI's *Journal*. Branch resolutions from around the country showed that there was little support for his position, and Johnston was obliged publicly to withdraw his letter and to resign the presidency.[62]

Negotiations between the chief secretary and the CHA occupied the first half of 1913, with Birrell continuing to try to give effect to his promise to 'raise the standard' of life of Irish lay secondary teachers. For their part, Fr Murphy and the CHA chose to regard the £40,000 as an allocation to Irish secondary education generally, with Lloyd George's commitment of 1911 providing a basis for their position. They were anxious that school authorities rather than the board have discretion regarding the distribution of the grant, and that staffing not be affected by the rules governing allocation of the money. From these conflicting objectives arose a particular difficulty regarding the requirement that each benefiting school should employ one lay teacher for each forty pupils. For the CHA, Murphy argued that it was the average for the Catholic school sector as a whole that should be taken into consideration – an average that was met as things stood – rather than the position in individual schools. This was unacceptable to Birrell. After negotiations broke down in mid-1913, in a context of growing impatience among teachers and the general public, Birrell published the correspondence between himself and Fr Murphy in an effort to show that he was not the unreasonable party.[63]

There were widespread fears in Ireland that the grant would be lost to Irish education, and a tendency to blame the Catholic authorities for this, but eventually, in August 1914, an exasperated Birrell pushed through the measure without agreement. 'Tentative rules', published in January 1915, enabled the board to make a payment for 1914–15, while firming up the procedures for subsequent years.[64] The money was paid through schools, accompanied by a declaration that its purpose was to promote the 'employment upon reasonable terms of an adequate number of duly qualified lay teachers in intermediate schools'. However, it was discovered that Catholic schools were not observing the 'tentative rules', but that they were diverting the grant to other purposes. Indeed in the first year, of the 300 that the ASTI estimated were eligible, only 46 teachers in Catholic schools were returned as being 'duly qualified'. In the non-Catholic sector 238 teachers benefited. Stricter rules imposed in the following years saw the number in Catholic schools benefiting increase to 264 in 1918.[65]

Years later, Joe O'Connor recalled for ASTI members the circumstances in which he received his share of the grant in 1915. Summoned to a meeting by his president, he and his colleagues – seven clerical, one lay – were presented with 'a lavish collation of wines and confectionery stood ready to put us in good humour'. The president began:

> I have received from the Board a paying order for three hundred and twenty pounds from the Birrell grant. With it came a set of

instructions which I have not bothered to study, but I am sure that we here are quite competent to make our own decisions, so I propose to divide it equally between us giving £36 to each of you and taking the balance which is £32 and some odd shillings myself.[66]

Handing each man a cheque, the president next proposed a toast to Birrell, but the two laymen refused to raise their glasses. O'Connor then pointedly asked the president to read the board's instructions, and handed back his cheque. The account continues:

> Next day, he waylaid Dick and me in the corridor between classes, treated us to a broad benignant smile, and gave us the Board's instructions to read for ourselves. 'This document has implications of which I was unaware yesterday,' he remarked, '*fiat justitia*'. Then he laid on the windowsill the four cheques, drawn correct to the last penny, and handed each of us the amount due to him under the rules.[67]

If there were similar scenes in other places, it is likely that many accepted a little, or nothing at all, rather than risk a confrontation with an employer. For the disappointed editor of the ASTI's *Journal*, the award had turned out to be 'a Teachers' Salaries Grant that is that in name only'.[68] But if there was disappointment, some principles were established and some improvements effected which might be built upon in the future.

The process of teacher registration which was integral to the salaries grant scheme was still awaiting attention, and it too would take several years to put into place.

Elizabeth Steele of the Belfast women's branch of the ASTI, and W.J. Williams, editor of its *Journal*, were among the twelve members of the new registration council for secondary teachers when it met for the first time on 8 December 1915. It was significant that the ASTI was recognised as the voice of secondary teachers, Protestant and Catholic, north and south, despite the claims of the longer-established IAAM and Teachers' Guild. The other bodies represented were the Intermediate Education Board, the Department of Agricultural and Technical Instruction, the universities, the CHA, and the ISA. Ominously, however, the business of this first meeting was to discuss resolutions protesting plans to change the council's composition. A second meeting in January 1916, boycotted by the CHA, was adjourned with little achieved. Not until the September 1916 meeting – of a board expanded to give greater representation to the Catholic interest – could it begin the work of drafting regulations. It was an inauspicious beginning for a body in which great hopes had been invested, and there would be further obstacles in the way of its work.[69]

It was in July 1918 that the registration regulations came into effect, on foot of agreement on elements necessary for the formation of a professional secondary teacher. These elements, which were required of principals as well as of assistants, were a degree from a 'university approved by the council', a diploma or certificate, and a minimum of three years' successful experience in schools meeting the council's criteria. It was necessary to allow for a transition period, during which those serving teachers whose qualifications did not meet the requirements might become qualified. Initially, a deadline of 1922 was set, but this was subsequently put back to 1925.[70]

The 'deadly grip of foreign fetters': Molony and the Education Bill

The Vice-Regal Committee on the Conditions of Service and Remuneration of Teachers in Intermediate Schools, and on the Distribution of Grants from Public Funds for Intermediate Education in Ireland, known for its chairman, the chief justice of Ireland, as the Molony Committee, sat between August 1918 and March 1919. These were months of considerable upheaval, which witnessed the ending of the First World War, the rejection by nationalist Ireland of the long-dominant Parliamentary Party, the establishment by Sinn Féin of a revolutionary Dáil which rejected vice-regal authority, and the first shots fired in what would become the War of Independence.

The ASTI had been an earnest advocate of such a committee, and it provided three of the eighteen members: outgoing president, and editor of the defunct *Journal*, W.J. Williams, honorary secretary Annie McHugh, and CEC member Elizabeth Steele.[71] Like its contemporary, the Killanin Committee on National Education, Molony completed its work expeditiously in taxing circumstances, generating a report, a minority report, and provisory notes from

individual members. For historians of education, Molony's significance is two-fold: it reviewed the situation then pertaining in secondary education and formulated an influential blueprint for its
improvement.

In treating the condition of secondary teachers, the report acknowledged the significance of registration, just introduced, in pro-
fessionalising secondary teaching, but added: 'If the state requires
professional services, it is but just that it should pay for them.'[72] In
a situation where seven years had to be set aside for education,
training and on-the-job experience before registration, conditions
would have to be considerably improved if young people were to be
attracted to teaching. The conditions were then considered under
four headings – tenure, working hours, pay, superannuation – giving rise to a number of recommendations. With regard to tenure,
it was agreed that the position had become 'more stable' since Birrell, but that the 'teacher is still liable to dismissal for no fault of his
own, and he has no redress'. It was difficult to agree a solution to
this problem, however, since the committee represented various interest groups, including employers anxious to retain their freedom
to hire and fire as they saw fit, and the outcome was a platitudinous
recommendation from which the ASTI members dissented, though
in different ways. It was the principal reason why Williams and
McHugh refused to sign the final report, and they were joined in
issuing a minority report by Professor Henry of Queen's, Belfast.
Steele signed the final report, but submitted a note of reservation
reflecting the ASTI demand for the establishment of an appeals
procedure for dismissed teachers. It is difficult to understand why
the ASTI members divided. Conceivably, it was a way of showing
that the Association broadly approved of the report, though it
seems more likely that it was a harbinger of the disagreement that
would divide Catholic from Protestant members later in the year.

With regard to working hours, the recommendation was that
timetables making excessive demands on teachers should not be approved by the educational authorities. Salaries, it was found, had
reached £160 for men and £110 for women, an approximate dou-
bling of the levels estimated by Dale and Stephens more than a
decade earlier. If examined in the light of wartime inflation of about
150 per cent, however, it will be seen that the purchasing power of
the teacher's wage was no greater, and perhaps rather less, than it had

been in the bad old days before Birrell. This situation was severely criticised in the Molony document. It was not possible, it stated, for 'men and women of culture to live comfortably on such salaries' or to teach effectively in circumstances where they were 'perpetually harassed by financial embarrassment'. The recommendation on salary was quite specific – a fully registered teacher should receive at least £180, and the salary should rise, in annual increments, to £450. It was envisaged that the basic amount would be paid by the school, and the incremental element by the state. On pensions, the precedents established for national teachers in Ireland, and, recently, for secondary teachers in England, were commended.[73]

The Molony Report, signed by only fourteen of the eighteen committee members, was published in early March 1919. Among its recommendations were that the several branches of Irish education be co-ordinated by a single central body, that the payment by results system should be ended, that Intermediate and Leaving Certificate examinations replace the three levels of the intermediate examinations, and that capitation grants, based on inspection, be paid to schools. In the shorter term, the report, along with that of the Killanin Committee, would influence the Education (Ireland) Bill which had its first reading in November 1919. That Bill was criticised by the ASTI for its failure to provide for an appeals procedure, and, more influentially, was roundly denounced by the Catholic hierarchy, which couched its opposition to greater public influence over education in resonantly nationalist terms. For Bishop Foley of Kildare and Leighlin, it was a 'brazen-faced attempt of a hostile government to impose on the mind and soul of an intensely Catholic people the deadly grip of foreign fetters',[74] by means of which a British minister 'responsible solely to an alien parliament' would exercise

> the enormous powers by which he is to be invested, over not merely paupers and lunatics, or seeds and manures, or the breeding of cattle or horses, but over the very heart and mind and soul of the Irish nation.[75]

As things turned out, Westminster's mandate to legislate for most of Ireland expired before the Education Bill could be made law. It will be seen, nevertheless, that Molony's recommendations would influence later developments in secondary education.

The ASTI becomes a trade union

When the ASTI voted to register as a trade union, and to seek affiliation to the Irish Labour Party and Trade Union Congress in July 1919, it was a clear signal that the world was changing. Adopted at the annual meeting on the narrowest of margins, twenty-five to twenty-four, it was a decision that was challenged, and that would ultimately lead to the resignation of a significant body of teachers.[76] The affiliation was one that would have been inconceivable a few years earlier, for teachers aspired to professional status, and most of them, ASTI members or not, had not identified with the burgeoning trade unionism of the pre-First World War era. Trade unions were firmly associated with the working class; teachers belonged, however insecurely, to the middle class. That is not to say that individual teacher activists, perhaps influenced by the egalitarian socialist ideas that were gaining wider acceptance in the years after 1909, did not see themselves as having something in common with trade unionists.

Egalitarian leanings, certainly, are indicated by the consistent use within the ASTI of the terms 'assistant master' and 'assistant mistress' to describe secondary teachers, with occasional mockery of the pretensions of those who styled themselves 'Professor'. There are some indications of identification with trade unionism in the columns of the *Irish Journal of Education* during the W.J. Williams editorship. Responding in March 1912, for example, to a remark from Bishop O'Dwyer of Limerick lamenting certain changes in the character of the teachers' organisations and to similar comments by others, Williams wrote simply: 'We have now and then heard ourselves scornfully referred to as a "trade union", as no doubt we are.' A few months later, in urging members to recruit their fellows to the ASTI, he wrote: 'The day for unorganised labour is past; everywhere, we see the various professions organising in defence of the their interests.'[77] General remarks like these hardly impinged unduly on *Journal* readers, but what of the disreputably militant face of trade unionism as represented by the ITGWU's Jim Larkin? It is indicative of the separate worlds occupied by the ITGWU and the ASTI that references to Larkin-directed class conflict are almost entirely absent from the *Journal*, but there is one oblique reference to the great Dublin dispute of 1913–14. In this instance, the revelation that a critic of secondary teachers was also a critic of the locked-out

Dublin workers seems to indicate where Williams's sympathies lay.[78]

It is noteworthy that with respect to another major conflict of those years, the 1916 Rising, references in the *Journal* are also somewhat oblique, with book reviews providing the main opportunity to engage with the subject. Thus Williams was able to pay tribute to his fallen ASTI comrade, Thomas MacDonagh, in September 1916 by including a very laudatory and exceptionally long review of the poet's *Literature in Ireland*, which was 'passing through the press [as] its author met his death at the hands of a file of soldiers in a Dublin barrack yard'. In their treatment of the rebellion, editors had to take account of official censorship at this point, but for the ASTI's *Journal*, the sensitivities of many subscribers also had to be taken into account. That there were many members who would have been very critical of the Rising is indicated by the tribute a few months later to the late Lieutenant C.P. Close of the Dublin Fusiliers, 'a much respected Limerick member of the Association'.[79]

The labour body to which ASTI sought affiliation in 1919 was founded, under the title Irish Trade Union Congress (ITUC), in 1894. The initiative was principally that of unions representing craft workers who felt that Irish labour interests were being neglected by the British Trade Union Congress. The new Congress remained narrowly based, and representative of this rather conservative and mostly Dublin- and Belfast-based 'aristocracy of labour' until the affiliation of the expanding ITGWU forced it to take account of the interests of the unskilled workers. The radicalising influence of James Larkin and James Connolly caused it to take a more overtly political stance in 1912, preparing to represent workers in the imminent home rule assembly as the Irish Trade Union Congress and Labour Party. Following the setback represented by the ITGWU's defeat in the Dublin lock-out, trade unionism revived in the conditions of the Great War, when a labour shortage improved workers' bargaining position at a time when runaway inflation gave them motivation to bargain. Labour moved leftwards due to a number of factors – the success of strike action, the growth in anti-war sentiment and radical nationalism, socialist advance in revolutionary Russia – and gained in confidence when the strike it called against conscription resulted in a complete cessation of business throughout nationalist Ireland on 23 April 1918. Amending its name again in 1918, the now Irish Labour Party and Trade Union

Congress announced it was going to contest the next general election. In fact, it stood aside from the December 1918 election because the unambiguous policy on the Irish constitutional question that it would have been necessary to put before the electorate would almost inevitably have caused a split between Labour's nationalist- and unionist-leaning components. Working people, however, continued to flock to the trade unions in the post-war period, with the numbers affiliated to Labour/Congress growing from 100,000 in 1916 to 250,000 in 1920. Most of the increase was accounted for by the expansion of the dynamic ITGWU, but a considerable part of it was due to new affiliations from clerical and professional associations that would not have previously identified themselves with Labour.[80] Following a ballot of its members in 1917, the INTO joined Labour/Congress, and the Representative Council of Associations of Officers of Agricultural and Technical Instruction Committees in Ireland, representing teachers and instructors in the technical sector, followed early in 1919. Civil servants, even bank officials in 1919, took the unprecedented step for the archetypally respectable of threatening to go on strike.[81] In a world seemingly turned upside down, many in the middle class were prepared to follow the lead of the hitherto disdained working class.

Despite the caution of Labour/Congress on the constitutional question, it was increasingly associated with Irish republicanism in the public mind, particularly in the unionist mind. In the case of the INTO, its affiliation, coinciding with a leftward shift in the Congress itself and its espousal of a militant stance against military conscription, had led to the resignation of members and to the establishment of an Ulster National Teachers' Union (later Ulster Teachers' Union) in 1919. For the secessionists, Labour was 'a body which is frankly bolshevist and Sinn Féin ... of which Larkin [is] the prophet and Connolly [is] the martyr'.[82]

In the ASTI – where the proportion of Protestant members was higher than in the INTO – the consequences of the identification with Labour were even more immediately damaging. Nuns dominated Catholic female education, so perhaps 80 per cent of non-clerical women teachers were in the Protestant sector. With the defection of the Ulster women's branch in 1919, and the resignation of many members of the Leinster women's branch, the ASTI's representative structures for women which had enabled many to serve as CEC members and as officers suffered a grievous blow and, in the reorganisation that followed in 1920, they were dispensed with altogether. Branches thereafter were not segregated.

The loss of many Protestant members was a predictable consequence of embracing Labour – there were discommoded Catholic members also – and it was not a decision that was taken lightly. The fall in the living standards of secondary teachers was greater than that of the primary and technical teachers who had received the so-called war bonus paid to compensate for inflation. It was natural that secondary teachers should have attributed their condition to their small numbers and to their isolation. In circumstances where pay increases were being reported daily – for bank clerks as for road workers – and where these increases were being secured through militant trade unionism, the argument that secondary teachers should seek allies outside their own ranks was persuasive. At the same time, a closer bond was established with the INTO in the form of a federation of the two teachers' unions in September 1919. The larger body, thereafter, took a more-or-less paternal interest in ASTI affairs, advising it on strategy, granting space for an ASTI column in its *Irish School Weekly* from February 1920, and, later in the same year, providing office space in its Gardiner Place headquarters.[83]

And the ASTI's affiliation with Labour, belated in comparison with other groups, was embraced with enthusiasm when it came. Members were urged by their leaders to develop links with other trade unionists at branch level, by joining local trades' councils and similar bodies. Moreover, secondary teachers came to be addressed more explicitly as workers in their Association's communications with them, as, in general, a more labourist vocabulary was adopted. Other developments of 1920 brought ASTI into line with orthodox trade union practice. A membership card was introduced, and T.J. Burke, general secretary, became an employee, the first full-time official in the Association's history.[84]

Strike

With the progress of the Education Bill halted, the urgent demands of the secondary teachers with regard to pay remained in abeyance. It was under intense pressure from below, therefore, that the ASTI held meetings with employer bodies in February 1920.

Much sympathy was forthcoming, but little money – the CHA offered a 'bonus' of £20, utterly inadequate from the ASTI perspective; the Christian Brothers schools offered nothing at all. To the argument of these employers that they were constrained by the low levels of fees in their schools, the teachers asked whether they were expected, through their low salaries, to continue subsidising the education of the children of those such as comfortable farmers who had made enormous profits from the increased food prices of wartime.[85]

With the employers showing no sign of reconsidering their position of February, the ASTI's standing committee served a demand for a cost-of-living wage increase of 140 per cent, following a warning from T.J. Burke, general secretary, that his members might be 'forced to take other steps'. What these 'other steps' might be was indicated in a resolution passed by the Munster Provincial Council in Cork on St Patrick's Day 1920 – the eleventh anniversary of the foundation meeting. The resolution stated: 'That ASTI have not given sufficient attention to the organisation of a strike as a weapon for redressing their grievances'.[86]

The initiative lay with Cork and, at a general meeting in Dublin on 7 April, the branch was given the authority to call a localised strike, and promised financial assistance if it were to do so. A demand for an £80 'bonus' was served on the school managers on behalf of the forty members of the Cork ASTI branch. The Cork Trades Council intervened to re-open negotiations but the improved offer that emerged fell considerably short of the demand, and a strike began on Monday 3 May 1920. It was the first strike by Irish teachers.

Support came from the INTO and from technical teachers, and reports in the ITGWU's *Voice of Labour* indicate that there was considerable support in the city from other trade unionists, but there was sympathy from non-Labour sources also, with *The Irish Times* commenting: 'The financial status of these educated men … is much worse than that of the Dublin Corporation scavengers.' The CHA responded with an improved offer – worth £40 a year to men and £30 to women – but this too was rejected as 'absolutely and unutterably inadequate'.[87] How inadequate it was is indicated by the estimate of the commissioners of education that a post-war salary of £200 had the same purchasing power as a 1914 salary of

£80. At a meeting of the CEC, it was resolved to call an all-out national strike on Monday 10 May to secure the demand for £80.[88] The decision was supported at regional general meetings held in Tralee, Fermoy, Limerick, Galway, Sligo, Letterkenny and Dublin.[89]

Realising that it had underestimated the resolve and the unity of its employees, concerned about the extent of public sympathy for them, and reluctant to open up a second front at a time when it was engaged in a struggle to obstruct the government's Education Bill, the CHA hastily sought its members' approval to make a concession. An offer of £75 was accepted by the ASTI on 10 May, but the matter did not end there, for a significant minority of CHA members were unhappy about the conduct of their representatives, and refused to be bound by the agreement reached.[90] The attitude of the CHA minority was expressed in a letter written on behalf of several Limerick managers:

> The secondary teachers have our Association (to use a vulgar phrase) 'on the run', and they will use their advantage to the uttermost. They [will] ... in a word employ all the tactics had recourse to against sweaters and profiteers. Are we, who are better positioned, to stand idly by and allow this brutal and unjust treatment without a protest?[91]

In Cork, likewise, there was some resistance to what was regarded as the CHA's abject surrender to militant trade unionism, but a threat to renew the strike brought around the few intractable school managers there. Two nuclei of opposition to the agreement remained: the authorities in three Limerick schools – St Munchin's, Crescent, Laurel Hill – who wished to make a stand against what they characterised as ASTI intimidation, and the Christian Brothers throughout the country who claimed inability to pay.[92]

In Limerick, the Trades Council intervened unsuccessfully to broker a settlement, whereupon it gave full backing to the teachers, placing an advertisement in the local papers supporting the teachers' demand 'for a living wage' and appealing to 'fellow workers organised under ... Limerick Trades and Labour Council ... for the assistance necessary to bring the struggle to a speedy and successful end'. This support – which must be considered remarkable given the very different social origins of teachers and the mostly manual workers represented by the Trades Council – extended to assistance at the picket line, and to a postcard from the Trades Council circulated to the homes of individual trade unionists asking them to withdraw their children from the affected schools for the duration, and concluding: 'Parents who cause or allow their children to act as strikebreakers will have to accept the consequences.' The presence of pickets outside schools affected the delivery of supplies, a potentially serious matter for boarding schools. In a context of growing bitterness, the school managers wrote to a local paper criticising 'efforts made to represent us as rich grasping employers who refuse to their employees a living wage', and claiming, somewhat dramatically, that

> little children who still insist on coming to our schools – many of them little girls – are being molested and terrorised by grown men, many of them fathers of families, some of them secondary teachers.[93]

Three weeks would pass before the intervention of Mayor O'Callaghan succeeded in bringing representatives of the school authorities and the teachers to a conference. The outcome was an arrangement to honour the national agreement of 10 May, but the Limerick school managers would take their pound of flesh later, and, by using their prerogative to freely dismiss employees, they totally excluded lay teachers from several of their schools for a period.[94]

The Christian Brothers schools (CBS) were not represented by the CHA, and not even represented when it came to matters of finance by their own co-ordinating Education Committee. They were not party, therefore, to the settlement of 10 May, and their particular structures made it difficult to conclude a satisfactory agreement with them. On 14 May, the lay teachers in their schools placed pickets, and displayed placards appealing to parents to keep their children at home. A time of rapid trade union expansion was one when people were more disposed than usual to take seriously the code of inter-union solidarity, and the message evidently had a considerable effect. In Cork, a group of schoolboys wrote a letter to the *Examiner* stating that they would not be passing pickets out of respect for their teachers and for a Cork Trades Council request for solidarity.[95] T.J. Burke left no doubt about how seriously the Association had taken the preparations:

Elaborate arrangements for picketing schools in Dublin, Cork, and other districts have been made ... and the ASTI is taking steps to induce parents, and in particular trade unionists, to withdraw the children from the schools until a settlement is arrived at. The teachers are prepared to conduct the struggle along trade union lines, and have been guaranteed support from various bodies identified with the Irish Labour Party as well as the primary and technical teachers.[96]

A high-powered strike committee was formed; a £2 a week levy was placed on members who had returned to work; speakers were sent to address trade union bodies, and promises of financial support solicited, so as to indicate to the Brothers that resources were available for a long strike. The largest such commitment, £1,000 from the INTO, came fortuitously on Saturday 29 May just as discussions were finally beginning between the ASTI and Brothers' representatives. It was agreed to recommend that the £75 bonus be paid by local superiors, this being as far as the authority of the Brothers' negotiating group extended. Arrangements were to be made to establish fundraising committees to raise the money needed to pay the teachers in schools fairly where this was necessary. For teachers employed in the Brothers schools, it must have been reassuring – and perhaps a little embarrassing – to read the following notice in the *Irish Independent*:

> Parents, past pupils, trade unions organisations, and other bodies interested in education are requested to inaugurate meetings in provincial towns on the lines of those already held in the Dublin area for the purpose of collecting funds to enable the Christian Brothers to meet the just demands of their lay teachers. As the matter is one of great urgency, local bodies are also earnestly requested to promote such meetings without delay.[97]

Progress with the fundraising in the Dublin area was reported during the following days from committees associated with Christian Brothers schools in Synge Sreet, Richmond Street, Westland Row and Marino, with past pupils of St James's having conducted a door-to-door collection to raise the £230 due to the three lay teachers of that institution.[98]

The agreement of 29 May marked the end of the 1920 secondary teachers' strike, a significant strike in many respects. Although it occurred in circumstances that were exceptional – extreme frustration among teachers; an acceptance to an unprecedented extent of the right of workers to use the strike weapon; a willingness among other trade unionists to express solidarity in tangible ways – success was by no means guaranteed. Clearly, among school managers, there was surprise at the extent of unity among teachers, and at the network of support that they were able to draw upon. And there was also anger among managers, with the ASTI being obliged to resort to legal action in several cases where retribution took the form of dismissal of a teacher.[99]

'We have asserted ourselves...'

Although it lasted for only one day in most schools, the strike of May 1920 was a milestone in the early history of the ASTI. While there had been earlier successes – the almost immediate recognition by all of the main interest groups of its right to publicly represent the views of lay teachers; the implantation of the Association in all four provinces and among both sexes within a few years of its foundation – to have directly confronted the Catholic religious employers would have been inconceivable any time before 1919. The ASTI's approach from its foundation had been to press the state to advance the reform agenda, which was pursued by securing public sympathy through lobbying and newspaper publicity. Progress had been made on the key issues of registration and pay, but it had been frustratingly slow and piecemeal. This was due both to the state's preoccupation with more vital matters in Ireland and elsewhere, and to the determination of the Catholic Church to maintain control over its own substantial segment of second-level education. The Association complained, but felt constrained from doing any more.

In a hypothetical strike situation, the ASTI might have been able to shut down Protestant-run schools, but, by and large, their authorities were not the ones that were being obstructive. Most Catholic-run schools would have been merely inconvenienced by the withdrawal of their lay staffs, with the predominant religious element available to see out any dispute. And the ASTI could not even be confident of its capacity to withdraw its members if it wished, given the pressure that isolated individuals in particular would have come under from their employers and the loyalty that many undoubtedly felt towards their schools. Their Association's weakness saw it being taken for granted, and resulted in secondary teachers falling behind other groups during the inflation-ridden later years of the war and its immediate aftermath. Even in seeking allies to compensate for its weakness, the ASTI was cautious, and understandably so, given the differing political standpoints of its members, but eventually it became part of an unprecedentedly powerful Labour movement, having first accepted the protection of the INTO.

The relative success of the 1920 strike was due to a number of factors, not least the extreme anger of secondary teachers who had seen almost every other category of employee win substantial increases while their own avowedly Christian employers allowed them to fall into penury. The sense of outrage was strong enough to ensure that the response to the strike declaration was solid, but solidity in itself was not enough to achieve victory – even with state examinations imminent; even with the particular vulnerability of the Christian Brothers schools which relied more on lay teachers than others. It was the solidarity from other trade unionists that was the crucial factor in persuading the Catholic authorities to concede. Even though the spirit of Fr Murphy manifested itself in Limerick and a few other places, the fact was that the Catholic hierarchy did not wish to find itself at odds with the mushrooming Labour movement at that particular point. That was why it opted for a strategic retreat. From the ASTI perspective the retreat gave grounds for the satisfaction expressed by T.J Burke, general secretary: 'We have asserted ourselves, we have the courage of our beliefs and convictions, we have abundantly demonstrated our determination to secure for ourselves a competent existence.'[100]

Securing a 'competent existence' would remain the key objective of the Association, but one which would soon be pursued in very different circumstances. The next chapter will trace ASTI's progress during the early years of the Irish Free State.

3

'Patient effort to effect an improvement'
ASTI in the Burke era, *c.*1920–37

The twenty-fifth anniversary of the foundation of the ASTI in 1934 was thoroughly commemorated, with the holding of a special convention, with the publication of a pamphlet, *Security of Tenure, 1909–1934*, and with the launch of a determined recruitment campaign. The centrepiece was a jubilee dinner in Dublin's Metropole restaurant on 8 December, where the capacity attendance of 110 included significant figures of state, Church and academy, as well as current and former Association activists.

What was most notable about the dinner was the profile of the dignitaries attending – there were so many ASTI veterans among them that one might have speculated that this small Association was taking control of the country: Éamon de Valera, chairman of the ASTI's Leinster Provincial Council in 1910, was head of government; Tomás Ó Deirg was minister for education; Frank Fahy was ceann comhairle; Séumas Davin was national secretary of Fianna Fáil; Frank O'Duffy was deputy secretary of the Department of Education; ex-ASTI president L.C. Murray was head of the primary branch of the Department of Education; Micheál Breathnach and Con Duane were both Department of Education inspectors; Cormac Ó Cadhlaigh, one of the founding sextet in Fermoy, was professor of Irish at UCD; E.W. Farrell was professor of Latin at UCD; ex-ASTI president W.J. Williams was a lecturer in Education at UCD; Michael Hayes, ex-ceann comhairle and ex-minister for education, was a professor of Irish at UCD. In addition, there were ASTI veterans among the spouses of several of the other dignitaries: Mrs MacEntee, married to the minister for finance, was former

CEC member Margaret Browne; Mrs Blythe, married to the Cumann na nGaedheal ex-minister for finance, was former ASTI national secretary Annie McHugh; Mrs Merriman, married to the UCC president, was also a former member.[1] The assembled evidence of success achieved by former secondary teachers was explained thus by Association president, G.D Daly:

> So intolerable, indeed, were the conditions under which we worked 20 or 25 years ago that many very highly qualified men were forced to abandon the profession, and we are not surprised to find that many of our former members are distinguished in other walks of life today. The loss to education has been the gain of other careers, and, incidentally, of our country.[2]

One might quibble with the analysis. Was it that these founding figures of the new state had been 'forced to abandon' teaching? Or was it that frustration caused by their social and economic position had led some secondary teachers down a revolutionary path? Certainly, their service in the national cause seems a more plausible explanation for the prominence of most of them than one stressing the superior attractions of 'other careers'.[3]

One of the two guests who addressed the gathering was Blackrock College president Rev. John Charles McQuaid, attending as chairperson of the CHA, the most important of the managerial bodies. There is no doubt that McQuaid was well aware that he was addressing a body which was, in his own phrase, 'constituted on a non-denominational basis',[4] but he chose to take no account of the sensitivities of the non-Catholic element:

> In the choice of this day for your celebration, we may well be allowed to find a gracious omen of future blessing. For is it not fitting that the heirs of the Catholic lay-teachers who have heroically preserved our Catholic and Irish culture should have decided to commemorate the founding of their Association on this feast of the Mother of God, Mary Immaculate? Under the protection of Her who gave us our Divine Teacher, may your members with increasing fruitfulness, continue in our midst the divine work of Catholic Education.[5]

In his own short address, de Valera alluded to the point made by G.D. Daly, allowing that, twenty-five years earlier, 'many who thought they had a vocation for teaching were compelled to leave it.' Things had changed greatly, however, because 'the more material aims of the Association have now been achieved'. The challenges facing secondary teachers in the future, he went on, would be educational ones resulting from ongoing social and technical development:

> The growth of mechanical processes in industry shows that there is a need for highly-specialised knowledge ... Now that the universities are becoming more and more professional, it must be realised that the secondary schools are becoming the universities of the common people. What we formerly looked for to the universities – culture – we must now seek from the secondary schools. With the need for specialisation, the question is whether we should not seek more general developments in education, leaving specialisation for a later stage.[6]

In setting out this challenging agenda for secondary teachers, de Valera admitted that his government had 'not been able to give as much time as it deserved to education' during its two years in office, because it had faced a 'difficult time in industry and economics'. The time had come, however, to devote attention to developing 'a system more in accord with modern conditions and conditions in our own country'.[7]

'Conditions in our own country'

The period 1932–34 was not the first during which de Valera found it expedient to postpone dealing with educational issues. In April 1919, as Joe Lee pointed out, the same ex-teacher, 'who claimed the mantle of the educationalist Pearse', appointed no minister for education to his revolutionary Sinn Féin cabinet. The omission was a deliberate one, shaped by the imperative of avoiding disagreement with the Catholic bishops who were just then contriving to lay to rest the unpalatable recommendations of Molony and Killanin.[8] That cabinet did have an Irish language ministry, however, reflecting Sinn Féin's Gaelic League-influenced policy, which was to Gaelicise Ireland. It was a policy that had an appeal also for certain Catholic thinkers, who saw in the language a prophylactic against the secularising influence of the Anglophone world.

The Gaelic League itself saw the education system as the key arena in its struggle – if English had been spread through the school system, could Irish not be revived in like fashion? Thus it developed a detailed educational policy which was designed to restore the language, and, rather less tangibly, to promote distinctively Irish modes of thought. Its 1921 policy with regard to the secondary sector, therefore, included the reasonable demands that all examination questions should be set in both Irish and English, and that candidates should be allowed to respond in either language, but also that the English literature curriculum be 'emptied of specifically English thought and culture' and that history and geography examinations be arranged so that 'full marks may be obtained by questions bearing directly or indirectly on Ireland'.[9]

In the unsettled conditions of the War of Independence, volunteer language activists began to visit schools to ensure that Gaelic League policy was being implemented, something that caused alarm in primary schools among teachers lacking Irish. Unease in its ranks led the INTO to pre-emptively convene a National Programme Council in 1921, which was attended by representatives of the League, of the Gaelic Athletic Association, of the Dáil and local government, of Labour/Congress, and of the ASTI. The report of the council recommended a number of reforms – though none that might unduly irritate the Catholic bishops – in a programme that was consistent with cultural revivalist sentiment, but that provided for gradual implementation so as to enable teachers to extend their linguistic competence. Significantly, for a trade union initiative, the council's report was adopted as policy by Dáil Éireann's Department of Education.[10]

By contrast, the Commission on Intermediate Education, which opened in September 1921, was an initiative of the Dáil itself. To devise a curriculum that 'would meet the national requirements while allotting to the national language its due place therein' was the objective of this body, which had former secondary teachers and ASTI members Michael Hayes and Frank Fahy as chair and secretary respectively. That the commission was not permitted by its terms of reference to examine the working conditions of teachers was unsurprising in the circumstances, but the ASTI's representatives – T.J. Burke and D. Greene, a CEC member – did succeed in persuading their colleagues to advise the government that it should attend to teachers' claims in tandem with the proposed curricular and organisational reforms. Its final report, completed in December 1922, was clearly influenced by earlier deliberations, in particular by those of the 1919 Molony Commission, and most of its recommendations would be accepted by the government and would come into effect for the 1924–25 academic year.[11] The detail of the changes will be discussed below.

Just as the commission was about to begin its business, the Dáil appointed its first minister for education, J.J. O'Kelly, who already had responsibility for the Irish language. O'Kelly, known as Sceilg, was a founder of Sinn Féin and was president of the Gaelic League during the period of his ministry. Editor of the *Catholic Bulletin*, he was a conservative Catholic.[12] Sceilg was also an inflexible republican, and his tenure was to be short, because of his opposition to the Anglo-Irish Treaty of December 1921. He was replaced not by one but by two pro-treaty ministers for education – one a member of the Dáil cabinet headed by Arthur Griffith, and one of the provisional government recognised by the British which was headed by Michael Collins.

In the context of the Civil War that broke out in June 1922, neither Fionán Lynch (a military associate of Michael Collins who had survived the 1916 Rising and several prison hunger strikes) nor Michael Hayes (another 1916 veteran, who was an ASTI member at CBS Synge Street before he secured a lecturing position at UCD) had much time to devote to educational matters, and civil servants were left to oversee them. The 21,000-strong civil service, significantly, hardly changed at all in terms of its personnel in the transition to native control. This was a surprising aspect of a revolution, which, according to one of its architects, Kevin O'Higgins, was carried out by 'probably the most conservative minded revolutionaries that ever put through a successful revolution', and arguably one that ran counter to the objective of eliminating 'English thought and culture'. One notable change in education, however, came with the dissolution of the National and Intermediate Boards, and the temporary transfer of their power to two pairs of civil servants. The National Board was dissolved in January 1922, but it was not until June 1923 that Proinsias Ó Dubhtaigh and Seosamh

Ó Néill (one of the primary schools' commissioners, and, prior to that, school's inspector J.J. O'Neill) took over the reins of the secondary system. The new Department of Education replaced both sets of commissioners from 1 June 1924.[13] Throughout the period, the ASTI was impatient with the slow pace of change, expressing 'profound disappointment' in January 1923, for example, about the failure 'to advance any educational policy or to promote legislation for the removal of the admitted grievances of the secondary teachers' and, a few months later, urging that the Free State follow the example of Northern Ireland which was 'recasting the whole system of education for its area'.[14]

A Free State government, composed according to Paul Bew of 'intellectually severe and brusque martinets', replaced the previous parallel administrations in December 1922. Minister for education was Eoin MacNeill, a UCD historian and cultural nationalist, who represented the National University of Ireland constituency in Dáil Éireann, and who is remembered as the Irish Volunteer leader who tried to stop the 1916 Rising. He was greatly interested in education, but was preoccupied with other matters during much of his term as minister for education.[15] MacNeill – a 'sincere and devout Catholic', according to his panegyrist, John Ryan SJ[16] – enjoyed the confidence of the Catholic bishops, mainly because he shared their conservative views on many issues. For a younger MacNeill, the tendency of the 'modern democratic state' was to evolve into a 'socialist regime' antagonistic to the Catholic interest, and he maintained his opposition to 'statism' in education. He was also sceptical of the 'great craze' for technical education, which he characterised as 'simply slave education ... an insult to human nature'.[17] On taking office, accordingly, MacNeill signalled that no major shake-up in the organisation of secondary education was envisaged. Indeed, remarks in the first annual report of his department might have been written by a bishop:

> The state at present inspects these schools regularly... but it neither founds secondary schools, nor finances the building of them, nor appoints teachers or managers, nor exercises any power of veto over the appointment or dismissal of such teachers or the management of the schools ... and the secondary system remains as hitherto one of purely private management.[18]

As a co-founder of the Gaelic League, however, MacNeill was committed to strengthening the position of Irish – even if he was less optimistic than many of his contemporaries about the likely contribution of the schools to this endeavour. For his government, accused of being anti-national by its republican opponents, its resolute commitment to the cause of the language was expedient proof of the opposite.

MacNeill's overall contribution to educational policy was less than it might have been, for, as the Free State's representative on the Boundary Commission, he was otherwise preoccupied during most of the period of his custodianship. And this did not go unnoticed, for in protesting about the minister's failure to meet undertakings given to its representatives, the ASTI sought to direct 'public attention to the fact that as Boundary Commissioner, the Minister appears to be unable to devote any time to his duties in the Education Department'.[19] When disappointment at the outcome of his commissionership brought an end to his ministerial career, MacNeill was replaced in Education by John Marcus O'Sullivan, also a UCD historian and a well-connected social conservative, who was as concerned as his predecessor about the 'harmfulness' of increasing state control in education. O'Sullivan, who had spent several student years in Bonn and Heidelberg, represented his native Kerry in the Dáil and served in Education until 1932. He differed from most of his colleagues in having played no role in the revolutionary events that led to the foundation of the state, but he was a far more effective and engaged minister than his predecessor. By Joe O'Connor's account, O'Sullivan could not even 'bless himself in Irish to save his soul' (despite being an accomplished linguist), but he oversaw the introduction of several significant developments in policy with respect to the Irish language, including compulsory Irish in state examinations at second level.[20]

Arguably more important for the pace and direction of education policy in the new state than any of the early ministers was Rev. Timothy Corcoran, the Catholic Church's own shadow – or phantom – minister for education. He merits a full introduction.

Corcoran, a Jesuit priest from a comfortable background in Offaly, was a vigorous defender of Catholic prerogatives in education. In 1908, he was appointed professor of education at UCD, becoming the first holder of an influential post which he retained through the nation-forming years that followed, until his retirement in 1942. His views put him at odds with the ASTI on the Registration Council for secondary teachers, of which he was an early member, and also on the Molony Committee. As the new state took shape, he was an important witness before the Dáil Commission on Secondary Education and the National Programme Councils of 1921 and 1924. And while it is difficult to accept that such an avowedly stern and inflexible man could have been captivated by the enthusiasm of the moment, his 'expert' testimony did mislead the Programme Councils with regard to the ease with which Irish might be revived through the schools.[21] An ASTI representative on one of these bodies recalled as follows: 'Fr Corcoran, as would be expected by anyone who knew that able and forceful educationalist, dominated the Commission and imposed the classical tradition on the language section of the report.'[22] Corcoran, therefore, was a pedagogical traditionalist, favouring classical over modern languages, and critical of liberal and child-centred educationalists like Montessori, Froebel and Pestalozzi for failing to take into account the 'effect of original sin' on human nature, and thereby 'perverting the whole professional mentality and action of teachers'.[23] He was a prolific polemicist, a founder of the periodical *Studies*, and a contributor to the *Catholic Bulletin* and the *Irish Monthly*. His articles in these publications conveyed his general outlook, but on occasion, they could be quite specific in their critique of proposals, and unambiguously directive in their tone. They were read, and were intended to be read, by senior public servants and political leaders. According to E. Brian Titley, Corcoran acted as a 'watchdog' for the bishops in educational affairs, and his comments precisely reflected their attitude in every respect. For Seosamh Ó Néill, secretary of the Department of Education, his influence was unparalleled: 'In the reconstruction of the Irish state, he was from the beginning the master-builder in Education.'[24]

If he was a master builder, Corcoran was also, as indicated above, an architect with regard to Irish language policy. And if he was naively optimistic, and lacking in competence in matters linguistic, he was not alone in this. There was an undoubted enthusiasm for the Gaelicisation project at all levels of society, alongside impractical notions of how easily it might be carried out. Joe O'Connor, in his own inimitable style, recalled the initial response of teachers:

61

Fired by the impatience of a newly emancipated people, the ministry made the extravagantly courageous decision to teach teachers Irish overnight, and the teachers, no less patriotic, and unaware of the magnitude of the task, undertook to tackle it at once. Centres of instruction were established all over the land from Donegal to Kerry, instructors qualified and unqualified were appointed to teach the thronging classes ... and the long summer holidays of 1922 were sacrificed to the forlorn hope of learning a difficult language before the schools reopened. How I remember the mad enthusiasm of it all, the good fellowship, the comedy of teachers playing pupil pranks on us 'professors'...[25]

(For at least one of his readers, O'Connor's jocularity on the subject was inappropriate, and it prompted a response which included the following jibe: 'The man who has a lifetime ... supposedly engaged in the promotion of Irish, and then gives his name as Joe O'Connor, advertises either that he has turned his back on his own beliefs or never understood them.'[26])

The status of Irish was integral to the recommendations of the Commission on Intermediate Education which were put into effect in September 1924, the beginning of the second academic year after the publication of its report.

In organisational terms, the principal change was the abolition of the system of payment according to examination result, and the introduction instead of capitation fees based on inspection – with bonuses for schools using Irish as the medium of instruction. So as 'to satisfy the department that he is sufficiently advanced in knowledge and intelligence', each prospective secondary student was required thereafter to sit an entrance examination in 'Irish, arithmetic, and at least one other subject'. The number of state exams was reduced to two, with prescribed periods of study for each: three or four years for the junior cycle leading to an Intermediate Certificate; two additional years in the senior course leading to a Leaving Certificate. Passes in five subjects were necessary to achieve a certificate in either case. From 1925, one of the five had to be Irish at Intermediate level, and, from 1934, success in Irish became mandatory for the award of a Leaving Certificate.[27]

By way of preparation for the new dispensation, and having previously established that a third of its members had no Irish, the

ASTI organised summer courses at Ballinskelligs in 1924. These ran until the state ceased funding them in 1929.[28]

The reforms of 1924 would have been welcomed on educational grounds by many teachers, but they did not satisfactorily address their grievances as employees. And with government accepting the status quo as far as the influence of the religious was concerned, the prospects for ASTI effort were inauspicious. The negotiating process would continue to be as labyrinthine as before, and agreements just as difficult to enforce in circumstances where there was a sometimes purposeful ambiguity in respect of where precisely lay the prerogatives of the state and of the several employer bodies.

Leaving Labour; leaving Gardiner Place

One vehicle that was available for the expression of reservations about developments was the Labour Party, a joint body with the Irish Trades Unions Congress until 1930 and the main parliamentary opposition between 1922 and 1927. The ASTI, following its decision of 1919, remained an affiliate, and general secretary T.J. Burke played a notable part in the movement, guided by INTO general secretary and TD for County Galway, T.J. O'Connell. (O'Connell, incidentally, credited the national teacher network in his sprawling nine-seat constituency with his own electoral success.) In 1923, T.J. Burke took steps to join his mentor in the Dáil, when, with the support of the Association, he sought a Labour nomination. He was not nominated, and even if he had been, it was unlikely that he would have been returned in an election where only fifteen of Labour's forty-five candidates were successful.[29]

Burke was also prominent in formulating Labour's policy on education which was published in 1925. While it accepted the desirability of strengthening the Irish language, and the goal of moulding 'civilised Christian human beings', the thrust of that policy was social democratic and secular – and not at all consistent with the view of the Catholic lobby. It called for an integrated and locally accountable system of free education at all levels from nursery, through primary, to secondary and technical, with adequate grants for those proceeding to university. For teachers, it recommended appropriate training, common salary scales, as well as employee protection and adequate pensions.[30] However, in circumstances where Labour's policy was largely aspirational, it is not clear that it even had the support of the general body of ASTI members.

There certainly remained considerable doubt about the wisdom of affiliation with the party and the trade unions, and the matter regularly forced itself onto the agenda of meetings. During 1926, disaffiliation from Labour was discussed in the context of recruiting teachers who remained outside of the ASTI, according to themselves, specifically because of the connection.[31] The following was recorded in the minutes of a meeting of the Dublin branch held in April 1926:

> Mr Keane stated that from inquiries, he gleaned that the objection to Labour was due to three causes: '1) that the connection was infra dig.; 2) fear of being involved in a strike; 3) that we were educators of middle classes, and as such, our connection should be with this class'.[32]

If such potential members were unfavourably disposed towards Labour, their views on secondary education itself were also out of step with the egalitarian policy of the ASTI.

That opinion was as evenly divided within the Association as it had been when the decision on the Labour affiliation was originally taken in 1919 was shown when delegates tied in a vote on a resolution proposing disaffiliation that was put before the annual convention in April 1927. That inconclusive outcome was followed by a ballot of members on the matter, which, on a margin of eleven votes, favoured disaffiliation. So as not to embarrass Labour ahead of an election, no public announcement of the separation was issued.[33]

There were several reasons why members might have voted to leave the Labour movement in 1927. Labour was a trade union centre, but it was also a political party, and there were teachers who had allegiances to other political parties. The consolidation of Fianna Fáil therefore, which had occurred during the previous twelve months, may have affected the attitude of some members towards the Labour affiliation. This was not the principal factor, however. Rather, the intermittent debate on the matter revealed different perceptions within the membership of the nature of the Association – for some its essential role was as a trade union; for others, it should act as a professional association. The decision of 1927 which, in a formal sense, settled the matter for several decades, did not alter the ASTI's dual role however. Arguably, it remained more of a trade union than a professional association, not least because the state and the school managerial bodies jealously guarded their prerogatives in educational affairs.

Similar debates were taking place elsewhere in the Labour movement during these years. The wave that had carried the movement forward in the 1918–22 period had ebbed, and with the launch of Fianna Fáil there was little prospect of a surge in the foreseeable future. A striking performance in the Free State election of 1922 was followed by disappointment in 1923, a recovery in the first election of 1927 and a serious setback in the second, after which T.J. O'Connell became leader. The organisational connection with the trade union movement was identified as a fundamental factor in inhibiting Labour's policy development capacity and in undermining its appeal to the electorate. The Irish Trade Union Congress and the Labour Party consequently went their separate ways in 1930. The ASTI by then, of course, had no connection with either.[34]

The cutting of the connection with Labour was not the most serious of the disappointments faced by T.J. Burke during these years, for it was also decided that the maintenance of a full-time office was not financially sustainable – even though the premises in Gardiner Place were provided at a nominal rent by the INTO. In September 1926, therefore, Mr Burke went back to the classroom, at Blackrock College. Until 1937, he continued to act as general secretary on a part-time basis from his home in Ballsbridge, keeping regular office hours each evening, and conducting business on a telephone paid for by the ASTI.[35]

At the root of the financial problems of the 1920s was the low level of membership. With 131 full-time members paying £2.10s.0d each, the key source of revenue would have generated at most £327 in 1926, the salary of a male teacher around the mid-point of the incremental scale, and clearly insufficient for the running of an office.

Why was membership so low? The division over the Labour affiliation from 1919 was certainly a factor, but the partition of the island immediately afterwards also contributed. The ASTI quickly became a twenty-six-county Association, notwithstanding the two-year term as president in 1921 and 1922 of Bernard Gillespie, a long-serving teacher at St Malachy's College, Belfast, and a veteran from the AIUT days. The loss of the six Ulster counties and, for a time, of Protestant teachers in the Free State made the ASTI reliant far more than formerly on the Catholic sector, throughout which the majority of lay teachers were scattered in ones and twos. Only 498 (34 per cent) of the 1,461 registered secondary teachers in the 283 schools in the Free State in 1926 were lay teachers, an average of less than two per school.[36]

On the face of it, the combination of declining membership and isolation from the Labour movement should have greatly restricted the ASTI's influence. Evidently, however, its representatives were able to overcome these shortcomings to some extent by drawing on personal connections with leading figures.

Pay and pensions

On one level, the status of the Association and of secondary teachers improved under the new dispensation. Half of the 'twelve apostles', the 1923 appointees to the new schools inspectorate were ASTI members – they included the memoirists Joe O'Connor and Micheál Breathnach. In 1924, a long-standing slight on the competence of lay secondary teachers was removed when, for the first time, they became eligible for positions as assistant examiners in the state examinations. It was gratifying too that several parliamentary commissions and committees sought expert input from ASTI members.[37]

The status that would accrue from adequate salaries, secure tenure and superannuation, however, had to be fought for. In the Dáil, the INTO's T.J. O'Connell was an effective advocate, while branch officers continued to lobby councillors as they had done since the foundation of the Association. Indicative of the continuity that there was between new and old, a system of so-called 'interim grants' to secondary education, on the Birrell model, was adopted by the Free State government. Due to the efforts of the ASTI, the money was paid directly to teachers for the first time in 1922. Further lobbying resulted in another reform in 1923 – the linking of the amount of this 'bonus' payment to the length of service – but it did not increase the total allocation.[38]

That scepticism remained among secondary teachers about their prospects under the Free State is suggested by Sean O'Faolain's recounting of the response he got in 1924 when he asked a fellow teacher at the Christian Brothers school in Ennis if he had ever thought of marrying: 'Marry? Are you mad? On my salary? With a mother and a sister to support? How the bloody hell do you think I could get married? Do you know anything at all about the facts of life?' The writer had no answer, but the questions prompted him to reconsider his career choice.[39]

The introduction of the new programme for secondary schools in 1924–25 did provide a focus for teachers' claims – if they were to co-operate in working more productively, could they not be properly paid? With the support of the management bodies, renewed pressure was placed on the relevant government departments of Education and Finance. During the summer vacation of 1924, Eoin MacNeill announced that a minimum salary would be set for teachers and that a system of incremental payments would be introduced – 'based on the length of service, and merit of teaching, and so calculated as to bring the teacher's salary up to a good maximum in, say, ten or twelve years'. Ernest Blythe in Finance, having only recently reduced old age pensions (and, not all that long before, married Annie McHugh, national secretary of the ASTI) was insistent that terms should not be too generous, arguing that taxpayers should not have to pay more for teachers than the amount necessitated by the operation of supply and demand. The finance minister's was a miserly hand in ordinary circumstances, but his authority over Education was even greater than over other departments, since Eoin MacNeill was totally preoccupied with Boundary Commission matters at this point, and it was Blythe who presented significant details to the Dáil in March 1925.[40]

Minimum salaries which were to be paid by schools in receipt of capitation grants to 'recognised' teachers were £200 for men and £180 for women. 'Interim grant' payments, meanwhile, were replaced by an incremental amount paid directly by the Department of Education to the teacher on a quarterly basis. Male teachers were to get £12 a year for each of the first ten years of service and £15 for each of the next six years, with a £40 allowance for holders of honours degrees (maximum total, £450); female teachers were to get £10 a year for each of twelve years, with a £20 allowance for an honours degree (maximum total, £320).

In the implementation of the proposals, there was annoyance

that the highest point of entry, regardless of service, was at the tenth incremental point and, when calculations were done, it was found that all women teachers and a majority of men teachers would receive, in total, somewhat less than they had under the previous ad hoc system. For Blythe, teachers should have been happy to accept a small loss in exchange for the regularisation of their status, and, objectively, the fixing of a regular salary scale in 1925 was a considerable advance in the professionalisation of secondary teaching.[41] To accept a drop in income was a bitter pill, however, and there was much consequent resentment.

In early 1926, the ASTI resolved to pursue the matter of pensions for its members, and a vigorous campaign of agitation and publicity ensued. Ministers indicated themselves well-disposed, and eventually, in May 1928, enabling legislation, in the form of a Teachers' Superannuation Bill was brought before the Dáil by education minister John Marcus O'Sullivan. It was a bill, the minister admitted, that was 'not over-generous', but teachers were private employees not public servants, and it was all 'the resources of the country will permit'. When the details of the scheme were announced later in the year, the ASTI concentrated on trying to win improvements. Several concessions were extracted but not the major one sought – that the pension be non-contributory. The scheme, which finally came into operation in August 1929, was voluntary and based on forty years' service. It required participating teachers to contribute 4 per cent of their salary, including its incremental element. Schools contributed 2.5 per cent of the basic salary, and the state provided the remainder.[42] There were elements of the scheme that the ASTI found to be unsatisfactory, and it became the task of its national representatives to address these in negotiations with governments during the following years.

Security of tenure: the 'last grievance'

By the twenty-fifth anniversary celebrations of 1934, considerable progress had been made on the founding demands of the ASTI, which it had inherited from AIUT. Not everyone in the Metropole restaurant on 8 December 1934 would have agreed with Éamon de Valera that the 'material aims of the Association' had been achieved, but it could be acknowledged by G.D. Daly, Association president, that secondary teachers had been enabled to play their part 'in the cultural and educational development of our country'. There was a system of registration, if not an entirely satisfactory one; there was a salary scale, even if it was less than adequate; there was a pension scheme which three-quarters of lay teachers had joined. Of the original demands of the Association, it was only in respect of job security that there had been negligible progress. This was why it was decided to highlight the issue on the twenty-fifth anniversary with the publication of a special pamphlet: *Security of Tenure, 1909–1934: a Statement of the Association's Efforts*. As the title promised, the various attempts to reach agreement on the issue were traced in a very detailed way, from the first meeting between the ASTI and the CHA in 1912, through the Birrell scheme, the Molony report, the Education Bill of 1919, to a 1931 pronouncement by the Catholic bishops.

In January 1912, the CHA had offered a limited right of appeal to dismissed secondary teachers – to the bishop of the diocese in the case of diocesan colleges; to the relevant provincial or superior in schools run by religious orders. This process was rejected by the ASTI as insufficiently impartial, and in circumstances where a lay teacher had been dismissed so as to make way for a religious, it could mean appealing to the individual who had ordered the dismissal. Teachers were rendered slightly less vulnerable to dismissal by the conditions attached to the payment of the Birrell grant, even if these conditions were unevenly observed. Thereafter, school authorities were obliged to give three months' notice of dismissal, and there were also other disincentives to replacing lay teachers with religious. For the ASTI, the establishment of an independent appeals body remained a key issue. As P.J. Kennedy, the first president, remarked, it was 'useless to give a good salary to a teacher if through no fault of his own, he may be deprived of it' and 'a mockery to establish a pension scheme if the conditions of service are such that no one can ever hope to qualify for a pension'.[43] At the Molony Commission in 1918–19, there was division between teachers' and managers' representatives on the matter, and definitive statements made outlining the perspectives of the two sides. Fr Marshall, representing the CHA, justified the Catholic opposition to an independent appeals board in the following terms:

Many schools, not placed as Catholic schools are, have historical connections with the State in Ireland ... [making] the acceptance of a state tribunal of appeal a natural course for such schools … It is quite otherwise with Catholic schools, deriving their origin from another source. And Catholic schools cannot but expect a teacher working in them to recognise and conform to their essential nature. There is no parity between the admission of the state as an authority on material structures and similar issues, or even as an authority on the attainment of a proper measure of secular knowledge … and the suggestion of a state or any similar tribunal of appeal on issues vital to the Catholic nature of the educative process itself.[44]

For his part, W.J. Williams justified the ASTI's insistence on an independent appeals body:

It is admitted that a teacher must, in his official capacity, be willing to submit to certain restrictions upon his conduct … and to a certain discipline of silence in regard to his opinions. But it is well-known that these necessary conditions of his calling may be, and sometimes are, employed as instruments of unreasonable repression. The dignity of the profession, and its usefulness as an organ of intellectual progress, can be impaired by undue interference with the personal liberty of its members … In asserting a right of appeal, we assert no more than that the private interpretation of his own rights by the head of the school should be controlled by the good sense of the community as interpreted by an independent tribunal sanctioned by a public authority.[45]

In the aftermath of Molony, ASTI concern was heightened when all of its members in Limerick were systematically dismissed by way of retribution for the 1920 strike, something that was regarded as an attack on the right of teachers to act collectively. Efforts by the Association to interest the state in the matter continued, but successive ministers for education proved unsympathetic. Indeed, in one respect, the situation was made worse in 1925 with the dropping of the obligation inherited from Birrell that schools receiving state funding employ a quota of lay teachers, on the grounds that it was unconstitutional to thus discriminate against religious. Some progress was made in discussions between the ASTI and management bodies during 1925, but a general meeting of the CHA later over-ruled its own negotiators.[46]

It was intimated by the Catholic bishops that the same protection available to primary teachers under the so-called 'Maynooth resolution' was available to secondary teachers, but from the ASTI point of view there were important differences. Under the terms of the 'Maynooth resolution', as amended, primary teachers in Catholic-managed schools were entitled to a hearing, with INTO representation, before the bishop of the diocese in which their school was located before notice of dismissal could be given. The appeal hearing offered by the CHA in 1912, and subsequently, was envisaged as taking place after notice had been given, and with no right to ASTI representation. In fact, unknown to anybody outside their own ranks, the bishops had passed resolutions in 1924 and 1925 extending the terms of the 'Maynooth resolution' to certain secondary teachers. The discovery of the existence of the resolutions prompted the ASTI in 1931 to investigate where precisely matters stood, but it did not prove to be a straightforward task, for a request to the secretary of the hierarchy elicited only the response that conditions differed from one diocese to another. Moreover, only three-quarters of the bishops replied to individual queries regarding which schools in each diocese were covered by the resolutions of 1924 and 1925. The replies that were received, however, revealed that they applied to diocesan colleges and to most convent schools.[47]

With the holding of a special conference and the publication of a special pamphlet, the silver jubilee year of 1934 marked a renewed determination to resolve the rankling 'final grievance' of security of tenure once and for all. Significantly, a few hours after the special conference ended, John Charles McQuaid, chairman of the CHA and, as such, a guest speaker at the jubilee dinner, hinted that his organisation was also anxious to see a resolution. The hint was heeded, and led to a change in the ASTI's approach to the issue. During 1935, there was recognition and some acceptance of the canon law objections to the sort of appeals board that had been sought by the ASTI since its foundation. T.J. Burke, in particular, became convinced that no significant progress was possible along the lines that had been pursued.[48] It was a realisation that may have been triggered by regular contact between him and Dr McQuaid, his headmaster at Blackrock College, who had been encouraging him to participate in Catholic discussion groups. The relationship between the two men requires exploration.

In the small Irish secondary sector, it was not all that great a co-incidence that the major figures on either side of the question for most of the 1930s should have been employed in the same school. Both men were careful to avoid giving any impression that there were 'off-the-record' understandings between them lest they lose the confidence of others, but that does not mean that the consid-erable figure of McQuaid did not exert influence over the other man, or indeed that Burke was not compromised by the relation-ship. In correspondence with a member of the hierarchy on an-other matter, McQuaid wrote: 'As Mr Burke has been for years a member of our teaching staff, I have had an opportunity of ob-serving him closely, and of proving that he is a very worthy Catholic.'[49] Furthermore, by McQuaid's own account, he initiated a private discussion with Burke in late 1934 in the hope of chang-ing ASTI policy with regard to a proposal to establish a federation of Irish voluntary bodies interested in education. He was very pleased with the outcome:

> When the situation was explained, [Burke] agreed at once to se-cede from the proposed federation. He anticipates little diffi-culty in persuading [the ASTI] executive. I believe he will fully succeed, for I know that his opinion is greatly valued by his As-sociation, and this year all members of the Executive happen to be Catholics.[50]

McQuaid's letters to Archbishop Byrne of Dublin on his progress in stalling the proposed federation are very illuminating in respect of his relations with the teachers' unions and his attitude to-wards them. For this reason, they are quoted here at some length:

> It has never appeared either from correspondence or conversa-tion or the proceedings of their meetings that the INTO or ASTI consider it in any way opposed to Catholic principles to establish a federation of educational interests comprising any and every belief. There is serious evidence that the INTO (which in principle is non-denominational) is endeavouring to

show itself as the dominant educational factor in the country ...
To meet the situation, an annual Education Day in Catholic
Truth Society Week is respectfully proposed to the consideration
of the hierarchy. This scheme while avoiding the undesirable result of antagonising the lay element in Catholic educational bodies, would seem effectively to avert at least to a considerable
degree, the danger latent in the proposed federation ...[51]

On hearing the reasons put forward, [T.J. O'Connell] also
agreed at once that the proposed federation must not be established. He however fears some difficulty from certain members
of his association, who may not readily understand the situation
... None the less, he is confident that by deft arrangements, and
without giving all the reasons, he will satisfy at least the reasonable element of his executive and association ...

... The interviews with these secretaries [T.J. Burke and T.J.
O'Connell] lasted each for several hours. I was thus given an
unusually good opportunity of receiving frank opinions upon
existing conditions. Both men gave courteous expression to a
certain dissatisfaction as felt in their associations with the aloof-
ness of the clerical element in education and both were anxious
to obtain for their bodies an assurance that the rejection of the
proposed federation did not mean a refusal of further collabo-
ration ... I assured both secretaries that my attitude was one of
great sympathy with the lay element in Catholic education ...

... As an instance of the very sympathetic interest of the Hierarchy in the problems of secondary education, I strongly emphasised the resolution to establish the Education Day at the
annual C[atholic] T[ruth] S[ociety] congress. The Education
Day would enjoy the patronage of the hierarchy, the lay and clerical element would be fully represented, all branches of education
would participate, the atmosphere would be one of moderation
...[52]

... It will please Your Grace further that at a meeting of the
CHA held on Tuesday, 2nd inst., it was agreed to collaborate
with ASTI in common problems of secondary education affecting Catholic schools. I believe this new gesture of sympathy
with the laymens' association will go far to conciliate the good
will of this body ...[53]

... Finally, in the case of Mr Burke, I was able further to

consolidate the Catholic position by obtaining his consent to form a Regnum Christi Guild of men and women among secondary teachers. It may be possible at a future date to obtain a similar success with primary teachers ...[54]

These letters reveal McQuaid to have been a crafty strategist, single-minded about achieving hegemony for his Church in educational affairs in the new state, but much more conscious than his predecessors about the necessity to cultivate allies among teachers' representatives, and about having them believe that they were respected partners. If in his reports to Byrne a degree of vainglory is discernible, it is evident that McQuaid sought to influence the activities of the teachers' unions through arguably improper pressure on O'Connell and Burke, with Burke's position leaving him more vulnerable to such pressure.

It is likely therefore that McQuaid had a role in persuading Burke, and through him the ASTI, that it was time to change the policy in respect to appeals procedures, but it was not the only relevant factor, for there were indications from two appeals during 1935 that it was possible to achieve an equitable outcome under the arrangements approved by the Catholic hierarchy. In the first case, where a teacher on the staff of St Jarlath's College had been given notice, the association decided to appeal the case to Archbishop Gilmartin of Tuam. The archbishop accepted the man's right to be represented by the ASTI general secretary at the hearing, the outcome of which was the withdrawal of the notice of dismissal. In the second case, which was in the Ferns diocese, Bishop William Codd's response to a written appeal from the ASTI was to instruct the convent school concerned to reinstate a dismissed teacher. He did not consider a hearing to be necessary.[55] While the outcome of these cases was positive, they arose from the favourable disposition of individuals, which could not be relied on in every instance.

Following the rejection of yet another proposal by the CHA in mid-1935 – a rejection, however, accompanied by a declaration of willingness to pursue a solution based on 'the principles of justice, equity and Christian charity' – the ASTI invited counter-proposals from McQuaid. While awaiting a response, Burke exchanged letters with Rev. Timothy Corcoran, and the ASTI engaged two canon lawyers, who advised, predictably, that the only form of appeals procedure permissible under canon law was of the type which had been offered intermittently by the CHA during the previous quarter century. Accepting this, the ASTI conducted a ballot of its members in February 1936, the effect of which was to allow greater flexibility to its negotiators.[56]

McQuaid's proposals, as expected, were almost identical to the scheme which had applied for decades to teachers in Catholic-run primary schools. The headmaster/mistress was obliged to inform his/her religious superior of any proposed dismissal of a teacher, together with the reasons for it, and to inform the teacher concerned at the same time. The teacher would be further advised that there was a right of appeal to the superior, and a right to ASTI representation at the appeal hearing. Dismissal procedures had to be pursued in such a way as to allow three full months' notice before the end of the school year for the individual being dismissed. The McQuaid scheme, with some slight amendments, was accepted by standing committee, and then by CHA members, which meant that a conclusion to the issue was finally in sight.[57]

There remained the intricate process of extending the scheme to Catholic schools outside of the CHA network. In general, their authorities looked to the CHA for leadership but, at the same time, there were jurisdictional niceties to be respected, which inevitably caused delays. There were many such with regard to the tenure agreement: for the Patrician Brothers, it was because of the absence of the superior general in India; for the Marist Brothers, there were difficulties in organising an internal 'council meeting'. There is a hint of the frustration at the lack of urgency in the way its concerns were processed in the following report to the 1937 ASTI convention:[58]

A reply from the Provincial of the De La Salle Brothers on 31 July 1936 intimated that, before signing, he would send copies of the agreement to the superiors of the secondary schools conducted by the order for their observations, but at the date of the compilation of this report, he had not signed, nor did he reply to the reminders sent him on 12 October 1936, and on 1 January 1937.[59]

There was a bizarre twist in the process when the CBS negotiator insisted that temporary and probationary teachers be excluded, a demand which the ASTI reluctantly accepted. For the sake of consistency, it then asked that the exclusion be extended to other schools also. In this instance, it was the crafty McQuaid who emerged as the champion of the younger teachers, and he insisted 'that every lay teacher, irrespective of class or grade, had the right of appeal to the major superior'.[60]

Almost all the Catholic schools were included in the scheme by the time of its effective ratification by the Department of Education in July 1937. The particular circumstances of convent schools had continued to be the subject of negotiations between the bishops and the ASTI until June 1937, but the protracted character of the deliberations proved useful in that it served to clarify a number of related issues with regard to temporary contracts and to restrict the circumstances under which nuns might replace female lay teachers. Even then, there were some convent schools which were independent of the major orders in Ireland and not under episcopal jurisdiction which were not covered by the terms of June 1937. It would take some time to conclude separate agreements with these.[61]

In important respects, the outcome was not a good one for the ASTI. In the first place, the terms of the agreed appeals procedure were such that they might have been negotiated at any time in the previous twenty-five years. Secondly, in the absence of a central appeals body, there continued to be arbitrariness and inconsistency in the outcome of appeals.

Arguably, the agreement of 1936–37 marked an acceptance by the ASTI of the particular character of the new state and of the strength of Catholic authority. In the Association's early years, British governments, for their own reasons, had been prepared to press for the extension of the role of the state in secondary education, and were prepared to use financial incentives to win concessions from the Catholic bishops. But even though they had ex-ASTI members in influential positions, neither Cumann na nGaedheal nor Fianna Fáil governments wished to quarrel with the Catholic Church regarding the limits of its authority in secondary education. Moreover, as one of its leading spokesmen on education indicated, the Catholic Church would accept no such limits in any case: 'On issues of Catholic education,' insisted Rev. Corcoran, 'there is no appeal to the civil state, least of all here in Ireland, where our schools have by all historic tradition, their title to existence from the Catholic Church alone, and not from any civil power.'[62] Irish self-government, in other words, did not change anything.

The end of the Burke era

The resolution of the tenure issue coincided with the rather acrimonious end of the T.J. Burke era in the ASTI – and the two matters were not unconnected. A pivotal figure, he had played a central role since the ASTI's establishment, when he was a twenty-year-old teacher in Limerick. As secretary/treasurer of the Munster Provincial Council, he may be credited with contributing to the continuing vibrancy of the ASTI in the south, and checking any tendency for it to retreat to the metropolis as its predecessor had done. Having led the Association into the trade union movement and into a close relationship with the much larger INTO during the period of his presidency in 1919, he was an obvious choice when the ASTI decided to appoint its first full-time general secretary in 1920. Continuing in his post when it became part-time, he remained central to Association affairs for another decade. For its strengths in 1937, as well as for its weaknesses, there was nobody who was more responsible.

He retained support in the Association, but there were some members who came to believe that he was altogether too accommodating towards the clerical employers. For this reason, there had been an abortive attempt to remove him from office in 1935 and to replace him with 'a member of the legal profession, who is not, and shall not be while holding this office, engaged in secondary school teaching'.[63]

There was further discord in respect of the agreement on the appeals procedure, with some members regarding it as a stepping stone rather than as a terminal point. Consequently, a resolution passed at the 1937 conference instructed negotiators to continue to seek security of tenure 'as set out in the ASTI booklet on the matter'. For Burke, that horse had long bolted, and he saw the agreement as conclusive. It would be an act of bad faith, from his perspective, to ask the clerical managers to revisit the issue. In deference to his argument, the incoming CEC immediately agreed not to actively pursue the conference resolution. However, as inevitably

happens when discord manifests itself, other grievances were revealed: there was the failure of the Association to adequately resource the general secretary's part-time office; there was a slight
from a president. An ultimatum on the provision of office facilities
was not met, with the result that Burke tendered his final resignation in September 1937. Circumstances surrounding the resignation led to the conclusion that other leading members had by then
come around to the view that he was no longer an effective representative, and that it was time for him to go.[64]

For the next fifteen years, Burke remained a member of the
Dublin branch and a teacher at Blackrock College, where he drew
on the qualities and skills that had enabled him to steer the ASTI
during several difficult decades:

> Reassuring seems the word to describe the effect of his manner
> and method … with his tall erect figure and resonant, low-
> pitched voice … He was alert and hardworking in class, but
> friendly, and the pupil could easily feel that Mr Burke was not
> only by his side, but on his side. His punctuality and orderly
> methods of working were a by-word, and his colleagues in the
> professors' room sometimes joked about it.[65]

While Burke devoted himself wholly to his responsibilities in Blackrock, new arrangements were adopted in respect of the administration of the ASTI. These will be outlined in the next chapter.

4

'Diligence and enthusiasm in the interests of secondary teachers'

The Association in the 1940s and 1950s

The sudden departure of the long-serving general secretary represented a 'grave crisis in the history of the Association', according to a report of the CEC, but scarcely had T.J. Burke departed than the reasonableness of his demand for resources was acknowledged, and city centre premises secured. At a special convention at the end of October 1937, moreover, it was accepted that a full-time officer was required, and advertisements were placed and interviews held for the post of organising secretary. Six individuals were interviewed in December, and Liam Glynn – an Irish scholar and a Quaker of Belfast, who had recently resigned a position at Newtown School in Waterford, and who had been involved in the efforts to remove T.J. Burke – took up the position in January 1938. The appointment was temporary, subject to ratification by convention, and the salary was so meagre that it was thought necessary to permit the appointee to accept other work, provided 'such work be part-time, outside of office hours, and neither political nor sectarian, nor of such nature as would … hinder the efficient performance of his secretarial and organising duties'. Glynn's tenure, however, would be short-lived, for when the candidates interviewed in December came before convention in April, his appointment was overturned. Instead, it was an experienced teacher, Florence Eva Quirke, MA, who was selected on a majority vote of delegates to fill the position.[1]

Quirke came to her ASTI post highly recommended. According to testimonials from principals of the several Mercy Convent schools in which she had taught, she was a 'high-principled, absolutely reliable, trustworthy' individual, who was notable for her 'personal refinement and gentleness', and was 'particularly qualified for any position which requires patience and industry'.[2] Her term in office would exceed even that of T.J. Burke, and nineteen years passed before she returned to the classroom, having been offered an opportunity to complete her teaching service for pension purposes. Her 'diligence and enthusiasm in the interests of secondary teachers' was recognised throughout the Association, but her talents lay in the administrative field as her testimonials had indicated, and her role was never quite as central as that of T.J. Burke's had been.[3] Presidents and other part-time officers were the principal negotiators during the Quirke era. It was an era that would see considerable progress, though little until the constraints of the 'Emergency' years slackened. ASTI membership would grow greatly and its work would be facilitated by new conciliation and arbitration mechanisms, while there would be significant improvements in pay and pensions.

That was all in the future and unforeseen in 1938, but, after an interval of more than a decade, the restoration of a professional ASTI with city centre offices in South Frederick Street was appreciated, and it became possible because of the modest success of the recruitment campaign inaugurated during the anniversary commemorations of 1934. While the ASTI still represented only a minority of lay secondary teachers, it was a growing minority. In 1926, the year in which it was decided to relinquish full-time office and officership, there were 131 full members and 20 associate members. By the time Florence Quirke took up her position in 1938, there were 270 full members and 90 associates. Though a marked improvement, it represented less than 30 per cent of all the lay secondary teachers employed in the jurisdiction. At the 1937 convention, it was reported that seventy-three members had joined or re-joined in the previous years, that new branches had been established in Castlebar, Dungarvan and Athlone, but that efforts to establish branches in Carlow, Cavan and Wexford had been unsuccessful. 'Many areas,' concluded the report, 'in which flourishing branches should exist are largely unorganised.' That convention had delegates from seventeen branches: Castlebar, Galway and Tuam in Connacht; Cork, Clare, Limerick, Roscrea, Tipperary, Tralee, Waterford, and West Waterford in Munster; Drogheda, Dublin, Kildare, Kilkenny and

Mountmellick in Leinster.[4] The war-time 'Emergency' years would see membership decline again, due, in some part, to the adverse effect on the *esprit de corps* of branch meetings being poorly attended due to the fuel shortage. Some branches went out of existence for a period, including the symbolically important Fermoy branch, as well as others in more populous place like Galway, Dundalk and Athlone. The impact of falling numbers on revenue was such that the abandonment of the Association's full-time office was again discussed during 1946.[5]

The pre-'Emergency' years which saw modest growth in the ASTI were years of considerable expansion in post-primary education generally. In the secondary schools, student numbers grew from 24,488 in 1926–27 to 35,111 in 1936–37, an increase of 43 per cent. During the same decade, the number of secondary schools rose from 283 to 327 (+15 per cent), while the total number of teachers rose from 2,298 to 2,948 (+23 per cent).[6] The religious element remained dominant within the system, however, especially in the female sector where 65 per cent of all teachers were nuns by the early 1940s. Increasingly, there was a feeling within the ASTI that it had become almost impossible for a Catholic lay woman to make a career in secondary education. The early career of the highly qualified and avowedly competent Florence Quirke might be taken as an exemplar of how difficult it actually was to secure a permanent position. During her thirteen years as a teacher, she worked in at least six institutions: five years in the Carysfort Training College, and shorter periods in the St Louis Convent in Monaghan, in the Loreto Convent in North Great George's Street, Dublin, and in the Mercy Convents at Ballinasloe, Ballinrobe and Ennis.[7]

Elsewhere in the post-primary sector, the Vocational Education Act of 1930 would bring order to the somewhat ramshackle system of technical education that had evolved over several decades. An element of secular and democratic local management provided for in the 1930 Act was not opposed by the Catholic hierarchy, as might have been anticipated, but the bishops did lobby to ensure that these schools would remain strictly technical and that they should not compete with secondary schools by offering anything in the way of 'general education', while also insisting that they should not be co-educational, and that they should provide denominational religious instruction. Restricted in some respects as the vocational sector was, due to their lordships' intervention, it proved attractive and there was a considerable growth in the number of teachers and students through the 1930s.[8]

Contracts and registration

Following T.J. Burke's departure, a major issue needing attention concerned contracts of employment. There was no standard contract; indeed, most teachers had no written contract at all. Fruitless approaches to the Department of Education on the matter led the ASTI back inevitably to Dr McQuaid and the CHA. McQuaid declared himself favourably disposed in May 1937 to a standard contract for lay teachers in Catholic schools which would incorporate the appeals procedures, although he dismissed a draft prepared by the ASTI. As he had done on the previous occasion, however, he prepared his own draft, which incorporated some ASTI-proposed changes. After some further refinements, the contract was accepted without enormous enthusiasm by the CEC in January 1940, and later by a majority of five to one in a ballot of the membership. The document was then despatched on a journey through the litany of Church organisations interested in education. By mid-1940, it had been accepted by the Catholic hierarchy and by the more significant of the management bodies. The ISA, however, held that the existing contract in the Protestant schools offered more protection; ASTI members in those schools agreed with the ISA, so the new standard contract was introduced in Catholic schools only.[9]

The agreement on a contract for lay teachers in Catholic schools was John Charles McQuaid's last major accomplishment as chairman of the CHA. The post itself he had valued for the influence it gave him in educational policy, and it was one that he had gone to some lengths to retain even after his term as president of Blackrock College came to an end, when, strictly speaking, he was no longer eligible even for membership of the Headmasters' Association.[10] Eventually, it was McQuaid's appointment as archbishop of Dublin in November 1940 that would terminate his leadership of the CHA. And if there were Dublin clergy who were apprehensive about his accession, there were secondary teachers who regretted his departure from his former office. Even though McQuaid had been disrespectful of the ASTI's non-denominational character and rather devious in his relations with its officials during his decade in office, he had been

far more amenable to dealing with the Association than his predecessors. He was an autocratic man, but a strategic thinker, and he
saw that a self-confident (but tractable) Catholic middle-class was
an essential bedrock of the Catholic social order that he was en-
deavouring to bring into being.[11] Where school managers and bishops of an earlier generation had seen only dispensable assistants and
their irritating advocates, McQuaid had recognised that the ASTI
was composed of educated men and women, some of them potential cadres in his own crusade for a particular type of social order.

One major concern that was not addressed during McQuaid's
decade in control of the CHA, however, was the growth in the number of unregistered teachers in secondary schools. Registration had
been regarded as a major achievement, and the improvements in conditions that had been won in the 1920s and 1930s had flowed from
it. The transitional period provided for when registration was introduced in 1918 expired in 1925, just as the Saorstát's educational reforms were introduced. From then on, only fully qualified teachers
could avail of the state's incremental payments, pensions and other
benefits. School managers, however, were increasingly evading their
obligations by employing unregistered teachers. In 1924–25, the first
year of full registration, 34 per cent of secondary teachers were in the
'unregistered' category. Ten years later, this had increased to 47 per
cent. In a decade during which the number of registered teachers in
an expanding system had increased by 115, the number of unregistered had increased by 613. It should be borne in mind, however,
that the unregistered included some probationary teachers, who
would qualify for registration on completion of three years' service.[12]

As in other matters, circumstances were worst in the female sector. According to one ASTI document, only 10 per cent of male lay
teachers were completely unqualified (if, for the purposes of the calculation, all graduates are regarded as qualified). For male religious,
the unqualified represented 37 per cent of the total; for female lay
teachers, it was 39 per cent and for female religious, 43 per cent.[13]

Many of the unqualified were part-time teachers, while some of
them taught subjects such as science where there was a shortage of
qualified teachers, and others taught art and music, subjects in which
it was difficult to acquire qualifications that met the registration criteria. Even allowing for such factors, it is clear that many schools followed a policy of employing unqualified teachers in order to save

money – in the case of religious orders, it may have been a matter of finding placements for some of their growing numbers in the decades following the establishment of the state. More than half of all schools were not availing of their entitlement with regard to the number of registered teachers they employed during the 1930s and 1940s.

As Tubridy has shown, the proliferation of the unregistered defeated the very purpose for which the Registration Council was formed, and that body might have been expected to intervene, to express concern at least. However, the annual reports of the nineteen-member council consistently avoided the issue, probably because the ASTI's three representatives were outnumbered by representatives of school managers. For their part, the ASTI representatives on the council focused on ensuring that the registration conditions themselves were not diluted.

The ASTI itself continued to be concerned, raising the matter regularly with the Department of Education and with the school management bodies. The department itself expressed occasional concern, but its efforts to tighten regulations in 1942 were thwarted by Church opposition. Insofar as the issue was brought under control during the 1940s and 1950s, with a gradual increase in the proportion of registered teachers, it was due to ASTI vigilance.[14]

A discrete group of 'unregistered' post-primary teachers was employed in so-called 'Secondary Tops', attached to national schools and offering the secondary syllabus. More than 3,000 students were being catered for in these schools in the late 1930s, and the numbers were growing.[15] Grassroots concern about this 'new and vigorous growth' prompted the ASTI to send a deputation to the minister for education in 1945, to ask him to 'discourage the addition of Secondary Tops to primary schools'. In many of these schools, it was stated, teachers were without qualifications, while those who were qualified were poorly paid, not being eligible for the increments paid by the department to teachers in secondary schools. In circumstances where the department was not insisting on the employment of qualified teachers, and arranging to have them properly paid, the 'Secondary Top was an inadequate substitute for, and detrimental to, the secondary school proper'. A case was cited concerning an ASTI member who could not qualify for increments under the existing quota system because of the operation of a Secondary Top in the same town, which was affecting enrolment in her secondary school.

The college staff, St Colman's College, Fermoy, 1907. Some of that college's lay staff members called the ASTI formation meeting in Cork, March 1909. Included in the photo are two founder members of the ASTI: P. Doody (back row, third from left) and Thomas MacDonagh (seated, second from left).

J. Kennedy, a founder member of the ASTI and its first president.

Thomas MacDonagh, poet and teacher; a founder member of the ASTI; signatory to the 1916 Proclamation; executed 1916. (Courtesy of the National Library of Ireland)

T.J. Burke, a founder member of the ASTI; president 1919–1920; general secretary 1920–1937. (Courtesy of Blackrock College Archive)

A science lab in St Colman's College, Fermoy, taken in the 1930s. St Colman's College had a great reputation for science subjects in 1930s and '40s; pupils came from all over Munster to avail of the modern curriculum on offer. (courtesy of St Colman's College Archive)

The Diocesan School for Girls, Adelaide Road taught science subjects to girls from as early as 1903. Pictured above is a science class from 1959. From Left: Diana Lowe, Gillian Kemp, Miss Lugton, Helga Prause, June Orr, Ruthie Rowe (courtesy of the Erasmus Smith Trust Archives).

Group of delegates at annual convention, 1926, which was held in University College Cork. This was the first annual convention to be held outside Dublin and the first at which invited speakers delivered addresses on education. Photo includes the president, T.P. Waller and T.J. Burke, general secretary (sixth and seventh from left in front row).

Delegates at the annual convention, 1935, which took place in University College Galway. Included are Liam Ó Buachalla, Dónal Ó Conalláin, Miss Forde, and T.J. Burke (general secretary).

Mr. de Valera at Teachers' Convention

The 1938 annual convention of the ASTI in University College, Dublin. Front row (left to right): Liam Glynn, (briefly) general secretary; T.P. Waller, vice-president; An Taoiseach Éamon de Valera, then chancellor of National University; F. Kennedy, ASTI president; Dr. D.J. Coffey, President of UCD; and Professor P. Larkin. Reproduced from the Irish Independent, *21 April 1938.*

Convention 1952, held at UCD, Newman House, St Stephen's Green, Dublin. President Dónal Ó Conalláin. Also included are Tom Waller, F.E. Quirke (general secretary), Tom Coppinger, Bill Meyler, W.G. Kirkpatrick, Cathal O'Gara, Charlie Dillon, Liam Comerford, Rita Murphy, Maurice O'Brien, Brian Devenny, Treasa Riordan, Anna O'Shea, Liam Hogan.

For his part, the minister defended Secondary Tops as being necessary in places distant from a secondary school, and he insisted that
his department was always careful about giving permission for their
establishment.[16]

'Wreckage to be sent adrift': a female teacher's perspective

How did lay secondary teachers see themselves and their work in the
late 1940s, as their Association approached its fortieth anniversary?
The minutes of meetings and the reports of committees give a general impression of moods and attitudes within the profession, but
personal testimony can often be far more revealing. A number of
anonymous articles in the *Cork University Record*[17] which were probably written by the same young female teacher, given the tone, content and provenance, indicate that registration, increments, pensions,
and contracts had not quite eliminated the feelings of vulnerability
and insecurity that were described by Hanna Sheehy-Skeffington in
the *Irish Review* in 1912. And the fact that features of the 'murder
machine' excoriated by Padraic Pearse in the same journal a few
months later were again presenting themselves was attributed to de
Valera's introduction of set texts for the state examinations:

> Thus, the average child leaving school is utterly uneducated: he
> knows a fair amount of poetry by heart – and never wants to see
> a poetry book again; he knows Latin verbs, but it is doubtful
> whether he is either able or anxious to read liturgical texts in
> Latin; he has a pretty thorough acquaintance with Irish – and
> how often does he speak it? It is the same for every subject: the
> most interesting material, if handled in the way in which unfor-
> tunate teachers are expected to handle it, becomes a mass of dead
> matter.[18]

Our anonymous teacher was no social revolutionary. She did not,
for example, argue that all teachers should be on the same salary
scale, only that women teachers should get as much as single men,
with married men continuing to get more. Moreover, while she criticised convent schools for their treatment of teachers, instancing an
advertisement in the *Independent* seeking 'a lady graduate to teach
Latin, Maths, Geography, and Irish to matriculation classes' at a
salary of £11,[19] she did not demand that a minimum quota of lay

teachers be employed, as her antecedents had done:

> The religious orders have an unquestionable right to staff their
> own schools with religious if they have them qualified in suffi-
> cient numbers. But if they employ lay teachers the orders must
> face their responsibilities: the teacher must get fair play and so-
> cial justice; be treated as a member of the Mystical Body, and
> not as wreckage to be sent adrift when a novice comes along;
> and to be shown the humanity that every decent lay employer
> shows, of payment during illness.[20]

There was a general feeling among women lay teachers, the
writer claimed, that 'the profession of secondary teaching is gradually being closed to them'. While the practice in Christian Brothers
schools was to have equal numbers of lay and religious on the staff,
she wrote, 'the ultimate aim of most religious orders (and especially
of nuns) is to run schools independently of lay teachers'. Unemployed teachers were emigrating to take up positions in the expanding British system, while positions in Ireland were held by
unqualified individuals, she argued, giving the example of the superior of a select boarding school, who, when challenged on appoint-
ing to a position a novice with only a recently-completed Leaving
Certificate to her credit, had responded that 'the class was small, and
the children were quiet'. Was the 'Department of Education afraid
of being called anti-clerical if it insists that all teachers in secondary
schools must be qualified?' this lay teacher wondered.[21]

Because he felt that the views expressed in the article were held
by many UCC graduates, the editor delayed publishing it while he
sought a response from 'certain organisations and individuals connected with secondary teaching'.[22] The only one received suggested
that the article be suppressed, and indeed it would not have been
unusual in post-'Emergency' Ireland if it had been, for there was a
tendency, as the contributor indicated, to regard any questioning of
practices in Catholic-connected institutions as being anti-clerical in
motivation. Just two years later, a letter from an emigrant to the editor of the *Connacht Tribune*, which criticised the education he had
received in a west of Ireland diocesan college and made some general
points about the shortcomings of the clerically dominated system of
secondary education, was suppressed. Not alone was it suppressed

but it was quietly forwarded to the authorities of the college that had been attended by the young man.[23]

In this instance, the request to suppress the article, which in large measure articulated ASTI policy, came, strangely enough, from the ASTI itself. The circumstances were that the ASTI was approached by the Conference of Convent Secondary Schools (CCSS) to 'use its influence' to block the article, which was embarrassing to CCSS members at a time when the ASTI was trying to improve its relations with the nuns. There was an indignant refusal from the *Record's* editor, UCC president Alfred O'Rahilly. O'Rahilly was a noted Catholic intellectual interested in Labour matters, and a promoter of National Labour which split from the Labour Party in 1944 on the rather spurious basis that it was communist-infiltrated. However, in this instance his strong views about the duty of Catholic intellectuals and Catholic graduates generally to be consistent upholders of the truth led him to resist the pressure from the would-be censors.[24]

If the article could not be suppressed, its contents could not be left unchallenged, and Rev. Thomas Foy, MA, wrote a rebuttal for a subsequent issue of the *Record*, which robustly defended the rights of the Catholic religious to manage their 'private schools' as they saw fit without interference from state or other institutions:

> In her private school, the headmistress is trying to give a good education as cheaply as she can … Every lay teacher employed must be paid a salary by the school. The state does not pay this: the school must find it. [The nuns and brothers] get a small grant now, and because they live in community without salaries they are able to exist on it. For every lay teacher they now employ, they not only lose the salary such a teacher would earn were she a Religious, but they also lose the £200 they must pay such a teacher … The money can only come out of the pockets of the poor, and as the headmistress does not want this, she is anxious, naturally, to get a qualified nun-teacher who will give her services freely …[25]

For Fr Foy, the claims of lay teachers were not worthy of serious attention. And he did not have a high regard for their qualifications:

> Do pass degree candidates drift into secondary education when they find that, on graduation, they had by accident and without

their knowing it, been all the time preparing to be secondary teachers? ... They find that doing a pass degree is not too difficult, and they frequently choose their subjects with little thought of teaching those subjects afterwards.[26]

For 'graduate teacher', Foy's attitude was 'reminiscent of the *laisser-faire* capitalists' who thought they could behave as they liked with regard to the businesses that they had built up. But, she pointed out, 'a "privately owned school" is not a "private" school, if it is in receipt of state grants – the acceptance of public money implies a corresponding duty to fulfil certain educational standards'.[27] It was a duty that was not fully recognised in practice, either by the recipients or by the disbursers of the public money.

Progress on pay and pensions, 1939–c.1959
The new minister for education listened sympathetically to the ASTI delegation on 18 January 1940, as they presented their reasonable claims. Secondary teachers had received no pay increase since the introduction of the incremental scheme in 1924, they told him, despite a considerable increase in the cost of living, and they had fallen far behind other professionals in the public service. A claim for an increase had been lodged with the department in 1938, but with no result, even though primary teachers had received a small award around that time. And their pension scheme was deficient by comparison with others, they contended, having no provision for the payment of a gratuity to the dependents of teachers who died in service, or, on their retirement, to those who survived.

The sympathetic minister was Éamon de Valera, who had given himself responsibility for Education in the restructured cabinet he appointed in September 1939 to respond to the 'Emergency'. The arrangement did not mean that education was being sidelined, for the taoiseach had strong opinions on the subject, and notwithstanding the many other demands on his time, he took the opportunity to make two changes that he considered to be necessary in the state examination system during his nine months in the department. In the event, both the involvement of university lecturers in the examination processes and the introduction of set texts were opposed by the ASTI, the latter because it amounted to a deskilling of the profession which might lead to an influx of unqualified teachers into the system.

To satisfy the ASTI delegation's pay demands would have involved some expenditure and would have raised expectations among other groups, so, in the straitened circumstances of the 'Emergency', sympathy was all that could be offered. In a crisis such as the state was going through, Mr de Valera advised, it was the duty of citizens to make economies. No increase could be countenanced.[28]

The wartime rationing of luxury goods – notably, tea and tobacco – left a strong impact on popular memory, but there were more critical shortages also, and the interruption in supplies of fuel and industrial raw materials greatly interfered with manufacturing. Many of those rendered unemployed as a result emigrated, finding employment in Britain's busy armaments industry or service in her armies. Those who had work in Ireland found their purchasing power greatly reduced – price inflation totalled 70 per cent during the six years of war, while wages increased on average by 13 per cent. The control of inflation was a key government objective and the Wages Standstill Order of May 1941 was the mechanism adopted. Despite trade union mobilisation against the measure the government held firm, although from January 1943 small regulated 'war bonuses' overseen by wages tribunals were allowed.[29]

Tomás Ó Deirg, who took over the reins again in the Department of Education in June 1940, had no more scope for giving concessions to his former ASTI colleagues than de Valera had. This TD for the Carlow–Kilkenny constituency, who was the longest-serving minister for education in the history of the state, deserves a full introduction. Ó Deirg had joined the Volunteers while a student at UCG, serving in the War of Independence and on the anti-Treaty side in the Civil War. Graduating with a Commerce degree after the Civil War, he worked as a secondary teacher and as principal of a technical school in his native Mayo. A founder of Fianna Fáil, he was appointed minister for education by de Valera in 1932, and served in that department, except for a few months in 1939–40, until Fianna Fáil lost office in 1948. Ó Deirg had strong interests in the promotion of Irish and in vocational education, and had some achievements as minister in both areas, but many of his ambitions in education were thwarted by resource limitations. His reactionary approach to the administration of industrial schools and reformatories has been criticised. Resources were never more limited than at the time of his reappointment in 1940.[30]

With little prospect of an increase in state salaries, the ASTI sought a raise in the basic salaries paid by schools, but sympathy was all that was available in that quarter also. Dr McQuaid had put the matter before those he represented in the diocesan colleges, and had also raised the matter with the authorities in convent schools, but an across-the-board increase was found to be unacceptable. Schools were having financial problems of their own, and their managements were averse to raising fees in what was a difficult economic environment for most parents. McQuaid did concede, however, that some schools were able to offer an increase. Ultimately, there was some success in persuading schools to pay wartime bonuses to those teachers who were entirely dependent on the basic salary. The level of the basic salary would remain at the discretion of the individual schools, although following representations over a period from the ASTI, the bishops agreed to 'recommend' to convent schools that they pay at least the £180 minimum to all their teachers.[31] There remained great differences in the amount of the basic salary, with men in some of the diocesan colleges receiving 40–50 per cent more than those employed by religious orders.

With regard to the payment of 'war bonuses' in January 1943, the ASTI lobbied Minister Ó Deirg for £30 a year for secondary teachers; most, in fact, were awarded little more than half that amount, but married men on higher points of the scale got nothing. Further lobbying eased the conditions attached to the bonus in the following year. Continuing demands for a wholesale salary review won no results in the short-term, but they did elicit a commitment to address the matter when the 'Emergency' had passed. A similar undertaking was given to the INTO.[32]

At war's end, the bottled-up frustration of the previous years saw a rush of pay demands, and a rash of disputes, with the INTO strike of 1946 being the most significant. To a detailed claim on behalf of primary teachers, the minister had responded with an offer which negotiators insisted would leave their members worse-off than they had been before the war. Despite an intervention by Archbishop Mc-Quaid, the government refused to offer any further concession, and following a ballot of members, the Dublin primary teachers went on strike on 20 March 1946 and were sustained by a levy on their fellows outside the capital.[33] It was to be a bitter strike which ran through the summer holidays, and which was marked by several at-tention-grabbing protests, notably a noisy demonstration in the vis-itors' gallery of the Dáil and a half-time invasion of Croke Park during the 1946 All-Ireland football final with a view to embarrass-ing the taoiseach who was in the stand. The dispute was one which saw national teachers win the sympathy of parents and the broader community; moreover, it was one which ultimately brought about a political shift in the country when radicalised teachers expressed their disillusionment with Fianna Fáil by rallying to the new Clann na Poblachta party. However, on 30 October 1946, the strikers returned to work, humiliated and many of them angry with their executive for having surrendered without achieving anything.[34]

The discussion at the ASTI's Dublin branch during the dispute does not indicate that there was any strong sympathy among mem-bers for their national school colleagues. Indeed, opposition was ex-pressed to demands from the INTO – whose members' wages had fallen behind those of secondary teachers – for a common salary for all teachers.[35] This demand would lead to serious disagreement be-tween the two bodies of teachers during the following decades.

While the INTO picketed the national schools, Minister Ó Deirg announced his salary scheme for secondary teachers in June 1946. It was less than the ASTI had sought, but it was not much less, as the following note from Daniel Buckley, ASTI president, to the minister for education, indicated:

I desire to state on behalf of the Association that the Minister for Education appears to have made a genuine and reasonable attempt to improve the salaries (and consequently the status) of secondary teachers. The Association is appreciative of the Min-ister's action and feels that the progress made augurs well for the future of the profession, and is indicative of a continuance of the cordial relations which have characterised the dealings between the minister and the Association in the past ...[36]

Increases in incremental salary and in honours degree allowances were welcome, as was the provision of a rent allowance for married men, and there was a significant concession to younger teachers who were given the opportunity to begin on the incremental scale after one year's service as 'provisionally registered' teachers, rather than after three years as had been the case since 1924. That the improvement, generally, was greater than anticipated was indicated by the ASTI's refusal of the minister's offer of a review in three years – there was a fear that any review might recommend that the 1946 package be trimmed. The decision would be regretted, however, for increases would be awarded to less cautious groups, including primary teachers, in 1949.[37]

By then, sixteen years of uninterrupted Fianna Fáil rule had come to an end, with the election of the first inter-party government in February 1948. It was an ideologically diverse government composed of five parties brought together only by a shared wish to drive Fianna Fáil from office, and was itself dependent on non-party deputies. As well as Fine Gael (successor to the pro-Treaty Cumann na nGaedheal), there was Labour and National Labour (the latter recently, and bitterly, split from the former), Clann na Talmhan (claiming to speak for small farmers, and strongest in the west) and Clann na Poblachta (a radical republican party with roots in militant anti-Treaty politics). The new minister for education was Richard Mulcahy, leader of Fine Gael and the logical choice for taoiseach but unacceptable to Clann na Poblachta because of his Civil War record.[38] The new minister was regarded as personally sympathetic towards secondary teachers but his government did not prioritise education, so he had little in the way of discretionary funds. As he bluntly put it himself, his department was 'governed by Finance'.[39]

The outcome of negotiations of 1950, consequently, was disappointing to male teachers, though females had the satisfaction of finally seeing the incremental element of their salaries brought up to the level of the single males to a maximum of £320, the maximum for married males being £470. A request from representatives of the Catholic school authorities that single male teachers – including, presumably, religious – be paid at the married rate had already been rejected by the department.[40]

Minister Mulcahy was able to use his influence, in the face of opposition from the Department of Finance, to introduce conciliation and arbitration schemes for both primary and secondary teachers, which representatives of both had sought. These new schemes, which were based on the existing civil service scheme, provided mechanisms for processing remuneration claims. Representatives of the Department of Education, of the ASTI, and of the management

bodies representing Protestant schools took part in the first temporary scheme of 1951, but the Catholic bodies declined their invitations. A further temporary scheme followed in 1953 under Fianna
Fáil, and permanent conciliation and arbitration machinery was introduced in 1955. The effect of the new approach was that salaries
and related payments were reviewed automatically at pre-determined
intervals. It was no longer necessary to initiate intensive political lobbying in order to have a claim heard. The maxima on the incremental scale as a result reached £620 for married males, and £452 for
unmarried males and females by 1952.

The new conciliation scheme provided the means by which long-
sought improvements in the pension scheme could be agreed in the
Secondary Teachers' Superannuation Scheme, 1951. Among the
changes were the introduction of gratuities on death, retirement, dis-
ability and marriage for females, to all paying a 1 per cent premium.
The pension remained voluntary, but as a result of the improvements
there was a higher take-up among teachers.[41]

There were renewed efforts to increase the basic school salaries
through the early 1950s, particularly in the aftermath of an increase
in school capitation in 1954. The basic salary was largely unchanged
since 1924, argued the ASTI, despite the fall in the value of the
pound. Asserting at first that the increase in funding was granted for
other purposes, the CHA eventually accepted the ASTI's argument,
and asked schools 'to do what they could' for their lay staff. The difficulty in negotiating with bodies that could do no more than offer
advice to their members was deeply frustrating for the ASTI's representatives, and this point was made in a circular to the various con-
gregations in 1955. Both CHA and CCSS recommended that their
members give increases and many of them did, though not in any
consistent way. However, the situation in Christian Brothers schools,
which employed a large number of lay male teachers, remained unsatisfactory until an incremental school salary in the range £240 to
£280 was agreed in 1961.[42]

The impression is that during most of this period ASTI negotiators remained quite ineffective in their dealings with the school
management bodies. Allowing for the Association's poor bargaining
position in a situation where lay teachers were in a minority in secondary schools, and for the fact that it was difficult for part-time
representatives to conclude binding agreements with a multiplicity

of agencies, each claiming to have only limited representational pow-
ers, one wonders nevertheless if there were other reasons for the lack
of results. Was the position of ASTI negotiators perhaps weakened
by the circumstances in which they worked? Were they predominantly individuals who worked in schools where lay teachers were in
a tiny minority? The indications are that this was not so, and that
most senior officials in the 1940s and 1950s had posts in elite schools
where the Association was secure. An examination of the circumstances of a number of presidents reveals that T.P. Waller (1938,
1939) and Owen P. Ward (1947) were employed in Castleknock
College, Charles Dillon (1943, 1944, 1959) in the Church of Ireland
High School in Dublin, William Kirkpatrick (1949) in the
Methodist Wesley College, and Thomas Coppinger (1952) in Blackrock College.[43] Many of the leading officers, therefore, worked in
leading colleges where, it was noted, above-average school salaries
were paid. The perception that positions and influence were being
shared out between the relatively privileged elements in the Association, both Catholic and Protestant, and to the detriment of other
members, caused tensions, and these led to an open split in 1943,
when frustrated teachers employed in Christian Brothers schools in
Dublin resigned from the ASTI to establish a Guild of Catholic Secondary Teachers. The initial cause of the resignations was the conduct of elections to the CEC, which was seen to favour the
'Castleknock men', but the disaffected ex-members in their efforts to
lure members away from ASTI placed the focus on the Association's
non-denominational character.[44] The guild met with little success,
but its abortive efforts to establish itself caused bitterness, as was
shown when one of its stalwarts sought re-admission to the Association in 1951. His application was blocked by a majority of the
Dublin members who still resented 'the small group of pseudo-
enthusiastic Catholics who had broken away from the Association
and tried to overthrow it by founding a rival organisation'.[45]

The Association and its membership
In an institutional labour history, there will necessarily be a focus on
the affairs at headquarters level, and on the interaction between the
headquarters and the headquarters of other organisations – of bodies representing employers, for example, and of mediatory agencies.
But the approach and effectiveness of headquarters will ultimately be

determined by the activism of its members, something that was especially the case with ASTI, a body that during its first half century had either little or no full-time apparatus. This section, therefore, will look at two aspects of the activity of the membership: (i) involvement at branch level through an examination of the affairs of the Desmond branch; (ii) the nature of proceedings at annual conventions.

(i) The Kilmallock (Desmond) branch: The survival of a full set of minutes facilitates the examination of the fortunes of the Kilmallock branch, the first meeting of which took place in the Central Hotel, Kilmallock, County Limerick, on 4 December 1948. Four women and three men attended, drawn from several towns in the vicinity, but none of them having any previous ASTI involvement. Despite finding procedures to be 'very mysterious', they succeeded in electing officers at that meeting – Tim Moloney of Kilmallock, chairman, and James O'Sullivan of Charleville, secretary – and in nominating Peg Wallis of Kilfinane to be the branch's representative on the CEC, and Miss Shortall of Charleville to be its delegate at the Easter convention. Thereafter, the branch met regularly three times a year, with occasional extraordinary meetings such as that held on 17 November 1951 to consider a pay offer. In October 1959 it re-named itself the Desmond branch.[46]

The officers showed considerable flexibility in the early years, arranging meetings in different towns within the branch's operating area with a view to recruitment. An early entry in the minute book sums up the approach adopted: 'It was suggested with the approval of all, more or less, that the next venue be other than Kilmallock, e.g. Charleville or Newcastlewest, the latter if members be found there willing to join the branch.' By these means, the branch grew quickly to more than a dozen, and gradually thereafter until it hovered around twenty in the late 1950s.[47]

Almost all members attended early meetings: to pay their membership fees, to share information and, no doubt, to socialise. There were no formal social events, however, until St Valentine's night, 1959, when the bill for a dinner for members in the Glentworth Hotel in Limerick was paid out of branch funds. It was not until January 1962 that branch members again treated themselves to a dinner in Limerick.[48]

As well as the regular selection of branch officers and delegates, the business of meetings included reports from conventions and CEC meetings, the provision of information for individuals, and re-minders of deadlines regarding teacher registration. Salary matters re-ceived attention intermittently, while arrangements regarding the scheme for ASTI members within the newly established Voluntary Health Insurance system raised a lot of interest in the late 1950s.[49]

Educational issues were frequently on the agenda, especially in relation to state exams, and the opportunity to articulate professional concerns must have provided members with a great incentive to at-tend branch meetings. In the early 1960s there was discussion about the introduction of a first-year curriculum in the Christian Brothers schools, the objective being, according to the minutes, 'to stimulate both the teachers and the boys to greater efforts during the year, the innuendo being that teachers (and consequently boys) were inclined to take things easier in this year than in other years'. The proposal was criticised on two grounds:

> It was educationally unsound as it gave no room for initiative in the matter of the syllabus during the only year in which there was an opportunity to do so. Besides, it could lead to less harmo-nious relations between the authorities and the lay staff.[50]

From time to time, the departure of members for other posi-tions was noted, as was the arrival in the district of potential mem-bers. And, as with all organisations, there were occasional votes congratulating members on their marriages and sympathising with them on bereavements. In the latter category were the poignant trib-utes paid to the 'unassuming, simple, and straightforward' Tim Moloney, founding chairman of the branch, following his death in 1955 at the age of fifty-eight.[51]

After some years, tensions developed between male and female members of the branch, which led to the women withholding sub-scriptions and boycotting meetings. The cause of the protest was the holding of meetings on Saturdays, which suited the men in the branch who were settled in the area, but not the women, who were mostly single and young, with some having commitments involv-ing travel at weekends. It must have been with the intention of ap-peasing this discontented element that James O'Sullivan proposed in 1953 that 'lady members be given refreshments at meetings', but, if so, the gesture did not have the desired effect, for the minutes of several subsequent meetings recorded that they had proceeded with 'no ladies' in attendance. Eventually, at the end of a year during which there had been no female presence at any meeting, it was resolved to write to five named women 'for arrears of subs, and for the views on date and venue of next meeting'. These conciliatory letters proved effective, and women were in a majority at the January 1955 meeting, where it was resolved to hold future meetings on week nights.[52]

Later in the decade, women played a very prominent role, with, for example, Eileen Scanlon elected chair in 1959, and Peg Wallis and Nora McCarthy as joint secretaries.

With generally good attendances at the once-a-term meeting, with participation of representatives in the leading bodies of the Association, with the attendance of delegates (and even non-delegates) at Easter conventions, with regular correspondence with head office, the impression is that secondary teachers in the branch area were well-integrated members of the national Association. Relations with headquarters were generally good, although occasionally there were disagreements. Errors with regard to subscriptions and in relation to an unreceived piece of correspondence, for example, caused irritation – 'not all inefficiencies (of secretaries, etc) was confined to the country branches,' complained James O'Sullivan.[53] The qualities desirable in a national organiser featured in a discussion of 1957, leading to correspondence with head office:

> The secretary of the branch, in his letter to HQ, referred to the desirability of having as chief organiser a person of tact and sound judgement, preferably with experience of CEC and Standing Committee. The letter, though cautiously worded, hinted strongly that the present incumbent is hardly suitable.[54]

The strong hint delivered may not have been to the branch's advantage in the medium term, and during the following year there was mild consternation when a teacher in Glin (regarded as being within Kilmallock's domain) received a letter from head office asking him to form a branch. A subsequent protest at the establishment of a West Limerick branch fell on deaf ears. The decision to change the name of the branch to the Desmond branch in October 1959 occurred as a result of this dispute, it being considered important in the circumstances to formally extend its jurisdiction so as to discourage any further secessions.[55]

(ii) Annual convention: As ASTI's leading democratic assembly since it superseded the AGM in 1923, the annual convention received a lot of attention at all levels of the organisation. The selection of delegates, discussion of resolutions, and decisions about the candidates to support for the various positions occupied a large part of the business of one of the three meetings that most branches held each year (though the Dublin branch held ten), while an account of convention proceedings formed part of the agenda of another. Its prominence on branch agendas shows that members believed that convention provided them with a real opportunity to have their views on conditions and on educational matters reflected in ASTI policy.[56] And the evidence indicates that this belief had a strong basis, for the record of convention proceedings reveals that debates were vigorous, that divisions were frequent and that decisions were acted upon.[57]

Indications are that convention arrangements placed considerable demands on administrative resources. Delegates would expect everything to be properly organised, and some of them might be quite demanding – advice sought from the general secretary, for example, included some regarding the proper attire for functions. Moreover, convention put the Association on public display, with invited guests attending from the various agencies and entities interested in secondary education, as well of course as representatives of the national and local media.[58]

For ordinary ASTI members, the social dimension of the event was important, and it attracted non-delegates as well as delegates, helping to maintain an *esprit de corps* throughout the association. In 1926, the first convention outside of Dublin was held in Cork, and thereafter it moved from one centre to another, often taking place at attractive seaside locations.[59] That delegates were welcome in such places is indicated by the following request to head office from Galway Chamber of Commerce in November 1956:

> I have been asked by the Conference City Committee to write to you to ascertain if your association would consider having their conference in Galway this coming year. The Committee

having just started work is most anxious to have as many conferences as possible for Galway next year.[60]

In the event, the ASTI accepted the Galway invitation for 1957 (as
did, incidentally, the Vocational Teachers' Association [VTA]). However, it was decided not to go back to the university – 'a spot which
was far removed both from the town of Galway and its very pleasant
suburb of Salthill'. Instead the Warwick Hotel in Salthill was chosen,
inaugurating a correspondence between the general secretary and the
manager about accommodation and other facilities for 120 guests, as
well as with Department of Education officials, the mayor of Galway
and local bishops about their availability. Church services had to be
arranged, as they had been on the opening morning of convention
since the mid-1940s, and it was a cause of concern to the general
secretary in 1957 that details of the Church of Ireland service might
not be available in time for inclusion in the conference programme.[61]

The Salthill proceedings of 1957 may be taken as representative
of conventions of the period, so a detailed examination of them will
be illuminating. There were fifty-eight delegates (but, additionally, as
many more sub-delegates and observers) representing twenty-seven
of the thirty-three recognised branches: Athlone, Carlow, Carrick-
on-Shannon, Clanwilliam, Clare, Cork, Donegal, Drogheda,
Dublin, Dundalk, Dungarvan, Fermoy, Galway, Kerry, Kildare,
Kilkenny, Kilmallock, Limerick, Midleton, Mullingar, Nenagh, New
Ross, Roscrea, Tipperary, Tuam, West Waterford and Wicklow. Two
new branches, Enniscorthy and Portlaoise, as well as others in
Mountmellick, Roscommon, Sligo and Waterford registered no delegates. Only six branches sent more than one delegate – including
the sizeable Dublin branch, which sent twenty-four. And Dublin's
central role was underlined by the outcome of the election of officers:
Mr L. Comerford (Dungarvan), president; Miss N. Kelleher
(Dublin), vice-president; Mr C.L. Dillon (Dublin), Mr T.C. Coppinger (Dublin), treasurers; Mr P.J. O'Reilly (Cork), Mr D. Ó
Conalláin (Dublin), trustees.[62]

Immediately after the special church services, the two-day convention began at 10 a.m. on Wednesday 24 April, with a closed session during which standing orders were agreed, elections were held,
and the treasurer's report was considered. Between noon and lunch
at 2 p.m., there was a public session, beginning with an address from

the ASTI president and continuing with addresses from invited guests. The afternoon was given over to 'golf competitions and other recreational activities'. During the second day, education and remuneration matters dominated the reports from leading bodies and subcommittees and formed the subject matter also of the resolutions discussed.[63]

Media coverage of the convention was divided between the address of P.J. Hardiman, outgoing president, and that of Dr Michael Browne, Catholic bishop of Galway and controversialist, known to many in his diocese as 'Cross Michael'.[64] Hardiman's contribution ranged over a number of educational issues, which may be taken as the ones that most concerned ASTI members in 1957. Criticising the Department of Education for not sufficiently consulting his Association with regard to the content of courses, he made a number of specific suggestions: Irish-language texts needed to be more 'modern' in their content; both Irish and English programmes should place greater emphasis on the spoken language; courses in the classics 'could be rendered far more valuable culturally than they now are'. He also expressed reservations about the Intermediate Certificate scholarship system, asserting that it 'led to cramming and premature specialisation in a minimum of subjects' and that 'in the number and value of scholarships there was serious discriminations against girl students' – who were now in a majority.[65] These were matters for which state agencies had responsibility, but the president also directed a message to school managers. There was widespread frustration among specialist and experienced teachers, he said, because they were offered no opportunity for advancement in the profession: 'Unless those men get adequate recognition for their specialist qualifications, the profession will eventually fail in its appeal to honours graduates in arts and sciences.'

For his part, the bishop wished to show that he had studied the convention programme, and he endorsed the position of the Association's sub-committee on English with regard to the retention of the question on 'parsing and analysis' on the Leaving Certificate papers. 'To abolish grammar,' Dr Browne said, 'seemed to be bringing the "rock and roll" spirit into education.' The main focus of the bishop's widely reported address, however, was on the urgent need for the state to greatly extend the secondary education system:

The principle of providing facilities for secondary education within the reach of every boy and girl willing and able to avail of them has been accepted in the North and in England, but not in the Republic … The state left that to private initiative and did nothing to put secondary education within the grasp of boys who lived away from the larger towns. About 1,000 more girls than boys were receiving secondary education in this country simply because their nuns had undertaken this public-spirited work … The contrast with the North in this matter is very pointed and is not such to attract the people there to join us.[66]

Some scepticism would have been aroused by these remarks, for, among educators, there were those who held the bishop's Church at least as responsible as the state for shortcomings in secondary education. But if the bishop was specifically critical of the parsimony of the state and of local authorities, there were no indications in his speech that he would accept any extension of the role of public bodies in education. In fact, he was seeking exactly what his predecessors had sought half a century before – greater public subsidies for a system under the control of religious. The references to Northern Ireland too might be regarded as disingenuous, for Catholic leaders there were critical – and remained critical in 1957 – of the post-Second World War educational reforms which, they said, by discriminating against Catholic-controlled schools, had obstructed their development.[67]

Nonetheless, to the extent that it shows an awareness on the part of an influential figure of the need to greatly extend educational provision at second level in the late 1950s, Dr Browne's address to the ASTI was highly significant. And it will be noted that his demands went considerably further than those of ASTI's President Hardiman.

Golden jubilee

The ASTI's golden jubilee, which fell in 1959, was an occasion for satisfied reflection. The approach of the anniversary had directed attention to membership, and a systematic and regionally based recruitment campaign had brought the number of branches to thirty-nine in time for the jubilee Easter convention in Sligo. That there was irritation with those perceived to be benefiting from the work of the ASTI, while remaining aloof from it, was indicated by

101

a resolution of the Dublin branch suggesting 'a boycott of secondary teachers who refuse (for no good reason) to join the Association'.[68] In the event, the somewhat less confrontational approach – 'an intensive drive against individual non-members' – adopted by the organising committee would bring membership past the 1,000 mark for the first time during 1959.[69]

Much of the jubilee preparation was handled by Galway woman Máire MacDonagh, who was appointed general secretary in 1958 to replace Florence Quirke. One of ninety-one applicants, she was unanimously recommended by the selection committee, being eminently qualified, with a BA (1st hons), and an MA from UCG, as well as an HDE, a Diploma in Public Administration and membership of the Chartered Institute of Secretaries. MacDonagh's career up to that point had included a few years as a temporary teacher followed by a decade in five different administrative posts, one of them with the Irish Trade Union Congress.[70] The appointment of a second woman to the senior post might be seen as evidence of an enlightened approach to gender issues in ASTI, but the indications are that the motivation, in part at least, was financial – it was cheaper to hire a competent woman than a competent man. The salary of £520 (£10 a week) was at the level of a young teacher's salary, and the hours of work were longer (5½ day week, minimal holidays). Pension arrangements also left much to be desired, while working conditions, evidently, were not very good either, if a resolution to the jubilee convention urging action on the 'dilapidated state of head office' is an indication. In fact action was soon taken with regard to head office, with the acquisition of premises on Stephen's Green in 1960. Moreover, within a few years, 'as a mark of gratitude for the very diligent manner she has served and continues to serve the Association' the executive raised MacDonagh's salary, and she was placed on the salary scale of 'a single lady secondary teacher', with an allowance for her honours degree – though not for her MA.[71]

Meanwhile, having returned to teaching for a few years in Dublin, Florence Quirke was one of those who established the Retired Secondary Teachers' Association in 1962. She served as one of its officers until her death in 1968.[72]

Another woman who was prominent in the lead-in to the jubilee was Nora Kelleher, a member of the Dublin branch and only the second woman to hold the ASTI presidency up to that time. In her presidential address to the jubilee convention, she reviewed fifty years of ASTI history and identified a number of necessary reforms in Irish secondary education. With the system overall, Kelleher articulated what was undoubtedly the attitude of the majority of her members: approval of the scheme of 'denominational education privately conducted, in which the adherents of all churches are treated alike'. It was right that the ASTI had sought to ensure that its members were well paid, she said, for the 'vocation to teaching needs to be nourished by at least a modicum of the things that go to make up gracious living', but the Association had always taken an equal interest in the development of secondary education. In this last regard, Kelleher argued that there was a need for a greater emphasis on the practical than there been up to then, and a lesser focus on examination performance. The founders of the state, she said, had been alert to 'the tyranny of the external examination', but in the intervening decades, their successors had lost sight of this enlightened attitude, with the result that the Irish had become the 'most examination conscious of peoples'.[73] The system had also neglected the development of 'civic sense' in young people, with unfortunate results:

> At present, some young people are affected by the prevailing mood of despondency and what is popularly known as cynicism. On the other hand, many of our young idealists are ready to adopt any method, however unwise or illegal, to attain the goal of national unity which they so ardently desire.[74]

The reference to the lack of scruples evident in the pursuit of 'national unity' was prompted by the IRA 'border campaign' of 1956–62, which had resulted in the deaths of several young idealists, and in the introduction by de Valera's government of internment without trial.

The centrepiece of the 1959 commemoration was a jubilee dinner in the Shelbourne Hotel on 31 October 1959, at which the guest of honour was the new minister for education, Dr Patrick Hillery. Coincidentally, the ASTI president welcoming him to the function was John Wilson, who himself would later become minister for education. In his address, the minister, who would soon lay the foundations for many of the reforms of the 1960s, modestly acknowledged that he was still learning about education.[75] Hillery, who was in his mid-thirties, was the first of a new generation of ministers appointed to cabinet by Seán Lemass, after he had succeeded de Valera as Fianna Fáil leader and taoiseach during the previous June. Lemass's succession presaged a changing Ireland, already mapped out in Whitaker's *Economic Development* (1958), and in the first *Programme for Economic Expansion* (1958), which would be critically dependent on a transformation in post-primary education.[76]

The minister's keynote speech paid tribute, as would have been expected, to the 'highly-qualified' and 'devoted' secondary teachers of Ireland, but it also alerted those who were listening to the necessity for change. If ASTI members were broadly satisfied with secondary education on the eve of the 1960s – and Nora Kelleher's presidential address, as well as a 1959 convention resolution from the metropolitan members of the Dublin branch arguing that 'it would be far more beneficial to reduce the size of classes than to raise the school leaving age', suggests that they were – the minister indicated that it would not long remain as it was:

A large part of the state's responsibility is also to foster the country's economic interests, and the first essential in this regard is that the system of education should, as far as possible, fit the pupils to face the modern world, by, for example, promoting the study of science … If we are to overcome the degree of underdevelopment at which we find ourselves, we must have more and still more education.[77]

That the provision of 'more and still more education' would have major implications for the ASTI and for all involved in Irish education will be seen in the next section.

Part Two

5

'And look at us now!'
Secondary teachers, educational change
and Irish society in the 1960s

For one writer on Ireland, the 1960s was 'the best of decades'; for another, it was 'the decade of upheaval'.[1] Both estimations, it will be readily agreed, contained more than a trace of truth.

The policies of the Lemass era, which opened the economy to outside capital, allowed the Republic of Ireland to share to some extent in an international boom, bringing an end to a long period of economic adversity. While the taoiseach promised that 'a rising tide would lift all boats', there were those who were sceptical, and, with a fall in unemployment which improved the bargaining position of trade unions, a wave of strikes ensued as working people in all sectors found their claim to a portion of the general prosperity was resisted by employers. Rising living standards along with easing emigration meanwhile brought about a more optimistic social climate, and there was a measure of openness to international cultural influences.

An important instrument for the dissemination of these influences was RTÉ television, which was launched on New Year's Eve, 1961. Notwithstanding the fact that BBC signals were already reaching homes in the east of the country, there was apprehension about the upheaval that the extension of the new medium might trigger, as was reflected in the remarks on the inauguration from 79-year-old President de Valera: 'I must admit that sometimes when I think of television and radio, and their immense power, I feel somewhat afraid. Like atomic energy it can be used for incalculable good, but it can also do irreparable harm.'[2] A 'good' use, of which the president would probably have approved, was Teilifís Scoile, which brought television into secondary school classrooms from February 1964.[3]

De Valera's fear that television would undermine traditional mores was well founded, but it was by no means the only source of such a challenge, for that great bulwark of tradition in Ireland, the Roman Catholic Church, was simultaneously dispensing with many of its own traditions in an effort to remain relevant in a changing world, under pressure indeed from many of its own members. Not without causing unease among many senior clergy, the Second Vatican Council (1962–65) introduced sweeping changes to time-honoured religious rituals and demanded also the abandonment of established attitudes. The central role of the Catholic laity in Church affairs was emphasised, and it was made clear that Protestants were no longer to be regarded as heretics, but as fellow 'members of the body of Christ'.[4] For Irish secondary education, where the institution of a rigidly denominational and clericalist system had long been the objective of the Catholic authorities, the new thinking had definite implications.

In a society where living standards and communications were improving, where censorship was being relaxed, where there was a less authoritarian religious climate than formerly, where trade unionism was being re-energised, there were opportunities for social movements to develop, with the result that there was a flourishing of activism in Ireland to a degree not seen since the early decades of the century. The ideas of civil rights, feminist, socialist, and other egalitarian movements, propagated through television and other media, reached a wide constituency during the decade, and many of their values were absorbed by a thriving youth culture.[5] Nowhere more than in the universities was there impatience with established procedures and power structures, and before the decade was out, newly qualified secondary teachers would bring some of the concerns of their generation into the ASTI.[6]

In the schools, of course, the egalitarian spirit of the decade often manifested itself as a challenge to authority, and this was something that concerned many teachers. For them, the modern age – with its beatniks, teddy boys and 'angry young men' – was presenting problems of an unprecedented character, personified in the phenomenon of the 'crazy mixed up kid'.[7] It was a reaction that was mocked at the very beginning of the 1960s by ASTI activist and humorous writer Tom O'Dea in an article in the *School & College Yearbook*. 'What modern and original trends in depravity,' he asked, were the hallmarks of the current cohort of school students? Arguing for tolerance of youthful idioms and of the youthful spirit from those of his contemporaries whom he characterised as belonging in spirit to 'the age which put stockings on piano legs', he asserted that the 'modern' youth was not that different to his predecessor:

> He is going through the same torments – some of them self-inflicted – which we experienced. He is encountering at the hands of his elders the self-same buffeting which made spells of our youth so miserable. He is subject to the same restrictions which tethered us; and he conforms to them no better than we did ... He is traduced and maligned by the press and the pulpit, and his sins are enumerated and magnified so often that he must by now have come to delude himself with their supposed enormity ... Have we forgotten that it was prophesied sorrowfully of us that we would never come to any good? And look at us now![8]

The argument about whether 'modern' teenagers were more than superficially different to earlier cohorts would continue through the 1960s, and beyond, but what about the 'modern' teacher of the same era?

Conditions, pay, and circumstances of employment in the early 1960s
In a careers booklet circulating in the early 1960s, the entry on secondary teaching included the following:

> Unlike most other occupations, a secondary teacher in term time has no set hours. There is considerable nervous strain in teaching a class, and the work is exhausting. Corrections and preparation take time, and the younger men and women will be expected to help with games in the afternoons; some member of the staff will be needed to run a debating society, or the school library, the school magazine or a musical society, to organise talks on careers or contemporary problems, even to keep the accounts of the tuck shop or school meals. For nine months of the year a secondary teacher works at high pressure and has very little free

time. But there are three months' holidays ... The profession is rather immobile. The young teacher can change schools freely, but the system makes a move rather difficult (though not impossible) after a number of years' service. The prospects for promotion are not very good ...[9]

If the picture painted was not a very appealing one, it had a certain timeless quality, for it represented routines and trials that would have resonated with teachers of earlier generations. But were there also features of the profession that had been positively affected by social and political advances, and by more than fifty years of ASTI activity?

At the beginning of the twentieth century, the most widely held grievances among secondary teachers were job insecurity, inadequate pay, lack of pensions, the absence of professional entry standards, low status, unfair competition for positions from religious and from 'birds of passage', poor promotion prospects, pay discrimination against female teachers, lack of consultation on educational matters, an over-competitive and grinding public examination system, and the marginal position of secondary education itself.

By 1960, as has been shown in the previous two chapters, there had been improvements under most of these headings. Secondary education had greatly expanded, with the number of teachers employed in the twenty-six counties of the Irish Republic having more than doubled since 1909 (though the system was accepted to be still inadequate to the country's needs). Reforms of the early 1920s had eliminated the worst features of the examination system (though the restoration of set texts in 1940 had allowed a revival of rote learning). The establishment of the Registration Council had seemed to address several grievances – by raising the status of secondary teaching; by reducing the number of casual practitioners; by lessening the likelihood of dismissal – though many employers evaded their obligations by hiring non-registered individuals. Such evasion, however, was becoming uncommon by the 1960s.

The pension scheme of 1929, which was regarded as deficient even by its architects, had been improved by ASTI effort during the following decades, while agreements between the ASTI and the religious employers on appeals procedures and contracts of employment in the second half of the 1930s, which had disappointed many teachers, had nonetheless contributed to job security. Women teachers were less discriminated against than formerly, having secured equality with single males in their incremental salaries in 1950, although they were still obliged to retire on marrying, even after the marriage bar in primary schools was removed in 1958.[10]

The question of pay remained very much a live one, but the situation of most secondary teachers in 1960 was utterly different to that which obtained half a century earlier, the most significant change being the introduction of a recognised pay scale. State payments, which had been introduced with the purpose of supplementing the amount paid by schools, had increased to the point where the 'incremental salary' formed the lion's share of the income of most teachers. There was considerable variety in the level of the school salaries – a source of dissatisfaction – but this was an ever-diminishing element of the whole. By several criteria, clearly, secondary teachers were better off in the early 1960s than the ASTI's founding generation, but how did their progress measure up against that of other groups in society? By way of an answer to that question, it will suffice to make a comparison with two of the occupations compared in Chapter 1 – primary teachers and policemen.

Primary teachers, whose average salaries had been somewhat higher than those of secondary teachers at the beginning of the century, had a salary scale in 1960, which, at maximum, was 88.5 per cent of the (acknowledged) secondary scale. Even though their opportunities for promotion remained far better, primary teachers were unhappy at the disparity. There was also dissatisfaction with salaries among policemen in the early 1960s, dissatisfaction that would lead the younger element of An Garda Síochána to adopt militant tactics during the November 1961 'Macushla revolt' (named for the Dublin ballroom where the said tactics were agreed). Up to that point, an un-promoted garda on the top of the scale received approximately 60 per cent of the salary of a married male secondary teacher.[11] This represented a considerable widening of the gap between the two groups, something which would perhaps have pleased Pádraic Pearse, who has already been quoted as asserting that secondary teachers ought to be paid better than policemen.

But if there were undoubted improvements with regard to pay, pensions, job security and, arguably, education itself, there was one significant set of grievances of lay secondary teachers in Catholic schools that had not been at all ameliorated. In Catholic-run schools,

Employers of male lay teachers, 1964

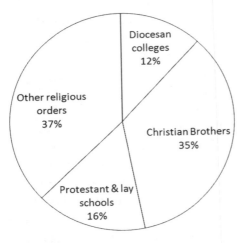

Diocesan colleges 12%

Other religious orders 37%

Christian Brothers 35%

Protestant & lay schools 16%

positions of responsibility continued to be arrogated by priests, nuns and brothers, with the result that there were few opportunities for the non-religious to advance beyond the status of 'assistant teacher'. Long-serving teachers continued to feel excluded in their own schools – it was commonplace among them to liken their position to that of a 'hired hand'.[12] Writing in 1966, the economist and future taoiseach Garret Fitzgerald argued that the 'downgrading of status' of the lay teacher, as well as the 'absence of opportunities for promotion' had been very detrimental for Irish secondary education.[13]

And lay teachers remained very much a minority in the system. By Patrick Duffy's calculation, majorities of both male and female full-time teachers were celibate religious up to the mid-1960s – 61 per cent of female and 54 per cent of male teachers. There were substantial institutions like the Convent of Mercy secondary school in Moate and St Jarlath's College in Tuam which employed no lay teacher during much of the 1960s. At the same time, however, there were other schools, like the Convents of Mercy in Limerick and Tralee, where lay teachers greatly outnumbered religious. If anything, indeed, Duffy's figures understate the extent of the religious presence in secondary education, for they exclude school principals and other functionaries who were invariably religious.[14]

The charts here show the extent to which the administration of secondary education was dominated by Catholic religious – 88 per cent of female and 84 per cent of male teachers were employed in their schools. There were dozens of religious orders involved, but only a few of them had spread widely throughout the country. More than a third of all male lay teachers in the state were employed in seventy-nine Christian Brothers schools; next in importance as employers of men were the De La Salle Brothers, with eighteen schools and under 6 per cent of lay teachers, and the Jesuits with six schools and under 5 per cent of lay teachers. In the female sector, the Sisters of Mercy employed 27 per cent of all female lay secondary teachers in their 110 schools, followed by the Presentation Sisters with 11 per cent in 40 schools, the Dominicans with 8 per cent in eleven schools and the Loreto with 6 per cent in twenty-two schools.[15]

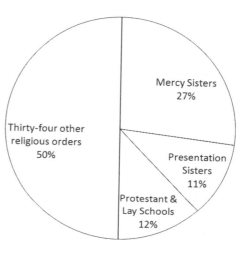

Employers of female lay teachers, 1964

Mercy Sisters 27%

Thirty-four other religious orders 50%

Presentation Sisters 11%

Protestant & Lay Schools 12%

Schools in the early 1960s were very much bigger, on average, than they had been at the foundation of the state. There was a notable development in the Christian Brothers secondary schools, which had an average enrolment in 1964–65 of 215. The average for diocesan colleges in the same academic year was 196, in the Presentation Sisters' schools it was 167, and in the Mercy Sisters schools it was 149. These averages conceal a wide range of enrolments, and it is evident that many schools were very small. The (US-based) Incarnate Word Sisters newly established school in Dunmore, County Galway, for example, had sixty-one girls and twenty-eight boys on its rolls, and was one of the few co-educational Catholic secondary schools.[16]

The Catholic Church's domination of secondary education continued to be reflected in the curriculum, which, in the words of one critic, was 'arranged to suit the minority of students who intended to proceed to Holy Orders'.[17] Latin was taken by almost 90 per cent of Leaving Certificate boys – four times as many as took a business subject. Science subjects were taken by a majority of Leaving Certificate boys, but, according to the OECD/Department of Education report, *Investment in Education*, 'few senior girls [took] science other than physiology and hygiene or domestic science'. In the same report it is found that 'no boy attending school in the City or County of Cork obtained honours in a modern continental language at the leaving certificate examinations in 1963', an omission that was regarded as grave in a 'context of the need for exports and of our possible entry into the European Economic Community'.[18]

Even within the structures of Irish Catholicism in the 1960s, there were those who were embarrassed by their Church's stranglehold over the secondary schools. The teachings of Vatican II raised certain questions: Was deploying trained religious in schools an effective use of Church resources? Why were priests, nuns, and brothers teaching secular subjects when there was a manifest need for competent people to give religious instruction in vocational schools? Was it ethical to deprive Irish lay secondary teachers of employment and promotion opportunities in their own country?[19]

To those questions, lay secondary teachers might have added a few of their own. Why are we not entrusted with any responsibility? Why are we never consulted?

In many schools, teachers had to refer even the most basic decisions to higher authority. This is highlighted in an account by former ASTI president Pierce Purcell, who describes a regime that was extremely autocratic, and one where lay teachers were expected to know their place. He attributed this tendency, for the most part, to the culture of religious orders, whereby a superior was entitled to unquestioning obedience from other members of his congregation. Was it so remarkable that a superior should treat school employees in the same autocratic fashion? One incidental effect of all of this was to make it difficult for lay teachers to play more than a marginal role in the life of their school:

> For the most part, lay teachers were not expected to engage in voluntary, extra-curricular activities because of the willingness of religious to train teams, organise debates, etc. However, they were not discouraged either, provided they knew their place in the scheme of things ... [I]t was most important for the religious order to be able to claim the credit for winning the cup, or raising the funds for famine relief. The lay teacher's place was in the background, no matter how much voluntary work he/she may have done.[20]

Sometimes, the reminder of his or her place in the scheme of things might come as a surprise to the younger teacher:

An attempt to organise a school tour to London by myself and a colleague was rejected by the Christian Brother manager/principal because he could find no Brother willing to participate in the tour. I remember his words well: 'a Christian Brother presence is essential'.[21]

Almost imperceptibly, however, things were changing, and the lay–clerical balance in secondary education at least would be very different by the end of the 1960s, due to the great expansion of the system itself.

Changing educational policies

There were profound changes in second-level schools, as in many other places in Ireland, during the 1960s, changes that were overseen by Fianna Fáil governments led by Seán Lemass and Jack Lynch, who succeeded him as taoiseach in November 1966. Educational transformation was implicit in the economic policies of the era, which were designed to 'modernise' the state. Indeed, it has been argued that a similarly instrumentalist perspective informed much of the subsequent educational policy in Ireland.[22]

Probably because of the perception that the role was important, ministers for education in the decade after 1959 were promising politicians in their thirties and forties. With the exception of Patrick Hillery's, however, which lasted six years, ministerial terms were very short: George Colley's ran from 1965 to 1966, Donogh O'Malley's from 1966 to his death in 1968, and Brian Lenihan's from 1968 to 1969.[23]

Historians have pinpointed a 1959 Dáil statement from Seán Lemass as marking the beginning of the 1960s revolution in Irish secondary education:[24]

Our immediate policy is to increase the facilities for postprimary education. We believe it will be possible to accelerate the rate of increase of the facilities. We think that by expanding facilities we can reach the goal of having all children continue their schooling until 15 years within a reasonable time, and certainly no later than it could, in fact, be reached by methods of compulsion.[25]

The taoiseach's reference to 'compulsion' was prompted by Dr Noel

Browne, whose private member's resolution on behalf of his National Progressive Democrats calling for the raising of the legal school-leaving age from fourteen to fifteen had initiated the debate. Little attention was paid at first – the Dáil was 'almost empty', according to one journalist – as Browne reminded his fellow TDs, and Fianna Fáil TDs in particular, of their republican obligation 'to cherish all the children of the nation'. For *The Irish Times*, it was a case of Browne riding 'his favourite hobby horse of education', and Minister Hillery was almost as dismissive, delivering 'a paean to the dedication and devotion to the work of our teachers', and appealing to those interested in education to be 'realistic'.[26] From the minister's point of view, Browne's costly proposal could not be accepted – if education was compulsory to age fifteen, it would have to be provided free of charge.

Lemass's intervention in the debate a few day's later was very different to Hillery's, and it may be regarded as extraordinary in the way that it seemed to undermine the authority of the neophyte minister for education. Unlike Hillery, he did not ask Browne's supporters to be 'realistic', rather, he declared that his government was 'not in disagreement with what the motion seeks to achieve', and went on: 'If the motion is put to a vote I would not ask Deputies on this side of the House to vote against it.' Providing more facilities, Lemass argued however, would be a more effective approach to increasing participation at second-level than simply raising the school-leaving age.[27]

In her pioneering study of the period, Sister Eileen Randles suggests that the approach articulated by Lemass in 1959 – that is, of incrementally improving facilities – was the one in fact that was pursued by the Department of Education during the 1960s. And while she declared herself wary of indulging in 'retrospective planning' by imposing a pattern on the educational policy which was not there in reality, Randles insisted that educational decisions were not quite as ad hoc as had been generally assumed, and that it is possible to identify 'a sequential pattern of events'.[28] But if one accepts that there was a pattern, it must also be acknowledged that there were several qualitative leaps in educational policy during the decade, most notably in Donogh O'Malley's announcement of free education in 1966.

Free education to Leaving Certificate level would have been regarded as an impossible dream by most in 1959, but the Department of Education did set about increasing second-level participation in ways that were consistent with the taoiseach's Dáil statement. In the vocational sector, the state was in a position to intervene directly and it did so by paying for the construction of dozens of new schools and school extensions, and by providing for an increase in current spending in the 1962 amendment to the Vocational Education Act. In the secondary sector, the intervention was necessarily an indirect one, but the 1961 amendment to the Local Authorities (Education Scholarship) Act did facilitate more children from poorer backgrounds in attending secondary schools.[29] And this amendment was followed in 1964 by a grants scheme to enable school authorities to extend their facilities.[29]

Undoubtedly, several of these measures contributed to the increase in full-time enrolment in the vocational sector between 1957 and 1963 of 24 per cent, and in the secondary school sector in the same period of 28 per cent (69,568 to 89,205).[30]

The reforms summarised above were all designed to expand the existing system, but an announcement from the minister for education on 20 May 1963 indicated a recognition that the existing system was deficient. Through the previous years, Dr Hillery and officials of his department had been exposed to new thinking on education, in ways that their predecessors had not, through participation in the Council of Europe's Conferences of Ministers for Education – the first of which was held in 1959 – and in the United Nations Educational, Scientific and Cultural Organization (UNESCO), which Ireland joined in 1961. Increasingly, senior politicians and state officials came to accept that significant educational reform was necessary, both in the interests of economic development and of greater social equality. The details of the May 1963 announcement, and Dr Hillery's defence of its contents in particular, showed that the exposure was having an effect.[31]

The establishment of a small number of comprehensive schools, offering both academic and practical subjects, was the centrepiece of the announcement, but their establishment, it was clear, heralded a general blurring in the demarcation lines between secondary and vocational sectors. The schools would be established in places that were poorly served by post-primary schools, and they would offer a three-year course, on completion of which pupils would be enabled to proceed to the Leaving Certificate in a secondary school, or to a technical course in one of a number of Regional Technical Colleges which Dr Hillery proposed to establish with a view to addressing skills deficits in the workforce. To accommodate those living some distance from the new schools, school transport would be provided, but those availing of it would have to pay. At the same time, there were to be reforms to the Intermediate Certificate, with examinations introduced in practical subjects. Moreover, it would henceforth be offered in vocational schools, whose full-time programme had heretofore finished after two years with the Day Group Certificate.[32]

The response of teachers, as represented in a joint statement from the ASTI, the INTO and the VTA, was to welcome the 'fresh thinking on education' that was apparent in the proposals, while criticising the absence of consultation. There was 'a grave danger to the whole education system', went the statement, if the Department of Education continued to ignore the views of teachers.[33]

For its part, in a leading article entitled 'The Hillery Schools', *The Irish Times* hailed the announcement as

> one of the most valuable steps taken by a member of the present government or any of its predecessors ... since they get away for the first time from the artificial division, tailored for a generation with different ideas on the strata of society from our own, between the academic and technical disciplines.[34]

The *Farmers' Journal* was also enthusiastic:

> For the farmers' children who are coming home to work, the new plan provides for a more liberal post-primary education, but the real value is there for their brothers and sisters who can use it as a guide and a ladder to better positions in other fields ... Initially, the new comprehensive schools, embracing technical and academic education, will be confined to a small number of areas but they appear to be the means of providing a sporting chance for every man's son and daughter.[35]

Before the first of the 'Hillery schools' opened in 1966, Patrick Hillery had moved into fresh pastures. His successor, following the 1965 general election, was solicitor George Colley, an ambitious and capable new member of the cabinet who would contest the Fianna

Fáil leadership on Lemass's retirement.

Other fruit of the Hillery era which was delivered during Colley's term included the OECD/Department of Education report *Investment in Education*, described by one historian as 'one of the foundation documents of modern Irish education'.[36] Published in November 1965, it was a 'critical examination of the Irish educational system', in the words of one of its overseers, 'a system that for long years lacked positive direction, ignored research, and neglected any adequate self-assessment'.[37] The report's details on existing conditions were invaluable for educational planners, but, according to one such, its projections on future needs would be 'shattered' by Donogh O'Malley's September 1966 announcement.[38] In general, *Investment in Education* was well-received, but its technocratic thrust provoked some criticism and the following cryptic warning from ASTI president Daniel Buckley: 'What we must seek to ensure is that the economist occupies the place he should in education and that is, of course, a minor place.'[39] Colley's objectives during his fourteen months in office were long term, according to one who worked closely with him. He was concerned in particular to introduce greater efficiency, and it was in this pursuit that he encountered considerable Catholic Church-led opposition, when he proposed the amalgamation of smaller primary schools. At second-level, in a similar spirit, he championed cost-saving co-operation between vocational and secondary schools.[40]

Donogh O'Malley, who succeeded Colley as minister for education following the 1966 general election, was a civil engineering graduate of UCG who had been a TD for his native Limerick since 1954. Gifted, strong-willed and impetuous, he had an egalitarian impulse despite his relatively privileged origins. Before he could advance politically, however, he had to overcome an alcohol problem, a problem that was forcefully drawn to the attention of his Oireachtas colleagues during the course of one important vote. In that instance, O'Malley found that he was locked out of the chamber, having tarried too long in the Dáil bar, whereupon he set about smashing the door, using a convenient bust of G.K. Chesterton.[41]

Another set of locked doors – the metaphorical doors blocking entry to post-primary education – attracted the attention of O'Malley on his appointment to Education, and his assault on them would also be unorthodox and dramatic. On 10 September 1966, in the course of what he described as his 'maiden speech' on education, he declared his hand:

> There is no problem in picking out the basic fault in our present educational structure – and that is that many families cannot afford to pay even part of the cost of education for their children ... Every year, some 17,000 of our children finishing their primary school course do not receive any further education ... I believe that this is a situation that must be tackled with all speed and determination ... I propose therefore from the coming school year, beginning in September of next year to introduce a scheme, whereby, up to the completion of the Intermediate Certificate course, the opportunity for free post-primary education will be available to all families. The free education will be available in the comprehensive and vocational schools and in the general run of secondary schools. Going on from there I intend to make provision whereby no pupil will, for lack of means, be prevented from continuing his or her education up to the end of the Leaving Certificate course. Further, I propose that assistance towards the cost of books and accessories will be given ... We must also face up to the position of making financial aid available to the pupil who because of the location of his home can have post-primary education available to him only if he enters a boarding school ...[42]

This 'maiden speech' was not delivered in the Dáil, nor even at a gathering of educators, but at a Saturday afternoon session of a National Union of Journalists conference, ensuring that its contents would dominate the Sunday papers. For O'Malley, press coverage of his announcement was strategically important, for he had not sought government approval for his potentially expensive proposals, knowing that such would not be forthcoming. While he had taken care to discuss the matter in general terms with the taoiseach, Seán Lemass' most authoritative biographer indicates that he was almost as surprised by the details as everybody else.[43] Minister for Finance Jack Lynch was furious as were senior officials of his department, including T.K. Whitaker, who found it 'astonishing' that O'Malley should have announced a policy that 'has not been the subject of any submission to the Department of Finance, has not been approved by the Government ... and therefore should have received no advance publicity ...'[44] Whether or not O'Malley had been intentionally Machiavellian, the manner of his announcement ensured that his proposals gained public support sufficient to over-ride any political opposition, and his scheme came into effect the following September, by which time Jack Lynch had taken the reins of government from Lemass.

'Surprise at the breadth of the scheme' was *The Irish Times* summation of the initial reaction to the announcement. And the surprise was accompanied by scepticism. Speaking for the Labour Party's Education Committee, Barry Desmond said that 'on occasion it was difficult to take Mr O'Malley seriously'.[45] A letter from a Mr Martin Marren to the editor of a national newspaper was in a similar vein:

> When Mr O'Malley was Minister for Health, he produced a White Paper on the health services which contained lavish promises of free medical care. None of these promises have as yet become facts, and the minister has left the Department of Health to continue making promises in the new field of education.[46]

The ASTI attitude to the O'Malley announcement, if leading articles in its *Secondary Teacher* are a guide, was similarly sceptical. They were ill-thought-out proposals, and therefore impractical, editor Tom O'Dea submitted, and they had been devised without any input from teachers' representatives. The handling by the Department of Education of the announcement, in fact, also gave offence – representative organisations in education had been advised on the Saturday afternoon that an important announcement was imminent, but they had not been given any details, not even a copy of the statement that was issued to the press.[47]

A considered response to the Minister's plan from Senator Dónal Ó Conalláin, a former president of the ASTI (1951–52) and a long-time editor of its *School & College Yearbook* (1953–65), was published in the *Secondary Teacher*. Placing O'Malley's announcement in the context of the educational reform of the preceding years and of the objectives and targets set out in *Investment in Education* just a year before, he wrote:

> The new Minister for Education proposes to take all the obsta-

cles in one colossal stride. School building programmes, teacher training schedules, balance of payments deficits – all are swept aside ... It is a magnificent gesture, and completely in character.[48]

Beyond causing disruption, however, Ó Conalláin seemed to believe that free secondary education would have little real effect:

> I have personally never been convinced that any significant proportion of our young school-leavers have been denied further education merely through lack of means. I can claim some familiarity with procedures ... and it is my belief that any boy or girl of promise is, at the present time, accepted into the local secondary school whether or not the parents are capable of paying the stipulated fee ... This does not mean that there is no problem to be solved, but it would indicate that nothing could be more distorted than the picture of hordes of budding geniuses boarding the emigrant ship to ply picks and shovels in foreign lands, having been denied the opportunity to flower at home because of lack of means.[49]

It was a rather elitist perspective, and, it transpired, a wrongheaded one. And it did not take into account evidence that school fees represented a real obstacle for families. Would the *Sunday Independent* have run summertime competitions with two-year scholarships to secondary schools as prizes if they had not?[50] Ó Conalláin's view that the elimination of fees would not greatly increase pupil numbers was shared by others, however, and this was a factor in reducing potential opposition to the scheme, and in allowing it to proceed.

In fact, the increase in enrolment would be beyond all expectations in 1967–68, and expansion would continue in the following years. Allocation of resources, however, fell far short of what was felt to be necessary by those involved in secondary education.

To a number of volatile ingredients in the secondary education mixture, therefore, many more were added during the 1960s. Teachers, already concerned about their status and their incomes in a rapidly evolving society, were presented with what they perceived as a series of ill-considered diktats. School authorities, just as most of them were adapting to religious changes, faced implied criticisms of their stewardship of secondary education along with fresh demands on their resources. The Department of Education, an ossified institution in many eyes, was put under pressure by demands from its political masters – and from the mercurial Donogh O'Malley in particular. Meanwhile, the largest ever cohort of young teachers, men and women who had come to maturity during the 'decade of upheaval', brought their own perspective and their own expectations into school corridors crowded with the largest ever cohorts of second-level students. The next chapter will explore some of the consequences.

6

'It could mean Mountjoy or hunger strike'
Teacher militancy, c.1961–71

A key objective of the ASTI throughout the 1960s was to defend the social and professional status of secondary teachers. This was not a straightforward task at a time when both profession and Association were expanding, and it would be a source of tension between ASTI and other teachers' organisations, between the ASTI and the Department of Education, and even between different generations of secondary teachers. In adapting to changed circumstances, however, the ASTI would be pressed into reconnecting with the trade union movement (tentatively at first) and into employing militant tactics – in an exams boycott of 1964, and notably in the first national strike of secondary teachers for almost fifty years in 1969.

The evolution of relationships around second-level education during this 'decade of upheaval' has been treated by other writers: by Charles McCarthy, who observed them from his vantage point as VTA general secretary and Irish Congress of Trade Unions (ICTU) insider; by a historian of the Teachers' Union of Ireland (TUI), John Logan; by a historian (and long-time treasurer) of the INTO, Michael Moroney; by a historian of the Catholic school managerial bodies, Eileen Doyle; by an ASTI leader of those years, Patrick Riordan; and most comprehensively by the earlier historian of ASTI, John Coolahan, who analysed the complex negotiations of the period and described the construction of the framework in which they took place. This chapter will necessarily draw greatly on Coolahan's work, but the approach will be somewhat different. While key episodes will be examined, the emphasis will be on conveying expectations and changing moods within the Association, as well as the reactions to them from other elements in society.[1]

A preoccupation with status, combined with the reality that secondary teachers derived their incomes from two distinct sources – the state and the school that employed them – meant that disputes might produce unlikely alliances and antagonisms. Two episodes, illustrating that point, will provide insights into the industrial relations environment in which the ASTI laboured in the early 1960s. The first, from the beginning of the decade, was a movement among students taking the Higher Diploma in Education (HDip) to secure state salaries for new teachers. These students won support from some employers but, significantly, not from the ASTI. The second was a long-running contretemps about school salaries between the ASTI and the Catholic school managers, which would culminate in a 'secret agreement' of 1964.[2]

The mobilisation of the HDip students was a response to the fact that secondary teachers were not entitled to the incremental element of their salary until they became registered after one year's service, with the result that they had to get by on a school salary of £4 a week during that first year. It was an arrangement which, when introduced in 1950, was an improvement on the previous requirement to serve three years before registration, but what had been acceptable in 1950 became unacceptable, as rising prices reduced the purchasing power of the school salary.[3] Yet there was little incentive for those affected to mobilise because, due to the short-lived impact on the individual, a resolution was unlikely to be reached soon enough to benefit the group that began an agitation. It was realised, however, that student teachers might expect to gain from a successful campaign.

During 1960–61, resentment about the issue surfaced among students taking the HDip in universities in Dublin, Cork and Galway, and a campaign was launched by a number of UCD students including Louis O'Flaherty, later an ASTI president. With some earlier experience of trade unionism, O'Flaherty assumed that the ASTI would provide an appropriate forum to raise the issue, especially since during a recruitment drive in the previous decade the Association had decided to accept HDip students as members. Joining the Dublin branch, and attending meetings, O'Flaherty would meet disappointment, however, for older members were dismissive of his complaint – 'Did we not have to work for three years for next to nothing?' was a characteristic riposte.[4]

Behind the glib reaction of individuals, there was an important strategic consideration. Secondary teachers had higher salaries than their colleagues in the primary and vocational sectors, but their entitlements in this regard were being challenged by advocates of a 'common salary' for all teachers, the most determined of which was the INTO. So as to maintain the salary advantage enjoyed by its members, the ASTI stressed the differences between the formation and the responsibilities of the several categories of teachers. Secondary teachers, went the argument, were graduates with specialist knowledge whose training took a total of five years, and it would be unreasonable to place them on the same scale as primary teachers who qualified in just two years. It was considered that this entire case, and with it the superior status enjoyed by secondary teachers, would have been undermined if the concession demanded by the HDip students was secured.[5]

Finding the ASTI a dead end for their purposes, the HDip students explored other avenues. A conscious effort was made to couch the demand in reasonable terms, according to Louis O'Flaherty, and not to appear in any way 'maverick', to which end, meetings were held in the most 'respectable' hotels. A high point came on 9 March 1961 with a well-publicised meeting at the Royal Hibernian Hotel in Dublin, chaired by O'Flaherty and addressed by other leading campaigners, Michael O'Higgins of UCD and Maurice O'Connell of Trinity College. Indicative of the effectiveness of the organisers, a letter of support was received from the provincial of the Christian Brothers and there were addresses of support from prominent figures in the Headmasters' Association and the Federation of Catholic Lay Secondary Schools.[6] O'Higgins put the case in reasonable terms:

> The minimum basic salary for the [one-year] period is £200, a figure fixed by the government over 30 years ago. While we are both aware and grateful for the sincere efforts made by various bodies, both lay and clerical, to have this state of affairs improved, the government has as yet made no effort to adjust this basic salary to a more realistic figure.[7]

This widely reported meeting gave credibility to the campaign and its co-ordinators and, not long afterwards, Minister Hillery received a deputation in Dáil Éireann and agreed to pay a state salary of £200 to probationary teachers, in addition to the school salary to which they were already entitled, from the beginning of the 1962–63 academic year. It was a significant victory for the young people involved, a victory achieved, they believed, in the face of ASTI opposition.[8]

The second episode to be highlighted here, the dispute over school salaries, lasted more than a decade. In the early 1950s, the ASTI had applied in vain for an increase to the various school management bodies and lobbied the minister for education to raise the minimum salary paid by the schools, set in 1925 at £180 for women and £200 for men. In 1954 came a small concession, when the department issued a circular raising the women's salary to £200. Thereafter, the ASTI continued to press its members' case with the Catholic employers' associations (Protestant schools, for their part, generally paid more). Frustrated by the lack of progress, the Association appealed to the Catholic hierarchy in 1955, but the bishops declared themselves unwilling to encroach on the jurisdiction of the headmasters and headmistresses. Their lordships, however, did commission a survey, which showed how things then stood: teachers employed by priests had an average school salary of £267, with those employed by brothers averaging £249 and those employed by nuns averaging £209. The ASTI was almost as keen to standardise pay as it was to increase it, but the school authorities wished to retain their discretion to vary the rate.

The ASTI's representations during this period were noteworthy for a tendency to base cases on Catholic theology, probably for strategic reasons, rather than on legal or trade union principles. The 1955 appeal to the bishops included supporting references to papal encyclicals, as did a subsequent petition to convent schools' managers. This was not a useful approach, however, for the religious judged these trespasses on their own sphere of competence to be impertinent. Nor is it likely that a 1962 proposal to involve the papal nuncio, which was entertained but not adopted by the ASTI, would have recommended itself to the Catholic authorities.[9]

While high-level negotiations proceeded at a frustratingly slow pace for the ASTI, potential frustration at rank-and-file level was relieved by local concessions, as the recollections of a veteran Munster member indicates. Michael O'Meara's account, which began with descriptions of discussions among colleagues and of a deputation waiting nervously on the president of their diocesan college, had a happy ending, with the president undertaking to seriously consider the request for a raise, and, a few days later, announcing that the raise was to be granted in full.[10] The outcome may have been exceptional, but the other elements of the episode were representative of general experience before 1964.

The end of such local arrangements came in 1964 with the so-called 'secret agreement', an arrangement that improved the relative position of teachers working in schools run by religious orders, and extended the advantage enjoyed by secondary teachers over other teachers. In that it marked a significant softening in the position of the Catholic management bodies, the agreement should be seen in the context of larger changes in the educational context – of an easing of financial pressure on schools, due to improvements in capitation and in grants for school improvement, and of a desire to mollify lay teachers at a time when the state was tentatively challenging the hegemony of the Catholic religious in secondary education.

In two respects, the 'secret agreement' represented a significant advance for the ASTI. Firstly, as the outcome of a single negotiation, in which the CHA, in effect, acted for Christian Brothers and convent schools as well as for its own members, it signalled an intention by Catholic employers to form a joint negotiating body. Indeed, a few years earlier, in 1959, a Joint Committee of Catholic Managers (JCCM) had been formed with a view to co-ordinating the efforts of these same bodies. Secondly, it provided a mechanism for automatic increases in subsequent years. The new school salary agreed was £200 plus 12.5 per cent of state salary, promising future increases linked to length of service and to cost-of-living. While this was less than the ASTI had sought, there was a sweetener in the form of back-dating (with a guarantee that the conditions of the more advantaged would be protected), and the deal was adopted by CEC, by convention, and by the membership in a ballot. All of this, remarkably, took place in conditions of strict secrecy.[11] It was not the sort of secret that could be kept for long, however, and when word leaked out it did nothing for the standing of either of the parties involved. Both the INTO and the VTA were incensed at what they regarded as a devious attempt by secondary teachers and their employers to retain an archaic demarcation in Irish education.[12]

Arguably, the pre-registration salary and 'secret agreement' controversies were harbingers for the way relationships within the ASTI, and between the ASTI and the Catholic employers, would develop during the 1960s. Within the ASTI, disappointment among the not-yet-registered teachers with their established colleagues was reciprocated – the self-conscious respectability of the agitators of 1961 might have impressed the minister and school managers but among older teachers, there was a lingering distrust of the 'young turks' who had risked all their futures for a few hundred pounds each. For young teachers, on the other hand, the salary controversy suggested that their own interests were not always identical with those of their elders.[13] As for relations between secondary teachers and the Catholic managers, the 'secret agreement' of April 1964 was a clear sign that they had improved. The managers, under pressure from their bishops, were engaged in a restructuring process which would result in them presenting a united face to the world in the form of a Catholic Managerial Committee. This would greatly simplify the task of ASTI negotiators, but it was not with a view to facilitating the ASTI that the bishops pressed their management bodies into closer unity, but rather to better equip them in their dealings with a newly assertive Department of Education. And that their lay teachers might prove to be useful allies in certain of these dealings was not an irrelevant consideration.

Pay relativity and the 1964 exam boycott

Just at the point when the ASTI's relationship with the Catholic authorities was improving, its relationship with the state was coming under strain. Salary levels were again at the root of the differences, with the question of relativities within teaching making it exceedingly difficult to find an acceptable resolution. That there was much more to the matter than negotiating arrangements that both the ASTI and the Department of Education could subscribe to was indicated by the 1957 letter from the INTO protesting against what it perceived to be an overly generous arbitration award to secondary teachers.[14]

The long-standing policy of the INTO, as discussed earlier, was that there should be a common salary scale for all teachers, with allowances for degrees and other relevant qualifications. It could justify its unfriendly intervention of 1957, therefore, by arguing that its policy obliged it to protest against a widening of the pay gap in education.

That was not the end of the matter for, as a result of persistent INTO lobbying, Minister for Education Jack Lynch established a Teachers' Salaries Committee in 1958, with the following brief:

> To examine and report on principles which might guide the Minister for Education in determining the relationship between the remuneration payable to trained National teachers, recognised Secondary teachers, and permanent whole-time Vocational teachers, respectively.[15]

The ASTI was among the bodies represented on this committee, where its nominees defended existing pay differentials. Secondary teachers, they reiterated, were graduates who had been longer in full-time education than primary teachers, and their responsibilities in the classroom were of a higher order. Moreover, they insisted that equity required that secondary teachers be compensated for two particular disadvantages: that their pensions were contributory, and that they had few opportunities for promotion. The INTO response was that academic entry requirements were higher for primary teachers, that their training was more intensive, and that the pedagogical skills required to do their job were greater.[16]

When the Salaries Committee reported in 1960 it recommended that existing salary differentials between primary, secondary and vocational teachers be maintained. Rejecting this, the INTO representatives issued a minority report. The majority position indicated, however, that the ASTI's arguments were accepted by most educational interests, including the Department of Education, as president Thomas Murphy told delegates at the 1961 convention:

> We should find it a source of pleasure and gratification that the studied opinion of the majority of this committee, including those not professionally interested, was that we, secondary teachers, deserve the little extra remuneration that we enjoy.[17]

Another significant recommendation of the Teachers' Salaries Committee was that a joint conciliation and arbitration scheme be established to replace the separate primary, secondary and vocational schemes that had been established at the beginning of the 1950s. This would become a controversial matter, that would sour relationships between secondary teachers and others in Irish education during the decade that followed. The change had been sought by the state, which wished to reduce the scope for catch-up claims, which were becoming an automatic consequence of a pay award to any group of teachers. In the interim, there was an aspiration to give a single arbitrator responsibility for the three existing schemes.

A number of arbitrated pay awards followed, including one accepted by the ASTI in 1962. Another, in 1963, brought the primary teachers' maximum to 95 per cent of the secondary salary. Significantly, when a subsequent claim from the ASTI was referred for arbitration to a board under Richard Cooke SC, the Department of Education argued that the differential between primary and secondary teachers should remain at 95 per cent rather than 88 per cent, a position, the ASTI protested, that breached the Teachers' Salaries Committee report. Worse, from the ASTI's perspective, was the acceptance by the arbitrators of the department's case.[18]

Dissatisfaction among the rank-and-file about the perceived threat to the status of secondary teachers was reflected in angry discussion at branch meetings in advance of the 1964 convention. (Significantly, this was a period of considerable industrial unrest in Ireland, just after a major bus strike and shortly before a major dispute in the building industry.) Anger notwithstanding, there were mixed feelings about a proposal to respond to the Cooke ruling with a boycott of the state examinations. While teachers were not contracted to do this work, and, strictly speaking, would not be engaging in industrial action if they refrained from applying for positions as supervisors and examiners, many were reluctant to take a drastic step which might adversely affect their students. The general disposition however (as expressed in a resolution of the Desmond branch) was to 'support the Association in whatever action would be adopted'.[19] The action decided upon – by a large margin, in a secret ballot at the 1964 convention in Limerick – bound members not to 'take part in the examining or superintending of the forthcoming Certificate examinations'. A decision at the same convention that the ASTI should register as a trade union was 'interpreted as an indication of militancy and determination', according to *The Irish Times*. For the government, Dr Hillery expressed an equal determination that the examinations should proceed, regardless of whether ASTI members 'decide to engage in the work'.[20]

The most suitable replacements were the teaching religious who were not members of the Association, and the Department of Education sought the co-operation of Dr John Charles McQuaid in this regard. The archbishop, however, thought it would be imprudent for priests, nuns and brothers to ally themselves with the department in opposition to lay teachers in their schools, and he advised management bodies against allowing this to happen. The religious, accordingly, decided not to break the examination boycott (although they did permit schools to be used as examination centres in the normal way).[21]

In accordance with the convention decision, ASTI members were instructed to complete application forms for superintendents' posts as usual, but to send them to the Association's head office rather than to the Department of Education.[22] And, with a view to inhibiting the department's capacity to run the examinations without the co-operation of secondary teachers, support was solicited from the Irish Conference of Public Service Associations, with which the ASTI was affiliated, and from that conference's other affiliates.[23] One of these, the INTO, very publicly refused the request. Its argument was as follows:

> To request the INTO, whose traditional policy has been parity of salaries as between groups of teachers, to cooperate in a campaign which might cause a movement in the opposite direction and might even result in a lowering of the relative position ... is unreasonable.[24]

The INTO's curtness was significant in itself, for it gave a carte blanche to primary teachers to act as supervisors and examiners. Many were to do so, and this would be a cause of considerable bitterness between these two arms of the profession, in some districts at least. For its part, the department was able to recruit personnel sufficient to hold the examinations. The ASTI, meanwhile, aired its concern about shortcomings in the organisation of the examinations and about inconsistency in their marking.[25]

Although ASTI did not succeed in halting the examination, or in forcing a concession from the department, the boycott should not be regarded as a failure. Insofar as it injected vitality into the Association and stimulated recruitment at a time of expansion in the profession, it had a beneficial effect. Arguably too, the discipline shown by ASTI members in 1964 strengthened its position in later talks, as did the fact that the teaching religious did not prove in this instance to be an Achilles heel. Other features of the dispute that would have longer-term significance were the worsening of relations with the INTO and the VTA, and the changing position of the Department of Education with respect to a common salary.

The Ryan Tribunal

The report of the Ryan Tribunal was one of the most controversial documents in the history of Irish education. Published in May 1968, the month of the Paris *événements*, it would spark considerable unrest in its own right. The tribunal, which was established by Donogh O'Malley just five months earlier, was given the task of recommending a common basic salary scale for teachers in the three established sectors, alongside 'appropriate additions' in respect of qualifications and responsibilities. To win universal acceptance for such a salary scale was going to be a delicate task – given the sensitivities involved – and the prospects of success were not improved by the urgency imposed on the tribunal members, or by the fact that they were deliberating during the turbulent first academic year after the introduction of free education.

Developments with regard to pay in the period since the 1964 examination boycott had been unsatisfactory as far as most secondary teachers were concerned. Taoiseach Lemass had raised hopes in January 1965 when he announced that the government was making money available for the purpose of 'raising the relative status of teachers' generally, but the allocation at conciliation proved divisive within the ASTI. The award, which was accepted by a large majority of the CEC, gave married men more than ASTI had sought, and women and single men considerably less. That this was out of line with the expectations of a changing membership was made clear by rebellious delegates at the 1965 convention. A rule change resulted – in effect, a reprimand for the CEC – requiring that future awards be voted on in secret ballots at branch meetings.[26]

A further anticipated award was rather slow in coming. The ASTI submitted a 'catch-up' claim in November 1965, following awards to primary and vocational teachers, but there were delays in the appointment of an arbitrator, a consequence of the department's wish that there be a common arbitrator pending the fusion of the three teachers' schemes. While the difficulty awaited resolution, the ASTI claim remained unheard, and fears grew among secondary teachers that their status was under threat.[27]

This was the situation when Minister O'Malley announced the establishment of the Tribunal on Teachers' Salaries, under the chairmanship of Louden Ryan, a TCD economist on secondment to the Department of Finance, a director of the Central Bank and an influential advisor on economic and structural change in 1960s Ireland. Other members appointed to the Ryan Tribunal were two officials of the Labour Court, an ex-official of the Department of Finance, and the general secretary of the Post Office Workers' Union. A Department of Education official acted as secretary. It was a very different type of body to the 1960 Teachers' Salaries Commission – where educational interests had been represented – and had far narrower terms of reference. Teachers' representatives soon formed the impression that the tribunal members were quite uninformed about the operation of the educational system and generally unsympathetic towards the needs of teachers.[28]

Protracted discussions within the ASTI resulted in a narrow majority in favour of co-operation with Ryan, a decision which, given the tribunal's brief, represented a de facto acceptance of (or at least an openness to) the principle of a common salary. Donogh O'Malley had facilitated the step with his guarantee that the Association could revert to its own conciliation and arbitration scheme if the Ryan report proved unacceptable.[29] In framing its submissions to the tribunal, the ASTI's focus was on maintaining the pay advantage of its members in altered circumstances. To this end, it proposed the introduction of special allowances for qualifications, and for new posts of responsibility in secondary schools which would be filled by lay teachers. In themselves, these were not especially controversial proposals, and they could easily be taken on board by the tribunal, but the attitude of the ASTI's members would be determined by their perception of the total pay package.[30]

In fact, the fears of many secondary teachers with regard to the effects of a common salary were confirmed with the publication of the Ryan recommendations. Evidently, the tribunal had accepted the government case that, in a context where educational provision was expanding, there was little scope for increasing teachers' pay. No relish was to be offered, therefore, to facilitate the digestion of un-palatable elements of the package. In the event, the most salient fea-ture of Ryan – that maximum points on the secondary teachers' scales were to be less under the new system than under the old – overshadowed all others, making it impossible to sell the recom-mendations to an already sceptical ASTI. They were promptly re-jected in a press statement:

> It is astonishing that any salary tribunal should, in this age of money devaluation and general salary increases, produce a re-port recommending a reduction in earnings for a whole sector of the teaching profession ... The fact that there are increases on the lower points of the scales, and that a number of graded al-lowances are made available, will not, in the majority of cases, compensate for the overall reduction in earnings due to the ac-tual reduction in salary on the higher points of the scales.[31]

Briefly put, the argument was that the recommended conces-sions, including an allowance of £75 per annum for a pass degree, a system of posts of responsibility and a requirement that one of the two senior posts in Catholic-run schools should be held by a lay man or woman, would barely outweigh the sacrifices demanded of sec-ondary teachers by Ryan – especially if the long-awaited pay increase was taken into account. And the suggestion that the state should re-lieve schools of their responsibility for part of teachers' salaries did not have widespread appeal within the profession either.

Donogh O'Malley, who had been so impatient to receive the re-port, did not survive to read it, and it was an evidently unenthusias-tic Brian Lenihan who inherited the task of trying to implement its recommendations. 'I didn't want it; I don't want it; I never wanted it; and now I'm stuck with it', was the new minister's reaction to the tribunal report, according to the ASTI's *Secondary Teacher*.[32]

If a sudden increase in activity is an indicator of heightened in-terest, the tribunal report galvanised ASTI members. There was an attendance of eighty-three members – about four times the usual level – at the May 1968 meeting of the Dublin North branch, held in the days after the publication of Ryan. Several of the members had prepared critical resolutions. Urging that the ASTI embrace trade unionism as unequivocally as the INTO had, one warned of permanent damage to the Association, if 'injustice was allowed to be suffered by even a small minority'. For another speaker, the tone of the entire report was 'antagonistic to secondary teachers', no account having been taken of cost-of-living increases since 1964, and provision for posts of responsibility being included 'only as bait'. The posts as proposed, he argued, were 'divisive to the unity of teachers' and offered no prospects to the majority. For a veteran of the 1964 dispute it was important that the secondary teachers' viewpoint was properly presented: 'The public must know why we are in dispute and that we are right ... The treatment meted out to us must be seen to be detrimental to education in Ireland generally.'[33] On a similar note, a unanimously passed resolution advised the leadership on how to approach the matter of publicity:

> That this branch asks that all statements, whether written or oral, issued in connection with the report of the Tribunal, should express in clear and unequivocal language the strong opposition of members to the Report's degrading of the salaries and status of secondary teachers as being grossly detrimental to the future development of Irish education, and that all statements of a neutral, academic or purely statistical tone are a great disservice to the Association at the present time.[34]

Working to rule, 'direct political action by voting against the government, especially in marginal constituencies' and 'non-co-operation with the Department in anything except salary negotiation' were among the suggestions made to overturn Ryan. One member, who was prepared to go much further, warned: 'It could mean Mountjoy or hunger strike.'

The tone of proposals and discussion at this first post-tribunal meeting were uniformly militant, and the decisions taken indicate that the speakers were representative of the attendance. The moderate voice of former president Nora Kelleher was heard on a few occasions, however, as she corrected other speakers on points of fact.[35]

Distrust of the Department of Education, as articulated at the Dublin North meeting, was widespread throughout the profession – as one senior member of the ASTI put it during 1968: 'One of the oldest activities of the Department of Education, and the one it pursues with greatest cunning, is the destruction and rejection of teachers' salary claims.'[36] There is no doubt but that young members were to the fore in opposing Ryan, but reservations were also held by venerable figures in the association. One of these, Owen P. Ward, an ASTI president more than twenty years before, explained why he opposed Ryan in an article in *Secondary Teacher*. The impression given is that he had many reservations about the general tendency of developments, and in particular about the way recent curricular re-forms had been handled: 'Changes are made first and when finalised the teaching body is then "consulted", but no change is allowed.' This state of affairs he attributed to the growing role of an officious state:

> I did not enter the civil service as a young man, nor do I want to do so now. I prefer employment in the private sector of the com-munity and I like the intimacy of the small community of teach-ers. I abhor the bureaucratic interference of the state in the existing secondary school system.[37]

It is unlikely that Mr Ward's sentimentality about the era of the 'small community of teachers' was widely shared, but some of his other points would have had resonance. Both the length of school holi-days and the lifetime earnings of teachers were under threat, he pointed out, and notwithstanding the guarantees that were given re-specting the conditions of serving teachers, they should not accept 'bribes in return for accepting a lower status for future secondary teachers'.[38]

Having rejected Ryan, secondary teachers were again coming to look to the established conciliation and arbitration scheme as offer-ing the most viable forum in which their grievances might be heard. Appropriately, in light of the county's role in earlier initiatives in the organisation of secondary teachers, the significant initiative of 1968–69 emanated from Cork.

A total of 124 delegates attended a special convention on 28 July 1968, held in UCD's premises at Earlsfort Terrace. The convention, held on foot of a petition from members of the Cork branch, had four items on its agenda: the amount of the ASTI claim to be sub-mitted for conciliation and arbitration; the date by which the claim was to be settled; action to be taken 'in the event of dissatisfaction'; action to be taken in the event of government acceptance of the recommendations of the Ryan Tribunal. The very specific character of the business, disconcerting for head office because it reduced the negotiators' room for manoeuvre, was indicative of rank-and-file distrust of the leading ASTI bodies. A proposal in respect of salary sought a scale reaching £2,496 at maximum, exclusive of responsibility allowances, and making no distinction as to marital status or sex. This figure, 40 per cent more than provided for by the tribunal, was adopted by an overwhelming majority.[39]

Notwithstanding an attempt from the platform to rule it out of order, a resolution on strike action proposed by Cork delegate and CEC member Deaglán Ó hÉallaithe opened the main debate of the day. The proposer was forthright:

> Working to rule would be useless and would only upset the school authorities, and one-day strikes or area strikes would not be effective either. The question to be decided was would the Association be prepared to strike? Would they consider it worth a strike? If not they were only worms ...[40]

Several speakers opposed the resolution, on the grounds that a strike was unlikely to have a successful outcome. The action of 1964 was unsuccessful, it was argued, despite support from the religious, and support from that source was unlikely on this occasion. Another speaker pointed to the difficulties encountered by the INTO during a recent strike, yet another to the ease with which schools could operate during a strike given that only two in every nine registered teachers were ASTI members.[41]

Replying to the debate, in particular to points made about the establishment of a strike fund and about religious support, Ó hÉallaithe scolded that there was 'no use thinking of strike action unless members were prepared to bear the hurt':

> It will not be possible to pay teachers out on strike, and they will have to look for jobs in England; a strike fund will not be available for paying salaries but for the purpose of organising and running the strike. I hope that the religious will support the Association if it goes out on strike; at best, they will close the schools; at worst they will try to carry on without the ASTI, but they would not break a strike.[42]

After the debate, an amendment to their resolution, committing the Association to conduct a strike ballot 'in the event of dissatisfaction', was accepted by the proposers and passed unanimously, while a resolution establishing a strike fund was passed by a large majority.[43]

The threat from the special convention notwithstanding, Minister Lenihan accepted the recommendation of the Ryan Tribunal in mid-September 1968, and soon after, in accordance with another resolution of the same convention, the ASTI submitted a claim to its own conciliation scheme. (Although Ryan had recommended the merging of the three schemes, six months' notice was required before individual schemes could be wound up, and, by that point, there had been no ministerial action in this regard.)

There came a conciliatory gesture, however, in the form of an invitation to the Association to meet the minister. Meetings took place in early October, at which no acceptable offer was made. As the ASTI negotiators prepared to face delegates at another special convention on Saturday 19 October, Minister Lenihan announced that the government was prepared to improve on the Ryan Tribunal. The offer, of approximately 7.5 per cent on existing scales, fell very short of the 40 per cent demand of the July special convention, and even the addition of £50 in the rate for degree allowances did not close the gap by more than a few per cent. A simultaneous ministerial declaration that the separate conciliation and arbitration scheme for secondary teachers was to be discontinued made the minister's announcement even less palatable.[44]

Retaining their initiative, it was the members of the Cork branch that had again called the special convention of 19 October. UCD again provided the venue. On this occasion, due to the growing membership and the fact that this meeting was held during term, the attendance of 180 was almost 50 per cent higher than in July. The key decision was to organise a ballot of the membership on the improved offer from the minister. Following that decision, the Cork members held their initiative by moving that the convention be adjourned for a period of weeks, until after the result of the ballot was known. With regard to the next scheduled gathering, they successfully moved the following: 'additional items to be added to the agenda by the president by agreement with the members of the Cork branch who had requisitioned the special convention'.[45]

As anticipated by those advocating it, both the conduct and the result of the ballot of ASTI members indicated the strength of opinion within the profession. And indications are that members of the Cork branch continued to be influential advocates of militancy, visiting other branches 'to explain any aspects of the whole situation not fully understood'. Three Cork members attended a meeting of the Desmond branch where they argued forcefully that acceptance of Ryan, even as amended, would 'depress' the profession. 'Now is a very favourable time to make a stand,' they assured members. 'With the support of the managers promised and affirmed publicly, it is now or never.' Their case was accepted unanimously in the ballot by the twenty-three members voting, two new members not being eligible to vote.[46] The pattern throughout the country was similar: fully 84 per cent of ASTI's 2,540 members voted on the offer at branch meetings during November. Of those voting, 92 per cent rejected the improved offer. The next special convention took place on 23 November.

A number of significant decisions were taken at this, the fourth ASTI convention of 1968. The existing negotiators were reappointed; it was accepted that a fresh ballot would be held ahead of any strike; the date of 1 February, previously adopted in July, was confirmed as a deadline for strike action. With only four delegates dissenting, moreover, it was decided to immediately seek affiliation to the Irish Congress of Trade Unions.

Another important decision of the day was one establishing an action committee – 'as representative as possible, but still small enough to function speedily and efficiently'. In line with these criteria, it was agreed to form a committee of five members, with elections on a regional basis. Joseph Gilmartin (Connacht), Pádhraic Ó Riordán (Munster), Thomas O'Dea (Dublin) and Macartan McCormack joining president Hubert Duffy as the members. There was a division, again reflecting distrust of a perceived ASTI 'establishment', in the matter of how the action committee would fit into the Association's power structure, and it was by a margin of only one vote that it was made subject to standing committee rather than to a reconvened convention. The roles defined for the five were, firstly, to act as watchdog – in the 'implementation of any course of action decided on by the members, in convention or by referendum; to advise and work in full co-operation with the negotiators' – and, secondly, to develop the Association, by means of the 'recruitment of the some 1,400 eligible teachers who are not members of the ASTI [and] the revitalisation of branches'.[47]

A trade union once again

The decision to affiliate to ICTU on 23 November was the second such of 1968. Evidently, the resolution on the issue from the Cork branch which was passed at Easter had not yet been acted on. By January 1969, however, the connection broken by ASTI forty-two years earlier was re-established. Éamon Ó hAllmhuráin, who was a young teacher at that time, remembers that many of his older colleagues were quite unenthusiastic about linking up with ICTU. But lest the Association be regarded as exceptional in its reticence towards trade unionism, it should be pointed out that the National Union of Teachers in Britain did not affiliate to the Trades Unions Congress until May 1970, after several years of discussions on the subject.[48]

In the ASTI's absence, the trade union congress itself had experienced many changes. At the time of the disaffiliation in 1927, the Congress and the Labour Party were a single body, but an amicable separation came in 1930. The following decade saw a considerable increase in trade union membership – which was attributable in part to Fianna Fáil's protectionism and its house-building programme – but tensions between the ITGWU on the one hand, and James Larkin's Workers' Union of Ireland (WUI) and British-based unions on the other, led to a damaging split in 1945. Between 1945 and 1959, there were two congresses, the ITGWU-dominated Congress of Irish Unions (CIU), and the Irish Trade Union Congress (ITUC). Obliged to co-operate by developments in industrial relations – notably by the establishment of the Labour Court and the beginning of national wage rounds in 1946 – the two congresses eventually came together to establish the Irish Congress of Trade Unions in 1959. The INTO had remained with the ITUC throughout, though it had disaffiliated from the Labour Party in 1945. The VTA, and its predecessor, the Vocational Education Officers' Association (1930–54) also maintained its affiliation with ITUC, despite internal pressure to switch to the more overtly Catholic and nationalist CIU in the late 1940s and early 1950s.[49]

The ASTI's isolation from the broader movement was not total in the years after 1927, for it continued to avail of the ITUC-affiliated INTO's *Irish School Weekly* which featured regular 'ASTI notes' until 1937. The Association next affiliated with the Irish Conference of Professional and Service Associations (ICPSA), which was established in 1946 to lobby on behalf of salaried workers. It has been argued that this body undermined the capacity of the trade union congresses to speak for employees in the professions, but that was not the light in which it was seen by the INTO and the vocational teachers, because they both joined the ASTI in the ICPSA without breaking their trade union links. For the ASTI, the connection was to be an intermittent one, for it disaffiliated in 1947, and did not re-affiliate until 1957, on foot of a resolution from the CEC to convention.[50] However, when it came to a clash between INTO and the ASTI, as it did in the course of the exam boycott of 1964, the much larger INTO prevailed, blocking the ASTI's request for ICPSA support. This was the main cause of the ASTI's disaffiliation in 1966. Before it forsook the ICPSA, however, the ASTI had already taken a decisive step towards re-engaging with trade unionism when convention voted to register as a trade union in 1963.

The re-united Congress was at the very centre of Irish life during the 1960s. Its affiliated membership expanded, both because of the growth of employment in the economy and because of the increase of white-collar trade unionism, while its formal influence on public policy became greater as a result of its participation in the work of government-employer-labour bodies like the National Industrial Economic Council. It was the unprecedented militancy of its membership, however, that was mostly responsible for keeping Congress in the public eye throughout the decade. As Charles McCarthy pointed out, more than half a million days were lost in strikes in five of the seven years after 1963, a figure that had been reached in only four of the years between the state's foundation and the early 1960s.[51]

The five members of the ASTI delegation that attended their first ICTU annual conference at Bundoran at the beginning of July 1969, therefore, were involving themselves in a vibrant organisation. And they were themselves already veterans of a strike, the Association having gone 'all-out' during the previous February. For James McNeive, who recorded his impressions in a subsequent issue of the *Secondary Teacher*, 'the most impressive characteristic of this great ICTU meeting ... which was attended by over four hundred delegates from virtually all the professional, craft, and general workers unions, was the superlative efficiency with which it was run'.[52]

All fifty resolutions on the agenda were taken – contrasting with the seven resolutions debated at the ASTI's 1969 convention – an achievement McNeive attributed to a 'mood of mature co-operation' among delegates, combined with a style of chairmanship, which, 'while good-humoured, was able to convey to the meeting the urgency of pressing on with the business'. The resolutions considered to be most relevant to the ASTI included one deploring 'the inadequacy of the conciliation procedures in operation in many parts of the public service', and another affirming that 'unequal pay for work of equal value by men and women [was] a denial of civil rights to women'. Struck by the 'consummate professionalism' of the officials leading other unions at Bundoran, our witness concluded that 'the day of the gifted amateur' had passed, and submitted that 'the ASTI with 3000 members can hardly expect to competently run its affairs with a highly efficient but over-worked office secretary and part-time staff'.[53] His conclusion suggested that experience of industrial conflict was changing perspectives in the ASTI:

> In sum, it can be said that Bundoran was well worthwhile not just because we showed the flag for the first time but because it revealed a whole new style of trade union leadership. We were able to have a say in such vital matters as equal pay for equal work and a prices and incomes policy. Useful contacts were made with delegations from other white collar unions and, finally, we carried away from Bundoran an urgent sense and a new understanding of the unity of all workers whether they be in craft, general, or professional unions.[54]

Efforts to bring about greater unity in the schools managerial bodies had also borne fruit by this point. Significantly, the CHA, the CCSS and the Christian Brothers, which had begun to co-ordinate their efforts under the umbrella of the JCCM in 1959, joined with bodies representing Protestant and lay schools to establish the important Joint Managerial Body (JMB) in 1964. A Teaching Brothers' Association (TBA) was formed in 1965, and it became part of the Catholic Managerial (Consultative) Committee (CMC) which replaced the JCCM in 1966. The authority of the CHA, which represented far fewer schools than the CCSS and the TBA, was much di-

minished in the post-Vatican II configuration. There was no immediate appetite among the school employers for engaging with employers outside of education, and it was not until 1982 that the JMB
affiliated on a trial basis with the Federated Union of Employers, a
predecessor of the Irish Business and Employers' Confederation,
IBEC.[55]

Out on strike: (i) the decision taken
With no progress made in negotiations, the action committee elected
in November circularised members in early January 1969, advising
that they prepare themselves for strike. An initiative of the Catholic
Management Committee, Secondary Schools (CMCSS) led to a
meeting between all of the parties at the Marino College in mid-
January. Conciliation, which re-opened as a result of that meeting,
produced a new proposal, but no extra money overall. The sum set
aside for posts of responsibility was to be allocated instead to a new
system of allowances, notionally tied to responsibility but in reality
related to the length of service. Recommending rejection, the CEC
put the proposals to ballot on 29 January.[56] The ballot papers circulated drew members' attention to the seriousness of the matter being
voted upon. A rejection of the offer, they were advised, would mean
a 'withdrawal of labour'. Acceptance, on the other hand, would en-
tail 'the surrender of many of our principles'. Also included on each
paper was a list of seven arguments in favour of the offer and eight
against.

The arguments against were as follows:

> It ignores the basis on which Claim 42 [i.e. the 40 per cent claim
> lodged on foot of decisions of the July special convention] was
> made; (2) It represents no increase on the offer of 18 October
> 1968 – merely a redistribution of money allotted for posts of re-
> sponsibility; (3) Though it offers some advantage to a larger
> number of teachers, it precludes any secondary teacher from get-
> ting a really worthwhile allowance; (4) It creates a disparity to the
> serious disadvantage of teachers on confined registers vis-à-vis
> graduate teachers [in the main, these were Music and Domestic
> Science teachers, who, as non-graduates, did not stand to bene-
> fit from the new degree allowances]; (5) It offers no increase in
> allowance for qualifications – pass degree and pass H.D.E. – de-

spite strong representations; (6) There is no proper recompense for level of work; (7) It implies that the 1964 agreement with the CHA will cease to operate; (8) It implies the acceptance of (a) a common salary for all teachers, contrary to the finding of the Teachers' Salary Committee, 1960, which were adopted by the government, (b) a common scheme of conciliation and arbitration for all teachers and this would mean the abandonment of our present scheme of conciliation and arbitration.[57]

The points in favour were summarised as follows:

(1) It applies equally to all teachers – existing and future; (2) Allowances do not depend on size of school and thus small schools are not at a disadvantage; (3) Allowances are based on absolute length of service and not on service in any particular school (4) The scheme of allowances will be reviewed each year but in no case will the teacher's allowance be reduced; (5) Existing teachers in receipt of £110 in respect of Hons H.D.E will receive £150 as a total qualification allowance instead the £100 due under Section B (ii) of the offer; (6) Existing teachers on confined registers [i.e. teachers of Art, Music and Domestic Science] in receipt of £110 in respect of Hons qualifications will receive £150; (7) The total remuneration is pensionable.[58]

As expected, the offer was rejected by a large majority, though with strike now imminent, the majority was rather less than in the two previous ballots. Some 15 per cent voted to settle, as against 8 per cent in November, but almost 300 more took part in the ballot – evidence of success with regard to recruitment. The way was cleared for strike.

'570 schools shut today', announced *The Irish Times* on Monday 3 February 1969, over a story detailing the final pre-strike statements issued by the parties to the dispute. School bus services would 'continue as normal', advised the Department of Education, but this position would be 'reviewed' in light of developments.[59] The significant development was the support which was forthcoming from school authorities for the striking teachers – support which was expected, and which led to the immediate closure of all secondary schools in the state except for St Columba's College in Dublin. School closure protected the position of vulnerable part-time teachers, who did not in consequence face pressure to break the strike. The school authorities' decision to continue paying school salaries eased, to an extent, the financial pressure on full-time teachers.[60]

The JMB, representing Catholic and Protestant schools, explained its position in a statement, while offering its assistance in finding a resolution:

> The managers are deeply conscious of how much the progress and well-being of their schools in the past were due to the loyalty and cooperation of their staff. In the present situation, they are equally conscious that the future progress of their schools must depend on a continuance of that loyalty and cooperation. Consequently in these present difficult circumstances they consider that they have no alternative but to suspend classes and other school activities until further notice ... The managers wish to pay tribute to the Minister for Education and his officials and to the ASTI for their ready cooperation over the past two weeks with the managers' efforts to avert this crisis. The managers wish to assure the Minister and the ASTI that their services as mediators are always available.[61]

For one leading educator, the 'alliance' between secondary teachers and school managers was 'a natural development'. In a letter to the newspapers, Augustine Martin (a former secondary teacher and joint founder of the Association of Teachers of English, who had joined the English Department in UCD as a lecturer in 1965) argued that the 'world of the secondary school ... [had] become one of close cooperation between the teachers and the managers ... largely because of government neglect'. Unless Minister Lenihan acted with 'swift and enlightened statesmanship', he predicted that the strike would be 'a prolonged and painful affair in which great harm will result to pupils, parents, and teachers'.[62] It was true that relations between the department and the school authorities had been deteriorating, due to a perception among the religious that traditional prerogatives were being challenged. The loss of some of the authority exercised by the religious was implicit in some of the Ryan recommendations and in the attitude of the Department of Education to posts of responsibility; it was explicit in an influential article by Seán O'Connor, a senior official in that department, which was published in the autumn 1968 issue of the Jesuit periodical *Studies*. The suspicions aroused by these developments led the management bodies into a position which was seen by some as an abrogation of their role as employers during the 1969 strike.[63]

Many of the strikers had already anticipated that the dispute would be 'a prolonged and painful affair' and, relieved of picket duty responsibilities by the closure of the schools, large numbers of younger teachers embarked for England to seek employment as supply teachers or as factory workers. This was an interlude that was vividly recalled almost forty years later by several of the ASTI members interviewed for this study, and it was an interlude during which at least one of them met with a future spouse.[64]

'Out on strike': (ii) responses of students, parents and teaching religious
Support for the ASTI position came from a number of sources. Significantly, the VTA instructed its members not to accept any duties that were ordinarily the responsibility of a striking secondary teacher. There were widespread expressions of support also from the young people affected by the strike, and in some of these, the influence of the youth rebellions that had broken out across the world during the previous months was apparent.

On Saturday 1 February, the day on which the strike officially began, more than 600 secondary school students in Dublin marched to support their teachers and to insist on their own right to an uninterrupted education. Two groups, the Secondary Students' Action Committee and Secondary Students Unity, which had mobilised separately at the Mansion House and in Parnell Square, joined together outside the Department of Education, chanting 'Teachers in; Lenihan out' and 'Close the department; open the schools'. Placards demanded respect for the needs of youth: 'The boys and girls of Ireland are people'; 'Education, not programming'. 'The demonstration was organised with all of the care of another Tet offensive', according to *The Irish Times*, which marvelled that 'there were schoolgirls there too', and that the 'children' participating 'represented most of the secondary schools in and around Dublin'.[65] A journalist tried to capture the atmosphere:

Youthful marshals shouted sternly through marginally efficient loudhailers. The youngsters milled about good naturedly, their school scarves collectively colourful as a tropical jungle. Someone let off a stink bomb ... Basically, it was a very orderly and dignified demonstration. A letter of protest and a petition supporting the teachers were handed in through the iron bars outside the Department of Education building in Marlborough St. One or two tomatoes were thrown half-heartedly in the direction of a garda cordon outside the building. Several boys staged a brief sit-down demonstration, but heavy sleet was falling and they were quickly on their feet again.[66]

There were disagreements between some of the organisers and a Young Socialist Group which, it was alleged, 'tried to incite the crowd'. Elsewhere, on the same Saturday, there was a demonstration through the centre of Cork organised by students at Rochestown Capuchin College.[67]

A demonstration outside the Department of Education on the following Monday morning was organised by representatives of students at St Declan's CBS in Cabra. A letter addressed to their local Fianna Fáil TD and to Minister Lenihan, which was signed by 280 Cabra students, posed questions and issued a warning:

> Where are all the fine words you spoke to us at Easter 1966, when you attended the ceremony to commemorate the Rising of 1916? ... Cast aside by the whim of a stubborn minister. Don't be mistaken. The government are faring worse. During many labour disputes, the conservative middle and upper classes will complain and favour government policy. But not here. These teachers have the sympathy ... The government is in dire straits. The swing is completely against you. Not to the equally conservative Fine Gael, but to Labour – and the full swing to socialism.[68]

An 'ad hoc committee', composed of students from Maryfield College, Baggot Street School, Beneavin College, Coláiste Mhuire and St Vincent's CBS, which called a demonstration two days later 'in support of the ASTI', was implicitly critical of the Cabra initiative: 'We are completely non-political, and intend to remain so ... Our committee contains only secondary school pupils.' This last committee further announced that, after the strike was settled, it would continue to campaign for school students' rights, and it seems likely that it was the antecedent of the Interim Secondary Students' Council (ISSC), which 'came into being at the time of the ASTI strike' and that entered into correspondence with the CHA during April/May 1969, claiming to represent students in schools in Dublin and Cork.[69] The ISSC also initiated contact with the ASTI, with the result that its case for the establishment of student representative councils in schools was published in the September 1969 issue of the *Secondary Teacher*. The following excerpt gives an indication of the new council's stance:

> We are not revolutionaries, we do not purport to be, but we feel that at times, some sort of action is necessary to spotlight the in-justices and wrongs in our present system of secondary education ... Education has always involved communication ... Everyone has a vital contribution to make before the ideal system of com-munication can exist. There are four groups to be considered: the managers and the teachers who maintain dialogue through school councils and teacher–manager associations, and the par-ents and students who maintain a dialogue in the home. How-ever, this, as it stands, is incomplete communication. In order to form a complete unit two things are needed: firstly, a teacher–parent association and secondly, and just as essential, a student representative council. Thus we would have dialogue be-tween every group involved and a real school association formed.[70]

The ISSC leaders may have had an exaggerated notion of the ex-tent of the existing channels of communication between teachers and managers, but the ASTI's dissemination of its arguments indi-cates openness, at the very least, to student representation in educa-tion. Moreover, the initiative was welcomed in the following issue of the Association's periodical by a well-known radical and second-ary teacher, John de Courcy Ireland:

> Some councils may be set up and sink into apathy or cause scandal. Yet, by and large, the movement to establish them is an encouraging echo ... The teaching profession in our country

will, in my opinion, be unworthy of its splendid traditions if, surprisingly, it fails to welcome this movement and help to direct it into channels leading to new and wonderful destinations.[71]

The council established by school students during the 1969 ASTI strike continued to issue occasional statements until early in 1971, some of them of an extremely radical character. During 1971, it was one of three groups that came together to establish an Irish Secondary Students' Union. It seems likely that this last body was a forerunner of the Irish Union of School Students (IUSS) which was active for several years from 1972, and which had some contacts with the ASTI.[72]

If the 1969 dispute led school students into establishing a representative organisation, it also prompted some parents to launch an abortive National Parents' Council. In this instance, it seems that the initiative came from Galway city, where there were two independent parents' associations. At a meeting in Salthill's Banba Hotel, called 'to obtain the views of parents on how best to meet the present situation', strong support for the position of the teachers was apparent. Despite a 'disappointing' attendance, which included more than a few teachers, it was resolved to proceed with a mooted meeting in Dublin, and to canvass for 'mass demonstrations' demanding a settlement of the strike, which would mobilise 'children, university students and parents'. The attendance at the Dublin meeting, held on 16 February 1969, was also disappointing, with representatives attending from only seven local groups – Salthill and Renmore in Galway, Newport in Mayo, Templeogue and Raheny in Dublin, Coachford in Cork and Carlow town. Nevertheless, it was decided to establish a National Council of Parents' Association, and two Galwegians, two Dubliners and a Carlovian were elected to a committee.[73]

The dispute also prompted teaching religious who were not in managerial positions to establish their own representative organisation. Some wished to join the ASTI, but a resolution from the Sligo branch to the 1968 convention which would have allowed them 'associate membership' was rejected. It was a matter that had arisen several times in the Association's history, but the argument had prevailed that the religious, not least because of their vows of obedience, would have brought the perspective of school managers into the Association. There were religious in 1969–70 who argued that this was not the case, especially not since Vatican II, and some of them favoured a legal challenge to the ASTI's right to exclude certain secondary teachers from membership 'on the grounds of canonical or religious status'.[74] Discussion of the issue among Catholic managers shows that the ASTI's reluctance may have been well founded. There is no evidence that the managers felt in any way threatened by the establishment of an organisation representing the teaching religious, or indeed that they had concerns about any relationship that such an organisation might develop with the ASTI. In fact the Association of Clerical/Religious Assistants received encouragement from the CHA, and, evidently also, from the CCSS.[75]

Out on strike: (iii) compromise settlement and after-effects

During the dispute, the Catholic Church found itself in an awkward position. One of its branches – the school managerial component – was conniving with a strike called in opposition to government policy, at a time of great social tension in the state, when 'respectable' professionals like bank officials and teachers seemed to be taking their lead from manual workers and embracing militancy. For those wary of social radicalisation, moreover, there were dangers in a prolonged secondary teachers' strike, something that was underlined by the spontaneous demonstrations organised by teenagers in several parts of the country. In the second week of the strike, therefore, the Catholic bishops intervened through their Episcopal Council on Post-Primary Education – bypassing their managerial bodies. The intervention resulted in a meeting between the ASTI and the minister on Thursday 13 February, and in further meetings involving the various interested parties.[76]

The discussions generated a fresh offer which represented a slight improvement on that of late January, and this offer was refined in conciliation. Increases in the proposed degree allowances, together with a mechanism for automatic increases in their value in future pay rounds, and a slight shortening of the incremental scale were the main changes. The significant improvement on the Ryan proposals, however, was one that had been available before the pre-strike ballot – this was the conversion of responsibility allowances into 'special function' allowances (which were essentially long-service allowances) of £100 to £300 a year for teachers who reached the tenth point of the scale. It was little more than what had been comprehensively rejected in late January, but the offer was accepted by the CEC, overwhelmingly on a vote of sixty to five. The feeling, after nearly three weeks of strike, was that no better deal was negotiable, and that vital support – from the management bodies in particular – would be risked if the dispute continued. For their part, the managers were happy with any settlement that left the existing school administration systems largely undisturbed.[77]

In a ballot, the members accepted the improved offer, on a vote of 1717 to 538. That the turnout was 20 per cent lower than in January is explained by the fact that many of the members were still in England. On Monday 24 February, three weeks after the strike began, most of the secondary schools re-opened their doors, though some boarding schools remained closed for one more day.[78]

There was widespread dissatisfaction among the younger teachers, however, with the way the dispute had ended. For nine members of the staff of St Paul's secondary school for girls in Greenhills, Dublin, 'irreparable damage [had] been done to the prospects and prestige of all secondary teachers by the complete capitulation of the Central Executive Council to the Minister for Education and the Department'. For probationary teacher Michael Corley of Tullamore, who believed he spoke for 'most of the younger teachers', the settlement was 'unsatisfactory and inexplicable', having been reached in circumstances that remained mysterious and that were contradictory of everything that had been argued in advance of the strike. While calling for greater transparency, he suggested that it was already too late and that the ASTI had 'dealt itself a body blow from which it may never recover'. He concluded: 'It has driven from the ranks many members who expect, as I do, that an association of secondary teachers will be run with more efficiency than a local GAA club.' Corley, who, according to the secretary of his branch, contributed to meetings to an extent that was 'unusual for new members', was one of those temporarily 'driven from the ranks', in his own phrase. Returning, however, he would serve as ASTI president over three decades later.[79]

In the immediate post-strike period, there was a more general bitterness against the few secondary teachers who had breached ASTI discipline by working through the dispute, specifically those employed by St Columba's College in Dublin. St Columba's was a

Church of Ireland institution, and there are indications that the reservations of its staff were shared to an extent by teachers in other Protestant schools, due to a perception that it was Catholic rather than secondary teacher objectives that were being advanced by the dispute. In this regard, the evident acquiescence of the school management bodies in the strike was a cause of suspicion.[80]

Because they gave expression to Protestant sentiment, and because their case took up an enormous amount of ASTI's time before, during and after the dispute, the stance of St Columba's teachers in relation to the dispute merits some attention. St Columba's connection with the ASTI was historically strong, with prominent members there having included George Lodge, a founder in 1962 of the Retired Secondary Teachers' Association and an early president of that body. With Lodge's retirement, the connection was broken for a few years, until an approach from the ASTI during a recruitment drive yielded a few members. According to St Columba's history, the combination of rising militancy and increasing membership fees alienated the new members, but they decided not to totally abandon the Association. Instead, the entire body of masters combined to pay the membership for three so as to keep an eye on developments on behalf of all. Within St Columba's, concern about the deteriorating relationships in secondary education deepened as 1968 gave way to 1969. The school authorities made it clear to staff that the college would remain open during any dispute, lest boarders be lost to schools outside the jurisdiction during a prolonged closure.[81] At the same time, the three designated members did not allow their lack of enthusiasm for trade unionism to stand in the way of using trade union mechanisms to prevent the strike. But rather than arguing for their position at branch meetings, they lobbied head office asking that alternatives to the withdrawal of labour be considered. Ultimately they joined, with one other member, in a complaint to ICTU's Appeal Board, which was lodged very soon after the ASTI's affiliation to that body took effect in January 1969. Basing part of their case on the allegedly unrepresentative character of the July 1968 special convention, the petitioners argued that the conduct of the strike ballot of January 1969 was not in line with proper 'standards of democratic procedure', because 'the executive of the association and its various committees did not provide to the members full and unbiased information'.[82] It was a vexatious petition, and one that was not even fully consistent with the personal views of those lodging it. That some of them at least considered it morally wrong for teachers to strike in almost any circumstance is indicated in a list of seventeen points in defence of his decision to work through the strike submitted to ASTI headquarters by one of the St Columba three.[83]

The affair culminated in the expulsion of the men concerned but, before that happened, they tried to donate the wages that they received during the strike to the ASTI benevolent fund, so as to demonstrate that their stand was a moral rather than a venal one. When that donation was returned, they sent it, pointedly, to a charity run by a Catholic bishop.[84]

With all schools having been closed except for St Columba's, disciplinary cases overall in the aftermath were even fewer than they had been in the case of the 1964 exam boycott. Another breach of Association discipline, however, came to the attention of the CEC on foot of a complaint from the colleagues of an individual who had given grinds during the dispute on the basis that 'as he had these classes all year he was obliged in conscience to continue them'. Objecting to this act of 'scabbing', and finding it 'most repugnant to be obliged to work along with him', the complainants asked that this member be disciplined.[85]

While business arising out of the strike was still occupying its leading bodies, the ASTI concluded an agreement on school salaries in March 1969, a successor to the deal struck with the CHA five years earlier. A flat £400 a year was to be paid to all teachers in secondary schools which, although subsidised by an increase in the amount of capitation paid to schools, maintained the authority of the school managers as the employers of the teachers. In the same month, the department and the ASTI signed an agreement based on the terms which had brought the strike to an end in February.[86] This agreement seemed set to mark the definitive end of the dispute. It marked only the end of its first phase, however.

Reservations about the terms of the settlement were articulated again during a closed session at ASTI's annual convention at Easter. An injustice to the Music and Domestic Science teacher members on so-called 'closed registers' who would not benefit from the recently negotiated qualifications allowances gave particular concern, and it was resolved that parity be urgently sought on their behalf. But there were other teachers' congresses that same Easter where the agreement between the ASTI and the department was even more emphatically criticised. In the VTA, which had a far lower percentage of graduate members, there was opposition to the proposed allocation of qualifications allowances. Even more was the concern in the VTA about the 'tragedy' that the minister and his department had, by the February/March agreement with the ASTI, repudiated the 'principles' established by the Ryan Tribunal.[87] At the opening session of the INTO congress at Kilkee, the president referred to 'the serious situation facing our organisation arising from the settlement made to end the recent strike of secondary teachers'. Two days later, the 600 INTO delegates unanimously adopted a resolution from their CEC, committing themselves to a series of area strikes before the end of the month should the government not agree to pay primary teachers salaries that were equal to those of secondary teachers.[88] In fact the VTA was first into the breach, with a two-day strike on 26 and 27 May, culminating in a national demonstration in Limerick. On 27 May, in a move characterised by *The Irish Times* as a 'cat and mouse game' between that organisation and the department, the INTO followed suit with the closure of 350 primary schools in Dublin and Wicklow.[89]

An agreement broken
Following these displays of determined militancy from the INTO and the VTA, the Department of Education was enabled to revisit the strike settlement terms of February/March, terms which were becoming increasingly unpalatable in official circles as the full costs were calculated. Louden Ryan was brought back into the maelstrom, with an invitation to assess whether in fact that settlement was consistent with the earlier report of his tribunal. It came as no surprise to the ASTI when he found that it was not. Ryan recognised that sensitivity was required if the agreement was to be superseded by alternative arrangements, so he recommended that the phantom 'special functions' rewarded under the strike settlement terms be gradually transformed into the 'posts of responsibility' advocated by his tribunal just over a year previously, suggesting that national pay agreements be used as a carrot to facilitate the transition.[90]

It fell to Pádraic Faulkner, the TD for Louth (and, it was noted, in an ASTI publication, a member of the INTO[91]) who was appointed minister for education in the aftermath of the Fianna Fáil

155

victory in the 1969 general election, to formally break the post-strike settlement. With Ryan's adjudication as his point of departure, he issued new salary proposals in mid-September 1969. There was to be a common salary scale for all teachers, with a system of allowances as recommended by the Ryan Tribunal. The pay and conditions of newly appointed secondary teachers would be in line with the new Faulkner proposals, while those enjoyed by serving teachers would be incrementally altered until they too were brought into line. To begin the process, those in receipt of 'special function' allowances would not receive an increase due under the terms of the national pay agreement.

The ASTI's leading bodies deplored the announcement as breaching the terms of an agreement reached in good faith, and accepted by its members in a national ballot. Their attitude was backed by delegates at a special convention, and subsequently, a claim was submitted to the secondary teachers' conciliation and arbitration body, whose abolition had been announced by Faulkner's predecessor but had not yet come into effect. The department held fast in conciliation, insisting that no advance on the minister's proposals could be countenanced.[92]

During November, the JMB met with representatives of the contending bodies in an effort to end the stand-off. In January 1970, following efforts by the department to show that there were unrecognised advantages for teachers in its proposals, there were meetings between the ASTI and the CHA to explore how a system where responsibilities were rewarded might operate in the schools. Significantly, the Catholic managers were also now indicating that they would not close their schools in the event of another strike – which meant that there was a considerable change in the balance of forces in the ongoing dispute between the ASTI and the Department of Education.[93]

Nevertheless, because it was forced into a corner by the department's intransigence, the CEC issued an ultimatum in mid-January, threatening to take 'whatever action may be necessary' if satisfactory concessions were not made within three weeks. That deadline passed, forcing the ASTI into deciding on some course of militancy. In mid-February, the CEC voted to ballot members on a series of one-day strikes during the remainder of 1969–70, culminating, if there was no resolution, in an all-out strike at some point during the 1970–71 academic year. A series of well-attended regional meetings indicated that the caution of the CEC was reflected among the membership – in straw polls conducted at these meetings, an estimated 1,000 indicated that they favoured an all-out strike, while 700 indicated that they did not.[94] Another indication of reticence is found in an excerpt from the minutes of the large North Dublin branch from January 1970: 'On the question of a full immediate withdrawal, 49 members voted in favour, and 67 against. A very large majority voted in favour of an accelerated withdrawal, culminating in a full withdrawal if necessary. There was little support for the idea of "going sick".' But if the idea of 'going sick' won little support from the branch in January, it was only narrowly defeated in February when reformulated as follows: 'That the Association should make maximum and organised use of the rule about illness which would give most of the effects of a strike, and yet would cause little appreciable loss financially to members.'[95]

For some members, the fact that such 'objectionable tactics' could be considered was due to a lack of leadership from the CEC and standing committee, and some of the more militant of these set about calling another emergency general meeting to press for an all-out strike. Ahead of this meeting, which took place on 3 March 1970, branch discussions showed no shift in favour of the all-out strike advocated by the militants, and this course was rejected by over 70 per cent of the delegates attending. Also rejected was the one-day strikes proposal. The combined effect of the 3 March decisions, therefore, was to leave the ASTI without any clear strategy with which to pursue its objectives, and this situation was not corrected by the annual convention which followed four weeks later.[96] No further progress was made in discussions with the minister, or with Labour Court intermediary Dermot MacDermott, and matters came to a head as teachers were preparing for their summer holidays.

Exam boycott, 1970

The specific catalyst for what followed was a circular from the department to school managers, advising them that the terms of contracts for new teachers from 1 June should be consistent with the now slightly amended Faulkner proposals of September, rather than with the strike settlement of the previous February. The ASTI president Tom O'Dea swiftly condemned the circular, with its 'implied threat of differentiation between existing and future teachers and ...

apparent attempt to create a cleavage between them'.[97] At a meeting of the standing committee, it was decided to convene a special CEC meeting to consider a response. The decision taken was to boycott the correction of the state examinations, which were already underway. Accusing the minister of irresponsibility – 'with his eyes open, he has deliberately provoked us into our present action' – Tom O'Dea stated that the boycott was an attempt 'to throw the Department of Education into utter confusion'.[98]

Many members were unhappy with the boycott decision, which had been reached with rather less consultation than they had come to expect. However, according to the reports of standing committee representatives who attended regional meetings in the week after the decision was taken, 'the vast majority ... had agreed loyally to support the decision'. A proposal to place a notice in the press, 'similar to the advertisements published in 1964, informing the public that anyone who undertook examining the certificate examinations 1970 would be regarded as a scab', was rejected on a majority vote at standing committee, on the grounds that it would be a 'confession of failure' which would 'antagonise the public'. Subsequently, however, more mildly worded advertisements were placed.[99]

But the department was able to recruit enough examiners to grade the Leaving Certificate papers. According to the minister, who was eager to reassure the public about the competence of those engaged, 'a very considerable number of those who had contracted to mark papers had elected to mark them'. The ASTI insisted that none of its members was breaking the boycott, and pointed out that 'in any year, the examining force included religious, vocational, primary, and former teachers'.[100] With a great increase in the number of public examination candidates in the interval since the boycott of six years earlier, however, there were difficulties in grading the Intermediate scripts, and at a meeting in Marlborough Street on 16 July 1970, the secretary of the department made a request, on behalf of Minister Faulkner, that the ASTI lift the boycott. The request sparked a heated debate at standing committee a few days later, and on a vote of 6–5 was turned down.[101]

Subsequently, Minister Faulkner issued a public appeal to the ASTI president to lift the ban, undertaking that if the response was positive, the opening of schools would be delayed by three weeks to facilitate the work. A further announcement on salaries from the minister a day later contained conciliatory gestures – amounts due under the national pay agreement would be paid to teachers and a new long service increment would be payable to those not receiving responsibility allowances. Without reference to standing committee (for which he faced criticism), Tom O'Dea put the matter to a ballot of the CEC members who had taken the original decision in June. In a somewhat changed climate, there was an overwhelming vote to end the boycott.[102]

'Voting kills your taste for strike!'

As secondary teachers returned from their extended summer holidays late in September 1970, their dispute with the department was no closer to resolution. Some concessions had been offered during the summer, and it may have been calculated that their extended paid break would have made rank-and-file ASTI members more amenable. However, the major stumbling blocks to a settlement had not been removed, there being as yet no sign that a majority of teachers would accept either the replacement of the 'special functions' allowances or the winding up of their own conciliation and arbitration scheme. The position of their 'confined register' colleagues remained a concern of some, but one senses that this was not as intractable an issue as the others. Room for manoeuvre on all of these matters was reduced by the straitened fiscal circumstances of late 1970.[103]

It was not surprising, therefore, that the mood of delegates who gathered for yet another special convention on 17 October was 'one of anger – a deep, cold anger', in the words of the *Secondary Teacher*. Commenting again on the department's volte face with regard to the 'special function' allowances, that periodical's editor wrote: 'If any other group of workers were treated in this fashion, it would be reasonable to suspect that they would have gone on strike months ago, and would have stayed on strike until their claim was met in full.'[104] The key decision of this October convention was that preparations should be made for an all-out strike from 2 February 1971 if no agreement was reached by 15 December.

The JMB tried to break the deadlock in mid-November with a proposal that the department take account of the 'genuine grievances' of younger secondary teachers, and it suggested that raised allowances and a shortened incremental scale might alleviate these. Constrained by the Department of Finance, Education refused to even entertain the suggested improvements, and while secondary teachers were encouraged that their concerns were recognised by a third party, the ASTI walk out from a joint meeting with the Department and the JMB on 18 November was indicative of continuing frustration. Subsequent initiatives from the CHA and from the minister failed to break the impasse.[105]

The department, meanwhile, was pressing ahead with its plans to establish posts of responsibility: threatening to bypass the ASTI by communicating directly with its members on this issue, reaching an agreement with the school authorities, circularising school managers with details of the implications for each school and asking them to make this information available to their staff. Following the advice of their own representative bodies, managers complied. In a counter circular, the ASTI asked members not to co-operate with the arrangements.[106]

There is some indication of public support for the Association's claim in correspondence on the issue received by the taoiseach in late 1970 and early 1971. Individuals and representative organisations urged Mr Lynch to intervene – either to secure a compromise solution or to press the minister for education to concede the secondary teachers' claim. It would appear that there were very few, even in his own party, who were asking him to stand up to the ASTI. A letter and several telegrams from the secretary of Fianna Fáil in Salthill, Galway, advised his leader that cumann members had unanimously adopted a resolution urging him to 'instruct the Minister for Education to honour the signed agreement with ASTI'. There were letters also from parents' associations and groups of parents in several places in Dublin, Munster and the midlands, asking the taoiseach to intervene personally. Letters from individuals carried less weight, but some of them were interesting. One 'housewife', for example, appealed to Mr Lynch 'as a graduate himself', to accept the ASTI's case that graduate secondary teachers should be better remunerated than non-graduate primary teachers, and suggested that it was inappropriate that a mere primary teacher like Mr Faulkner should hold the post of minister for education.[107]

As Christmas 1970 approached, the CEC was making preparation for a strike ballot, though some softening of positions was apparent in the framing of the text to be balloted upon, with the intimation that a solution based on the JMB's proposal of November would be acceptable, provided that the concerns of members on confined registers were addressed. A slight softening of the department's line during last-ditch talks in mid-January further bridged the gap between the ASTI and the department. However, it opened a gap within the ASTI, with younger members generally favouring an uncompromising approach. That the mood of the majority on the CEC was for compromise as the 2 February deadline loomed was indicated by the defeat of a resolution rejecting the department's most recent offer. Accordingly, the strike ballot proceeded without any recommendation from the CEC as to how members should vote.[108] In respect of the disposition of the CEC majority at this time, one is drawn to conclude that it was affected by the prevailing attitude among the longer-serving teachers with whom the CEC members would have had most contact and most empathy. Their extreme caution in 1970–71 may also have been affected by the knowledge that there had been mass resignations from the Ulster Teachers' Union after that union's executive had called a one-day strike in January 1970 in pursuit of a pay claim.[109]

Continuing controversy, meanwhile, was driving ASTI membership upwards – of forty-five attending a special meeting of the Desmond branch in January 1970, twelve were new members.[110]

The layout of the ballot paper circulated to members seemed to reflect the disposition for compromise within the CEC. There were three questions, framed in a way that allowed voters to show irritation at the way they had been treated, while stopping short of supporting strike as a response. When the votes were counted, 96 per cent had voted 'no' to the proposition that the offer represented a 'full and fair settlement', while 76 per cent had voted 'no' to the offer itself. The vote on strike action produced a narrower margin, with only 56 per cent in favour.[111]

Further urgent talks followed the vote. Because of an intervention from the INTO, which had raised an objection to any discussions on teachers' salaries taking place outside of the now functioning common conciliation and arbitration scheme, these talks involved the VTA and the INTO as well as the ASTI and the department. Some further concessions emerged. While all agreed that these were insignificant, there was again a serious division within the CEC, which rejected the offer on a margin of only one vote. Strike was deferred, and another ballot of the membership was carried out on 9 February, which reduced the total in favour of strike still further, to 53 per cent.

Combative younger teachers were becoming more cynical about an ASTI 'establishment' which they saw as determined to wear them down with procedural manoeuvres and behind-the-scenes deal-making. 'Voting kills your taste for strike', a catchphrase adapted from the Department of Health's 'Smoking kills your taste for life' advertising campaign of 1970–71, was one encapsulation of rank-and-file cynicism during the early months of 1971.[112] And that there was a certain basis for the cynicism is indicated by the following excerpts from a report to his members from the CHA chairman explaining why an agreed statement was not circulated to the media:

> I spent some three hours on Tuesday with Mr O'Dea and some of his Standing Committee seeking possible ways of keeping the schools in operation ... They formally assured me of their appreciation both of our statement and of our readiness to seek with them avoidance of a strike. None of those I met wants one; nor do they see it as likely to accomplish anything. You will be interested to know that the members of the Standing Committee of the ASTI whom I informed of the decision to withhold publication were *relieved*: they felt that the statements would simply encourage the militants. I judge that on Monday, going on such information as was published in the Sunday press, and on Saturday's TV news, we were misinformed. The ASTI Central Executive committee issued no statement; what appeared were 'leaks', pretty obviously from the militants. The *sanior pars* were/are disturbed. Maybe we could in a quiet way help to win over the less committed to a more peaceful frame of mind ...[113]

The 'statement' referred to in the report was one agreed at an earlier CHA meeting, drawing attention to the likelihood that member schools would be forced to close in the event of a strike. The suppression of this statement by the CHA's chairman strengthened the argument of strike opponents in the ASTI leadership who purported to believe that schools would remain open, and that the withdrawal of lay teachers would only serve to undermine the bargaining position of the Association by revealing its weaknesses.[114]

In support of their argument the anti-strike element in the ASTI were able to cite a CCSS statement of 15 February indicating that convent schools would remain open (a statement, incidentally, which caused distress to some CCSS members). Changed circumstances within the Catholic Church in the 1960s allowed representatives of convent schools to adopt a more independent stance than formerly. The long-time CCSS president, the Dominican Mother Jordana (who, incidentally, was Máire MacDonagh's first cousin) had reservations about the longer-term implications for school employers of continuing to give support to their striking 'employees'. Mother Jordana's stance was one that made her unpopular among secondary teachers in the 1970–71 academic year.[115]

For his own part, the CHA's Fr John Hughes could hardly be blamed for agreeing to a secret meeting with a section of the ASTI leadership, but, arguably, his use of the term *sanior pars* to describe 'Mr O'Dea and some of his Standing Committee' reveals something of the CHA's attitude to ASTI democracy. Literally 'the sounder part', *sanior pars* was an allusion to Catholic conciliar practice, whereby the validity of decisions was dependent on consensus among senior members in addition to a decision of the majority or *maior pars*. Evidently, religious managers considered that the authority of the longer-serving members of standing committee was greater than that of the more 'militant' *maior pars* of the ASTI.

In the week following the 9 February ballot, there was tremendous pressure on the ASTI to call off the strike. Much of the pressure came through ICTU and, eventually, on Monday, an undertaking from ICTU president Maurice Cosgrave to give priority to the ASTI's problem if the strike was postponed for a fortnight was considered by standing committee. On a vote of 13–2, the postponement was agreed.[116]

The siege of Hume Street

Most members learned of the postponement of the strike on the night-time news of 15 February (which was an auspicious date for another reason, being the day when the long-anticipated decimal currency was introduced).

Some were socialising after attending meetings; others, expecting a long strike, had already embarked on journeys to England or to their native places for the duration. In the North Star Hotel in Dublin, 200 mainly younger teachers were meeting to co-ordinate activity in the capital during the following day. According to Michael Ward, secretary of the ad hoc action group that had organised the meeting, placards were being crafted and teams of 'flying pickets' were being formed, to be despatched to any school that tried to open on the morrow. In light of the earlier CCSS statement, it was anticipated in particular that some convent schools would try to open, and there was much resentment in the North Star and elsewhere at the apparent determination of the CCSS president, Mother Jordana, to thwart the strike. Michael Ward recalls that 'a tremendous feeling of anger' swept through the crowd in the North Star when the news of the postponement broke, directed against an ASTI leadership that was perceived to have been 'completely out of touch' with the views of younger teachers, and against the ICTU officials that were blamed for placing pressure on standing committee to call off the strike. With suitable materials to hand, a banner was quickly improvised, reading 'Broken agreement', and the 200, along with some reinforcements, marched behind it to the union headquarters in Hume Street. A meeting of the standing committee was just ending, and there were angry exchanges between the North Star contingent and those that they blamed for 'selling out'. 'It was evident,' commented journalist John Horgan, 'that some members of the Standing Committee were far from popular with the crowd.' If they were unpopular, they were also nervous enough to phone An Garda Síochána. When gardaí arrived, the protestors quickly dispersed.[117]

Speculating about how representative the crowd was of secondary teachers generally, Horgan predicted that 'few of the people who waited in the icy cold outside Hume St last night will be in school this morning'.[118] The prediction was accurate, and during the following day, there were hastily arranged 'meetings at several venues' in Dublin to discuss the situation. Several hundred members, including some who travelled from Cavan, Drogheda and Galway, blockaded the ASTI building, and a picket was placed on ICTU headquarters on Raglan Road. According to John Walshe, education correspondent of the *Irish Independent*: 'Angry teachers shouted "sell-out" and waved placards.' An accompanying photograph showed placards with the following messages: 'Majority rule', 'Total betrayal', and 'Standing Committee resign'.[119]

In other parts of the country there was also intense activity. The Sligo branch issued a statement declaring itself 'highly indignant at the postponement of the strike', announcing that 'action would be taken against certain headmasters and headmistresses who had stated that they would keep their schools open', and demanding the resignation of the ASTI's standing committee. In County Tipperary, the ASTI branch formally protested to the heads of the eight convent schools that had arranged to remain open. 'We regret this lapse of loyalty,' went the statement, 'and cannot guarantee our cooperation in the future.' From the city of Limerick, it was reported that all secondary teachers had turned up for work, but the branch there was one of those that protested against the standing committee decision.[120]

In several places, teachers clearly did not go to work. In County Cavan, twenty-four ASTI members absented themselves on Tuesday 16 February, though their schools were open. In Monaghan, the principals of four schools denied that twenty of their teachers had embarked on an unofficial strike, with the head of the St Louis Convent stating that she had 'an understanding' with the twelve ASTI members of her staff that they were 'relieved of duty yesterday pending a meeting of the Monaghan ASTI branch last night to consider headquarters' action'. John Mulcahy – then in his first year as a teacher in the North Monastery CBS; later an ASTI president – recalls that most members of the Cork branch stayed away from work for one day, but that members of the Carbery branch stayed away for several days. The superior of Coláiste Iognáid in Galway told journalists that, due to 'confusion and the short notice of the calling off of the strike', he had decided not to hold classes on Tuesday, and there are indications from that city that several days passed before things returned to normal.[121] According to the *Connacht Tribune*, the assertions from school managers that there was 'business as usual' in their schools during the rest of the week were contradicted by teachers and by representatives of students who organised an Eyre Square demonstration so as to show that they 'objected to being used as a pawn in a power struggle' and to display solidarity with their teachers. School managements were accused of 'painting a picture for the public' by these students, who insisted that there was 'serious disruption of classes and absenteeism', despite the postponement of the strike.[122] There were student mobilisations also in Cork and in Dublin, where students of one school were suspended 'for absenting themselves from classes without permission', according to their principal, and not 'for taking part in the demonstration as such'.[123]

On Wednesday 17 February in Dublin, an estimated 700 ASTI members 'from all parts of the country' gathered for what the *Independent* characterised as a meeting of 'dissident teachers'. In the event, nearly 90 per cent of the 'dissidents' voted to go back to work, 'under protest', a decision that was criticised as showing 'cowardice' by members of the thirty-strong Galway contingent. It is likely, however, that the votes of the 90 per cent were cast in the light of experiences like that of Éamon Ó hAllmhuráin, who had been rebuffed by senior colleagues in his inner-city Dublin school when he tried to persuade them to leave their classrooms on the day following the decision to call off the strike.[124]

The impression overall is that there was widespread absenteeism of teachers in the days following 15 February, but that school authorities took a tolerant view in the expectation that tempers would become calmer, given time.[125]

The same days saw a flurry of activity on the part of the ASTI, Department of Education, and ICTU negotiators. New proposals were presented to the CEC on Wednesday 24 February which, it was generally felt, had little to recommend them. The CEC vacillated, with members voting first against a resolution rejecting the proposals and then against a resolution accepting them. Yet another national ballot was held on 26 February – without any recommendation from the national leadership – in which the alternatives were a national strike beginning on 2 March 1971 or acceptance of the offer. On this occasion, members voted to accept on a margin of 57 per cent to 43 per cent. There was much anger among the advocates of strike. Among younger teachers, John Mulcahy recalls, the final package was perceived to represent an effort to 'buy off the older group ... with little bits and pieces' of concessions. The anger found an outlet in yet another special convention convened by the Cork branch and held in the ITGWU's Liberty Hall on 27 March. A vote of no confidence on the standing committee was defeated by only six votes at an extremely heated convention where the subjects of the censure ignored appeals that they themselves should abstain.[126] One commentator summed up the outcome as follows:

As far as the Association leadership was concerned, the snake has been scotched, not killed, and the deepness of the division in the ranks was accentuated by the high proportion of speeches in favour of the resolution and the small number defending the standing committee and negotiators – none of whom spoke in their own defence.[127]

Peter Kerr, one of the 'militant' minority on standing committee, did resign, however, in protest at the 'Munich-like compromise' of 15 February. His letter of resignation expressed the extreme frustration and disappointment felt by many members:

> I am no longer content to be associated with the decisions of those who, in my opinion, have abused the trust of those who elected them, and by caustic arguments have taken it upon themselves to flaunt decisions of the special convention of October 1970 and to ignore the views of the 53% of members who voted for strike action on February 9th 1971, who have used their influence to persuade the teachers of today to sell out the teachers of the future and the teachers on the confined registers, just as was done in 1964 and 1969 to other sections of the association.[128]

Kerr himself would be back on standing committee a year later, but there were others of similar views whose disillusionment led to a longer disengagement from ASTI activity. There was even discussion in some quarters about establishing a rival secondary teachers' union. Over the course of a few years, however, many more of those associated with the 'militant' position moved into positions on the leading bodies of the Association, where they found themselves having to make the most of the 1971 agreement.[129] The only mechanism through which progress could be achieved on the several outstanding issues, it seemed, was the common conciliation and arbitration scheme for teachers, which had been operating without the ASTI's participation for the previous year. Accordingly, its representatives joined in discussions, charged with the task of negotiating such improvements in the scheme as would make it a more suitable vehicle for considering secondary teachers' claims. Discussions with the other teachers' unions and with ICTU produced a set of proposals that, in turn, provided the basis for discussions with the Department of Education, which resulted in a document that could be recommended to a special conference on 24 March 1973. Having been accepted overwhelmingly, the agreed scheme came into effect before the end of that year. The process, it may be noted, repaired to an extent the damaged relationships between the ASTI and the other teachers' unions.[130]

It transpired that there was no easy solution to one major source of fraught relationships within the ASTI, however, for the grievance of the non-graduate teachers on the so-called 'confined registers' (about 15 per cent of the membership in the early 1970s) remained unresolved, and could not be satisfactorily resolved, even in the medium term. Having been cut adrift from their colleagues with the introduction of qualifications allowances, they remained adrift and resentful that they were so disregarded.

Decade of upheaval

With hindsight, it can be seen as almost inevitable that there would be unrest in secondary education during the period discussed in this chapter. Indeed, to have placed so many fresh demands upon a system that was so tradition-bound without giving rise to conflict would have been an achievement in ordinary times. And the 1960s and early 1970s were not ordinary times. While social unrest was manifesting itself on almost all conceivable fronts, the weapon of strike had been seen to prove itself time and again in industrial relations. That there was at the same time an unprecedented influx into the profession of secondary teaching in Ireland, and that this influx was of young men and women in their early to mid-twenties was a further dynamic factor. Quite how 'radicalised' these young men and women actually were may be an open question, but they certainly had not yet fully absorbed the notions of middle-class respectability that had constrained their elders in the profession.

Inevitably, it was to these elders that leadership devolved – and they were judged to have been inadequate in carrying out their responsibilities. If 96 per cent of ASTI members in the ballot of December 1970 voted that an offer from the department did not constitute a 'full and fair settlement', then the acceptance of a not-substantially-different offer a few months later must be considered a serious and conclusive defeat in a three-year-long struggle. And that was how it was regarded, even by many of those who promoted its acceptance. Notwithstanding the real gains in salary that had been won for most secondary teachers in the previous few years, therefore, the overwhelming feeling in ASTI ranks in March 1971 was one of failure.

The real failure of leadership, however, pre-dated the struggles of 1969–71. The fact was that the long-standing preoccupation with status within the profession led the ASTI to join a battle that it probably could not have been won, because the forces ranged against it were too formidable. Properly marshalled, secondary teachers might well have extracted significant and sustainable concessions from the government in the conditions of the late 1960s – many bodies of trade unionists did so. But to have secured what was actually sought, it would have been necessary to defeat the VTA and the much larger INTO as well as the government. The ASTI had successfully won privileges for its members during the decades when the secondary sector was a small redoubt in the Irish education system, when the relative cost of a concession to secondary teachers was small. The failure of the *sanior pars* of standing committee was not to recognise that circumstances had become different with the reform and expansion of post-primary education in the 1960s. There is no evidence that the new ASTI recruits of the 1960s were hung-up about maintaining their special status, only that they were persuaded that mechanisms like separate conciliation and arbitration were required so as to ensure that they enjoyed a decent standard of life. They might just as easily have been persuaded to join in a common cause with other teachers for the benefit of all.

But in assessing the major disappointment of 1971, it is important not to lose sight of the even more important success of the period. The reality was that in the period between the exam boycott of 1964 and the abortive strike of 1971, the ASTI became a really vibrant organisation. Teachers were drawn to meetings in unprecedented numbers to learn about the issues, to express opinions about them, and to vote upon them in increasingly frequent national ballots. Those of them who held strong views competed with one another for delegateships to annual convention and to the many special conventions. The vitality of the debate and the ever-present danger of strike ensured that enlistment in the ASTI became almost automatic for many entrants to the profession. With the concurrent decline in the proportion of teaching religious, it became more difficult to dispute the Association's claim to speak for the body of Irish secondary teachers.

7

'Properly and fully organised'
ASTI expansion and development, c.1970–90

According to one authority, 'secondary teachers derived the same collective psychological benefit from the 1969 strike and the associated controversies as their colleagues in the INTO derived from the unsuccessful strike of 1946'.[1] There were other factors, but it is undeniable that the period between the Ryan Tribunal and the abortive strike of 1971 marked an important transition, during which seeds for future development were planted. It was not inevitable, however, that the harvest would be bountiful.

Membership grew in the late 1960s, but perhaps not quite as much as it might have done. There were still problems in reaching the *cadhain aonair*, individuals working alongside religious in small schools, and there remained a tendency for members to drift away, either because they overlooked the payment of dues or because they wished to quietly register disapproval of ASTI action or inaction.[2] About a thousand eligible teachers, therefore, were not members at the end of 1969. However, grounds for optimism existed, for almost a thousand had joined during the previous two years, providing a source of income for further development. Recruitment was discussed at convention in 1969 and 1970, and again in 1971, when it was determined that a full-time organiser should be recruited. When Michael Cahill accepted the position of organiser/negotiator later in 1971, the ASTI had two full-time officials for the first time in its history.[3]

Months later, there was a further strengthening of head office when an agreement that ASTI presidents would be granted sabbatical leave during their terms came into effect. It was a concession that had been sought for many years, and the memoir of Limerick-based president Tony Bromell shows how onerous the responsibilities had become by the mid-1960s and how difficult it was to fulfil them alongside teaching duties, especially for a president based outside Dublin. It fell to Kevin Meehan, president in 1972–73, to be the first to benefit from the new arrangement, and he and his successors greatly enhanced the Association's capacity to maintain contact between branches and headquarters.[4]

The actual headquarters themselves, which had been located in Hume Street since 1965 (following a short sojourn in Stephen's Green), were now inadequate and, in 1973, new premises were acquired on Highfield Road, Rathgar. That the Association was able to purchase its own building, for the first time, was evidence of financial health and of confidence in the future. Further development necessitated another move in 1982, to Lower Baggot Street, but within a few years, the continuing expansion of the Association rendered that building inadequate. In 1992, at the official opening of the new purpose-built headquarters in Winetavern Street, in central Dublin, president Joe Whyte declared that the Association's days as a 'peripatetic organisation' were at an end. These premises would later be named Thomas MacDonagh House in honour of the revolutionary poet and scholar who was one of the founders of the Association.[5]

It could not be said that the sense of confidence indicated by the purchase of its own premises found expression in Michael Cahill's first report to convention in 1973. Rather, that document presented 'a rather dismal and disappointing picture', in the words of an organiser who was trying to cajole activists into becoming more methodical in their ASTI work. He identified the following shortcomings:

(a) Low paid up membership; (b) Low morale and little enthusiasm reflected entirely in the attitude 'what can the Association do for me?'; (c) Numerous pockets of unorganised teachers who are not members and have not been canvassed; (d) Schools left completely outside of the existing branch structure for recruitment and other branch activities; (e) Inter branch and internal branch bickering and dissent in a few cases; (f) Jealous protection of certain branch advantages to serve parochial ends rather than the national ends of the Association; (g) A reluctance to accept division, amalgamation, or restructuring of branches for the betterment of all.[6]

The list, arguably, exaggerated the problems, but it underlined the determination of the organiser, who was realistic enough to re-alise that it was impractical to think 'of tackling all of these problems simultaneously'. His strategy was to begin with a pilot scheme in-volving eight branches, with a view to ensuring that 'all schools within these branches will be properly and fully organised', and then to use the results to encourage others.[7] Subsequently, a 1975 survey identified gaps in the organisation and sought to ascertain why some teachers remained aloof. If the reasons given for non-membership were not so enlightening from an organisational perspective – 'fi-nancial, personal, dissatisfaction with lack of service or progress, anti-union' – it was useful to be able to identify the lacunae. The regions with the highest penetration, it transpired, were Monaghan/Dun-dalk, Kerry and Wicklow/Wexford, in each of which there were few non-members. Conversely, non-members were plentiful in Galway, in Fermoy/Desmond and in Dublin North.[8]

Cahill's subsequent organisational reports were more upbeat. In 1974, he recorded a substantial increase, notwithstanding the diffi-culties caused by the petrol shortage, and in 1977 he reported that the Association was 'nearing maximum membership' among its base of lay secondary school teachers. Reaching that maximum necessi-tated a degree of pragmatism, and such was indicated in Cahill's sug-gestion that there be an amnesty of arrears for lapsed members. If membership was to be maintained at near the maximum level, it was vital to prevent arrears in the first place, and providing for deduction

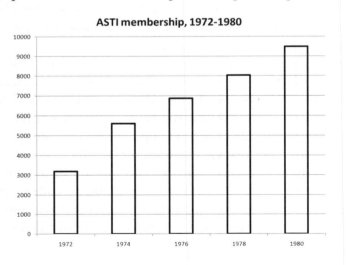

ASTI membership, 1972-1980

of membership fees at source through a 'check-off' system was an obvious means of achieving this, even if it was recognised that there would be a consequent loss of contact between members and branch officers. Convention approved the 'check-off' in 1976, but it was not until 1980 that the necessary arrangements were completed. About 70 per cent of members switched to the new system on its introduction, and this rose to over 90 per cent by 1984. From the head office perspective, the efficacy of the 'check-off' was illustrated by the fact that the Association maintained its membership, even as numbers of secondary teachers fell due to cutbacks in the mid-1980s.[9]

In the period between Michael Cahill's appointment and his departure in 1979, there was a phenomenal growth in membership, fruits of an expanding system and of well-judged recruitment strategies. A survey showed that the number of 'eligible non-members' was reduced to 250 in 1979 – that is, 3 per cent, compared with perhaps 30 per cent at the beginning of the decade. If the decline in the proportion of teaching religious is taken into account, it will be seen that the ASTI's voice in secondary education had become far stronger. In 1970, it spoke for 40–45 per cent of secondary teachers; by 1980, the figure had reached about 80 per cent. And membership might have been even higher had the teaching religious been accepted into membership. The matter was passionately argued at conventions during the 1970s, but there was a consistent majority against, delegates continuing to believe that nuns, brothers and priests would be constrained by their vows in acting independently of their superiors, the employers.[10] That there was considerable anger among the teaching religious at their exclusion was indicated by responses to a survey conducted among Galway teachers in 1979–80. Two quotations selected from the responses of the participating religious will convey their feelings about the issue: 'At the very least, the TUI will have you – time ASTI respected people's intelligence and independence'; 'Not allowed to be in a trade union – a serious sore point'.[11]

As it happened, an issue arose in the mid-1970s which might have presented problems for the religious had they been ASTI members, in that it had the potential to oblige them to choose between obeying a union directive and a superior's instruction. This was the Association's campaign for a 22-hour week, which was prompted by the Department of Education's desire to bring about uniformity in teaching hours across the post-primary system. Under the terms of the 1957 contract, up to 26 hours might be demanded and this was identified as a source of weakness in any negotiations with the department – hence, the emergency resolution passed at the 1974 convention instructing members not to accept a teaching load of more than 22 hours in the forthcoming year. School stewards and branch officials were left to work out the details at local level. Most school managers accepted the new regime, and evidently they were encouraged to do so by the JMB, but there were difficulties in about 15 per cent of schools at the start of the 1974–75 academic year. Sustained pressure, however, brought about almost full conformity within months. The success of the ASTI ultimatum dismayed the main Irish employers' organisations and they protested to the government and to ICTU about breaches of procedures and of national wage agreements committed in the course of the short campaign. Obliged to reprimand its wayward affiliate, ICTU met with ASTI officials, an encounter that was recounted as follows for Pierce Purcell by Liam Hogan, ASTI president in 1974–75: 'They ticked us off, tongue in cheek, for being such bad boys.'[12]

The standardisation of hours at an acceptable level and brisk growth in membership were both sources of satisfaction, but the Association faced other challenges, some of them consequent on growing membership, others arising out of broader social change. Two of the challenges were large enough to deserve separate treatment in the next two chapters: the efforts at co-ordination between the ASTI, the TUI and the INTO, and the efforts to achieve greater participation by the female majority in the affairs of ASTI itself. This chapter will concern itself with the Association's responses to the increase in its own membership and to developments in the educational context, with a focus on the following: reforming the ASTI's structure and infrastructure; developing communication with members and training for local officers; addressing problems presented by the establishment of the community school sector. Before proceeding to these issues, however, it will be instructive to glimpse developments from the perspective of rank-and-file members.

'Code word "horse"': branch life in the 1970s

The transformation of the late 1960s and the 1970s affected the life of the Association at all levels. For most members, the primary point of contact was their local branch, so a scrutiny of developments at this level is necessary. The availability of branch records from the period drew this writer's attention to branches in Carrickmacross and Clare.[13]

The Carrickmacross branch was established in May 1964, at a meeting in the Farney Hotel on the town's Main Street. Its minutes for the early 1970s, when they were kept by Art Agnew, have some of the vividness and telling detail of a Pat McCabe novel, for they convey the atmosphere at meetings as well as the attitudes of members, who were few enough in number and often absent. Poor attendances, according to one veteran, were attributable to the fact that 'they knew each others views too well on several items'.[14]

When members did turn up, they were often unruly, chatting among themselves and interrupting speakers, making it difficult for the chair to keep order and for the secretary to record proceedings. It was a cautious branch, however, where there was an absence of enthusiasm for the regular balloting that was so much a feature of the period, the consensus being that it was unsatisfactory 'to have their views expressed consistently by answering "yesses" and "noes" and vice-versa'.[15] That the significance of these ballots was recognised nonetheless is underlined by the amount of information recorded about their conduct, right down to the process of sealing and registering envelopes before their despatch to head office. And if the outcomes of votes at branch level were not nail-bitingly close, drama was not completely absent, as the following minute of 26 February 1971 shows: 'The outcome of the ballot was sixteen for acceptance and one against. The result was then phoned through with our code word 'horse', and the meeting ended.'[16]

The frequency of inquorate meetings, combined with a failure to attain the membership target of twenty (the minimum necessary for representation at convention), led to discussions about the viability of the branch during 1971 and, to the disappointment of several of the founders, it was decided to dissolve it with effect from 27 November 1971, when members transferred to the Dundalk and Monaghan branches. The final meeting, we are told, ended with the singing of 'Auld Lang Syne'.[17]

A more typical branch, insofar as it was viable, was the Clare branch, centred in Ennis, but with members scattered throughout the county, as well as in Gort, County Galway. It was a branch with a history stretching back to the mid-1930s – when its establishment was attributed to the 'activity and enthusiasm' of the Limerick branch

– but its surviving records reach only as far back as 1973. Older members recall branch meetings being held in the village of Lissycasey, so as to facilitate teachers in both Kilrush and Ennis, who would share car hire expenses. During the 1970s, meetings were always held in or around Ennis, often in the Auburn Lodge Hotel, a few miles outside the town. In mid-decade, the branch met for a period in the newly established Ennis Teachers' Centre. This was one of the many such centres established by the Department of Education from 1972, and ASTI headquarters encouraged branches to make use of them.[18]

There were veterans, like Michael O'Meara who had joined in the 1940s, but the profile of the ASTI in Clare was youthful during the 1970s as, reflecting the rapid growth of the Association generally, new members were proposed at almost every meeting. Membership in 1975 reached 100, and during the same year, the branch approved the departure of members who wished to establish a West Clare branch.[19] This new branch was not established, however.

It did not always prove easy to integrate new members, and concern arose about the level of attendance, just as it had in Carrickmacross, there being rarely more than fifteen present at the seven or so branch meetings that were held each year. Their lack of contact with the branch, moreover, led many to fall into arrears with their subscriptions – thirty-two individuals were regarded as lapsed in May 1974. Little wonder then that Clare was an early proponent of deduction at source of ASTI contributions. Various suggestions were made as to how participation might be improved, but a proposal that meetings 'rotate' among the towns within the branch's jurisdiction, one that had a reasonable chance of success, was defeated on a vote of 7–5 in January 1976. The alternative adopted, which was that the agenda should have a more 'local' focus, did not have any noticeable impact. Visits by dignitaries, however, did improve attendance, with twenty-nine members being present to hear president Derek Nolan address a meeting in 1979. As always, the possibility of industrial action of some sort was the most effective mobiliser, and this was the circumstance which caused seventy-two members to throng the December 1979 meeting, the last of the decade and the best attended.[20]

For those who did attend them, the Clare branch meetings must have been useful, in providing a forum where Association policy might be interpreted, where the implications of this or that departmental directive might be explained, and where advice in respect of the predicaments of individuals might be found. Long-running national issues were discussed – the department's (ultimately abortive) regionalisation plans, for example, were of concern to members during 1974, while corporal punishment was debated in 1978 when, on a division, a majority voted that it should be retained.[21] Some causes of indignation were of the quickly forgotten kind, in which category one might place the following minute:

> The secretary was instructed to write to Mr Cooney, Minister for Justice, and request that he either substantiate or withdraw his allegation of IRA propaganda indoctrination of students by teachers. The secretary was also instructed to send a copy of the letter to head office and to the *Clare Champion*.[22]

A striking feature of branch life in the 1970s was the amount of business generated by the annual convention; a similar observation was made, it will be recalled, in relation to the affairs of the Kilmallock/Desmond branch during the 1950s. The necessity of formulating resolutions, of selecting delegates, of deliberating over the final agenda and over requests for support from candidates for office, of receiving post-convention reports meant that convention business was transacted at a majority of all meetings. Active members were thereby kept in close touch with the national Association, but did the arcane character of much of the agenda dissuade some teachers from attending meetings?

Becoming active

If there were difficulties in integrating new members in the 1970s, there were many young teachers who gradually took on responsibilities within the structures of the ASTI. The recollections of several of them will indicate how this came about.

The first teaching position of future president P.J. Sheehy was in 1973 in Dingle CBS. In 1974, he moved to Arklow CBS. Very soon, he was drawn into ASTI activity:

> One of the teachers in Arklow told me that you had to join [the ASTI]. In Dingle, nobody had mentioned it to me. In Dingle indeed, it seemed to me as a 22-year-old that the teachers were prepared to accept things that they shouldn't have accepted. They

weren't really able to speak up for themselves. In Arklow, on the other hand, the staff was younger, and people were open about the ASTI, all going to meetings and that ... There was a certain social aspect to meetings at that time because afterwards you'd have a few drinks. People actually saw them as enjoyable occasions. At first, you'd almost need a glossary to explain the terms, but like so many other things there was a process of osmosis almost, and you got to know what it was all about ...

I didn't set out to be a school steward, but fairly early on I found myself in that position. About 1979, I attended Convention for the first time, and the scale of it all made an impression. I was used to speaking out at meetings, but it was a different thing looking down a hall at a few hundred people. And then I was proposing a motion that I personally didn't really believe in, but I had to speak on it on behalf of my branch. From there on it got easier ...[23]

After completing the HDip in 1977, Christina Heneghan found employment in school in Clontarf. Soon she was attending ASTI meetings:

When I went to my first meetings, I found it all very intimidating. There was one man there who seemed to have opinions on everything and he dominated the meetings ... On the other hand, I didn't understand a lot of the procedural stuff. I mean, teaching is full of jargon. At first you'd even have to ask yourself, what exactly was an increment and questions like that. But I picked it up ...

Then, further along, I shared a house with a bunch who were teaching in Fingal. Now, the hottest union branch in Dublin to this day is in Fingal. They were really on top of the issues in Fingal; they were at the cutting edge. One of the girls used to spend hours writing minutes, making phone calls, and she was big into it. I suppose it was rubbing off on me, but at first I thought she was mad to be doing all this extra work. You might say I served my apprenticeship there. When I came back to Mayo then, I was elected school steward.[24]

Paddy Daly, who became active in the Tipperary branch, took up a position in Rockwell College in 1973, after a period teaching in

Africa. Getting involved in the ASTI was a natural process for him:

> The man I replaced in the school was John Buckley who was an ASTI stalwart, going back to the late 1920s I think. He was one of those who built up the Tipperary branch ... It seemed to me that the obvious thing to do was to get into your teachers' union. At the time everyone in Rockwell was a member, so it was easy to join, but I would have joined anyway. I started to go to meetings straight away ... We used to pool cars, so there would be four or five of us in the car from Clonmel going over to meetings, which were held in Cashel.[25]

In 1975, just qualified as a secondary teacher, Lily Cronin received a phone call offering her a position in Balloonagh secondary school in Tralee. Joining the ASTI, she attended branch meetings, especially when there were important issues on the agenda:

> The officers and CEC people were older, and as a young teacher, you'd sometimes ask yourself: 'What are they trying to do to us?' I suppose, the younger ones today look at us, and say the same thing. Early on, there was a pay offer, and I remember going to a meeting to vote against it, because it favoured those on the top of the scale, and the younger people were getting nothing. There was often fantastic discussion at the meetings. Any time there was a national debate, we certainly had people on opposite sides of the fence in Kerry. People would stick to their guns – we even had tied votes. The Kerry branch was absolutely very vibrant ...[26]

After a few years, there was an occasion which led to deeper involvement:

> In 1980, when Convention was held in Tralee, I got involved in the organisational side of things, helping out with stands and with registration. There was a friend of mine in Dublin, who was very involved before that, and she said, 'That'll be you rounded into ASTI forever'. And it was. She was right ...[27]

Responding to change (i)
If in Clare the need to integrate a rapidly expanding membership

posed questions about the relevance of the agenda and about the desirability of splitting the branch, it is not surprising that growth prompted somewhat similar discussions at national level. And rapidly increasing numbers was not the only novelty, for the membership was also changing in other ways. The average age of ASTI members was lower than before and, arguably, the mentality was also different – affected by the cultural shift of the era, by the militant engagement of 1969–71, and by a new diversity in an Association which, as shall be seen, was beginning to represent men and women who worked outside of traditional secondary schools as well as individuals in positions of authority.

However, agreement on the most appropriate response to changed circumstances was not always easily reached. The Kerry branch was deputed to formulate proposals for restructuring the Association in 1971, and it set about the task with vigour in co-operation with the new organiser. Its 'plan' which, among other measures, proposed the establishment of six regional councils, the abolition of standing committee, and the reduction of CEC membership to fifteen, won majority support at the 1972 convention, but it did not secure the votes of the two-thirds of delegates necessary for implementation. Reform proposals met with a similar fate at a 1973 special convention. After an interval, the issue was addressed again in 1977 by a CEC subcommittee, which produced proposals not very different to those set aside a few years earlier, proposing nineteen regional councils and a twenty-five-member CEC. In the intervening years, the CEC had grown in proportion with membership to a point where it rivalled Dáil Éireann in size, but sufficient support could not be marshalled to bring about what many regarded as necessary and rational restructuring in a series of votes in 1979, 1980 and 1981.[28]

Similarly intractable was another contemporaneous issue that took up a considerable amount of the Association's time and energy. The contract negotiations with the managerial bodies were not strictly internal matters, but the frustrating lack of progress in this regard shows that the difficulty in introducing necessary changes during this period was part of a wider problem. Efforts were made over several years to replace the 1957 contract with a document reflecting the new relationships in education – one that would provide for appeals procedures for probationary teachers and recognise the reality of the twenty-two-hour week, among other issues. It did not

ISSN 0790-6633

70p

Volume 18

Number 3

1989

The SECONDARY TEACHER

Is Co-Education the answer?

Published by the Association of ondary Teachers Ireland

ASTI

See article by William Gardiner and submission from A.S.T.I. Equality Committee

A cover of The Secondary Teacher *from 1989. The Secondary Teacher was published by ASTI from 1966 and dealt with the key education topics of the day. This issue asks, 'Is Co-Education the answer?'*

Handing over the reins: Kieran Mulvey and Máire MacDonagh pictured at Máire MacDonagh's retirement celebration in 1983. Maire MacDonagh was ASTI general secretary from 1958 to 1983. Upon her retirement, Kieran Mulvey took over the position and served until 1991.

The female presidents who held office during Máire MacDonagh's time as general secretary, pictured with Máire MacDonagh in 1983. Left to right: Mary MacCarthy, Máire MacDonagh, Margaret Walsh, and Nora Kelleher.

ASTI treasurer, Michael Ward (third from left) pictured in 1983 with five of his predecessors. Left to right: Noel Keane, Dan Buckley, Michael Ward, Bill Kirkpatrick, Dónal Ó Conalláin and George Lyons.

Past presidents of the ASTI pictured with Máire MacDonagh, former general secretary, on her retirement in 1983. Back row (left to right): P. Purcell, T. Bromell. Standing: H. Duffy, D. Buckley, G. Lyons, M. MacCormack, K. Meehan, G. Ó Maoilmhichíl, L. Hogan, A. Sheehy. Seated: P. Finnegan, W. Kirkpatrick, M. MacCarthy, M. Walsh, M. MacDonagh, J. Wilson, N. Kelleher, D. Ó Conalláin.

A group of former ASTI presidents with Minister for Education Gemma Hussey and President of Ireland Patrick Hillery, (front row, third and fifth left, respectively) pictured at the launch of The ASTI and Post-Primary Education in Ireland: 1909–1984 *by John Coolahan in 1984.*

A high point of teachers' trade unionism in Ireland was Thursday, 5 December 1985, the day that an unprecedented number of teachers came together in one place for a common purpose. The cause of the mobilisation was the government's decision to withhold an arbitrated pay award of 10 per cent, on the grounds that public finances could not bear the cost. (Photo by Derek Spiers)

Louis O'Flaherty, ASTI president, welcomes a 20,000 strong crowd of teachers to Croke Park on 5 December 1985. The mass rally made its way from Croke Park to Government Buildings. 'In the interval between O'Flaherty's welcome and the march from Croke Park to Dáil Éireann which concluded proceedings, the freezing protestors were treated to more than a dozen speeches, from home-grown trade union leaders as well as from representatives of international teachers' organisations, and to a rousing musical performance. (Photo by Derek Spiers)

An ASTI member holds a placard depicting Gemma Hussey, then minister for education, during the 1985 Teachers United rally at Croke Park. (Photo by Derek Spiers)

Crowds gather outside the Dáil during the 1995 ASTI demonstration. (Photo by Tony Parkes)

Delegates pictured at Convention 1994, held in Cork.

Former ASTI presidents John Wilson and Mary MacCarthy pictured during celebrations for ASTI's ninetieth anniversary. Mary MacCarthy was president from 1979–1980. John Wilson served as president following the death of C.L. Dillon in 1959. Mr Wilson also held the position of minister for education between 1977 and 1981 and was tánaiste 1992–1993. (Photo by Tommy Clancy)

Bernadine O'Sullivan, ASTI president 1999–2000, Micheál Martin, minister for education and Charlie Lennon, general secretary, pictured at the signing of the revised Conciliation and Arbitration Scheme in 2000. The scheme set out procedures for dealing with claims relating to salary and conditions of service of teachers. (Photo by Tommy Clancy)

On 5 December 2000, the fifteenth anniversary of the great Teachers United rally, 12,000 ASTI members attended a pay protest outside Leinster House in Dublin. The protest was held as part of a pay campaign pursued in the belief that ASTI members had specific grounds for a pay increase beyond that provided for in national agreements. When the government ignored the thrust of this ASTI argument, and imposed the Partnership for Prosperity agreement, ASTI members voted in favour of industrial action, which included two one-day strikes on 14 November and 5 December and a ban on the supervision of students outside of class.

prove possible, however, to come to an agreement on a document acceptable to ASTI members, with the result that 'custom and practice' increasingly provided the framework in regard to contractual matters.[29]

Within the ASTI itself, some reorganisation eventually did take place when the proposals of a Branch Rationalisation Committee, which was also established in 1977, won acceptance. Branches in areas of growth like Dublin and Cork were divided, and a number of small branches were merged.[30]

At the same time, there was long-overdue support for activists in the form of a *School Stewards' Handbook* which became available for the first time in 1977. It was further recognised by that point that training for stewards was necessary, but its introduction was delayed by the department's unwillingness to release teachers. Eventually, an agreement with the department and with the JMB allowed courses to proceed, 'provided classes were not left unattended'. The first series of courses, held in nine centres throughout the country between October 1981 and March 1982, was fully subscribed. Developed in association with ICTU, partly funded by the European Social Fund, and designed to run from Thursday at 5.30 p.m. and all day Friday, the course addressed the following topics: 'Introduction to the union and how it works', 'The functions of the school steward', 'Grievance handling procedures', and 'Policy formation'. Éamon Ó hAllmhuráin, national organiser and later president, was one of the ASTI volunteers who delivered the courses. He recalls having to photocopy the course materials, and having to get his own children to assist him in collating them.[31]

Following the success of the first round of courses, a training committee was established in 1983 which oversaw the organisation of courses for branch officers as well as for members and prospective members of national committees.[32]

Communication with members was another challenge – a recurring one throughout the ASTI's history, indeed. The *Irish Journal of Education* had ceased in 1917, and there would be no comparable publication for almost fifty years. However, the Association was not without a voice for most of that time. First, there were 'ASTI notes' in the INTO's *Irish School Weekly* in the 1920s and 1930s; then, between 1939 and 1965, there was an annual publication which settled on the title *The School & College Yearbook*. The replacement in 1966 was the monthly *Secondary Teacher* in tandem with an annual *Bliainiris*, edited by future president Tom O'Dea, with future minister for education Dick Burke acting as business manager. Seán Ó Riain took over as publications editor in 1969, and under his stewardship the frequency of the *Secondary Teacher* was reduced, and a new title, *ASTIR*, appeared on a pilot basis in December 1970. Ó Riain's reports to convention suggest that he was an energetic editor, ambitious for his publications. Reporting in 1971, that it was 'comparatively easy to get articles and advertisements', he advised that several contributions to the *Secondary Teacher* had prompted wider discussions in the press. However, some frustration was apparent in the following comment of 1973:

> The *Secondary Teacher* has been highly praised by publishers, journalists, and by educationalists and teachers outside the second-level schools. We have received no critical comment – good or bad – from members of the ASTI ... I believe that given proper support the *Secondary Teacher* and an enlarged *ASTIR* could become the leading educational journals in the country ... The publication I envisage would be on public sale and would be actively promoted. The publication would be of benefit to teachers, managers and parents.[33]

But if there was frustration in the comment, there was also a sense of confidence about the ASTI's place in the scheme of things. Ó Riain clearly believed that he and his colleagues were full partners in education, and their perspective gave them insights that were useful to one another, but also to others involved in the system.

It may be that this confidence reflected the 'collective psychological benefit' of the recent militant engagement as suggested earlier, but there were other developments that were serving to draw secondary teachers in from the margins. The introduction of posts of responsibility had been a cause of great contention, but it undoubtedly affected the way that lay secondary teachers viewed themselves. The most senior posts remained off limits, generally, but the prospect of promotion and the associated responsibilities made it difficult for teachers to any more regard themselves, or to be regarded indeed, as mere 'hired hands' in their schools. And if impressionistic evidence had not convinced lay teachers that their hour was at hand, the religious employers would go a long way towards con-firming that this was indeed the case.

The revelation came in a report commissioned by the Episcopal Commission on Post-Primary Education and the Catholic Major Religious Superiors, entitled *Future Involvement of Religious in Edu-cation* (*FIRE*). It was an acronym that, intentionally or not, reflected the sense of alarm that prompted the investigation in the first place. *FIRE* was circulated privately in February 1973, but its contents were leaked and most of the report appeared in the *Education Times* a few months later. Showing that the percentage of lay teachers in sec-ondary schools had grown from 43 per cent to 66 per cent in a decade, the authors projected that they would form 72 per cent of the total by the mid-1970s. In the opinion of one theologian, *FIRE* was 'a depressing report' for the commissioning bodies, in that it un-derlined 'the lack of planning and the lack of foresight in the past, as well as painting a gloomy picture for the future'. Throughout its pages, however, he found 'a heavy underscoring of the seriousness of the situation, and of the urgent need for action'.[34] *FIRE* was signifi-cant in that it recognised that the role of the religious in education would have to change, circumstances having made it necessary to 'share management of religious schools with lay people', something which, moreover, was considered to be 'fitting ... particularly in the light of Vatican II'.[35]

The ASTI: a school management view

In an appendix to *FIRE*, entitled 'Relations between schools and lay staff', there were assessments of the ASTI's historical role and of its disposition in 1973.[36] In that the perspective is that of the religious managers, and that the deliberations that produced them took place at an important moment in Irish educational history, these assess-ments clearly merit close examination.

The ASTI emerged in circumstances of 'great insecurity of job tenure, relatively low salaries, negligible career opportunities, and a situation where satisfying work was generally given to religious rather than lay teachers'. These conditions notwithstanding, *FIRE* ac-knowledges that the Association did not 'adopt a militant attitude' with the result that it was largely ineffective until the 1960s. Their acquiescence, however, the report advises managers, should not be taken as indicating that the 'older generation teachers' had been satisfied with their lot.

Two reasons were identified for the hardening of the ASTI approach in the 1960s: 'First, the opportunity created by an excess of job opportunities over the number of teachers by the so-called "free education scheme"; and secondly, the example of the success of other teachers' unions, and other white collar workers'. The report proceeded with an analysis of the Association which located it within a model of trade union development:

> The past ineffectiveness of the ASTI should not be assumed as continuing into the future. This union reflects five main characteristics which are to be found in most trade unions in the history of their growth. These characteristics are, first, a long period in which the majority of the members are passive towards the problem put before them by the trade union and slow to respond to any form of militant action. Second, an emergence of a younger age group in control of a number of branches within a trade union, and their success in winning over certain branches to their ideas. Thirdly, a crisis situation develops in which the trade union, despite its loose organisation and apparently diffuse autonomous branches unites to the extent of taking a concerted strike action, as in the first quarter of the century, Fourthly, from the apparent or real success of the strike action there emerges a more vocal and powerful group within the union which is able to reorganise the trade union usually around a smaller executive, so that decisions become more clear-cut, and apparently more unified than before. And fifthly, a sharp difference of opinion between the younger more progressive and more publicity-oriented members of the branches and the older, perhaps more work-oriented majority of the members.[37]

Many concessions had been secured by teachers in the recent past, in respect of pay, of working conditions, and of training courses. This did not mean, the *FIRE* authors warned, that the relationship between the ASTI and employers would improve, because it was 'the essence of trade unionism' that 'every achievement is used as a base for making further claims'. Nor should school managers take comfort from the uneasiness felt by many lay teachers with regard to trade union militancy. There was a 'conflict of loyalty' certainly, but it would be wrong to interpret this as indicating willing-ness to 'go against the trade union policies'. Moreover, the perception among headmasters and headmistresses that lay teachers had been far more loyal to their schools in the past than they were in 1973 was not a fully accurate one either: 'Their former loyalty was prob-ably in fact more superficial than appeared and those in authority over them rarely, if ever, heard the real views, the real convictions, the problems, difficulties and frustrations of the teachers in their schools.' Furthermore, the halcyon days when tranquil obedience reigned in schools were not likely to reappear: 'In the absence of pe-riodic slumps ... no effective deterrent to the trade union's constant pressure for more concessions in the secondary schools can reason-ably be expected.'[38]

Sharing management?

FIRE pronounced that it was 'fitting ... to share management of re-ligious schools with lay people', but how willing in practice were the religious to share authority? How keen, for their part, were second-ary teachers to assume authority? And who were the 'lay people' that the religious authorities envisaged bringing on board? In his study of the administration of post-primary education, Louis O'Flaherty pointed out that the religious did not necessarily mean the lay teach-ers in their schools. And the *FIRE* appendix establishes that they cer-tainly did not mean the union representatives of their lay teachers. Warning that 'trade unions will seek representation on boards of management' when such were established, *FIRE* urged that board members should be selected in their personal capacities, and 'not as representatives of this or that body'.[39]

The question of the composition of boards of management of secondary schools was one that assumed importance a few years after *FIRE*, but in the meantime there were several issues that served to test the attitude of the Catholic religious to the prospect of sharing of responsibility with lay teachers and others. Negotiations surround-ing the introduction of posts of responsibility into secondary schools underlined the differing priorities of the ASTI and the religious man-agers in the matter, while in the long-running controversy on man-agement structures for the comprehensive and community sector both groups sought to maximise their own influence.

Posts of responsibility had been topical since 1966 when the

ASTI had formulated a detailed policy on the matter, but they were put into abeyance by the short-lived agreement on special functions allowances of 1969. The posts were central to the conflict between the ASTI and the department during the next two years, but the settlement of February–March 1971 moved the issue back into the sphere of ASTI/JMB responsibility, and as early as March 1971 it was discussed at a meeting between the two representative bodies. The ASTI position was refined at its 1971 convention, where a new policy was adopted which included three elements that would prove contentious: that there should be no expectation that post-holders (other than principals) would work outside normal school hours; that in those schools where the principalship was held by the managing religious body, all other posts, including vice-principal, should be allocated to lay teachers; that in making the allocation, the manager should be advised by a committee elected by the staff. As might be expected, given the stance articulated subsequently in *FIRE*, these points were not acceptable to the employers. However, further meetings with the JMB and the department took place during the summer of 1971 which resulted in an agreement, papering over the outstanding differences. At this point, it was envisaged that appointments might be made, with effect from before the end of the 1970–71 academic year, but the issue remained a highly charged one during most of 1971–72. During a period of tense negotiations, punctuated by two ASTI special conventions, the ASTI threatened the withdrawal by its members of 'all forms of voluntary co-operation in the running of schools', and the JMB tetchily reminded the Association that it represented only a minority of secondary teachers (which was still true). The ASTI acted on its threat of withdrawal of cooperation on 1 March 1972.[40]

Acting to save the scheme, the department intervened to broker an agreement, enabling the ASTI to remove its co-operation ban within weeks. The new agreement, which was accepted by 62 per cent of ASTI members in a ballot of late March, included the following terms: in schools where the principalship was held by a member of the controlling religious community, that the vice-principal and a 'substantial majority' of other post-holders would 'normally' be lay teachers; a 'posts' appeals board with equal representation of the ASTI and the JMB would be established; there would be no requirement that post-holders work outside ordinary school hours.

That feelings remained strong about the issue, however, was shown by the adoption at the following convention of an unenforceable policy that only lay teachers who were ASTI members should be eligible for posts.[41]

The acceptance of the agreement on posts of responsibility in April 1972 was significant, but, before that resolution was reached, another contentious matter presented itself when the Department of Education circulated a document on community schools late in 1970.

Community schools were a new concept, and their introduction would have implications for the key power relationships in post-primary education: those between the state and the religious authorities, between the religious authorities and the secondary teachers, and between the secondary teachers and the state. As the debate developed, moreover, the place of parents would assume greater importance. The issues have been examined, in a scholarly context, by two former ASTI presidents, Louis O'Flaherty and David Barry, and their published works will inform the discussion that follows.[42]

A shake-up of the established order in post-primary education, it has been shown earlier, was signalled on several occasions in the years prior to 1970: by Patrick Hillery's 1963 announcements of comprehensive schools and of a softening of the boundaries between secondary and vocational schools; by the resource-conscious minister George Colley when he pressed for closer co-operation between secondary and vocational sectors; by the important article in *Studies* in 1968 by senior Department of Education official Seán O'Connor. Both management and teachers in secondary schools were apprehensive about the direction of developments, alarmed even by the increasing use of the term 'post-primary', seen as threatening the 'top dog' status of secondary schools.[43]

As it transpired, the ASTI's concerns about comprehensive schools eased, because they were few in number and because few ASTI members worked in them. All the previously felt apprehension was reawakened, however, by the department's unexpected policy announcement in respect of a new category of community schools, to be formed either by the amalgamation of existing vocational and secondary schools or as an alternative to new schools. The policy itself had been signalled earlier in Seán O'Connor's article, and its implementation had been facilitated by the Vocational Edu-

cation (Amendment) Act of 1970 but, nevertheless, the announcement of community schools surprised most of those involved in education.[44]

The ASTI's relationship with the department being very poor
in late 1970, it was not very surprising that its initial reaction was defensive. Why was there no consultation in the formulation of such
far-reaching policy, asked an ASTI statement. The Catholic authorities, already involved in negotiations on comprehensive schools, had
their own concerns and they were quick to raise them. Over the following months, as information about the department's intentions
seeped out, it was clear that these were changing in response to lobbying. The Catholic intervention was having an effect. One contemporary observer summed up the process as follows: 'An apparent
attempt by the government to take over Catholic-owned secondary
schools had ended up as an actual takeover of the vocational schools
by the Catholic hierarchy.'[45] The writer was referring mainly to the
model for community schools' trusteeship announced by Minister
Faulkner in mid-May 1971, which would empower the Catholic
bishop of the diocese where the school was located to nominate all
three trustees: one of them from a list provided by the relevant Vocational Education Committee (VEC). This model arose from a pre-
sumption that most community schools would be established
through the merger of a vocational school and two secondary
schools, one male and one female.

In addition to the trusteeships, the proposed management structures of the community schools were also of great interest, and these too
evolved in the six months following the original announcement, in response to lobbying by the Catholic authorities.[46] For the ASTI, the CEC
established a sub-committee to examine the department's 'working document', but its work was overshadowed by preparations for strike (and
for avoidance of strike), so the examination took some time.

The following motion from the Dún Laoghaire branch was
passed at the 1971 convention: 'ASTI demands representation on
the management boards of the proposed community schools should
they be established, in accordance with the social teaching of Pope
John and the stated policy of the ICTU.'[47] It may be regarded as significant that those who composed the motion deemed it necessary
to locate their essentially secularist objective within Catholic social
teaching.

Convention also reappointed the sub-committee and its report, completed a few months later, was interesting for the insight it seemed to give into ASTI thinking at a time when much attention was being paid to reconfiguring Irish post-primary education:

> We would reject control of secondary education by local authorities. We are employed by individual school managers, and wish to retain this characteristic of our employment ... We believe the term 'community school' should be abandoned in the entire educational discussion at present ... Existing secondary schools have well served their communities in the past – and continue to serve them.[48]

Rather than the replacement of some secondary schools, the sub-committee recommended their expansion, also expressing concern about the size of schools, in particular about the proposal in the department's community schools 'working document' that the optimum number of pupils in a school should be in the 400 to 800 range. Insisting that smaller schools of 200 to 400 were preferable 'both from a teaching and a sociological point of view', the sub-committee argued that from 'a community point of view' schools smaller than the minimum in rural areas should be allowed to survive. There were strong commitments to denominational education and also to the Irish language, which was essential, it was contended, for the protection of 'our collective identity in that which makes us what we are – Irish'. As well as this genuine concern about identity, there were worries about autonomy in educational matters, possibly prompted by apprehension about the consequences of joining the European Community. Should 'any international bank or agency' such as the World Bank provide funding for education, the report insisted that 'this must not mean that our Department of Education concedes to such agency the right to decide the structure of Irish education, to dictate the size of our secondary schools, or to impose on our existing schools an alien educational philosophy'.[49]

The ASTI's initial response to the community schools concept was quite negative, therefore, but there is evidence that it may not have been a considered response. Other issues had occupied the attention of leading members and leading bodies in 1970–71, and one might ask if the reactionary tone of the report of the sub-committee on community schools reflected the attitude of the membership. Moreover, if it was accepted by the 1972 convention, so was a resolution from Dún Laoghaire which struck a very different note:

While ASTI welcomes in principle the genuine community schools concept for social and educational reasons [author's emphasis], it rejects the arrangements envisaged for the control and management of the proposed community schools at Tallaght and Blanchardstown.[50]

The contradictory policies adopted at the 1972 convention indicated that ASTI members had differing attitudes to community schools, and that there was a middle-ground prepared to politely accept both a report representing the outlook of a traditionally-minded faction and a resolution from a progressive branch (suggesting, perhaps, that the *FIRE* analysis discussed above was not that far wide of the mark). As events unfolded, it seemed that the sentiment in the resolution more accurately signalled the ASTI approach to the community schools issue, until deeds of trust on behalf of most of the community schools were eventually signed in April 1981. The spheres of 'control and management' remained the contentious ones in respect of the community schools issue generally. And if the Catholic authorities intervened very effectively at the initial stages of the process, other viewpoints soon demanded attention – trade union, secular/liberal, minority religious, and VEC.[51]

Pádraic Faulkner, the minister for education who had overseen the development of the community schools policy, left office with the defeat of Fianna Fáil in the 1973 general election. A different approach to community schools was expected from the 'national coalition' government composed of Fine Gael – which had argued, echoing the ASTI, for parent and teacher representation on boards of management – and Labour, the most secular of the major parties. The new minister for education was Dick Burke, a prominent ASTI activist until his election as Fine Gael TD for Dublin South County in 1969. He was to be a conservative minister, who had a 'personal commitment to private denominational education' according to Louis O'Flaherty.[52] With regard to community schools, his views were out of line with the pre-election platform of his own party. Nonetheless the draft deeds of trust for community schools, published in May 1974, showed some traces of the debates of the previous three years, during which criticism of the proposals of 1970–71 had been expressed by Protestant and vocational education bodies, and the community school model had been rejected by several bona fide communities.[53]

Under the terms of the draft deeds of 1974, boards of management would consist of six members, four nominees of secondary school authorities (including two parents) and two VEC representatives, with the school principal as a non-voting member. Not only was there to be no teacher representation, but such was specifically excluded by the following clause: 'No person employed for the purposes of the school shall be a member of the board.' Both the ASTI and the TUI would work hard for the removal of this clause, but there were also two other matters of great concern that arose from the deeds of trust document. These were the 'reserved places clause' and the 'faith and morals clauses'.[54]

'Reserved places' referred to teaching posts in new schools, to which religious managers might nominate qualified members without their facing normal selection procedures – possibly leading to redundancy for Association members in no-longer-needed secondary schools. Of the 'faith and moral clauses', the most alarming from the ASTI perspective because it was potentially so intrusive, was the following: 'No teacher shall at any time do or say anything which may offend or weaken the religious belief or the moral training or practice of pupils in the school.' Much discussion was sparked by the publication of the draft deeds, but little progress was made regarding their implementation during the three remaining years of the 1973–77 coalition, either by Dick Burke or by his short-serving successor Peter Barry.[55]

The new Fianna Fáil minister for education in 1977 was another ASTI stalwart, John Wilson. Regarded by teachers' representatives as a conciliator, Wilson was a former Cavan football star and a lecturer in classics at St Patrick's, Drumcondra. He had taught at St Eunan's College Letterkenny and Gonzaga College, and, in 1959, when ASTI president C.L. Dillon died in office he was the serving vice-president, so he assumed the presidency for the remainder of the jubilee year. Pressed by his former Association, as well as by the TUI and others, Wilson announced in April 1978 that he was initiating fresh discussions on the management of community schools.

He had already indicated that he favoured teacher representation.[56]

By this point, ASTI policy was being strongly influenced by its own members in community schools. From nineteen by 1976, the number of these schools rose gradually, reaching forty-one in 1982 (when there were fifteen comprehensive schools). It was in response to pressure from teachers in these new schools that an ASTI Advisory Committee on Community and Comprehensive Schools was established in May 1978, its members elected at an Athlone meeting of teachers from the sector. Paddy Carolan of Ardee Community School was the first chairman of this body, and Colette Shaw of Tallaght Community School the first secretary. They and other committee members, including David Barry who was elected ASTI president in 1980, were part of subsequent negotiating teams on this issue, beginning with a meeting with Minister Wilson in May 1978.[57]

Other key encounters in 1978 were those with the TUI which resulted in a broadly similar approach being pursued by the two unions, and with the Conference of Major Religious Superiors (CMRS) representing religious authorities, who finally accepted the principle of teacher representation on boards of management, though not of union representation. (Separate discussions on the question of boards of management for secondary schools are treated later in this chapter.) The importance of the deeds of trust issue was underlined by the special convention on community and comprehensive schools in April 1979, called by members in those schools who thought it necessary to firmly define 'ASTI policy on several issues before we can begin to make any progress at meetings with the Minister for Education, the CMRS and the TUI'.[58] Progress thereafter was swift, and in July 1979, a revised draft deed was circulated by the department which took account of the outcome of discussions during the previous year. For ASTI members, the important differences with the 1974 document were the considerable dilution of the 'moral clauses' and the acceptance of teacher representation. Ten-member boards would now consist of three representatives of religious, three of the VEC, two of parents, and two of teachers. It was not stated in the draft deeds, but Minister Wilson assured the ASTI and the TUI that the teacher representatives, in practice, would be union representatives. This proved to be the case, leaving the two unions to work out the system whereby one representative would be allocated to the smaller of the two unions in schools where it had a minimum of 25 per cent membership among the teachers. The 're-served places' clause was perceived to be far less threatening in 1979 than it had been earlier in the decade due to falling numbers of religious in education, so the unions were able to withdraw their objections to its retention.[59]

The revised trust deeds of 1979, which would be accepted by all parties, were an advance for the ASTI and for secondary teachers: at the beginning of the 1970s, posts of responsibility remained to be negotiated; by their end, secondary teachers were making their way onto school boards. In the interim the ASTI had been centrally involved in discussions on educational policy, an arena from which it had been previously excluded, and it was accepted, both by department and religious managers, that the ASTI's consent was required if deeds of trust were to have legitimacy. This was due principally to the ASTI's increasing membership, numerical and proportionate, but the tenacity of its representatives was also an important factor. It was significant too that the ASTI was able to present a policy on this issue that was compatible with that of the TUI – disagreement between the teachers' unions would have greatly weakened the case, as it had in the 1969–71 period.

Responding to change (ii)
Two events commemorating important ASTI milestones took place in the first half of the 1980s. The first, held on 11 March 1983, was a banquet for Máire MacDonagh, who had steered the Association through twenty-five challenging years. Marking her silver jubilee, and her imminent retirement as general secretary, were representatives of government, of teachers' unions in Ireland and elsewhere, and of ASTI branches throughout the country. The second event was the launch in the Mansion House of the first published book-length history of the Association on its seventy-fifth anniversary. Among those attending were Uachtarán na hÉireann, Dr Patrick Hillery, and recent minister for education, John Wilson, who had both been prominent at the golden jubilee celebration when one was minister for education and the other ASTI president. Wilson's successor, Gemma Hussey, attended, as did Mary O'Rourke, Fianna Fáil education spokesperson, and Michael O'Halloran, lord mayor of Dublin.[60] ASTI president Henry Collins paid tribute to the author of *The ASTI and Post-Primary Education in Ireland, 1909–1984*, the

educationist and educational historian Dr John Coolahan, before reflecting on the Association's history:

> The ASTI has a long and distinguished tradition in its contribution to the educational, social, cultural, and political development of Irish education. We are proud to have counted among our members two of the 1916 leaders, a Taoiseach and President of Ireland, a European commissioner, five Ministers for Education, and at least three secretaries of the Department of Education ...[61]

Responding, Coolahan compared ASTI's former and current relationships:

> In the early years, ASTI and the INTO were very close. In the 1930s, it seemed as if a federation of the teaching associations might take place. Later on, in the 1970s, it seemed as if ASTI and its sister union, the TUI, might federate. Eventually in 1981, a Council of Educational Unions was established which has great potential in the years ahead to improve conditions for teachers.[62]

There will be an opportunity, later on, to address Coolahan's theme of teacher unity, a major aspiration of the mid-1980s. Of his book, it may be said that it became an indispensable resource for those writing on Irish post-primary education. Reviewing it, Professor John A. Murphy wrote:

> We have here not only the history of an organisation but the chronicle of the chequered fortunes of a profession, and the book goes a long way towards justifying the blurb's claim that it is also 'a history of post-primary education from the perspective of the secondary teacher ...'[63]

The ASTI's regular publications, meanwhile, continued to inform members about negotiations, entitlements, policy, and developments generally. Both the *Secondary Teacher* and *ASTIR* were adaptable, changing format occasionally and publishing special issues on themes of particular interest. After Seán Ó Riain relinquished his editorships in 1978, Seán Beausang of the Cork branch took re-

sponsibility for the *Secondary Teacher* on a temporary basis, before
passing the task to the new full-time education officer. Her term,
however, was short and there was an interval during which the periodical did not appear. Accordingly, when the new editor, Michael
McCann of the Galway branch, took over as editor in 1982 he could
write that the *Secondary Teacher*, 'like the phoenix', had 'arisen from
the ashes'.[64] Galway also provided editors for *ASTIR*, with Paddy
Boyle succeeding Seán Ó Riain in 1978 and, more than ten years
and ninety-three issues later, passing the baton to Bernie O'Connell.
Through the recession of the 1980s, advertising revenue kept the
publication in profit, while the adoption of new technology – in the
form of computerised labels – improved distribution to members.[65]

In general, the 1980s was a grim decade, during which high unemployment, emigration and public indebtedness, as well as the continuing conflict in the North, combined to create an atmosphere of
near crisis. Teachers were presented with the consequences, and both
ASTI publications and convention proceedings reveal that members
were concerned about their students' prospects, and that some of
them at least had given thought to how the rising generation might
be better equipped to face the challenges that lay ahead. The same
proceedings show teachers grappling with new issues – drugs awareness, sex education, computers in schools, remedial education, guidance and counselling policies, among others.[66] The profession suffered
from the fiscal stringency imposed by the government in response to
the crisis – the total number of teachers increased only marginally,
young teachers were unable to find full-time positions, while cutbacks
had an impact both on school resources and on the salaries of those
with positions. It was a reaction to cutbacks, indeed, that sparked the
major movement of teachers during the decade, a movement involv-
ing all the teachers' unions that will be discussed in the next chapter.

Constrained by the level of entry into teaching, the ASTI grew
only modestly during the 1980s – from 9,495 in December 1980,
membership reached 11,259 in December 1988, an increase of 18
per cent, compared with 228 per cent in the eight years before that.[67]
But the Association did not stagnate, for there was a great improvement in its capacity and in its professionalism during the 1980s. In
this respect, the ASTI was not unique, for with ICTU encouragement, there were similar developments in Irish trade unions generally at around the same time.[68]

That change was necessary was indicated by a large-scale survey, conducted by a prominent ASTI activist, of Galway teachers in 1979–80, which showed that there was great dissatisfaction with the Association among its membership (compared with the TUI). While male and female members were about equally dissatisfied, their explanations for their dissatisfaction were somewhat different in tone. A comment, typical of the disgruntled males, read, 'Reflects the average teacher, does not lead, reacts to situation and has no guts', while the female members surveyed felt that the Association was too preoccupied with teachers' salaries, and was neglectful of educational issues and of working conditions.[69]

In the light of these sentiments, it may not have been a coincidence that it was the Galway branch that tabled a successful resolution at the 1979 convention calling for the establishment of a sub-committee, which would have access to 'expert opinion if necessary', to investigate the staffing and equipment needs of head office. Up to that point, there had been a tendency 'to add another person to the head office staff whenever the work got beyond the existing staff', according to an interim report from the sub-committee (which was composed of members of the proposing Galway branch). 'That kind of growth,' it insisted, 'will serve no longer.'[70] The sub-committee made recommendations on the need for computerisation, for larger premises and for new functionaries. It was especially important, it was suggested, that the Association should have a full-time education officer:

> If ASTI is to promote the interests of secondary teachers it must give due attention to the educational and professional side of secondary teaching. Unlike the primary level, teaching at secondary level is characterised by the diversity of education and professional training of the teachers ... ASTI should be equipped to speak out of real knowledge of ... trends in other countries. ASTI should be researching, developing, and propagating educational policies re teacher training ... to ensure that secondary teachers get the best possible preparation for their work. In parallel, ASTI should be researching, developing and propagating policies re second level students – the needs of pupils, the needs of society, the suitability of courses and their contents ...[71]

The discussion demonstrated an appreciation of the opportunities that existed for teachers to play a more assertive role in Irish education than they had in the past. This was an impulse that was as old as the Association itself, for it had striven to serve the professional interests of its members from its foundation, as indicated by the content of its publications, by the work of its education sub-committee established in 1925 and of the various subject committees, and by the attention devoted at branch meetings to curricula and examinations. Through the years, representations were entertained by the department on matters like examinations and textbooks, but it could not be said that the ASTI was consulted to any great extent with regard to Irish education policy between 1925 and the end of the 1960s. The establishment of an Education Committee in April 1970, on foot of a convention decision, marked the beginning of a more determined effort in this respect, and this committee would oversee the work of a growing number of specialist sub-committees as the decade advanced. With its greater capacity to assert itself, the ASTI won greater influence in educational affairs, but it was restricted by limited resources, its officials, full-time and voluntary, having many other commitments. A specialist education officer would add weight to the Association's efforts with respect to policy. The case was accepted, and Rhoda O'Connor was appointed as ASTI's first ever full-time education/research officer in 1981.[72]

The appointment of an education/research officer came in a context where there were increasing opportunities for ASTI to make its mark educationally. In this regard, the recommendation in the *White Paper on Educational Development* (1980) that a curriculum council be established was welcomed, but progress was slow during these years of political instability. When eventually, in January 1984, Minister Hussey made her announcement on the composition of an interim Curriculum and Examination Board (CEB), there was both disappointment and annoyance in the ASTI that it was to have only one representative on the nineteen-member body. This was reflected in the adoption at standing committee of a policy of non-co-operation with the interim board. ICTU was able to break the impasse, however, by offering to nominate an additional ASTI member as its own representative. The work of the CEB was continued by the National Council for Curriculum and Assessment (NCCA) established by Hussey's successor, Mary O'Rourke in 1987, on which the ASTI has also been represented. In light of his subsequent experience as a member of the NCCA, John White came to believe that there was an over-emphasis in the mid-1980s on the level of the ASTI representation on the CEB. Votes are seldom taken in such bodies and therefore, he argues, the effectiveness of trade unionists is determined more by the ideas and arguments they bring to the table than by their numerical presence.[73]

Responding to change (iii)

These were years that also witnessed developments in the relationship between the Association and the religious employers. In the words of one writer, discussions about three issues were 'beginning to mesh' in the late 1970s: redeployment, boards of management in secondary schools, and parent–teacher meetings.[74] Disagreement about parent–teacher meetings dated from the early 1970s, when convention resolutions had insisted that teachers should be paid for attending. Asserting that schools could not afford the expense, the JMB sought funding for the purpose from the department. This was not forthcoming, with the result that parent–teacher meetings did not take place in most secondary schools. The necessity for an agreement on redeployment arose from continuing school amalgamations and school closures. The ASTI members affected had successfully found employment in other schools, but fears that ongoing rationalisation might result in redundancies were heightened by a unilateral announcement by the Sisters of Mercy that their school in Borrisoleigh, County Tipperary, would close in 1978. ASTI's demand was for redeployment of teachers to a nearby school in such cases – as happened with primary teachers – and internal discussions on the issue culminated in a special convention in May 1978, where it was decided that industrial action would be taken to defend members' interests in the case of any unilateral closures. In respect of the third issue in the 'mesh', boards of management for voluntary secondary schools, discussions had begun during the long-running community schools controversy treated above. *FIRE* had raised the issue in 1973 and two years later, at an ASTI convention, Dick Burke urged the religious to establish boards in their schools. Insisting that he was not advocating interference in the conduct of secondary schools, the minister urged that the school authorities 'reach out for help and encouragement' from parents and teachers. For some ASTI members, any change in the management structures of secondary schools which might change their fundamental character was undesirable; for others, who saw that change was inevitable, the objective was to ensure that teachers had substantial representation in the new structures.

Concerned about declining numbers of religious, the CMRS published its model for boards in 1976. However, it proved to be unacceptable to ASTI delegates who debated the issue at special conventions in 1976 and 1977, voting at the second to take strike action in the event of any boards of management being formed without agreement, and forcing the disbandment of a board that was established at St Paul's of Greenhills in Dublin.[75]

The 'meshing' of these three issues came about in negotiations during 1981–82, when the CMRS undertook to support ASTI's position on redeployment/redundancy at conciliation if the Association accepted parent–teacher meetings and a modified model for boards of management, providing for two representatives of teachers, two representatives of parents and four nominees of the trustees including the chairperson. Agreement on an interim redeployment scheme came in April 1985, and in ballots later in the same year, ASTI members finally accepted boards of management and parent–teacher meetings during school hours. Discussions on a permanent redeployment scheme for Catholic-managed schools were not concluded until 1988, when teachers were guaranteed employment within their panel area, of which there were eleven in the state. As a result of hardship in individual cases, an amendment of 1990 guaranteed that no teacher would be redeployed to a school more than thirty miles from his/her original place of employment.[76]

The agreement on boards of management presented challenges and opportunities for the ASTI. Advice was issued to members, which was intended to ensure that teacher representatives were, in practice, ASTI representatives. In 1986, the Association began to provide training for those of its members elected onto boards of management in secondary, as it was already doing for those in the community/comprehensive sector.[77]

A new broom

Much of the development of the 1980s was overseen by Kieran Mulvey, a significant recruit to the Association who took up the new post of assistant general secretary in April 1980. Mulvey was a former student radical who was associated with the Workers' Party – until that party's policy came into conflict with the ASTI's – and he had impressed as a trade union organiser and negotiator during five years' working for the Irish Federation of University Teachers (IFUT). Joining the Association, he anticipated (correctly, as it turned out) that he would succeed to the top position on Máire MacDonagh's retirement. While relishing the fresh challenge, by his own account, he took up his new post with some apprehension, having been alerted to the ASTI's 'fractiousness'.[78]

The extent of the fractiousness, he found, had been somewhat exaggerated. While there were 'passionate' arguments at meetings, Mulvey recalls, these did not adversely affect personal relationships between men and women who, after all, were committed to defending the interests of teachers. His relationships with the elected officers of the Association were good on the whole, and he was impressed by the calibre of individual presidents:

> All of them were outstanding teachers in their own right. You didn't get to be president of ASTI just by being an agitator. These people had reputation and standing in the profession and were well-respected by the owners and managers of the schools, namely the religious orders, as well as by the Department of Education ...[79]

These were presidents, moreover, who had spent gruelling years, as members of committees and as organisers, rushing from their classrooms to meetings in Dublin and around the country and driving through the night to get back home in time for early morning classes. They had prevailed in elections that were extremely hard fought, notably those for standing committee, where aspiring presidents had to serve their time. In the days before these were conducted on a regional basis, campaigning was country-wide, culminating frequently in an all-night canvass at convention on the eve of the election. Disappointment was not uncommon, but unsuccessful candidates recovered, many of them to fight another day.[80] In addition to maintaining good relationships inside the Association, Mulvey was also concerned to develop links with other organisations, recognising that allies were necessary if ASTI's objectives were to be advanced. He was committed, in particular, to strengthening the Association's connections with, and position within, the trade union movement. In the decade since its affiliation, the ASTI had participated in ICTU, but in a somewhat desultory fashion. It had sent delegates to ICTU conferences, nominated members to its various sub-committees and, through an agreement with the TUI, had had occasional representatives elected onto the ICTU executive. It had also joined in demonstrations and work stoppages during the trade union campaign for fairer taxation in the late 1970s and early 1980s. For its part, ICTU had encouraged the ASTI to provide more training for its representatives at all levels, assisted in the development of that training, and was active in encouraging greater involvement by women. The relationship was given far greater priority after Mulvey's appointment. He himself was elected to the ICTU Executive in 1982, and quickly won respect among other members of that body. As a result, he was able to secure re-election, with ITGWU support, when, due to competition for members, relations with the TUI came under strain in 1983. Greater continuity of representation thereafter enhanced the ASTI's status within the movement, and, increasingly, its nominee represented the Congress at important events, both in Ireland and abroad. Within two decades of its reaffiliation, therefore, the ASTI was at the very centre of the Irish trade union movement.[81]

Mulvey's interest in coalition-building extended beyond the trade union movement and he was a strong advocate of partnership between the teachers' unions and representatives of parents and school management bodies. He recalls that relations with the latter group improved greatly once the agreement on redeployment was concluded, and that the support of the 'partners' was important to the unions in the course of the 1980s disputes with the government about the resourcing of education. Parents were becoming more organised and more independent, and consequently it was desirable to establish good relations with their representatives.[82] Traditionally, the Catholic Church, while stressing the rights of Catholic parents in education, had in effect arrogated that right to itself. During the 1960s, however, genuine parents' associations were established in a number of schools. At the time of the teachers' strike of 1969, efforts were made to establish a national parents' council, but these efforts, as shown in the last chapter, were not successful. An active Parents'

Federation had emerged in the Christian Brothers schools in the early 1970s and, in 1976, a Catholic Secondary School Parents' Association was founded. Evidently, there was some displeasure in the ranks of the latter that it was not adequately consulted by Gemma Hussey before she announced the establishment of the National Parents' Council in 1984.[83]

While ASTI was deepening its links with the trade union movement at home and developing relationships with other partners in the educational system, its international profile was also rising, and Kieran Mulvey was ultimately elected president of the International Federation of Secondary Teachers (FIPESCO). The Association had affiliated to both FIPESCO and the World Confederation of the Teaching Profession (WCOTP) in 1967, and was involved in hosting conferences of both bodies during the following year. Thereafter, it sent delegations abroad annually, and received delegates. During 1984, to give an example, the ASTI sent one representative to the European Trade Union Committee on Education in Brussels, two to the FIPESCO congress in Lisbon, four to the WCOTP conference in Ayr, three to the AGM of the Educational Institute of Scotland in Rothesay, four to a joint meeting of the teachers' unions in Ireland and the United Kingdom, and (through ICTU) one to an OECD Council of Education Ministers in Paris.[84] These international links were important, Kieran Mulvey believes, not least for the sense of perspective they gave to those involved:

> By the time I left ASTI, we had the best-paid teachers in Europe ... When I was president of FIPESO, and Gerry Quigley was on the executive of the WCOTP, we'd listen to teachers from other parts of the world, and we'd look at our own teachers. We could see how professional our teachers were, how important three and four year degree programmes and post-graduate programmes were, how well-rounded our teachers were as a result of their training. And when we discussed the discipline problems that were emerging around us, we knew that there were places in other parts of the world that were totally undisciplined.
>
> ... We could see how important the retention of a proper state examination system was – a system whose integrity could be accepted – because we knew that there were places where the idea of a terminal examination was little more than an interview

done by the teacher. One thing we were always conscious of was that the Irish system had professional standards. It mightn't have the same money, the same resources, as the Scandinavians, but by golly, by comparison with our near neighbours in Britain, even with the US, the quality of Irish education was top class. I don't think the Irish people realise how good the Irish Leaving Cert is ... We were a shining light. You went from some of these conferences very secure in the knowledge that we had an all-graduate profession, that we had a good distribution of subject teachers ... What I always felt was that our teachers were being paid an adequate salary, a fair salary, for the work they were doing. Not all members would have agreed with that but I feel that Irish education was in a position where it could attract and retain good quality teachers.[85]

If the Irish educational system could be described as 'professional' by the late 1990s, and its workers paid accordingly, it had faced several challenges. Notwithstanding Mulvey's very positive portrayal of Irish secondary education, he had led a succession of campaigns during his decade with the ASTI for adequate remuneration for teachers and for adequate resources for education generally. These campaigns will be considered in the next chapter.

8

'We are the gentle angry teachers'
Teachers' unity and resistance to cutbacks in the 1980s

A high point of teachers' trade unionism in Ireland was Thursday 5 December 1985, the day that an unprecedented number of teachers came together in one place for a common purpose. The cause of the mobilisation was the government's decision to withhold an arbitrated pay award of 10 per cent, on the grounds that public finances could not bear the cost. News of the decision, in August 1985, followed an announcement that there was to be a public sector pay freeze. Widespread resentment had greeted that decision – ICTU's Donal Nevin memorably commented that it 'out-Thatchers anything that has been done by the present British government'[1] – but teachers were doubly indignant because they stood to lose out twice. And their indignation was deepened by the insensitivity of the minister, Gemma Hussey, in communicating the decision to block their special award. Scolding teachers, she urged them to 'address themselves to the morality of what they are about', and alleged that their representatives were 'so bound up in self-justification and media attention' that they were unable to 'stand back for the sake of the country'.[2]

In September, a national co-ordinating committee of the teachers' unions announced the establishment of a 'Teachers United' campaign to secure the 10 per cent arbitration award. *Teachers United* bulletins were published, local co-ordinating groups were formed with representatives from each union, a series of one-day regional stoppages was organised, and a national one-day strike was announced for 5 December.[3]

That an estimated 20,000 men and women, drawn from the ASTI, the TUI and the INTO, were prepared to travel on a cold winter's day to Croke Park by car, coach, and special train from all corners of the country – and by boat from several off-shore islands– testified both to the depth of feeling and to the effectiveness of the preparations. And the attention to detail on the day impressed journalists covering the event – even if several of them were taken aback by the firmness of the conviction among participants that their case had been treated unfairly in the media. For *The Irish Times*, Christina Murphy wrote:

> Organisation was superb. There seemed to be stewards everywhere muttering into walkie-talkies: 'Croke Park to Heuston Station. Come in Heuston'. 'Molesworth Street to HQ; come in HQ' … Croke Park looked like All-Ireland day. From early morning, teachers streamed down the Clonliffe Road, and coach after coachload were deposited outside the Hogan Stand Gate.[4]

Some of the protestors, evidently, were lured to Dublin by the opportunity presented of spending a few post-rally hours doing Christmas shopping, but overwhelmingly, the mood was of good-humoured determination. Not surprisingly, in the rhetoric and the banter of the day, sporting analogies were drawn, beginning with ASTI president, Louis O'Flaherty, who opened proceedings by welcoming the crowd in the manner of sports commentator Micheál Ó hEithir: 'Fáilte romhaibh go léir, a chairde Gaeil.'[5]

In the interval between O'Flaherty's welcome and the march from Croke Park to Dáil Éireann which concluded proceedings, the freezing protestors were treated to more than a dozen speeches, from home-grown trade union leaders as well as from representatives of international teachers' organisations, and to a rousing musical performance. The next day, the *Irish Independent* showed Kieran Mulvey and the INTO's Gerry Quigley singing along with Connolly Folk who had composed the following chorus for the occasion: 'We are the gentle, angry teachers, and we're singing for our rights / Where are the teaching TDs today – are they marching for their rights? / Garret and Gemma are you listening? We are singing for our rights. / There will be an election soon ...'[6] If there was paradoxical quality to the lyric, it was because Teachers United wished to convey distinct messages to different audiences. To parents and the public generally, whose support was solicited, it was necessary that teachers should appear to be conscientious and mild-mannered professionals; to the government, who had to be forced into making a concession, it was important that they be seen to be driven by feelings of righteous determination.

Teachers United?

The sense of elation triggered by the enormously successful joint endeavour of December 1985 raised hopes that co-operation between the three unions might be deepened, and that this might lead eventually to organisational unity. Insofar as there was such harmony, it was a rare moment in the history of Irish teachers' trade unionism. Almost seventy years earlier, as observed in Chapter 2, the ASTI, the INTO and the association representative of technical teachers had all subscribed to trade unionism for the first time. For an extended period thereafter, there was close co-operation between the ASTI and the INTO, and the latter – much larger and longer established – provided valuable support for the infant Association of the secondary teachers. In large measure, the co-operation was due to the good personal relationship between the general secretaries, T.J. Burke and T.J. O'Connell, and the departure of the former in 1937 brought it to an end. Already, the ASTI had begun to plough an independent furrow, which had yielded some small successes, and if it could not maintain a relationship with the INTO, there was little possibility that it would co-operate with the representatives of vocational teachers. While technical education had gained a foothold in the intermediate system following the establishment of the Department of Agriculture and Technical Instruction in 1899, the legislative intervention of Saorstát Éireann in 1930, very much guided by the Catholic Church interest, had placed the systems on resolutely separate paths.

Secondary teachers, it was shown above, remained aloof during the bitter national teachers' strike of 1946, and the relationship over the next two decades was affected by conflicting attitudes to a common salary scale. The belief that many primary teachers carried out examination duties boycotted by ASTI members in 1964 did not help to mend fences.[7]

Educational developments of the 1960s brought about conditions where there might have been useful co-operation between secondary and vocational teachers, but the former were suspicious of any development that might equalise them downwards. Moreover, there were attractions for vocational teachers in a common salary scale, and in the controversy that surrounded the publication of the Ryan Tribunal the VTA aligned itself with the INTO and against the ASTI. While there were aspirations towards teachers' unity, especially at post-primary level, and even some gestures in that direction, during the 1960s and early 1970s, the circumstances of the period obstructed progress.[8]

When the ASTI eventually did join the common conciliation and arbitration scheme for teachers in October 1973, its pursuit of its members' interests required it to liaise closely with the representatives of other teachers. With relations thus improved, the Association was able to respond positively, in May 1975, to a TUI invitation to consider closer co-operation. To this end, a working group of representatives from the two unions was established under the chairmanship of ICTU's Donal Nevin – ICTU itself being particularly keen at this time to promote trade union rationalisation through mergers. The extent of progress in this forum was indicated by the vote in favour of a merger of the bodies at the TUI Congress of 1976. The ASTI followed suit in 1977 on a delegate vote of 125 to 64. In early 1979, having continued to consult widely within the two unions, including at regional meetings, Nevin circulated a document suggesting structures for a merged organisation. The process exposed some differences between the two unions – the TUI, for example, had a policy of accepting the teaching religious into membership, while the ASTI wished to keep them out. These differences, together with tensions arising out of competition for members, hindered further progress. In an effort to reinvigorate the discussions, the TUI initiated contact with the INTO and IFUT, but this served only to complicate matters, and further divisions materialised in respect of what would constitute the most appropriate joint approach to relations with the government.[9] The prospects of a merger between the ASTI and the TUI now seemed remote, but other dynamics were serving to strengthen bonds between the teachers' unions.

New co-operation

To fully appreciate the reasons for the great mobilisation of late 1985, it is necessary to look at the immediate background, at the political context and at the movements in teachers' pay during the previous few years. These were years of economic difficulty, during which there was rising unemployment, high rates of inflation, and political instability. They were the GUBU years, during which four different governments held office within three years, with power alternating between administrations led by the swashbuckling Charles Haughey and the donnish Garret Fitzerald.[10]

After a decade of explosive growth in their individual memberships, and of necessary co-operation in respect of conciliation and arbitration, these were years of increasing cohesion among the teachers' unions – notwithstanding the loosening of the mutual embrace of the TUI and the ASTI. It was a cohesion that was assisted by a generational shift at leadership level. Kieran Mulvey's assumption of an influential role in the ASTI in April 1980 came shortly after Gerry Quigley's election as INTO general secretary and just before Jim Dorney's appointment to the same role in the TUI.[11] The working relationship between Mulvey and Quigley in particular reprised in some respects that of their long-ago predecessors, T.J. Burke and T.J. O'Connell, although a more equal partnership was possible in the 1980s. Quigley's background was in Belfast: he had trained as a primary teacher in that city, and taught there for a period before becoming Northern Ireland secretary of the INTO at the age of twenty-six in 1954, in which position he served until he was elected general secretary.[12]

Their cohesion enabled the teachers' unions to become an influential bloc within the trade union movement, and it is argued that as a result teachers' concerns were more fully taken into account in the negotiation of national agreements.[13] If this was so, there are also indications that national agreements were regarded by teachers merely as starting points during this period of high inflation.

With the national wage agreement about to expire, negotiations between government and ICTU to find a successor began early in 1979. In the circumstances, a simple wage deal was not considered adequate, and there emerged instead the portentously titled National Understanding for Social and Economic Development. This document, negotiated in a context of government and employer concern about the negative economic impact of previous pay agreements, signalled a more corporatist and consensual approach to the matter of remuneration. Instead of simply determining gross pay as formerly, the government sought a deal that would place the focus on net pay, committing itself to fiscal measures which would allow for increases in take-home incomes while bringing total pay costs under control.[14] For one ICTU negotiator, the new approach represented 'a golden opportunity … for trade unionists by enabling them to have an impact and an input on the development of social and economic policies'.[15] Another leading trade unionist would go even further in stressing the important departure represented by the first National Understanding:

> I said in March and I said in April that the breakthrough we had achieved was historic, in that for the first time in this country, and indeed in any other country – and I include the socialist countries – we now had an acknowledgement that the trade union movement not only had a voice to be listened to but had to be brought into the circle where the decisions are made.[16]

The majority of trade unionists were not so impressed – there was a general feeling that the 1979 deal did not adequately address the major grievance of the over-taxation of PAYE workers, an issue that had brought thousands onto the streets. Among teachers, moreover, there was a perception that it did not take account of the fact that 'they had been left behind over the last ten years in a whole variety of ways'.[17] It was rejected therefore by a majority of almost three to one at an ICTU special conference in late May 1979, with all of the teachers' representatives voting against. A very slightly revised agreement was accepted two months later, however. The ASTI and the other teachers' unions did not change their position but, accepting the majority decision, they entered into the fifteen-month agreement, which provided phased increases totalling about 16 per cent and a tax rebate of £175 for Christmas.[18]

A second National Understanding, providing for increases totalling about 15 per cent over fourteen months, came into effect in November 1980. The increases were large, but they will be seen to have been less impressive if annual inflation rates of about 20 per cent during these years are entered into the equation.[19]

There was a clause in the first National Understanding which specifically prohibited the processing of any additional claim for its duration, but the teachers' unions chose to regard that provision as an inconvenient obstacle rather than an absolute impediment. Therefore, when a joint claim, submitted before the acceptance of the 1979 agreement, fell as anticipated at conciliation late in October 1979, it was determined that other avenues should be pursued. The ASTI proceeded to arbitration, while the INTO and the TUI prepared for industrial action to secure the establishment of a review body on teachers' pay. Subsequently, the ASTI's standing committee decided to ballot members on strike action in pursuit of its pay claim.

Support for the establishment of a review body came from clerical managers and, in late January 1980, there was a meeting between representatives of the three teachers' unions and Minister John Wilson. On Wilson's recommendation, the government established a review body. Under the chairmanship of Justice Ryan, the five-member body began meeting in mid-April 1980, with instructions to issue an interim report by September, and a final report by the end of January 1981. Like the earlier Louden Ryan Tribunal, the review body received oral and written submissions, including several from the teachers' unions emphasising that their members were deserving of considerable increases, both to compensate them for the fall in the purchasing power of their wages during the 1970s and to give them their deserved share in the increased national prosperity of that decade. There were, however, some differences in the submissions: the ASTI's placed a particular emphasis on the need to address the long-standing grievance of the non-graduate specialist teachers (discussed in Chapter 6), and while the TUI's and INTO's sought an integrated scale, the ASTI argued for the retention of the common basic scale with allowances, in which view it was supported by the secondary school management bodies.[20] Despite their differences, however, there was close co-operation between the three unions.

As it turned out, the final report of the Ryan review body never appeared, due to the extremely adverse reaction to the contents of the interim document which was made public on 9 October 1980. In a co-ordinated response the teachers' unions declared themselves 'positively outraged' according to *The Irish Times*, which quoted a teachers' spokesperson as describing the review body's proposals with respect to increments as 'absurd'. 'A teacher would be 56 years old before he would benefit from the top increment', and it was further asserted that 'several of the recommendations would actually worsen the working conditions of teachers'.[21] That the sense of outrage was widespread is indicated by the remarks of ordinary teachers during a discussion on the interim report at the very well-attended AGM of the Clare branch which took place on the day that the interim report was published. One member detected in the report an 'attempt to divide established teachers from their colleagues', another regarded it as 'an insult to the teaching profession', a third warned that its impact would be to 'demoralise the profession and hunt people from it', a fourth described it as 'hypocritical because while it put a high value on teaching, the report recommended larger increases to those in administration'. At the end of the discussion, the consensus was in favour of 'industrial action ... in which all three teachers' unions should be involved'.[22]

It was not apparent from the reaction, but the interim report of the review body did make two important concessions. It recommended a substantial salary increase at the top of the scale, and also facilitated future teachers' negotiators by recommending that the established pay relativity between teachers and (the generally non-graduate) executive officers in the civil service be broken. The problem was that the benefits were to come in the longer term. There was no facility for retrospection, which would have generated an attractive lump sum, and the substantial increases would go to those coming to the end of their careers in a series of long-service increments, the last of which was payable on completion of thirty-four years' service. There were no increases in qualifications or in A post allowances, while there was a recommendation that B post allowances be discontinued.[23]

Following their rejection of the interim report, the minister for education, John Wilson, complied with a request to meet representatives of the executives of the three unions. At that meeting, he agreed to open negotiations between the unions concerned and officials of his department. Thus undermined by the minister who appointed them, and resentful of the tone and the content of teachers' reaction to their report, the members of the review body resigned. They did however assent to the minister's request to postpone the public announcement of their resignation.[24]

In the meantime, negotiations proceeded at a brisk pace, under the chairmanship of the minister himself when matters became delicate, and agreement was reached on 23 October – a mere two weeks after the publication of the interim report. Further improvements in pay were conceded and, significantly, the period of the incremental

211

scale was reduced by ten years over what was recommended in the interim report. Some of the unpopular features of the 9 October document were retained, however: there was to be no retrospection, and B posts were to be phased out with allowances for existing post-holders being subsumed into the new long-service increments. The loss of promotional opportunities, in particular, was a cause of disappointment and the agreement was received with little enthusiasm by teachers. It was accepted, however, by the three unions, the outcome of the ASTI ballot being 54 per cent to 46 per cent in favour.[25] Outstanding issues – notably matters relating to the level of allowances, and the non-graduate specialist teachers' claim – were referred to conciliation, where the teachers' case was rejected early in February 1981. The rejection however cleared the way for arbitration on the claim. It was November 1981 before the arbitrator presented his report, and it contained some good news: qualifications allowances should be increased by 25 per cent, and responsibility allowances by 30 per cent; the holders of these allowances should not be deprived of them for as long as they remained in post. There was ambiguity with respect to the subsuming of the B post allowance, ambiguity that would not be cleared up until late in 1984, when a later arbitration ruling found in favour of the post-holders, although some individuals were disadvantaged. The non-graduate specialist teachers, however, faced disappointment once again in 1981, for the arbitrator ruled that their claim fell outside his terms of reference. The grievance of the specialist teachers, which arose from recommendations in respect to degree allowances made by the Ryan Tribunal in 1968, would remain unresolved for quite a few more years, indeed. Lacking degrees, although most of them had equivalent qualifications, these teachers were deprived of the allowances. At conciliation and arbitration, their claim became linked to that of non-degree primary teachers who had trained prior to 1977, making resolution more difficult. Ultimately, twenty-eight years would pass before a final settlement was reached in the context of national pay negotiations in 1996.[26]

A third National Understanding was still-born, due to the attitude of the employers' negotiators, who were vehemently of the view that workers in the public sector should receive a lesser award than those in the private sector. Negotiations between the minister for labour and ICTU's Public Services Committee resulted in a phased increase over fifteen months. It was accepted by ASTI members by a margin of 90 per cent to 10 per cent, but the reception was not as enthusiastic as the margin suggests, for only 22 per cent participated in the vote. By way of comparison, there were 60 per cent turnouts – and similar margins – in the other teachers' unions.[27]

Another issue of concern to post-primary teachers during these years was the fall in the real value of remuneration for examination duties. In October 1978, the ASTI lodged a claim for a 100 per cent increase in the 'pittance' paid to assistant examiners, subsequently advising its members to make applications for these duties conditional on 'satisfactory' remuneration being offered. There was the prospect then of an examination boycott in 1980, which was averted by an arbitrator's recommendation of a 60 per cent increase. While the 60 per cent was accepted, it was not regarded as satisfactory – in any case, inflation quickly reduced its worth – so a fresh claim for increases of 40–50 per cent was lodged jointly by the ASTI and the TUI in 1980. The government offered an increase of 16.6 per cent, the same as the percentage increase provided for in the second National Understanding. This was reluctantly accepted by ASTI, but a further claim was served which yielded a 30 per cent award at arbitration in good time for the 1981 state examinations. The total increase in the payment for examination work between 1979 and 1981 therefore was more than 140 per cent, which must be regarded as significant.[28]

The three-year period between the spring of 1979 and the spring of 1982, therefore, was incredibly complex from the industrial relations point of view. It was a period of proto-social partnership, marked by frequent ballots, during which ASTI representatives had been involved in negotiating three national agreements, one re-negotiation of a national agreement, and the negotiation of a public service pay deal, as well as engaging with a pay review body and Department of Education officials, and processing several claims on salaries and examination remuneration through conciliation and arbitration. There was not complete agreement on every issue between the teachers' unions during the period but the nature of many negotiations made it desirable and strategically sensible that there be close co-operation between them. The joint publication in 1981 by the ASTI, the TUI and the INTO of *From School to Work*, to mark the United Nations' International Year of the Disabled, was one of the fruits of this co-operation.

That there was a general willingness to strengthen the bonds be-tween the unions was indicated in the case of the ASTI, by the adop-tion at its 1981 convention of a resolution in favour of a federation of teachers' unions. Even those who were strongly in favour of such a development were very conscious of the failure of the proposed merger between the ASTI and the TUI in 1979, so there was cau-tion. A significant step was taken in November 1981, when a Coun-cil of Education Unions (CEU) was formed by the INTO, the TUI, IFUT, the Northern Ireland section of the British-based National Association of Teachers in Further and Higher Education (NATFHE) and the ASTI. Kieran Mulvey was the CEU secretary. The declared objective was as follows: to 'provide for structured li-aison and exchange among ICTU unions engaged exclusively in the education sector and to assist the development of an overall trade union view of education'. It was significant that there was finally es-tablished a body which was equipped to advance an integrated pol-icy on educational affairs, drawing on the experience and expertise of men and women involved at all levels of education on the island.

Hard times
'The £120m sting' was how the *Irish Independent* described the mi-nority Fianna Fáil government's decision on spending cuts an-nounced on 30 July 1982, in which a public sector pay freeze was the central element of a response to what the same paper characterised as 'a thirties style recession'. Other measures included education cuts totalling £7.5m and the lifting of subsidies on staple foods. Because it was handled by government officials rather than by ministers, the manner of the announcement attracted comment: 'Mr Haughey, and most of his cabinet were well on their way to their holiday des-tinations yesterday ... when the bombshell on public service pay was dropped.'[29]

The decision to freeze pay amounted to a reneging by the gov-ernment on the public sector agreement negotiated by its predecessor, and which had been accepted by ICTU's Public Services Committee less than six months earlier. And in respect of teachers' pay, the July 1982 announcement marked a turning point after three years of steady progress. Indeed, apologists for the several rounds of educa-tional cuts that followed would highlight the teachers' unions' achieve-ments on pay during 1979–82, and suggest that these lay at the root of the budgetary problems of the Department of Education.[30]

Threats from the unions to call national demonstrations and work stoppages, however, had their effect in what was a period of political instability, and the taoiseach agreed to renegotiate the public service pay deal rather than set it aside altogether. The renegotiation produced an agreement in early October 1982, acceptable to the public sector trade unions, which provided for a delayed phasing in of agreed increases. Significant clauses in the renegotiated deal allowed for the processing of special claims, but precluded the setting of a date for their implementation.[31]

The government fell soon afterwards, and was replaced by a Fine Gael/Labour coalition, but teachers were soon presented with further challenges, for one of the first acts of the new minister for education, Gemma Hussey, was to announce further cuts, cuts which impacted in particular on remedial education, on guidance counselling, and on the free school transport service. There was angry response from representatives of students, parents and teachers. Following a meeting with Gemma Hussey, members of a joint deputation from Catholic parents' organisations criticised the minister's 'intransigent attitude', and announced that they intended to challenge some of the cutbacks in the courts.[32] The TUI called a one-day strike of its members and a demonstration outside the Dáil, which was attended by up to 7,000 teachers, including representatives of the other teaching unions who were not on strike. Addressing the demonstration, the ASTI president Margaret Walsh referred to the promises of all of the parties during the recent election campaign to maintain and protect education, yet within weeks the new government had 'undermined and eroded … the principle of free education'.[33]

Discussions on a successor public sector pay deal took place a short time later, and a deal in three phases, over fifteen months, beginning with a six-month pay pause, was agreed. The previously adopted limitations on special claims were retained. In 1984, a delay in the filling of the vacancy for a public service arbitrator prompted the unions into announcing a one-day work stoppage. The announcement had the desired effect.[34]

On the expiry of the 1983–84 pay agreement in mid-1984, the government cut across arrangements for a successor by publishing its economic plan entitled *Building on Reality, 1985–1987*. For teachers, a salient feature of the plan was that there would be only minimal increases in public sector pay during the following three years, and the determination of Garret Fitzgerald's government in this regard was underlined when its estimates for 1985 did not make any provision for wage increases. The teachers' unions responded by jointly making the case that there had been a loss of 15 per cent in the purchasing power of their members' wages during the previous few years, and that inflation would lead to a further loss in the year ahead.[35] And joining a chorus of critics of the estimates' implications for education generally – including Fianna Fáil, who criticised their 'sterile smugness' – the teachers' unions predicted serious adverse effects if the projected 5 per cent to 7 per cent cut in expenditure was implemented.[36]

In a pessimistic climate, there was relief in trade union circles when the public service arbitrator recommended some movement on pay – albeit on a very modest scale – in January 1985. The recommendation was for a nineteen-month settlement, beginning with a seven-month pay pause, to be followed by two increases of 3 per cent each. The government initiated contact with ICTU's Public Services Committee with a view to agreeing a reduction, but later agreed to pay the full amount. The teachers' unions, with their separate arbitration scheme, were not bound by the agreement, but they accepted it nonetheless.[37]

In the meantime, a long-standing 'catch-up' claim on behalf of teachers was proceeding through conciliation and arbitration, the arbitrator having rejected the government's plea of penury on the grounds that a refusal to consider their claim would amount to 'quite unjustified discrimination against teachers'. Eventually, the arbitrator came to a decision which he circulated, in confidence, to the interested parties. The recommendation, for a 10 per cent increase in two phases, quickly came into the public domain accompanied by rumours that the government would refuse to pay it. The rumours were confirmed by Minister Gemma Hussey in her combative statement which initiated the chain of events that led to the enormous demonstration of 5 December 1985.[38]

Relations had been poor between the ASTI and the TUI since the latter had complained, unsuccessfully, to ICTU in November 1983 that the Association was 'poaching' members in the community colleges which the TUI regarded as being in its own sphere.[39] Significantly, the resulting tensions were pushed aside in the exhilaration generated by the Teachers United campaign.

In the immediate aftermath of the December 1985 demonstration, the government sought to enter negotiations on the disputed award, in the context of a new pay round. The minister offered the teachers' unions the 7 per cent offered to other public service workers on condition that they agreed to a postponement of their own arbitrator's special 10 per cent. Refusing to concede, the three unions continued their campaigns, lobbying individual TDs at their clinics and elsewhere and encouraging individual members to initiate a correspondence on the issue with TDs in their own constituencies.[40] That the combined membership of the three unions was a formidable force when mobilised is confirmed by several of those involved at the time. According to Kieran Mulvey:

> The teachers' unions collectively, between them, had become the most powerful group in Congress – notwithstanding the industrial power of the ITGWU and the FWUI [Federated Workers' Union of Ireland]. As a professional body, when they moved politically, they were akin to the IFA [Irish Farmers' Association]. They had that solid institutional political clout, insofar as they permeated every parish in Ireland, every political party in Ireland, every cultural, sporting and recreational body. This stood to them in the pay battle of the early 1980s, it certainly stood to them in the battle over the arbitration award in 1985–86, and in the fight-back against cuts.[41]

Garret Fitzgerald, who was on the other side of the barricades in 1985–86, was in substantial agreement with Mulvey:

> The teachers' unions have always been a powerful force, and their efforts had led to a higher valuation being put on the work of teachers in Ireland than in many other countries. I believe that over the years that this had been one of a number of factors contributing to the quality of Irish education.[42]

But if, as Mulvey asserted, teachers had clout equal to that of the farmers, the *Farmers' Journal* disapproved of the fact that teachers were choosing to apply that clout:

> The teachers are in open conflict with the government (in other

words the tax payer) ... They are giving the young in their care a practical lesson in pressurising the guardians of our money to spend some of it on themselves. In a year or two these young folks will be in a position to lay on a bit of disruption on their own behalf.[43]

And the *Farmers' Journal* was not alone in its concern, for Gemma Hussey's diaries from the period reveal that she was alarmed at the impact the lobbying was having on the resolve of TDs, especially Labour TDs. They also show that she had become quite emotional about teachers' pay: 'But the more I think about it, the more indignant I am at the thought of teachers getting 10 per cent on top of all the public service increases. If we had a really strong government, they couldn't possibly get it ...'[44] An impasse having been reached, Minister Hussey took the unprecedented step of introducing a Dáil motion which would have the effect of deferring the arbitration award. She need not have worried about the Labour backbenchers, for her motion secured the support of the opposition Progressive Democrats, a new party advocating policies that would later be described as neoliberal. The minister's moment of triumph was brief, however, for a week later she lost her post in a cabinet re-shuffle. For Christina Murphy, *Irish Times* education correspondent, it was her handling of the conflict with the teachers' unions that brought about the downfall of this most energetic of ministers for education.[45] Hussey herself was despondent:

Garret has made the most appalling mess of the re-shuffle and I am the victim to expediency and am now Minister for Social Welfare. I ... seriously considered resignation ... If Garret had thought I was a bad Minister for Education, surely he would have had the guts to tell me.[46]

Fitzgerald, evidently, did not think she was a 'bad' minister, and he would acknowledge later that he made a 'mess of the reshuffle': 'On the pay issue itself I was totally supportive of her stand and in moving her I had no intention whatever of easing the way for a government climb-down, as subsequent events were misleadingly to suggest.'[47] There was no immediate sign of a 'climb-down' from Hussey's successor, Patrick Cooney, a TD for Longford–Westmeath, a solicitor, and a man of 'conservative bent', according to his party leader.

Cooney had earned a reputation as a hard-line minister for justice in the 1973–77 government, and on his appointment to Education he showed no inclination to compromise.

A round of regional strikes followed in March 1986 with another scheduled for May, while ballots of the TUI and the ASTI produced majorities for a ban an examination work. The new minister's statement of determination that the examination would proceed prompted Teachers United to place an advertisement in the Sunday newspapers which called on parents to 'use their influence with government TDs to bring this dispute to an end', and questioned the judgement of the government in relation to the examinations:

> The government is proposing to recruit untrained and inexperienced people to supervise and mark the public examinations. These people do not have the skills and experience of practising teachers. The government cannot guarantee proper standards unless the teachers are involved. A massive effort is underway that the same standards of exactness and fairness can be reached. No similar effort was put into finding a resolution to the dispute.[48]

The beginning of a resolution came on 16 April 1986, in the middle of a very eventful week in Irish education. Five days earlier, an estimated 300 students had walked out of the Shannon Comprehensive School, declaring themselves on strike. Professing neutrality in the dispute between the teachers and the government, they protested that they were being 'treated unfairly' by both parties, that they were 'being used as pawns in their battle'. In order to preserve the credibility of the 1986 examinations, they urged students in other schools to protest against the introduction of 'inexperienced examiners'. On Monday 14 April, there were further large-scale student walkouts in Dublin, Kilkenny, Ennis and Galway.[49] In all instances, the students were scrupulous about declaring their neutrality, but those of them that were quoted in the press seemed generally sympathetic towards their teachers – if not necessarily towards their unions. Their demand for 'experienced examiners', moreover, placed them on the same side of the argument as the teachers. Six students from St Mark's Community School in Tallaght gave voice to their feelings in *The Irish Times*:

Let's face it, anybody can supervise the exams without it making too much difference, but the correcting, that's different ... If you got an A or a B in those circumstances, nobody would know for certain if you were worth it ... We are being used, of course we are, and students feel strongly about this, and about what is happening to us.[50]

All six seemed appreciative of their own teachers, and of the fact that they spent an 'enormous amount of extra time with us, unpaid', but they had different attitudes to the union action. While one thought that the teachers 'had to ban the exam work, they had no other weapon', another doubted that 'ordinary teachers got to voice their opinion in the unions'. Parents of students at the Greendale Comprehensive School followed the example of their sons and daughters in a protest at government and union buildings on the Wednesday, and the National Parents' Council followed suit on the Saturday, with a march of 150 people – small, judged the *Sunday Independent*, due to the rain. On the same day 500 students insisted on their right to properly organised examinations. 'The only way this can happen,' went their statement, 'is for the government to pay the teachers their just claims.'[51]

One reason for the poor turnout of parents on the Saturday was that the government had already begun the 'climb-down' referred to by Garret Fitzgerald, having been put under pressure by a Fianna Fáil motion debated in the Dáil on Wednesday 16 April. The motion required the government to enter negotiations with the teachers' representatives, and in order to retain the support of its own backbenchers – and to ensure its own survival – the government put down an amendment committing itself to accepting third-party intervention in the dispute. During the following week, talks began under the auspices of the Employer–Labour Conference. They continued for ten days but ended in stalemate.[52]

Early in May, pressure forced the government and the unions to enter direct talks. By this point, there was widespread disruption of practical examinations, mostly because stand-in supervisors changed their minds about breaking the boycott, but in one Limerick school, it was because students refused to accept examination material from non-teachers. The disruption was represented in the press as a success for the unions, but there were tensions nonetheless between the

TUI and ASTI about the enforcing of the practicals' boycott.[53] In the course of the talks, improvements offered by the government in respect of the phasing of the arbitration award, along with a series of *ex gratia* payments to partly compensate for the delayed phasing, were accepted by the teachers' negotiators and were put to ballot along with the general public service pay offer.

The package was accepted by large majorities in all three unions, the largest, in the order of four to one, being in the ASTI. It was less than had been offered by the arbitrator the previous August, but it was seen as a good compromise by teachers who had fought an academic-year-long campaign but who held reservations about boycotting the state examinations.[54]

The most salient effect of the Teachers United campaign of 1985–86 was that it served to show the impact of co-ordinated action by teachers. At all levels and in all parts of the country, teachers in the different unions had met together, protested together, and had got to know one another.

Council of Teachers' Unions

The sectoral boundaries that had divided secondary teachers from their counterparts in vocational and primary schools had become fainter and there was a real appetite for a deepening of co-operation. It was the impression of Tony McKernan, who became active in the ASTI in Limerick, that many previously passive members were drawn into activity and pressed into accepting positions at branch and national level in the course of the great mobilisations of 1985–86. Their experience of Teachers United persuaded these new activists of the advantages of unity and, for a period a single union for teachers seemed a real possibility.[55]

Donal Nevin of ICTU, who had been involved in a similar way in the 1970s, was invited in May 1989 by the three unions to facilitate discussions between them. The outcome was the establishment of the Council of Teachers' Unions (CTU) in 1990, with its own chief executive and representation from each union in proportion to its membership. The first meeting of the twenty-four member council took place in Dublin in December 1990, with Billy Fitzpatrick of the TUI in the chair. According to a statement from that meeting, the goal of unity was to be pursued in a sensitive manner, respecting the 'separate traditions and identities' of each of the three unions.[56]

It would be significant that the inaugural meeting of the CTU took place in the same month that Kieran Mulvey informed members of standing committee that he would soon be leaving the ASTI to take the position of chief executive of the Labour Relations Commission. His resignation coincided with the unexpected retirement of the INTO's Gerry Quigley, removing from the arena a second key promoter of co-operation between the three unions. Senior figures, with different union backgrounds, suggested that the changed circumstances now made unity more difficult to achieve for two main reasons – influential individuals feared that their own prospects might be damaged in a post-merger configuration, and the capacity to overcome the inevitable obstacles was reduced by the dissolution of the Quigley–Mulvey partnership.[57]

The CTU's efforts continued however. Three working groups were established and there were a number of inter-union initiatives – CTU year-planners and diaries, for example, courses for safety representatives and retiring members, and an equality conference in May 1992.[58] Work proceeded, meanwhile, on devising agreed structures, and out of this work a resolution was agreed, which was accepted by the three executives, and placed on the Easter agenda of the three annual delegate meetings. The resolution included the following points:

> That a union be established to represent the members of the three teachers' unions; that this union have a federal structure with divisions and subdivisions as appropriate ...; that a union conference of delegates representing all branches decide policy on matters affecting members of more than one division; that a central executive, with divisional representation, as appropriate, be responsible for the running of the central business.[59]

It was further proposed that 'an outline of a constitution reflecting such a structure be presented ... not later than the annual convention of 1994'. The acceptance of the resolution by three bodies of delegates would have represented a significant step forward, but it was not to be. Against the advice of their executive, the INTO delegates placed an obstacle in the way of further progress by insisting that the other two unions modify their policy in respect of the points system for promotion. Faced with what they interpreted as an ultimatum, the ASTI and the TUI refused, bringing an effective end to the prospects for three-way unity, though the CTU maintained a legal existence for a time.[60]

The TUI remained keen to pursue a merger with the ASTI, and two-way discussions took place almost immediately. The ASTI proceeded cautiously, urging on occasion that the door to the INTO be left open, at least ajar. The TUI–ASTI relationship deepened during 1994, with joint executive meetings and joint meetings at regional level. From general meetings in Cork, Galway and Dundalk, it was reported in December 1994 that the response of ordinary members to the proposed merger 'was generally positive'. There were some tensions at grassroots level, however, for TUI members who attended a joint general meeting in Waterford alleged that 'condescending' comments were made about their union by ASTI members.[61]

The joint working group continued to devise an agreement on appropriate structures, but history was about to repeat itself, when submerged tensions came to the surface in the course of a conference debate. The result was that the momentum towards unity was broken.

On this occasion, the debate was prompted by a resolution submitted to the 1995 TUI conference calling for an interruption in the merger discussions pending a satisfactory outcome to a local controversy in Swinford, County Mayo. The controversy itself arose from an unusual form of amalgamation between a vocational school and a secondary school, where the outcome was to be a new secondary school. TUI members felt that they had not been adequately consulted, placing their colleagues in the vocational school at a disadvantage under the new regime. The depth of feeling stirred by the issue is conveyed by the strong language used by TUI delegates: for Dan Dillon of Mayo, it was time that the ASTI was 'flushed out from behind the skirts and cloaks of the religious'; for Tom Dooley of Dundalk, it was necessary to take a stand to avoid the emergence of 'an amalgamated union where we are second-class citizens'. Despite an appeal from the platform not to 'conduct national issues on the back of local problems', the delegates voted in favour of the resolution.[62] A matter-of-fact minute of a subsequent internal ASTI meeting hardly concealed the resulting sense of disappointment: 'Standing Committee noted TUI Congress motion 58 on teacher unity which has the effect of suspending unity discussions with

ASTI.' Early in 1996, there were further ASTI–INTO contacts, but there was little in the way of tangible results.[63]

A full decade after the heyday of Teachers United, and the elation surrounding the great mobilisation of 5 December 1985, the organisations involved were again on resolutely separate paths. Extremely close co-operation at all levels between the three unions in 1985–86 and 1992–93, and between the ASTI and the TUI in 1994–95, had fallen casualty to long-standing rivalries and to mutual suspicions between the three sectors. There would necessarily be an interval before the teachers' unity project could be resuscitated.

9

'Highlighting the imbalance'
Equality and Women's Issues, *c.*1970–95

Attention fell on the employment conditions of women secondary teachers in the mid-1980s due partly to the travails of Eileen
Flynn, a UCG graduate and a young teacher of Irish and History at
the Holy Faith Convent School in New Ross. Because it occurred
during a period of adjustment in the relationships between religious
employers and their lay staff, her dismissal brought 'into national
focus the whole question of Catholic mores and standards for the
teaching profession', in the words of the *Irish Independent*.[1] Flynn
had neglected to join the Association, so she was not represented by
it at any of the three stages of her appeal. Nevertheless, her case and
its implications preoccupied ASTI officials and activists during 1984
and 1985, and they were closely followed by the membership. To
Kieran Mulvey, general secretary just a few months when it became
public, it would present several challenges.

Flynn was dismissed in November 1982, the school authorities
citing a 'lifestyle' that 'ran contrary to Catholic morals and opinions'.
For the teacher, her pregnancy and her relationship with Richie
Roche, a local publican who was separated from his wife, were private
matters. In the view of the nuns, however, her 'position as a teacher
in a convent school in a country town had become untenable, in that
her personal conduct and attitudes towards the authority of the school
was inconsistent with the nature, status and function of the school'.
While Flynn's work was regarded as satisfactory, her relationship had
caused tongues to wag in both town and convent.[2] In this regard, in
addition to the matter of the marital irregularity, there were other
senses in which her choice of partner might have been seen to challenge the settled 'respectability' represented by the Holy Faith convent

– Roche's bar, which could be seen from the school, had a somewhat bohemian reputation, and Richie Roche himself publicly identified with the anti-establishment Sinn Féin party.

In December 1983 the case became public, when it came before an employment appeals tribunal. According to an ASTI informant, Flynn impressed as a woman doing 'her best to tell all the truth'. Questioned on whether she held ASTI membership, she responded: 'No, I thought about joining but did not get around to it. Then, when the trouble started, I did not want to "jump on the bandwagon". I didn't want to cause industrial action.'³

In February 1984, the all-male tribunal ruled for the employing nuns, on a split decision, with the chairman finding for Flynn, and his two colleagues – including an ICTU nominee – determining against her. It was the opinion of the tribunal majority that 'her employers were entitled to expect a certain code of behaviour and standards from someone responsible for children of an impressionable age … [and] the claimant did not measure up to what was reasonably expected of her'. Critical for the tribunal was whether the dismissal was a response to the pregnancy, thereby contravening unfair dismissals legislation. In the chairman's view, Flynn was 'effectively' dismissed when her employers learned she was pregnant, but his colleagues' reading was more nuanced: 'Miss Flynn was not dismissed because of her pregnancy, but her pregnancy was a confirmation of all the rumours regarding her association with a married man.'⁴ Reacting, Leo Donnelly, SJ, provided a glimpse into the attitudes of religious employers:

Ms Flynn's pregnancy is significant only as being incontrovertible evidence that her relations with the man in whose house she resided were in fact immoral. Had her immorality remained genuinely private, it might have been overlooked.⁵

According to commentator Nell McCafferty, Donnelly's remarks were an admission that in the application of the 'Catholic ethos', women were discriminated against because of the nature of what was 'incontrovertible' in such matters. 'Male teachers … don't have babies,' she wrote, 'they're away on a hack.'⁶ Because it occurred at a high point in what Gene Kerrigan characterised as Ireland's 'moral civil war', the case outraged feminist and liberal campaigners who had mobilised to oppose the pro-life constitutional amendment referendum of September 1983. For them, Flynn's dismissal, and the death of pregnant schoolgirl Ann Lovett in January 1984 were manifestations of the worst hypocrisy. Where now, they asked, was the 'compassion' for pregnant single women advocated by Catholic spokespersons during the referendum campaign?[7]

Kieran Mulvey referred to this context in an uncompromisingly-worded article in the *Sunday Independent*:

The recent decision ... clearly points to all the inherent contradictions of this divisive but necessary debate on private morality and indeed on the implications of the pro-life argument itself. It has not been a good week for Irish education and neither has it been a good week for Irish society. A child and her child both die in giving birth in the most appalling circumstances and a teacher is dismissed for making an essentially pro-life decision ... Increasingly within the profession, and particularly because the profession is a young profession in its age profile, major flash-points are now developing which are a mirror of those conflicts which exist within our society. We are a young nation, with a young teaching force – a teaching force educated in the liberal values of the Sixties and Seventies, and the post-Vatican II liberalisation of Church teaching ... There is a real and legitimate concern among teachers, perhaps more in rural than urban areas, that a gossip and moral watchdog society will begin to take over their management and management boards. Is a teacher who enters into an adult relationship to be dismissed? ... However, the implications of the New Ross decision are not confined to teachers alone, but have further and broader implications for all employees – particularly for those employees in whatever institution or agency that may have a passing or prominent involvement with the 'Catholic ethos' ... The ASTI itself was founded in 1909, largely to counter the unjust and cavalier treatment of lay teachers by the religious employers ... Seventy-five years later, has the situation really changed? The New Ross case clearly points to the need for an overhaul and review of both the Employment Equality and Unfair Dismissals legislation. This Association will be recommending to the ICTU that this takes place as a matter of urgency ...[8]

The article, along with a statement from the president, Ray Kennedy, fulfilled the ASTI's formal responsibilities in the matter, but in the circumstances of the mid-1980s, there were those who would urge that the Association should go further. However, a resolution debated in private session at the 1984 convention, and passed by a six to one majority, did not commit it to any specific action. From Wexford, a branch with a radical reputation, the resolution read: 'That it be ASTI policy that a teacher's private morality and lifestyle should not be grounds for dismissal where they conflict with the views of the school management.'[9] Michael Waddell, who proposed the resolution, recalls that the case caused great nervousness and indignation among younger teachers, and that there was a determination to send 'a shot across the bows' of the religious managers. Because of this, there was apprehension in the upper echelons of the Association about what delegates might say during the debate. However, according to Waddell, there was an acceptance, even among the more radical element, that the Association's role was limited by the fact of Flynn's non-membership. Activists of the County Wexford branches, who took pride in recruiting every eligible teacher in their jurisdictions, were dismayed that Flynn had remained a non-member, but nonetheless they formed a committee with members of the other teaching unions in the locality to raise funds for her appeal.[10]

Throughout the trade union movement, indeed, the ruling attracted attention, and delegates to ICTU's annual women's conference supported a motion from Kathleen Lough of the TUI committing them to resist 'any attempt to deny women the right to work on spurious pretexts related to their private lives' and demanding the resignation of ICTU's nominee to the employment appeals tribunal.[11]

For the ASTI, Kieran Mulvey remained adamant that it was 'specifically precluded under its rules from any financial or legal involvement in this case, particularly since the individual in question was not a member of the union'.[12] The prevailing view was that Flynn would have been protected if she had been an ASTI member, and this was reflected in several statements from the general secretary. Her dismissal was an isolated incident which was not typical of general trends in schools, he indicated, and the ASTI had successfully defended its members in a number of similar cases, cases where he had encountered 'a degree of fairness among management'.[13]

Flynn's appeal to the Circuit Court was heard in July 1984. That it was unsuccessful was not altogether surprising, but a comment from Judge Ryan as he delivered his judgement ensured that the issue became more of a *cause célèbre* than it was already. 'In other parts of the world, women are being condemned to death for this sort of offence,' he remarked, seeming to forget that Eileen Flynn was not on trial.[14]

Responding to the judgement, Mulvey again forcefully defended the teacher's right to 'a private life'. Well aware that some members regarded his approach as too meek, he would be reminded by responses to the statement that there were many others for whom his attitude was outrageously libertine. Because unusually crude language was used, a sermon from a Sligo priest attacking his position received extensive coverage. Accusing the general secretary of making 'a virtue of adultery', Fr McDermott described his arguments as 'bullshit'.[15] Meanwhile, long-standing ASTI members were writing in protest to newspapers and directly to head office. The following is an excerpt from one letter:

> I am a member of ASTI and I do not support Eileen Flynn. In taking that attitude, I am not making any moral or subjective judgement, hypocritical or otherwise, contrary to what Mr Mulvey and others suggest. It is my view that those responsible for running a school, and the parents associated with it, need not apologise for their religion. If a teacher in the school openly and publicly contradicts those values by his/her personal arrangements, then he/she is honour bound either to leave the school or to change those arrangements.[16]

Judge Ryan's verdict came as delegates were gathering in Waterford for the annual ICTU conference, where it prompted both an emergency debate and the coming together of an ad hoc committee of concerned trade unionists for the purpose of fund-raising for Ms Flynn's High Court appeal. Encouraged by this committee, Flynn now sought membership of the ASTI, but was found to be ineligible (not then being a serving teacher).[17] The committee, which included some ASTI members, caused further argument when its request to commend the appeal to its eighty-eight affiliates was considered by ICTU's executive council in January 1985. Kieran Mulvey opposed the request on two grounds: firstly, that Ms Flynn had 'never been a member of a trade union' and, secondly, that ICTU should not support 'unofficial ad hoc groups', a position in which he was supported by the INTO general secretary. The INTO activist Joe O'Toole passionately disagreed, arguing this was 'a matter of principle which goes beyond a person's trade union affiliation'. In the event, O'Toole's view prevailed, and ICTU urged individual unions to support the £50,000 appeal. Evidently, there were units of the ASTI where the prevailing view was closer to O'Toole's than to Mulvey's. In the Clare branch, there was agreement that the unofficial appeal should be circulated to members on the following grounds: 'It was felt that as she was fighting a case for all Irish teachers it was worth supporting and therefore important that contact should be made with all teachers, even though it is not an official branch policy as she was not a member of ASTI.'[18]

The High Court decision came on 8 March 1985 (ironically, it was pointed out, International Women's Day). Rejecting the appeal, Mr Justice Declan Costello stated that the appellant should have known 'from her upbringing as a Catholic, and previous experience as a teacher, the sort of school in which she sought employment and she should have been well aware of the obligations she would undertake by joining the staff'.[19] There was a jubilant response from the management bodies, prompting an ASTI statement rebuking one of their spokespersons for being 'unnecessarily provocative' in his comments, and pledging to fight for amendments to equality legislation.[20]

The ASTI faced criticism, implicit and explicit, for its response to the Flynn case. For critics – feminists, socialists and liberals dismayed by the triumph of conservative Catholic activism in the pro-life referendum and anxious at preparations to resist divorce – the dismissal presented an opportunity to make a necessary stand for a secular profession and a secular Ireland. For the ASTI, it was not so simple, since its members included some conservative Catholics, and there was no groundswell in favour of an interventionist approach among the more secular activist members, due to their disapproval of teachers remaining outside the Association. Any measure stronger than verbal support, it might be argued, would have been divisive internally. In the event, it proved possible to maintain a united front within the ASTI around statements of general principle. Moreover, the Flynn case did not prove to be the harbinger of intrusive clericalism that many predicted, even in the short term. In the medium term, the censorious impulse would be blunted further when prominent Church figures were revealed to have 'lifestyle' issues of their own.

Looking back, Flynn regretted she had not joined the Association when she became a teacher: 'I think it would have made a difference, but to what degree I can't tell.' And she did not blame the ASTI for the outcome of her case, stating that 'they did give me the maximum help that they could, they raised funds and issued statements'. Her life, thereafter, was lived largely in the private domain, but in 1997, she spoke at a press conference against exemptions for religious employers from the Employment Equality Bill. In the 1990s, after divorce was introduced, she married Richie Roche, continuing to work in the family pub business while volunteering on an adult literacy project. At the time of her tragically early death in 2008, she was back in the classroom, in a primary school in New Ross.[21]

Women in the Association before 1970

The Flynn controversy reflected lingering tensions between religious employers and their lay staff but it was seen to have important equality and women's rights aspects. What was genuinely shocking about it, however, was that it seemed to belong to an earlier time – to 'an age that put stockings on piano-legs' in Tom O'Dea's phrase, to a time when lay secondary teachers 'behaved as if they had actually taken vows of obedience', as another ASTI president, Pierce Purcell, put it.[22] The extent to which vestiges of that age survived into the 1980s and 1990s will be considered later in this chapter, in discussing efforts to win representation for women and to make the Association more relevant to its female members. Before proceeding to that, it will be useful to look backwards, to review how things actually stood before the impact of 'second wave' feminism was felt.

From its foundation in 1909, ASTI had included women. Between 1911 and 1920, women's branches, which enjoyed substantial autonomy, had the right to nominate members onto the Association's executive. The defection of Protestant members in response to the decision to affiliate with Labour/Congress in 1920 weakened the women's branches to the extent that they were no longer considered viable. Women remained active in the ASTI's affairs, nevertheless, and one of them, Miss A.J. Mulligan of the St Louis Convent in

Rathmines, became its first female president in 1926. By way of comparison, Catherine Mahon, the INTO's first woman president, took office in 1912, while Louie Bennett was elected as the first woman president of the Trade Union Congress in 1932.[23]

There would not be another woman president of the ASTI until Nora Kelleher took office in 1958, but, as mentioned earlier, the post of general secretary was filled by women from 1938 to 1983 (with one short interval). Arguably, however, the selection of Florence Quirke and, after her, of Máire MacDonagh did not indicate any ideological commitment to gender equality. The fact was that a male administrator would have required a higher salary – an important consideration in cash-strapped times – and he would probably have needed a secretary. Moreover, it might have been anticipated that a male official would be more likely to encroach on the authority of the part-time elected officers.[24]

Similarly, it was pragmatically defensive rather than idealistically egalitarian motives that prompted the ASTI to adopt a policy of equal pay for women as early as 1914, the concern being that low-paid women teachers might replace men in boys' schools. Although the matter of equal pay was not always actively pursued (this would have been difficult given the infrequency of pay negotiations in the decades after 1922), there were some advances. In 1926, due to ASTI efforts, the allowance for women with honours degrees was raised to the male level. And the Association negotiated a further degree of equality in the state salary for women in 1950 when they were placed on a par with single men, though single men maintained an advantage in school salaries until the 1964 'secret agreement'.[25]

If there were women at the top levels of the ASTI, one might ask how prominent they were at other levels of the organisation. In considering that question, however, it is important that the broader context be borne in mind, and the fact was that in the decades after the state's establishment, women became less inclined to play public roles than they had during the revolutionary period. While Irish women acquired equality in voting rights, the view that 'a woman's place was in the home' was promoted, and it was a view that was buttressed constitutionally and legislatively. Nor was Ireland exceptional in this regard in the 1920s and 1930s, for in other western states also, women came under pressure to leave the public sphere, having been encouraged to fill positions vacated by men during the

First World War and to take part in political affairs by the egalitarian ideologies of some of the revolutionary movements that gained ground in the wake of that conflict.[26]

Broader social attitudes were reflected in trade unions and professional organisations. Even though Congress remained formally committed to equality of the sexes, it accepted measures like the 1934 Conditions of Employment Act which provided for the exclusion of women from certain industries. Its executive, moreover, was overwhelmingly male, with even unions representing strongly female occupations sending men to represent them, causing Louie Bennett to remark sardonically on the 'touching and flattering confidence in the male sex' that this showed. Over the decades, Bennett's Irish Women Workers' Union (IWWU) represented the female point of view – placing an emphasis on working conditions and safety, for example, while others focused on pay – and highlighted instances of discrimination against women. It should be noted, nevertheless, that the IWWU adapted itself somewhat to the prevailing ideology of state and Church, for it accepted the principle of the 'family wage' for male workers, so that married women need not work.[27]

Given this context, the level of female participation in ASTI affairs was relatively high, especially during the 1930s and 1940s.

After the disbanding of the female branches in 1920, women members participated in the ordinary branches. In an earlier chapter, the example was given of Kilmallock, where it was shown that women members successfully asserted themselves when the male officers ignored their views in setting the times of branch meetings. The Kilmallock women also acted as branch officers and as convention delegates, as did large numbers of their sisters in other branches. Taking attendance as a branch delegate at convention at ten-year intervals as one barometer of participation, the following is found: 43 per cent of those registering for the 1937 convention were women; in 1947, it was 40 per cent; in 1957, it was 31 per cent; in 1967, it was 34 per cent. The percentage was lower in later years, but it was not that low – especially if one takes into account that, until the mid-1960s, only 40–45 per cent of those eligible for ASTI membership were female, due to the preponderance of nuns in schools for girls.[28] In any case, branch delegates were not the only voices at conventions, for members of CEC, where the profile was rather more masculine, also participated.

So, how does one account for the relatively high level of representation of women at ASTI conventions in an era when men dominated public discourse? In all probability, it was related to the fact that women secondary teachers were mostly single, due to the accepted practice that they resigned on marriage, even if they were not subject to the marriage bar imposed on women primary teachers and on other public servants in the 1930s. The marriage bar, insofar as it affected primary teachers, was lifted in 1958, because of a shortage of qualified people. Belatedly, however, the informal marriage bar affecting secondary teachers had been made 'official' in the previous year when the ASTI agreed a revised contract for teachers in convent schools, which included the following:

> Upon the marriage of any lady lay teacher, it shall be lawful for her headmaster or headmistress to give her notice terminating her contract of employment at the expiration of the school term expiring next after the expiration of three months from the date of such notice of termination. Notice of termination served upon a lady teacher under the provisions of this agreement shall be final and conclusive ...[29]

Not all women secondary teachers worked in convent schools, of course, and even some of those who did worked after marriage, as will be shown below. Pressed by a convention decision, accordingly, the ASTI negotiated some improvements for its married women members in the early 1960s.[30] But the exclusion of married women from the public sector workforce had wide support in society at that time, as was indicated by the fact that delegates to the VTA conference in 1960 rejected a resolution seeking an end to the marriage bar in vocational schools. 'The home,' argued one of the women delegates who spoke against change, 'is the most important of all societies.'[31]

Throughout the period, then, ASTI women, being single and independent, and having fewer domestic responsibilities than their married contemporaries, were in a position to at least attend conventions and regular branch meetings. And, quite probably, the fact that the secondary system was so rigidly segregated would have facilitated their selection as branch delegates. There were, in addition, social reasons why it would have been desirable to have both sexes in attendance at convention.

And women had some success in placing their concerns before convention during what was a very difficult era for the female teacher. In 1932, for example, a resolution was passed which reduced the annual subscription for women (reflecting their lesser pay); in 1938, a resolution demanded action to ensure 'that initial salary and scale of increments for women teachers be the same as those paid to men teachers'; in 1946, 'the inadequate salaries paid, especially to women' in Catholic schools, was raised; in 1947, a resolution was discussed which stressed the need for a sick pay scheme for women teachers 'based on Christian principles'.[32] The evident recognition by the men of the plight of their colleagues in the convent schools rarely resulted in an effective response, however.

This, quite probably, was due to the fact that at the policy-implementing levels of the Association – CEC, standing committee, elected officer – women were under-represented. They may have won acceptance as delegates and even as speakers at convention, but societal norms, and the internal culture of the ASTI itself, made it harder for women to join the leading bodies. The following table shows, again at ten-year intervals, the percentage of women who served on the CEC and on the more important standing committee:

1936–37	CEC 15%	Standing Committee 25%
1946–47	CEC 24%	Standing Committee 10%
1956–57	CEC 20%	Standing Committee 17%
1966–67	CEC 17%	Standing Committee 15%

In line with the position in the trade union movement, then, women were much less likely to be found at the upper levels. Moreover, the general trend, as far as female participation was concerned, was in a downward direction.

Change during the 1970s: (i) A right to work?

From the mid-1960s, there was a marked rise in the percentage of women in the Association, reflecting a growth in the number of female lay teachers. By 1974, they were already a majority, comprising 52 per cent of lay secondary teachers and accounting for 55 per cent of ASTI membership. The shift in gender balance was due to a decline in female religious vocations at the moment of expansion in secondary education and, apparently, to the fact that the profession was proving less attractive to men than to women.[33]

At the same time, the great demand for qualified teachers, post-1967, had an effect on the prospects of women in the system who got married. Under the terms of their own marriage bar, which prevailed more or less until that point, women secondary teachers were required to resign within months of marrying, but they might be re-employed in a temporary capacity, as the account of Mayo teacher Kathleen Ryder reveals:

> In 1958 I resigned from teaching on marriage. I duly accepted marriage gratuity of £480 … On the 1st of February 1959, a teacher left Sacred Heart, Ballinrobe, quite suddenly and I was at hand to replace her the following day. On September 1st 1960, an appointed teacher failed to turn up in St Louis, Balla, and again I was close by and very available. 'If Balla can have you, you can come back to Ballinrobe,' the principal [in Ballinrobe] said, and the following September I returned in a very temporary capacity and on the usual £200 per annum paid by the convent employers. Marriage gratuity was now the bar to incremental salary paid by the Department of Education … With the characteristic compliance of a woman of the times, I adjusted to teaching subjects outside my brief during subbing periods. Although English and Latin were my specialist subjects, in one school I 'stood in' for a Commerce teacher. In another, I replaced a Geography teacher for a year … Another demand on my teaching resources came with the demise of Latin. I retrained in French (of course during holiday time and at my own expense).[34]

Married women teachers, then, who managed to continue working were deprived of entitlements to state salary and to pension. The pressure to resign on marriage came from the religious employers – copper-fastened by the 1958 contract of employment – but it was the state that denied incremental salary and pension rights to women who had claimed the marriage gratuity. On foot of a decision of its 1961 convention, the ASTI pursued a claim on behalf of married women teachers, and in January 1964, the state conceded that they might be granted rights to incremental salary and pensions, provided they refunded the marriage gratuity. Kathleen Ryder recalls: 'I gladly repaid my marriage gratuity with compound interest, and it never dawned on me that men received marriage gratuity also, and to wonder if they ever had occasion to return this *deontas*.'[35]

From the late 1960s, the expanding system needed more married women to stay on in employment, and in 1967 and 1968, one finds the ASTI negotiating a 'married lady teachers' contract with the religious employers. These negotiations, however, were subsumed into the larger discussions regarding a new contract for teachers appropriate to the conditions of the 1970s, which were treated in Chapter 7 above. The situation for married women remained unsatisfactory, therefore, as Susie Hall discovered in 1971:

> I started teaching in 1969 in a Roman Catholic convent school in the leafy suburbs of South County Dublin ... In the spring of 1971 I got engaged and was promptly sacked by my school ... I felt sure the ASTI would call on all the teachers in the country to down tools until I was reinstated. How wrong I was! I was informed by my branch officers that this was what women had to accept. Schools did not have to continue your employment if you got married, even if you had a permanent position. I couldn't believe it and determined that once I found another teaching position, I would do everything in my power to fight this injustice.[36]

In fact, Hall did secure a position in another school in 1971, and her fight against injustice in education continued throughout her career. In 2004–05, she served as ASTI president.

The continuing expansion of the system following the introduction of free education ensured that there was a demand for the services of young women teachers like Hall, but convention resolutions indicate that there was frustration during the first half of the 1970s regarding the contractual position.[37] In the meantime, however, the context was changed by the removal of the marriage bar in the public service in 1973.

The increasing number of married women in secondary teaching raised the question of maternity rights – in 1972, the Commission on the Status of Women (CSW) had recommended a minimum entitlement to twelve weeks' paid leave. In 1973, the ASTI and the JMB agreed that employers would pay half of the cost of a substitute teacher during maternity leave, with the teacher herself paying the other half. The two bodies, meanwhile, jointly petitioned the Department of Education to bear the full cost of maternity leave substitution. For its part, the department was reluctant to set a precedent which would have implications throughout the public service, but an agreement covering all teachers was reached at conciliation in March 1975. With effect from the beginning of 1975, the department agreed to bear half the cost of the maternity leave substitute, with the school paying the other half. Several years passed before the Maternity Protection of Employees Act (1981) came into effect.[38]

Change in the 1970s: (ii) Policy and social attitudes
The removal of the marriage bar and the introduction of paid maternity leave were two reforms of the period that facilitated working women. There would be others and, in this regard, the work of the Commission on the Status of Women was important. Established in 1970 by a Fianna Fáil government, on foot of a United Nations recommendation and under local pressure from an ad hoc committee of women's groups and from ICTU, the commission sought submissions from interested organisations and individuals.

In its submission to the CSW, the ASTI reiterated its policy that there be 'equal pay for equal and the same work', before outlining the position for secondary teachers as it stood in the early 1970s, and putting forward arguments for change. The secondary school salary, it was pointed out, had three elements: (i) an incremental salary paid by the state; (ii) allowances for qualification and functions, also paid by the state; (iii) a school salary. Rates for (ii) and (iii) were the same for men and women; only in the incremental salary was there a difference, between married men on the one hand and widows, single men, and women on the other. Justifying its demand for full equality, the ASTI pointed out that standards of entry, length of training, and registration requirements were the same for both sexes, and that the work undertaken – teaching the same courses and preparing students for the same examinations – was also exactly the same.[39] Perhaps because their case provided the most blatant example of discrimination, perhaps because it offered the best opportunity for redress, the situation of widows was given prominence in the submission. Teaching widowers, it was pointed out, remained on the higher 'married man' scale, while widows, who had equal family responsibilities and expenses, were placed on the lower.[40]

When it was published in 1972, according to Linda Connolly,

the CSW report 'directly challenged the main thrust of discriminatory legislation that had been progressively institutionalised after 1922'. Equal pay received attention, but so did other issues. Indeed, the impact of the CSW is illustrated by a 1976 estimate that thirty-six of its forty-nine recommendations had already been implemented. A Council for the Status of Women, formed in 1973, was diligent in keeping attention focused on the commission's recommendations.[41]

Equality in pay provided a significant incentive for married women to stay at work, though its introduction was a protracted process, beginning with the Anti-Discrimination (Pay) Act of 1974 but not completed for teachers until 1981. The taxation system, it has been pointed out, continued to discourage married women from working.[42]

The changing position from the early 1970s was, in large part, a response to the transformation in Irish society during the previous decade. The growing economy required a larger and more 'flexible' workforce. Revived feminism, and associated inchoate social movements, drew attention to a range of inequities, and it was easier for the political system to concede a modicum of workplace equality than to tackle issues like contraception and divorce. Most of all, there were obligations to bring Irish employment law into line with the directives of the European Economic Community, which Ireland joined in January 1973. But if laws changed, embedded conservative social attitudes remained, and there were recurring appeals to married women to relinquish their positions, especially when the job market tightened in the wake of the first oil crisis.[43] One such appeal, from Brother Vivian Cassells, leading educationist and guidance counsellor, caused something of a stir in education circles in 1976:

> There are still a high percentage of married women working for no valid reason, though they realise they are depriving many young people from starting their careers in the civil service, banking or teaching. These people are not willing to forego the added 'perks' that a second salary can provide, like the trip to the Costa Brava, that second car, or that well-stocked cocktail cabinet ...[44]

Teachers responded by pointing out that their family's 'second job' was necessary to pay for mortgage and other outgoings, and that in any case, married women were as entitled as others to seek fulfilment in a career. A forthright feminist response to the Marist brother went as follows: 'I am a married woman and a practising teacher; I will consider giving up my career, when he decides to give the "good example" and give up his.'[45]

If the tendency towards equality impacted on teachers' pay and contracts it also had implications for teaching itself. The CSW report identified differences in educational formation as a root cause of inequality, pointed to a disparity between the sexes in respect of science subjects and mathematics, and suggested that steps be taken to secure 'the future supply of female teachers capable of taking Leaving Certificate classes to honours mathematics level'. A degree of flexibility would be required in the brave new world:

> The school authorities have a responsibility to ensure that girls are encouraged to participate in these subjects to a greater extent, and they should try to ensure this by whatever means are available to them. For example, it may be possible to make arrangements for girls' schools to join in mathematics and science classes in neighbouring boys' schools ...[46]

During the 1970s, in any case, the system was becoming less rigidly segregated than formerly. Comprehensive and community schools were co-educational, and other smaller schools were moving in that direction, while single-sex schools had begun to employ teachers of the 'other' sex.

More generally, there was a growing recognition that the roots of much of workplace inequality were in the classroom. As one prominent equality advocate put it in 1979: 'A balanced curriculum should not limit options for any pupils, whether boys or girls.' That advocate was Sylvia Meehan, who in 1977 was appointed the first chairperson and chief executive of the Employment Equality Agency, a body established to oversee the operation of the Anti-Discrimination (Pay) Act 1974 and the Employment Equality Act of 1977. Prior to her appointment, Meehan was a well-known ASTI activist, and that background, arguably, would help to ensure that the educational dimension of inequality continued to be accorded due recognition.[47]

Promoting equality

The trade union movement itself became a strong advocate of equality in the workplace, and the debate on equal pay was one of those that impressed the first (all-male) ASTI delegation to an ICTU conference in 1969. ICTU itself had a Women's Advisory Committee, to which the ASTI began nominating women members, and in 1976 that committee adopted a Working Woman's Charter encompassing thirteen 'principles of equality', which indicated a commitment to women's rights that looked beyond conditions in the workplace itself to the social barriers to genuine equality.[48] However, the trade unions' commitment to equality was not reflected in their own structures. That men continued to dominate as before was shown by ICTU's *Report on Women in Trade Unions*, published in 1981. Only one woman, it was admitted, had been nominated to ICTU's own executive during the previous five years. The responsibility for this state of affairs lay squarely with the affiliated unions, and they were urged to examine their own structures, with a view to implementing corrective measures including the establishment of equality committees and positive discrimination in favour of women. To promote these tasks, ICTU inaugurated a Programme for Equality in 1982, which was followed by further programmes in 1987, 1993 and 1999.[49] An ICTU initiative that future ASTI president Catherine Fitzpatrick found to be particularly beneficial was its training programmes for women activists in the 1970s and early 1980s. She considers that these courses were useful in terms of personal development, but also in encouraging herself and others to think about putting themselves forward for positions on union executives.[50]

The scrutiny of trade unionism's own practices would find an echo within the ASTI. Throughout the 1970s and 1980s, representation of women on standing committee remained low – only twice between 1973 and 1990 were more than two women elected to that body – but it came to be recognised that it was necessary to correct this. Some progress was indicated by the election as president in 1979 of Mary McCarthy – the first woman to hold the post in twenty years – and, in relatively quick succession, of Margaret Walsh in 1982, Kathleen O'Sullivan in 1988 and Mary Dowling Maher in 1993.

The impression is of a genuine commitment to allow women to participate in ASTI affairs on equal terms with men, together with some puzzlement that they proved slow to come forward. As far as the association's representative on ICTU's Women's Advisory Committee in 1973 was concerned, 'women's lack of interest and lack of participation in trade union affairs is justly criticised – one good reason why we have not achieved equity.'[51] The connection with ICTU's committee at least ensured that women's issues found a place on annual convention agendas – even if they did not prompt much debate. In ASTI discussion generally from the 1970s, it has been observed that a more gender-neutral language was employed, indicating that a consciousness with regard to equality was gaining ground. Such consciousness was occasionally reflected in the content of conference resolutions, such as those commending co-education in 1975, criticising the delay in implementing equal pay in 1977, proposing improvements to the maternity leave scheme in 1978, and demanding the provision of crèche facilities in schools in 1982.[52]

Because other matters took precedence in the early and mid-1980s, there was little urgency about establishing the type of structures seen by ICTU as necessary for the promotion of equality, something that was a source of frustration to feminist-leaning activists in the ASTI. As a result of pressure from members who wished to develop a women's network within the Association, a course was organised in 1984 to provide training for female members of the CEC. Although this was a once-off initiative, there were some indications of the existence of an informal women's network in the programme of the 1987 convention when similarly worded resolutions on female participation were submitted by Galway, Desmond, Limerick South and Dublin North 1 branches. The resolution adopted – in the face of some opposition – committed the Association to investigate 'the imbalance that exists in the representation within the formal structures of ASTI and report back to Convention 1988'.[53] An equality sub-committee established on foot of the resolution conducted a survey of a section of the membership, male and female, with a view to ascertaining the impediments to participation. The most significant difference in the response of the sexes was in respect of their familiarity with trade union affairs. Of regular attendees at branch meetings who were unwilling to take an office of any sort, 51 per cent of the women, but only 32 per cent of the men cited 'lack of experience in trade union matters', while 44 per cent of women and 18 per cent of men cited 'lack of knowledge in trade union affairs and procedures'.[54]

A tangible outcome of the investigation was the establishment in 1988 of a fully fledged ASTI equality committee – five years after the TUI, and just one year after the INTO. The members of the committee – five women and three men, including the president and general secretary – had prepared a detailed draft policy document for the 1989 convention, with recommendations under three headings, as follows: Working conditions; Promotion of gender equality within the union; Equality within the curriculum and in the school. The equality committee was superseded by an equal opportunities committee with a rather wider remit, by decision of the 2000 convention.[55]

How equal was the ASTI?

In the period under review, there was a marked 'feminisation' of teaching, alongside a growing consciousness about the rights of women. Was there at the same time a feminisation of administration and decision-making in the ASTI? Or, rather, was there a sense in which the Eileen Flynn case might be regarded as metaphorical for the position of ASTI women generally – as an issue that attracted a lot of attention but brought no tangible benefit to those directly concerned? A study of women's role in the Association during the period 1974–94, carried out by Sheila Parsons, a long-standing activist who would later become president of the Association, and a report from a workshop held under the auspices of the Council of Teachers' Unions in 1992, both shed light on these questions.[56]

For the ASTI women participating in the Parsons study, the establishment of the equality committee in 1988 was an important step, because 'by continually highlighting the imbalance of participation', it forced members at all levels to consider 'ways of redressing the balance'. Other work of the committee that was identified as useful included its contribution to the formulation of an Association policy on sexual harassment, which was seen as important both for female members and for their female students in mixed schools. An understandable impatience at the rate of progress was also apparent however, as well as some scepticism about the depth of the commitment to equality of many males on the leading bodies.[57]

Within the ASTI, there was an acceptance of what has been characterised as a 'gender-neutral' approach to internal affairs, but results here were slow to manifest themselves as far as increasing female involvement in decision-making was concerned. Gender neutrality, it came to be recognised, did not take sufficient account of the social restraints on women's participation, and this led to demands for positive action, including specific training for would-be women activists. Similar circumstances pertained in other trade unions during the 1970s and 1980s, but there was a view within the ASTI at the end of the period that its own practices were enlightened by comparison with others.[58] If this was so – and there is some evidence that it was – the argument was made that much remained to be done and that, in any case, the Association's responsibility to get its own house in order was greater than that of other unions, given that its members were involved in educating others in equality principles. By way of comparison, it might be pointed out that the pattern of gender representation in the other teachers' unions in the state in the early 1990s was quite similar to that in the ASTI (allowing for differences in the membership profiles).[59]

When members of the three teachers' unions came together to discuss the matter in 1992, a number of barriers to women's participation were identified, and suggestions were made in respect of appropriate positive interventions. That the duties of branch officers and executive members were both onerous and ill-defined, and that branch meetings tended to be long and boring due to overly bureaucratic procedures and unnecessarily rigid agendas were seen as major factors in maintaining the imbalance in gender representation. The necessity for crèche facilities at meetings – *especially* equality meetings – was reiterated, while there was agreement on the need for reserved places for women on union executives. Technology was identified as potentially contributing to reducing the workload of office-holders, but it was also seen as important that the extent of duties and of the necessity for travel be re-evaluated. The imposition of limits on how long an individual might hold a particular office was also identified as a way of allowing new talent to develop. Training was seen to be necessary – both of women in political skills, and of male office-holders in 'sensitivity' – while meetings, it was felt, might be made more relevant to women if their agendas were to provide for more discussion on educational and equality issues, and their structures were to be made flexible enough to allow for the operation of discussion groups and workshops.[60]

At the time this discussion took place, 57 per cent of the members were female and the evidence of their participation in the ASTI's affairs was mixed. At local level, it was quite high; at national level, it remained low. Returns show that 55 per cent of branch secretaries and 46 per cent of school representatives were women, but only 28 per cent of branch chairpersons and 36 per cent of conference delegates. In 1992, only one member of standing committee was a woman.[61] Arguably, the difficulties that women faced in breaking through the 'glass ceiling' onto standing committee were compounded by the method of election, which tended to favour those with a macho temperament. Elections, for as long as they took place on a national basis at convention, were extremely hard fought. Participants during the 1980s and early 1990s recall that canvassing might continue through the night in the hotel bars and lobbies. It was a rough and ready form of democracy, and it was one in which women were at a disadvantage.[62] Catherine Fitzpatrick recalls how challenging the process was for her:

One of the things that struck me at the time was that it was all very much 'back-room boys' stuff – and it suited the 'boys' mainly. You'd have people campaigning late into the night. I'd have felt that I needed to go to be in bed at one o'clock or thereabouts, but the following day someone would say to you: 'Where were you at three o'clock when so-and-so was doing a deal?' The various branches would be doing their deals and trading block votes and so on. It was very difficult.[63]

When reforms agreed at a special convention of 1993 expanded standing committee somewhat and determined that elections take place on a regional basis, more women were successful. For example, ten women were elected onto the twenty-three-member body in 1997.[64]

Clearly, there was considerable progress with regard to female involvement and female representation, but the statistics on these matters represent only the tip of an iceberg of the Association's engagement. The reports of the equality committee show that it had a very extensive programme of work in promoting equality within the Association, as well as in relationships between teachers and their employers, and in the education system generally. In 1994, for example, its activity included the following: developing a model pol-

icy on gender equity for schools; formulating a response to the report
of the Second Commission on the Status of Women; examining the
implications of ICTU's *Mainstreaming Equality* document; making
recommendations as to responsibilities of equality officers at branch
level; co-organising equality seminars with the Department of Education; assessing the applicability to teachers of equality legislation;
and making submissions to an Economic and Social Research Institute (ESRI) project on co-education.[65]

The extent of the Association's engagement with state agencies in
addressing equality issues was an indication of considerable progress
by the 1990s, but constant vigilance remained necessary at other levels nonetheless, for teachers' personal lives continued to be subjected
to scrutiny. Speaking in 1997 in opposition to exemptions for religious employers contained in the Employment Equality Bill (echoing some points that Eileen Flynn had made earlier), the ASTI's
industrial relations officer Máire Mulcahy stated that, during the
previous decade, three secondary teachers had lost their jobs, and
three more had been threatened, because their private lives were
deemed to be 'in conflict with the religious ethos' of the schools in
which they worked. Mulcahy described these cases:

> Two of those who lost their jobs were temporary or part-time.
> One, a religion teacher from a large provincial town was living
> with her boyfriend, although this was not the reason given. The
> other, who was later reinstated after the union intervened, was
> living with his girlfriend in a small provincial town. Two teach-
> ers who were threatened were divorcees, again from small towns,
> living with second marriage partners, and in permanent jobs.
> Both were told that if they did not also apply for Catholic
> Church annulments, their jobs might be in danger. One was told
> by her principal that she should at least be seen to be applying for
> an annulment, even if she did not intend to go through with it.[66]

The problem was not regarded as 'widespread' in 1997 – more
than a decade after the Eileen Flynn case – but occasional threats
like those described would have had a wider impact. Even after the
introduction of divorce in Ireland, evidently, many teachers were
obliged to be secretive about their private lives.

Part Three

10

'As if education was a commodity'
Secondary Teachers in the 'Celtic Tiger' era

For the greater part of a week each year, the Irish public joins a conversation about education, the cue being the Easter-time gatherings of teachers' organisations. The ASTI convention and its counterparts, which originated as vacation-time opportunities for teachers' representatives to confer with one another, were modest affairs for many years, but they have developed since the 1960s into great showcase events, attended by ministers for education, by representatives of the major media, by invited guests from dozens of organisations, as well as by hundreds of delegates. There were 437 delegates, for example, at the 1993 ASTI convention.[1]

That these events receive such extensive press coverage may be partly explained by the fact that several ordinarily newsworthy institutions are not in session during Easter. The main reason for the attention, however, is the intrinsic importance of the meetings themselves, both as occasions for debates on educational policies and philosophies and for the airing of occupational grievances. But there has not always been unanimity in the teachers' unions in respect of what constitutes a proper balance between professional and trade union concerns, as the following pithy analogy drawn by one delegate at a 1980s ASTI convention indicates: 'Do you think that, when miners have their conference, they talk about coal?'[2]

Convention organisers are conscious of public relations when arranging agendas and schedules, but press coverage is difficult to manage and, almost invariably, the grievances capture the bigger headlines. These relate to pay and conditions, broadly speaking, and in essence they are not very different to those raised at other union gatherings. However, because the teachers' deliberations receive more

attention than, for example, those of building workers or bank officials – and perhaps also because everyone has some experience of the
school system – their grievances loom larger in the public consciousness and are subjected to more critical scrutiny on radio
phone-ins and in the newspapers. A characteristic reaction came in
1991 from the writer Nuala O'Faolain:

> Every year … the news of what they're talking about filters
> through to me. And I start muttering to myself. Don't they ever
> stop whingeing, I ask myself. Does nothing ever satisfy them?
> Do they go collectively mad when they get together at these con-
> ferences even though they're individually sane?[3]

The cause of the writer's irritation was a discussion about stress
among teachers, an issue that had been highlighted at convention
by former ASTI president Senator Joe Costello, who had advocated
a facility for early retirement on full pension as a solution. Were not
other occupations more stressful than teaching, protested O'Faolain.
And did teachers not have more control over their working days than
most, did they not have longer holidays to recover from stress, did
they not have more powerful unions to protect them? Being somewhat more reflective than the typical convention-time critic of teachers, however, O'Faolain proceeded to consider the demands that had
been raised in the course of the week. Concluding that these were
generally reasonable, she speculated about why her initial reactions
against teachers, and those of many others also, had been 'so venge-
ful' and 'exaggerated'.[4]

If much of the public reaction around convention time is vis-
ceral, the heightened awareness of educational issues around Easter
offers an opportunity for others to join the debate in a strategic way.
During the convention period of 1993, for example, the business
organisation, IBEC, launched its educational policy, which, among
other changes, sought a lengthening of the post-primary school year,
an end to compulsory Irish, and the development of a more positive
attitude towards 'enterprise' throughout the curriculum. Anticipat-
ing a negative reaction, the spokesperson criticised 'vested interests'
– he meant the teachers' unions – which, he said, had in the past
wilfully misrepresented IBEC as a body that 'wanted the schools to
produce robots trained only for work'.[5]

IBEC did not address itself in 1993 to the problem of stress among teachers, a problem that was widely and deeply felt, as research commissioned by the Council of Teachers' Unions had established.[6] It was a recurring issue at ASTI conventions of the 1990s, and it was an issue that was mentioned by a number of teachers who were interviewed for the purpose of providing a 'human interest' dimension to press coverage of conventions. An anonymous Geography teacher with twenty-eight years' service spoke to *The Irish Times* in 1995 about the pressures of his job, and about why he wished to be allowed to retire at the end of thirty years, like 'the guards, the prison officers, the fire officers, the army'. Disagreeing with the way the ASTI presented the solution, he urged that 'we should stop calling what we want an early retirement scheme, and start calling it a proper retirement scheme'.[7] The causes of his own periodic 'headaches and stress' he outlined as follows:

> The stresses are different from any other job. At 9 o'clock each morning, teachers must be in tip-top shape – to meet as many as 30 or more pupils who, frequently, will make life as difficult as possible. If you are not on top and motivating pupils they will lose interest and this gradually gives rise to disciplinary problems. You have to entertain them (although I am reluctant to use that word because I don't think teaching should be about entertaining). To maintain interest, class after class, is very demanding ... We have pupils with special needs, but we don't have the services to meet them – that can cause disciplinary problems. Alcohol and drug abuse are also increasing. The vast majority of sixteen-year-olds take a drink. Teachers may have to deal with pupils with hangovers ... The points race is another pressure.[8]

Another who took an opportunity to talk about his work was Gerry Murphy, a teacher of Latin and Music at Gonzaga College, a fee-paying Jesuit school that was rather different to the one employing the Geography teacher quoted above. While insisting that Gonzaga was not as exclusive a place as it was perceived to be, Murphy did acknowledge that most students there were high performers, due to the school's admissions procedure, there being an entrance exam, as well as interviews with prospective pupils and their parents.

With twenty years' service, Murphy was not yet longing for

retirement. But while he enjoyed teaching, he feared growing stale, admitting that 'if he got the chance to do something else' he would. The points race, he suggested, was a key source of pressure and stress, on teachers and on the school itself, with some parents withdrawing their sons so as to send them to grind schools and others advocating a strictly academic emphasis which would have sacrificed the social outreach programme and certain other extra-curricular pursuits. In general, he felt that teaching was becoming more difficult, both because more individual students were troubled as a result of familial problems like marital breakdown and because young people in general were less receptive due to conditioning by the changing media: 'You have to compete with television, but you cannot teach in sound-bites.'[9] For Murphy, the task of teaching was as demanding as acting, something that he felt was not appreciated by people outside his profession:

> It is part of you but not all of you ... You cannot bring your personal problems into the classroom and, like an actor, you must show a certain amount of detachment. But when you finish teaching for the day, you must leave and say 'that's it', and be someone else.[10]

These snatches of Easter-time discussions from the early 1990s, prompted by, but not part of, official deliberations of the ASTI, the TUI and the INTO, convey something of the temper of the times. They show teachers feeling unappreciated and under strain from the increasing demands placed upon them; they show influential business interests trying to cast teachers as inflexible defenders of outmoded methods and theories; they show a public in part, at least, disinclined to sympathise with the teachers' predicament. In the following sections of this chapter, there will be an examination of the changing economic, ideological and social contexts during that decade in which the so-called 'Celtic Tiger' entered public consciousness, followed by an assessment of how changes impacted on teachers.

Leap-frogging 'to a post-industrial high-tech economy'
By the time the 'Celtic Tiger' phenomenon acquired its name in 1994, Ireland's economic recovery was already underway, even

if those who had endured the 1980s were sceptical of the likely resilience of the good times. And there were grounds for caution, for, despite high growth in GNP in several of the years between 1987 and 1993, it was not until 1994 that the period of consistently high growth began. Statistics demonstrate the extent of the shift that occurred between 1987 and 2000: unemployment fell from 17 per cent to 4 per cent; the standard of living rose from two-thirds of the EU average to surpassing that average; Ireland went from being the only EU state where emigration exceeded immigration to being the state with the second highest level of immigration. Given that a remarkable transformation took place, there has been much discussion about 'how a predominantly pre-industrial economy leap-frogged to a post-industrial high-tech economy so abruptly.'[11] There is agreement that the leap occurred due to the coincidence of a number of factors.

Near the top of any list of explanations for the 'Celtic Tiger' must be placed the education system and its teachers. Since the 1960s, the state had been committed to advancing education, but the end result was dependent on the proficiency and commitment of the men and women at the chalk-face.[12] That Irish teachers were effective, and that the quality of their accumulated efforts greatly contributed to the increase in prosperity of the 1990s, is indicated by the following observation from the Canadian economist Pierre Fortin:

> Irish education policy has been to encourage free secondary and low-cost higher education. Interacting with a late baby boom, this policy has made available a plentiful supply of well-educated young workers. The performance of Irish pupils in international comparisons of proficiency in mathematics and science is respectable and close to that of Canadian pupils. A recent United Nations survey of literacy and numeracy indicates that young Irish score significantly above average ... These developments have been highly instrumental in making Irish domestic firms more productive and in attracting multinational corporations to Ireland.[13]

The ASTI was alert to the contribution made by its members, and in a 1996 feature in *ASTIR* iar-thaoiseach Garret Fitzgerald and Dave Young of Hewlett-Packard were quoted in this regard. According to Fitzgerald, a crucial factor in the recent Irish success was 'our non-specialised educational system, and not just the system it-self, but above all the high motivation and commitment of parents, pupils, and teachers alike'. For Young, the 'young, highly-educated workforce' had been a strong inducement for his firm to locate in Ire-land, but he expected that the arrival of Intel and other high-tech-nology firms would lead to a shortage of qualified workers. He was concerned in particular that the system was not producing 'a suffi-cient number of women who are qualified as engineers and techni-cians'.[14] The two could agree on the important role of the education system, even if they differed on whether it was preferable that it be 'non-specialised' or technological.

An education-related factor that facilitated the boom was the growth in labour productivity: averaging 3.3 per cent per annum in the period 1976–2000, it was surpassed only by South Korea. Less tangibly, a case might be made for the impact of the attested increase in Irish cultural confidence.[15]

There were qualified workers available therefore when the tide turned and circumstances became favourable; when a telecommu-nications revolution made Ireland's insular location less disadvanta-geous than it had been; when EU structural and cohesion funds could be applied to the upgrading of the telecommunications net-works; when the imminence of the single market pressed US firms wishing to trade in the EU to locate in a member state; when the Northern Ireland peace process signalled the ending of serious po-litical discord on the island. And besides the propitious educational and logistical factors, the fact that Ireland's inhabitants spoke Eng-lish made it attractive to US investors. That some of these investors identified with an Irish diaspora was also an advantage.

Nonetheless, it was remarkable that over a third of US investment in the EU in 1992–96 came to Ireland, given that she accounted for only 2 per cent of the EU population. For this, a substantial share of the credit has been accorded to Irish industrial policy.

Incentives had long been offered to encourage firms to locate in Ireland, including low taxation, grant aid, and easy repatriation of profits. In the 1980s, efforts were specifically directed at attracting information technology (IT) and pharmaceutical enterprises, which was prescient – or lucky – for these proved to be the most consis-tently profitable sectors through the 1990s. These were sectors also for which access to educated workers was a powerful incentive influencing their location.

Several writers cite other domestic factors as having contributed to prosperity in the 1990s. One was a budgetary policy that focused from 1987 on tackling the state's indebtedness by means of very painful cuts in public spending.[16] Another was the deepening of 'social partnership', beginning with the 1987 Programme for National Recovery (approved in an ASTI ballot by a margin of two to one, on a 15 per cent turnout), resulting in modest wage settlements and relatively few working days lost due to strikes.[17] To compensate workers for 'pay discipline', as it came to be called, there was a progressive reduction in income taxation, with the public finances being replenished by revenue from the thriving property sector. (In the longer term this fundamental adjustment to the taxation system would have serious adverse consequences.) For the trade union negotiators, 'social partnership' remained a mechanism through which their movement might retain political influence in a difficult economic and ideological environment. Seeing it as a consensual 'European' and social democratic approach to collective bargaining, in contradistinction to the more confrontational 'British' model, they were willing to progressively extend the scope of 'partnership' through successive agreements. Moreover, the national 'social partnership' agreements became a vehicle for achieving the sort of consensus at workplace level that was being advocated by human resource management theorists. This was formalised in workplace partnership structures established under the terms of the Partnership 2000 agreement of 1997–99.[18]

While Ireland seemed to ride on the crest of an economic wave, it was subject also to the influence of broader ideological trends. Being 'the gateway to Europe … for corporate America', as one tánaiste put it, was challenging, for it was not always easy to reconcile the role of 'good European' with that of recruiter of US corporations.[19] At the wider social policy level, there was the 'Boston or Berlin' dichotomy highlighted by the same tánaiste, Mary Harney, in an address to the American Bar Association in 2000. For the Progressive Democrats leader, Ireland was 'spiritually' more in tune with the non-interventionist social model she associated with America than (social partnership notwithstanding) with the social solidarity model that had been espoused by the European Community. Unlike many other Europeans, she told the lawyers, the Irish believed in 'the incentive power of low taxation', in 'economic liberalisation', and in 'essential regulation but not over-regulation'.[20] If not all of Harney's ministerial colleagues would have publicly agreed with her, the fact was that while Ireland was being utilised as a 'gateway' by corporate America, corporate values became more and more embedded in the political culture and throughout civil society.

Trans-national corporations were advocates of a set of policies associated with 'Chicago school' economists that would be labelled 'neoliberal'. In the 1990s, having been championed for more than a decade by Washington and by international trades bodies in which it had influence, these policies won wide acceptance. Accordingly, deregulation, the removal of restrictions on the movement of capital, the privatisation of publicly owned enterprises and utilities, and the marginalisation of trade unions came to be regarded in influential quarters as key public policy goals. Bodies representing business interests were active advocates of the new order, promoting scepticism about the public sector and seeking to impose an 'enterprise culture' on its workers.[21] IBEC, quoted earlier, was one of the key organisations articulating such views in Ireland. The extent to which Irish governments adapted to neoliberalism was illustrated by the fact that, by one measure, Ireland's was one of the most open or 'globalised' economies in the world by the end of the 1990s. Ireland was also near the top of the 'Worldwide Index of Economic Freedom' compiled by the *Wall Street Journal* and the neoliberal Heritage Foundation.[22]

Even as job prospects improved and average living standards increased, the atmosphere generally became much less hospitable for trade unions than it had been in the 1980s.[23]

Declining influence of religious

In circumstances where the economy, the nature of employment and modes of communication were being transformed, it was to be expected that social mores would also change, and indeed the number of extra-marital births and the rate of marriage breakdown continued to rise throughout the decade. Irish citizens accepted that changed conditions necessitated changes in family law, and on the narrowest of margins, they voted to allow divorce in 1995, having rejected a similar proposition on a margin of 63 per cent to 37 per cent as recently as 1986. In part, this reflected the loss of influence of the Catholic Church, a process under way for several decades, and which would have significance for education. Given the other changes that were taking place, it might have been anticipated that the gradual ebbing of Church influence would have continued, but this was not what happened. Instead it seemed to evaporate very quickly as a result of a series of scandalous revelations, beginning with the flight of Bishop Casey in May 1992, and continuing with the dissemination of details of the abuse of children in Church-run institutions.[24]

Even before the Casey episode, there were already lay principals in many Catholic secondary schools, most of them members of the ASTI. In 1988, there were forty lay principals in religious-run schools, and the pace quickened after that. During 1991–92, for example, there were twenty-one such appointments. Only a decade earlier, prominent religious had been apprehensive about handing over management of their schools to men and women who were not subject to religious discipline, but the decline in their own numbers left them with little choice.[25] The changeover, when it occurred therefore, was not as orderly as many would have wished.

At a special ASTI meeting for lay principals in 1990, there were complaints about a 'lack of standardisation' in the contracts of lay principals, and about the fact that some principals had not formally agreed to a contract of any sort. Some of those attending expressed the view that their allowances were inadequate, while others were aggrieved that there was no provision for principals to return to classroom teaching.[26]

A largely unanticipated consequence of change was a decline in the number of women in positions of authority in post-primary education, for, in a majority of instances, male teachers succeeded nuns as principals in convent schools.[27]

In handing over to lay principals, the religious sought to maintain their influence, establishing trusteeships, and ensuring that appointees were sympathetic towards their beliefs and their traditions.[28] According to one researcher, formerly prominent in the ASTI:

> Candidates for such posts are furnished with pamphlets, which outline the official thinking of the order about the ethos or, to use a recent phrase, the 'charism' of the founder. During these interviews, which typically last for about one hour, the candidates

257

are questioned searchingly about the content of these publications ... About one third of the typical interview for principal is concerned with the 'nuts and bolts' of running a school.[29]

Post-primary education in the 1990s

The creation of educational structures appropriate to the changed circumstances was the focus of considerable discussion during the 1990s, much of it prompted by the consultative Green Paper in 1992, the National Education Convention in 1993, and the White Paper in 1995. The ASTI participated in the convention, and published its considered responses to both of the government documents.[30]

The long-awaited Green Paper appeared during the short term as minister for education of Séamus Brennan, a Fianna Fáil politician with a background in accountancy who represented Dublin South. In educational circles, there was disappointment at the document's espousal of a narrowly technocratic and business-driven agenda. During the ensuing Dáil debate, Garret Fitzgerald described as 'misconceived and dangerous' the emphasis it placed on enterprise and technology, arguing that 'it was found that people trained to do specific tasks were unable to convert themselves to other tasks when their work environment changed'. For Michael D. Higgins, it was inexcusable that no account was taken of the various reports on arts and education, and that there was no reference to 'ecological responsibility, interdependency, aid, trade, debt, the contribution of feminist theory ... the new work on equality'.[31]

The ASTI's detailed response to the Green Paper, the result of extensive consultations within the Association, echoed these criticisms but its greatest emphasis was on the necessity for increased investment in education. Reflecting concerns about the extent of stress in the profession, it made the case for a reduction in teachers' workload, which was achievable, it pointed out, by means of a progressive reduction in class sizes. Signalling apprehension over suggested reforms in the conduct of state examinations (and of the Junior Certificate in particular), it argued against requiring class teachers to undertake assessments of their own students.[32]

The White Paper of 1995 was more positively received. Published during the tenure of Niamh Bhreathnach, a remedial teacher representing Dún Laoghaire and the first ever Labour Party minister for education, it was seen to have taken account of some of the criticisms of the 1992 document made at the education convention and elsewhere. It was also the case that familiarity had rendered more palatable some of the novel proposals that had caused concern in 1992. For *The Irish Times*, the White Paper was the fulfilment of a liberal dream:

> The publication of the first White Paper from a Labour Minister for Education nudges Ireland into the mainstream of liberal pluralistic education systems found elsewhere and heralds the end of a long era of Catholic education in this country.[33]

Plainly, the case was somewhat overstated here, and the reaction of Catholic agencies was generally positive, as was that of bodies representing parents, who were pleased about several of the promised changes: that the establishment of boards of management was to be made mandatory in all schools receiving state funding, that there was to be parental representation on all of these boards, that parents would have the right to view school records on their children, that there was to be greater subject choice at primary and second level, that there was to be more in-service training of teachers, and that the school-leaving age was to be raised to sixteen.[34]

In that it focused on the need for increased investment, the ASTI's response to the White Paper was similar to its earlier response to the Green Paper. Speaking at convention in 1992, president Willie Ruane had argued: 'The fundamental question in the debate on the Green Paper was whether the ensuing changes would result in the schools being able to deliver a better service. Devolution of responsibility without authority and resources will not be the answer.' Three years later, general secretary Charlie Lennon struck a similar chord, when he suggested that the White Paper was missing a chapter: 'That chapter is the chapter on implementation which should outline the programme of additional investment necessary to implement many of the proposals.'[35]

As teachers anticipated the fresh challenges signalled in the White Paper, they might well have reflected on the many challenges that they had already faced.

In an earlier chapter, it was suggested that, while remuneration and job security had improved, many characteristics of the ASTI member's work did not alter very much during the first fifty years of the Association's existence. The typical lay secondary teacher was a member of a very small profession who taught several subjects from a rather narrow academic range to students of his or her own sex who came, by and large, from relatively comfortable backgrounds; he or she was answerable to a religious principal/manager and could not realistically aspire to a status other than that of 'assistant teacher'. By the early 1990s, things were quite different. Indeed, it was hardly possibly at the later date to talk about a 'typical teacher', and the overlap with the vocational sector – which was entirely distinct in the early 1960s – was so extensive that one might conclude that a new profession, that of post-primary teacher, had been created. It was an almost entirely unionised profession with more than 20,000 members in 1993 – 13,000 of whom were members of the ASTI, with almost all of the remainder being members of the TUI. This represented a five-fold increase in thirty years in the combined number of full-time lay secondary and vocational teachers.

If secondary and vocational education were fusing in some respects, the economic and ideological environment of the 'Celtic Tiger' era supported the challenge from a growing 'grind school' sector. Fee-paying and narrowly focused on examination performance, 'institutes' and 'colleges' in this sector prepared up to 4,000 students for the Leaving Certificate by the mid-1990s. There was advice from the ASTI to parents to be wary of 'spurious fifth form colleges', and a speech from President Mary Dowling Maher in which she was very critical of the nature of their appeal: 'These institutions exploit the fears of parents about their children's future; they promise them achievement ... which their children would be equally capable of attaining in secondary school.' The Association was reported in 1994 to have investigated a claim that one of its members was teaching in such a school and to have secured a commitment from the individual concerned to relinquish the part-time position.[36] In an *Irish Times* interview in 1997, the ASTI's deputy general secretary, John White, was critical of the 'offensive Darwinian hierarchy of results' that was being promoted by grind schools' publicity material which focused on the high Leaving Certificate points of individuals. With regard to the ASTI's philosophy, he said: 'We take the proper and human view that we should cherish all of our pupils and that we should not exploit the results of particular pupils.'[37]

The ASTI member in the 1990s was to be found working along-side colleagues of both sexes, some of them perhaps members of the TUI, reporting to a lay principal who might also be an ASTI member and, to an increasing extent, teaching in a co-educational context. Domestic Science teachers, whose subject had evolved into Home Economics, had boys as well as girls in their classes, something that would have been almost inconceivable in the 1960s, while Latin and Classical Greek, mainstream subjects then, survived only in isolated redoubts thirty years later. There were new programmes, including the Junior Certificate which replaced the Intermediate Certificate and the Day Group Certificate in 1992, and transition year, piloted since 1974, which was introduced into the mainstream, following ASTI pressure, in 1994. There were new subjects, including Civic, Social, and Political Education which was introduced in the junior cycle as an examination subject in 1996.[38] There were new functions in the schools, including those of guidance counsellor, remedial teacher, and transition year co-ordinator, and some opportunities outside of the traditional classroom – thirty post-primary teachers were seconded by the Department of Education to train their colleagues in Relationships and Sexuality Education in 1996.[39]

That the ASTI was alert to the many new challenges facing its members is indicated by the unprecedented number and the sheer variety of its publications during the 1990s. These included handbooks on gender equity, sexual harassment and school discipline, as well as on transition year and on technology in the Junior Certificate. In 1996, in a significant initiative, the Association launched a new journal entitled *Issues in Education*.[40]

Another significant change that had occurred was the abolition of corporal punishment in 1982. The ASTI had accepted a resolution from the Cork branch in 1978, condemning 'the use of any form of corporal punishment' in schools, and the cane was only rarely used in most schools thereafter. Nonetheless, its final decommissioning prompted discussion about discipline in schools, which was generally felt to be in decline.[41]

Like many of the changes in teachers' working conditions, the ending of corporal punishment was a reflection of changing social mores – of a broadening of conceptions of democratic rights, of a greater acceptance of equality principles. But if schools were becoming less hierarchical as a result, there remained an expectation that teachers should maintain discipline of a traditional kind over their classes, with sometimes unfortunate results, as one veteran of the classroom told a journalist in 1997:

> Some teachers are terrified to let down their guard, and be themselves. They maintain a stiff upper lip and refuse to allow jokes in class, believing that if they do, they will lose control … If you can't laugh at a trick that's played on you, it can get out of hand and sour relationships. An innocent joke can end up as a major incident.[42]

There is evidence, moreover, that the attitude of students to classroom management, and discipline generally, was changing. That the school students of the 1990s had been raised according to more liberal principles, in the main, than preceding cohorts was undoubtedly relevant in this regard, but it has been argued that this was not the only factor responsible. A study by Kathleen Lynch and Ann Lodge established that a substantial minority of second-level students found paid employment during the boom – of their representative sample of second-level students at the turn of the millennium, 41 per cent had part-time jobs.[43] The authors argue that young people's sense of autonomy and independence was affected by their experience as workers, and that this was reflected in their expectations of how they should be treated at school. The respondents were resentful generally of the perceived absence of democracy in schools, and sceptical of those consultation mechanisms which they saw to be staff-dominated. Girls in particular resented intrusions in their privacy and at what they felt was a lack of proper confidentiality in schools, the perception being that any information disclosed to a teacher about family background or personal difficulties was liable to be discussed with teaching colleagues. The view that students' dignity as human beings was not sufficiently respected was articulated forcefully by one fifth-year student:

> In my opinion, if you're not treated like a child, you won't act like a child. Take for example teachers who make us stand up when they come into the class … I mean … who do they think they are! We're seniors and we don't need to be treated as if we are in baby infants. The teacher says it is to get our attention, but it is more about intimidation than anything else … I think a

school should be a more democratic place where we have a say in what is done. Treat us like adults![44]

Conflicting pressures from students and school authorities contributed to the stress felt by many teachers, and the demand for an early retirement scheme, which had been identified as a partial answer to the problem, remained a priority. During 1994, a joint position on the issue was agreed by the ASTI, INTO and TUI. Progress thereafter, however, was slow for a number of reasons – including a change of government and a delay in the appointment of a new public service arbitrator – and this was a source of frustration. Eventually, it was determined that industrial action was necessary if progress was to be achieved, with the result that the ASTI and INTO embarked on a series of 'days of action', beginning on 23 May 1995. For its part, the TUI postponed action until autumn.[45] To begin industrial action just a week before the post-primary school holidays was to offer a hostage to fortune, and, predictably, there was some adverse reaction. Kevin Myers of *The Irish Times* – a strong advocate of neoliberal orthodoxies and a habitual detractor of public servants – took the opportunity to mock: 'For the shocking truth remains, teachers on holiday are unable to make much industrial impact. Can you imagine how powerless they feel? … Their working day is over when others might only be getting into the rhythm of a strike.'[46] Myers' derision notwithstanding, militancy did concentrate minds, and negotiations resumed in mid-September. Again discussions were rather protracted, but an early retirement scheme was eventually agreed, which came into effect at the end of July 1996. There were a number of restrictions, among them the condition that no more than 300 teachers in total, across all the sectors, might avail of the scheme in any one year.

A potential mechanism for the relief of the stress of teaching, short of resignation or retirement, came in the form of a job-sharing scheme, which was introduced on an experimental basis in 1993, and was made permanent three years later.[47]

Provisions for job sharing and for early retirement represented important improvements in conditions, but salary remained the key measurement of the value that society accorded their work as far as most teachers were concerned. By way of assessing their relative success in this regard, comparisons were made in previous chapters between secondary teachers and other groups of public servants. A similar comparison for the 1990s would be less meaningful, not least because of the introduction of the common basic scale in teaching. The matter of relativity with groups like gardaí and nurses received attention for a specific reason in the late 1990s, but increasingly, during the Celtic Tiger era, it was with groups outside the public service that teachers made comparisons – for example, with workers in IT and finance. Statistics from 1999 showed that starting salaries in teaching compared well with those in IT, but that a gap opened up within a few years. After five years' service, an average teacher's salary would have been less than £20,000, while a software engineer would have expected more than £30,000. After five years, a database designer would have been on a higher salary than the principal of a middle-sized secondary school.[48] Other statistics from the period show that Irish teachers were well paid in comparison with their colleagues in other countries. Figures presented by the ESRI showed that starting salaries for Irish secondary teachers were the fifth highest in the advanced OECD countries, that they were third highest for teachers with fifteen years' service, and that they were sixth highest for those on the maximum.[49]

If there was satisfaction for teachers in discovering that they were reasonably well paid by international standards, it was tempered by awareness that such comparisons do not take account of differences in cost-of-living. After all, it was not with their German colleagues that Irish teachers were competing when it came to buying a home, but with Irish people employed in sectors like IT and finance. Indeed, the spiralling property prices of these years, which kept young teachers out of the housing market altogether or obliged them to commute great distances, contributed to the dissatisfaction that emerged over pay.

Another source of dissatisfaction, and of demoralisation, was the growing ascendancy of a flatly functionalist view of the educational process and of educational systems, under the influence of the philosophy of 'new public management'.[50]

An educational 'product'?

In a well-received address at the 1995 ASTI convention in Ennis, historian Gearóid Ó Tuathaigh located the challenges faced by teachers in the broader societal context. The contemporary emphasis on public accountability was perfectly legitimate, he acknowledged, but it was important that the approach be appropriate:

> The critical question for us is how these ideas of accountability and systems management are discussed, determined and implemented in the educational sphere. The dominant language of systems in recent times has drawn its models and metaphors from engineering, financial control and accountancy. You know them yourselves –'input-output models', 'quality assurance and quality control', ... 'bottom-line evaluation' ... More generally, and I regret to say not only among the downmarket tabloids but also among senior academic commentators, we hear discussion of what an excellent 'educational product' we have in Ireland ... – as if education were a commodity to be produced to standardised size and form. I know from my conversations with teachers at every level that they are uneasy at the disproportionate emphasis on education as a 'product'.[51]

And the perception of education as a 'product' had very real implications for the work of teachers. There would be a greater emphasis in quantitative measurement and less weight accorded to professional judgement. In devising benchmarks and performance criteria, Professor Ó Tuathaigh urged, it was important not to lose sight of the nature of teaching itself:

> Teaching is not an action but a transaction, not an outcome but a process, not a performance but an emotional and intellectual connection between teacher and learner. It cannot be assessed by any single dimension of quality; nor can it be assessed at all without deep knowledge of its setting, styles and the orientations of the teachers ...[52]

11

'Singing from different hymn sheets'
The pay battle of the new millennium

On 5 December 2000, the fifteenth anniversary of the great
Teachers United demonstration, 12,000 ASTI members attended a pay rally outside Leinster House.[1] In a newspaper article
that morning, under the heading 'Bad old days when teachers called
the shots', Gemma Hussey compared the challenge facing education
minister Michael Woods with the one that she had faced in 1985:

> In the year 2000 the three teaching unions are singing from dif-
> ferent hymn sheets, but in 1985 and 1986 ... a solid united front
> was designed to strike fear into any minister's heart ... The peo-
> ple are different: Joe O'Toole succeeded Gerry Quigley as head
> of the INTO and is now heading into leadership of ICTU – and
> wants peace. That other skilful teachers' leader, Kieran Mulvey,
> who was the *bête noire* of governments, is now the head of the
> Labour Relations Commission. Today, the Programme for Pros-
> perity and Fairness has followed a succession of such general
> agreements between the social partners – and the ASTI find
> themselves isolated outside it ... In the Dáil, the opposition,
> while criticising the present government on aspects of their han-
> dling of the dispute, is not advocating that the ASTI should be
> given its demands.[2]

Hussey seemed excessively pleased at the constellation of forces
ranged against the ASTI on this occasion, but her principal point
was irrefutable. The teachers were not united on 5 December 2000
– something that was clearly demonstrated when INTO leader Sen-

ator Joe O'Toole stepped out of Seanad Éireann to listen to the speeches, only to be hissed by people in the crowd.[3] Arguably then, the appropriate comparison in 2000 was not with 1985–86, but with 1969–71, when the ASTI position had been actively opposed by other teachers' unions, and when an important section of the Association itself had been less than half-hearted about the strategy that was being pursued. But even that judgement must be tentative, because the events concerned occurred so recently. If the twentieth-century Chinese revolutionary, Zhou Enlai, could respond to a question about the impact of the French Revolution by saying, 'It is too early to tell', how precarious must be any historical evaluation of events of the past few years, especially when their substance and meaning are contested? The effort must be made, however, even if few firm conclusions may be drawn.

Questioning social partnership and leaving ICTU

The origins of the dispute may be traced to provisions of social partnership agreements of the 1990s, so the early part of the following account will necessarily be sprinkled with acronyms. Relevant agreements were the Programme for Economic and Social Progress (PESP) of 1991–93, the Programme for Competitiveness and Work (PCW) of 1994–97, Partnership 2000 of 1997–99, and the Programme for Prosperity and Fairness (PPF) of 2000–02.[4] Because it had not proven possible before that agreement's expiry date to agree on the implementation for teachers of a 3 per cent 'local bargaining' clause in PESP, this residual business was subsumed into the negotiations on its successor. Under the terms of the PCW, the increase was conditional on unspecified 'restructuring', but a long-awaited initial offer was rejected in an ASTI ballot in 1996 by a margin of 60 per cent to 40 per cent. A revised version worth 5.8 per cent was accepted in the spring of 1997 by a margin of 63 per cent to 37 per cent.[5]

Throughout these years, the Association's representatives were conscious of a degree of frustration among the membership about the low level of pay increases that were negotiable under partnership, and they tried to make progress in the alleviation of other grievances.[6] In this regard, the department conceded in 1997 the long-standing claim of teachers that they be paid fortnightly rather than monthly. During 1997 also, there were significant concessions on the important – and related – issues of early retirement and pensions: under a 'buy back scheme', those who had made insufficient superannuation contributions for whatever reason were enabled to purchase teaching service for pension purposes at a greatly discounted rate; under an early retirement scheme it became possible for teachers with thirty-three years' service to retire at fifty-five. While these improvements were eagerly welcomed by many teachers, some of those involved in the negotiations that secured them felt that their value was not fully appreciated throughout the Association.[7] Indeed, not alone were the improvements not appreciated, but there was considerable resentment that the department had tried to exclude retired teachers from pension benefits secured by serving teachers relating to their acceptance of productivity provisions of the PCW.[8]

Concerns about pressures in respect of productivity contributed to disenchantment with the social partnership process in the ASTI, and there were even suggestions during 1997 that the Association reconsider its relationship with ICTU, on the grounds that it had neglected teachers' concerns.[9] Speaking at the 1997 convention, President John Mulcahy was adamant that national pay agreements were not an appropriate mechanism for the introduction of far-reaching changes in education through so-called 'restructuring', because the 'issues are far too complex and the sums of money available are far too restricted'. Mulcahy's views were representative of a membership which had voted three to one against Partnership 2000, in January 1997.[10]

Dissatisfaction was already widespread, therefore, when nurses and gardaí subsequently negotiated special increases that were far higher than 5.8 per cent. Teachers and other so-called 'early settlers' responded by insisting that they were entitled to supplementary awards. An 'urgent' resolution to the 1999 convention, proposed by President Michael Corley, made the argument succinctly:

In view of (a) the increase in pay for certain groups in the public sector since the teachers' unions' agreement on pay and conditions under Clause 2(iii) of the PCW, and (b) the financial benefits to employees of profit sharing and other bonus arrangements in the private sector, and (c) the wide-ranging implications for Teachers of the Education Act, Convention mandates the ASTI, in conjunction with the INTO and TUI, to pursue a salary increase which will address these issues and to take appropriate action if no progress is made.[11]

Pay, in fact, dominated the 1999 Killarney convention, and a few months later, in her first 'President's Message' in *ASTIR*, Bernadine O'Sullivan indicated that the issue would have high priority during her term of office, quoting Professor Anthony Clare in support of her views about the political neglect of education and of the needs of teachers:

> The content of the education that is going on in our schools is ... taken for granted ... The standard is good and the students coming out can hold their own with any in Europe, certainly in Britain. I have the feeling that the politicians live off this achievement. They would need however to be careful lest while everything seems to be ticking over nicely, behind the scenes everything is beginning to cave in.[12]

General secretary Charlie Lennon seemed to agree, for his column in the same issue was headed, 'Pay and staffing issues to dominate the new year agenda'. It would soon become apparent, however, that the harmony between the two senior figures did not run very deep, and, in the public mind at least, Lennon and O'Sullivan came to represent opposite poles in ASTI affairs.

A Donegal-born teacher of students with hearing impairments, Bernadine O'Sullivan had been a member of the Association since the 1970s, but her husband was more prominent in its affairs before she was elected to the CEC in 1992. O'Sullivan had always taken an interest in the educational side of ASTI work, and it was her determination to resist what she saw as the introduction into the Irish system of some of the undesirable educational innovations of Thatcher-era Britain that led her into more sustained activism. Through the 1990s, she took part in a number of campaigns in opposition to developments which she perceived as tending to undermine collegiality among teachers, and she was prominent among those who spoke out against the PCW in the mid-1990s. A spirited campaigner, she was elected to the vice-presidency by a margin of more than two to one in 1998, succeeding to the presidency in the following year. According to an *Irish Times* profile published in 2000, O'Sullivan was the latest of a number of presidents of that era who wished to change what was described as a 'top-down' culture in the ASTI.[13] She would also be a vigorous critic of the ICTU leadership.

The negotiations surrounding the PPF, in late 1999 and early 2000, sharpened existing divisions in the trade union movement, especially when ICTU negotiators conceded that progress on 'early settlers' claims might be linked to productivity.[14] Senator Joe O'Toole was an advocate of the productivity element of the programme – which would come to be described as 'benchmarking' – later arguing that the new arrangements were not too different to the old, in a much-cited analogy: 'It is no more than going to a different ATM: we will punch in the formula and collect the payout.'[15] Many teachers, however, were concerned that benchmarking might be used to introduce teacher appraisal and performance-related pay, and this was mixed with resentment that the grievances of 'early settlers' were to be diverted into the sidings while another disagreeable, and probably interminable, process was given the green light.

Deeply-felt dissatisfaction at the trade union strategy in the PPF negotiations came to a head at standing committee on 15 January 2000, where a resolution proposing that the ASTI should cut its links with ICTU was adopted. That such an important affiliate should threaten to leave represented a crisis for ICTU, and efforts were made during the following week to reach an acceptable compromise. The gravity of the situation was illustrated by the attendance of Peter Cassells, ICTU general secretary, at a special meeting of standing committee.[16] The ASTI was reported to be deeply divided, with Charlie Lennon strongly opposed to leaving ICTU.

From the ICTU perspective, this was an extremely delicate moment, for there were rumblings elsewhere also, as indicated by a statement from TUI president Joe Carolan in which he expressed his opposition to performance-related pay, and promised that his union would 'forge alliances with other public sector groups also opposed to it'.[17]

With no significant changes made to the objectionable elements of the PPF, the standing committee resolution was considered by the CEC of the ASTI at its meeting of 22 January 2000. This was a highly charged meeting at which even the agenda was disputed, and it must be regarded as one of the most significant in the Association's history. The resolution read: 'That Standing Committee recommends to CEC that in light of ICTU's obvious inability to satisfactorily resolve the early settlers' grievance as a stand-alone issue, that CEC decide that ASTI withdraw from ICTU forthwith'. An amendment, which would have had the effect of postponing a decision for three weeks while further talks took place, was defeated. At the end of a debate to which sixteen speakers contributed, there was a vote on the substantive motion. The result was 96 (64 per cent) to 54 (36 per cent), with a solitary abstention.[18]

Three further resolutions were adopted at the meeting. One committed the Association to opening direct talks with the government on the 'early settlers' claim as a 'stand alone issue with no strings attached', while another reiterated opposition to 'individual or school-based performance pay in all circumstances'. A third resolution, directing that a claim be lodged immediately for an across-the-board increase of 20 per cent, prompted two amendments and a heated debate. The first amendment, providing for a possible ballot on industrial action in the event that negotiations on the claim were not successfully concluded within twelve months, was rejected as being too meek. A second amendment – on the face of things more militant – proposed increasing the demand to 30 per cent. By several accounts, the suggestion that the figure be increased was made mischievously by a contributor wishing to make the point that the 20 per cent figure seemed very arbitrary and that the resolution tabled did not make clear whether it was to be regarded as additional to the 'early settlers' claim, the subject of the earlier resolution. Whatever the motivation, the amendment was successful, and the meeting ended with the Association committed to pursuing a 30 per cent pay claim, and to doing so outside of ICTU structures.[19]

While there were no such dramatic developments in the other teachers' unions, there were nonetheless internal divisions. According to *Industrial Relations News*, the ASTI's decisions stirred similar resentment against the PPF among INTO and TUI members.[20]

In the TUI, according to the same publication, key members became more favourably disposed towards the deal as a result both of commitments to increase staffing in disadvantaged schools and of the alleviation of their concerns about the likely implications of performance-related pay. But when the more positive attitude was reflected in a special issue of the union periodical issued in advance of the TUI ballot on the PPF, two executive members sought a court injunction preventing its circulation, arguing that the publication did not meet the union's obligation, under its own rules, to fairly present both sides of the argument in relation to the issue being voted upon. The two executive members lost that skirmish, but they won the battle, for TUI members rejected the PPF on a vote of 55 per cent to 45 per cent.[21]

In the INTO also, the question was hard-fought, notwithstanding the strong pro-agreement views of General Secretary O'Toole. Branches in Dublin voted against the PPF in early ballots, but a determined intervention by the leadership succeeded in turning things around and the final INTO tally was 50.5 per cent in favour to 49.5 per cent against. As things turned out, the PPF was comfortably endorsed at a special congress meeting in late March, and the INTO's delegates were not crucial to the outcome, but the fact that the deal was not rejected by all the teachers' representatives was very important from a political perspective.[22]

The strong views on either side of the question in the INTO and the TUI reflected divisions between industrial relations professionals and their allies in these organisations on the one hand, and sections of their memberships on the other. For the full-time organisers/negotiators, social partnership was an orderly mechanism with the capacity to deliver results for workers. While unions were being progressively and deliberately marginalised in Thatcher's and Major's Britain, it was felt by their counterparts in Ireland that they had been able to secure their position through their involvement in the 1987 Programme for National Recovery and its successors.[23] If there were concessions in respect of productivity and flexibility, it was argued that these were inevitable anyway, and that it was better that they be negotiated than imposed. As Peter Cassells, an architect of partnership, told the 1998 ASTI convention:

> … Change should be achieved through partnership. As your colleagues and fraternal delegates from the British trade union movement and teachers' unions will tell you, partnership and change can be achieved through different means. As we saw in Britain, they sought to achieve it through confrontation, deregulation and disagreement, whereas I believe we can achieve it through consultation, dialogue and agreement.[24]

It was an argument that had won wide acceptance within Irish trade unionism, but for many teachers it was wearing thin. They had nursed a pay grievance for much of the previous decade; they had found that their housing and other living costs were rising; they had seen that workers in the private sector had been able to secure increases additional to those provided for by partnership; they had been placed under pressure from dealing with the consequences of social problems and from having to adapt to the many changes in the education system. Therefore, they resented that, under the terms of the agreements now being negotiated on their behalf, they were obliged to accept a worsening of their working conditions in exchange for pay increases to which they felt already entitled.[25] In the ASTI, the CEC majority of 1999–2000 represented such grassroots sentiment among secondary teachers.

The contrasting attitudes of an industrial relations professional and of an elected representative of alienated teachers were personified in the pages of *ASTIR* during the first half of 2000, with Bernadine O'Sullivan in her 'President's Message' on page five and Charlie Lennon in his 'Comment' on page seven generally singing from very different hymn sheets. Moreover, an internal dispute that shook the Association in the spring of 2000 revealed that the mutual incomprehension between those holding different views about the ASTI's relationship with, and responsibility towards, the broader trade union movement had mutated into distrust.

The dispute was sparked by the publication of details of an ASTI discussion document dealing with pay strategy, which had raised the option of non-co-operation with state examinations. Subsequently, there was an allegation at standing committee (and in *Phoenix* magazine) that the document had been deliberately leaked by a member of the head office staff to the *Irish Independent*. Indignant, the officials, administrators and clerical workers responded by threatening industrial action through their own trade union SIPTU, which would specifically impact on preparations for the upcoming annual convention in Killarney. That threat was not acted upon but the sensitivities remained, and when 'personalised comments' made at both private and public sessions of the Convention, against ASTI employees, were allegedly 'left unchecked' by the chair, those employees who were present walked out in protest.[26] And tensions were not eased when one convention speaker reminded the employees concerned of their duty 'to implement the policy of the union' in the following terms: 'If any officer of the Association has a problem promoting ASTI policy, he or she should immediately resign – the door is down there on the left.'[27] The conflict continued back in Dublin, with a 'work to rule' in head office beginning in early May, the object of which was to secure an apology and a retraction from standing committee, in respect of the leak allegation.[28]

At the convention itself, the PPF was rejected, and a subcommittee was formed to pursue the 30 per cent, through conciliation in the first instance. Reporting from the eye of the storm – which his own report of the leaked document had helped to foment – John Walshe captured the atmosphere in Killarney for *Irish Independent* readers:

> There is no doubt that ASTI president Bernadine O'Sullivan has tapped into a deep well of discontent not just in her own union but also in the other unions. In the process she has become the best known teacher union president for years ... The other teacher unions are trying to divert the pressure by talking up the benchmarking element of the new PPF but ASTI is having none of it and in her presidential address O'Sullivan was scathing of this 'newfangled' notion ... Yesterday's opening session saw a long list of speakers alternatively bashing the media and talking about their own productivity ... The incoming vice-president Catherine Fitzpatrick was cheered when she declared: 'We do not rule out industrial action; we mean business; it's payback time.'[29]

That there was a 'well of discontent' right across the teaching profession was confirmed by another informed observer of Irish trade union affairs:

> Whatever about splits, the divergence on pay across all three unions appears to be between the members' mounting expectations and increasingly frantic efforts to leap again ahead of the guards and the nurses, and the union officials who are now welded to the ICTU/partnership process which, it is becoming increasingly evident, is not enough for the members.[30]

Pay campaign: (i) 'ASTI is not a party to such agreements'
By the autumn of 2000, as new president, Don McCluskey, took

over from Bernadine O'Sullivan, the ASTI was isolated and divided. Furthermore, for proponents of social partnership, it was important that it remain so for as long as it pursued its objectives outside the PPF. This was because that agreement was regarded as vulnerable even after its adoption by ICTU. As was shown by close votes in many unions – including the largest, SIPTU – ASTI members were not alone in their reservations, and there were fears about the possible impact of grassroots' pressure on other unions.[31] It was in this context that *The Irish Times* advised the government in the autumn of 2000:

> ... Government has an obligation to provide some comfort – and quickly – to the INTO and the TUI which are now under intense pressure from their grassroots to adopt ASTI's hard line. There is an obvious solution ... bringing forward the benchmarking process to the middle of next year. This would dampen the discontent in the INTO and the TUI. But it might have one other result. It could weaken the resolve of ASTI members to pursue a strike campaign ...[32]

In the battle for minds, the government had already made concessions to the TUI and the INTO, which had prevented them from making common cause with the ASTI. Subsequent efforts to restore teachers' unity were unsuccessful. At a joint meeting of the three union executives in June 2000, for example, each had remained resolutely committed to its own strategy: the INTO and the TUI to winning recognition for increased productivity through benchmarking; the ASTI to remaining outside the process.[33]

Conscious of their Association's isolation, the ASTI's pay strategy committee worked 'to develop a public relations strategy to influence positively all of the important audiences'.[34] While an opinion poll had shown that a slim majority of the public backed the ASTI's 30 per cent pay claim, it was anticipated that this support would melt away if industrial action was pursued. It was determined accordingly that a public relations campaign should be launched to coincide with the beginning of the school year (though evidently views were divided about the utility of such an initiative in the circumstances). The centrepiece of the campaign was an unprecedented, and expensive, television advertisement that did not directly address the pay issue, but that sought to win support by conveying just how complex and demanding the teacher's role had become. Here the message was that the modern teacher was not just an educator, but was also required to be a 'counsellor, psychologist, mentor, carer, motivator, diplomat, coach, and leader'.[35] There was criticism of the approach from at least one PR strategist who had advised trade unions during disputes. For Pat Montague, an effective PR intervention tried 'to bring out the underlying causes or reasons why a dispute takes place', and a campaign that did not engage with the central questions at issue would not have any significant effect on the outcome.[36]

If society placed great demands on teachers, circumstances placed even more on teachers' leaders, and with the new school year about to begin, the ASTI General Secretary Charlie Lennon faced a particularly testing time. Almost a decade in the position, he was considered by people that worked closely with him to have been an excellent and innovative administrator, if less gregarious than his predecessor, Kieran Mulvey.[37] Like Mulvey, Lennon had moved from student activism into trade union leadership, having been a founder of the student representative council at St Patrick's teacher training college, a secretary of the Dún Laoghaire branch of the INTO, and a full-time official of the INTO for ten years before he joined the ASTI as assistant general secretary in 1988. He was aged forty when he succeeded Mulvey as general secretary in 1991. At the time of the ASTI's disaffiliation, Lennon was a key member of the ICTU executive, and he advised that to break the links that had been painstakingly developed over the previous thirty years would be to needlessly marginalise the Association.[38] According to a profile published in November 2000, however, he had become reconciled to the changed circumstances, having 'skilfully readjusted his footing to fall in with the new direction and regularly denounc[ed] the PPF negotiated by ICTU earlier this year'. The same profile summed him up as 'an affable but private individual not given to verbal flourishes or colourful language'. The fact that he had little sympathy for militancy was well conveyed by the following quip from a trade union colleague: 'His name is definitely spelt Lennon, not Lenin.'[39]

The ASTI's submission to the arbitration body was eventually submitted in September 2000. It was a comprehensive document which justified the teachers' 30 per cent claim under several criteria – they were paid on average £9,000 less than other graduate profes-

The cover of ASTIR *September 2000, published following the launch of a nationwide ASTI advertising campaign to promote teachers and their work.*

AS TI
CUMANN NA MEÁNMHÚINTEOIRÍ · ÉIRE · ASSOCIATION OF SECONDARY TEACHERS · IRELAND

ASTI House,
Winetavern Street,
Dublin 8.
Phone: 671 9144
Fax: 671 9280
Email: info@asti.ie
Website: www.asti.ie

NUACHT

February 8th 2002
Issue No. 3

Members to withdraw from supervision, substitution

ASTI members rejected the Government's offer on a paid supervision and substitution scheme by 72% to 28%.

44% of members participated in the ballot, the results of which were announced on Friday, February 1.

Total Polled:	16,632
Turnout:	7,420
Total Valid Poll:	7,403
Spoilt Votes:	17
Yes:	5,326
No:	2,077

Following the rejection of the Government's offer, Standing Committee adopted the following resolution at its meeting on February 1:

That Standing Committee implement the directive to members to withdraw from voluntary supervision and substitution duties with effect from 4th March 2002 and that the Minister be advised immediately of the necessity of implementing his contingency plans.

ASTI will not inhibit Minister's plans

In adopting the resolution, Standing Committee emphasised that they did not wish schools to be closed and will not inhibit the implementation of the Minister's contingency plans. They called upon the Minister to ensure that schools were not closed over this issue.

The directive banning supervision and substitution will apply to voluntary supervision and voluntary substitution for absent colleagues.

Members will continue with teaching and other duties as normal.

Standing Committee will meet on Thursday, February 14th and Friday, February 15th to discuss the issuing of the directive and to clarify the operation of the directive. The directive and accompa-

An edition of Nuacht *published in February 2002, following a CEC decision that supervision and substitution would be withdrawn, in pursuit of improvements in the scheme.*

Standing committee, 1999–2000. Seated (left to right): Michael Corley, Don McCluskey, Bernadine O'Sullivan, Charlie Lennon, John White, Michael Ward. Standing, front row (left to right): Sheila Parsons, Monica Keane, Lily Cronin, Maire Collins, Mary Duggan, Helen Bhreathnach, Katherine Bulman, Irene Irish. Standing, back row (left to right): John McCourt, George O'Leary, Pat Cahill, P.J. Sheehy, Paddy Mulcahy, Brendan Forde, George Moran, Willie Lawlor, Damien Cooke.

Charlie Lennon, ASTI general secretary 1991–2003 is interviewed by RTÉ's Peter Cluskey.

John White, ASTI general secretary 2005 to present. (photo by Tommy Clancy)

Former ASTI president, Susie Hall (left) converses with the then minister for education and science, Mary Hanafin at annual convention, 2007.

December 2008: Teachers from St David's Secondary School, Artane, Dublin, prepare placards for the demonstration against the education cuts held on 6 December 2008.

THERE IS A BETTER, FAIRER WAY.

The four teacher unions are calling on all members and friends to participate in the national demonstration.

ACT!

THERE IS A BETTER, FAIRER WAY

JOIN US - 2pm - 21-02-09
PARNELL SQ.   DUBLIN

In February 2009 the four teacher unions placed a joint advertisement in the newspapers supporting the ICTU demonstration against the government's handling of the economic crisis.

Over 50,000 people participated in a march against education cuts in Dublin on Saturday, 6 December 2008. The march was organised by the three teacher unions – ASTI, TUI and INTO – as part of a lengthy campaign to reverse the education cuts announced in a budget the previous October. (photo by Tommy Clancy)

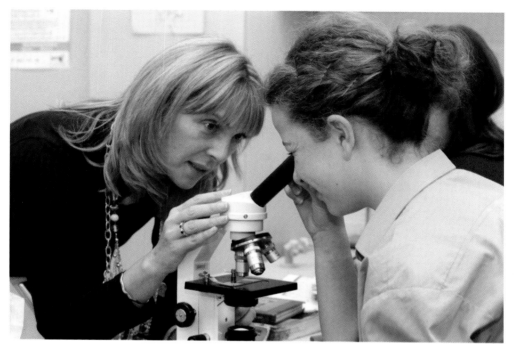

Margaret O'Riordan, a science teacher at Malahide Community School, 2008. This photo appeared in the ASTI 2009 Centenary Calendar, depicting the ASTI and teaching over the past 100 years. (photo by Dave Cullen)

(left to right) ASTI general secretary, John White; IFUT general secretary, Mike Jennings; and TUI general secretary, Peter Mac Menamin at the ICTU protest, 21 February 2009. (photo by Tommy Clancy)

The 2009 officers of the ASTI pictured with President of Ireland Mary McAleese at a gala dinner to celebrate the ASTI centenary held in March 2009. From left: Patricia Wroe, immediate past president; Joe Moran, vice president; Pat Hurley, president; President of Ireland Mary McAleese; John White, general secretary; and Ray St John, honorary treasurer. (photo by Dave Cullen)

ASTI standing committee 2008–2009. Fifth row, (left to right): Gerry Breslin, Christy Maginn, Philip Irwin. Fourth row: Patricia Wroe, Liam O'Mahony, Ger O' Donoghue, Diarmaid de Paor, deputy general secretary, Joe Moran. Third row: Gretta Harrison, Margaret Moore, Sarah Withero, Brendan Broderick. Second row: John White, General Secretary, Mary Lysaght, Elaine Devlin, Michael Barry, Colm O'Toole. Front row: Ann Piggott, Michael Ward, President Pat Hurley, Sally Maguire, Ray St John, Michael Moriarty. (Micheál O'Neill missing from photo.)

sions after fifteen years' service; it took them longer to reach the top of their pay scale than any other group in the public service; they earned on average 73 per cent of the wage, including overtime, of a prison officer, and 86 per cent of the wage of a garda. Younger teachers were unable to buy their own homes, the submission maintained, and this was reflected in falling morale, in falling numbers of applications for the Higher Diploma in Education, and in principals having to hire unqualified substitutes.[40]

Rather as expected, the arbitration body declined to take any of this into consideration, dismissing the claim on the grounds that it was not consistent with the current national pay agreement.[41] Charlie Lennon's response was hard-hitting. Referring to the fact that the arbitrator's ruling focused almost entirely on the PPF, he pointed out:

> The ASTI is not a party to such agreements, having left ICTU last January in order to pursue the pay interests of its members outside the restrictions of such agreements. The ASTI believes that its members have specific grounds for an increase beyond that provided for in national agreements. Secondary teachers have transformed the second-level education service over the past decade. They have shown considerable restraint in not pursuing pay rises while participating in large scale restructuring of the second-level system ... Secondary teachers are not a radical group. They preferred to pursue improvements in their pay through negotiations. They have been prevented from doing so by the government which ... is trying to preserve the wholly inadequate pay agreement associated with the PPF.[41]

Determined to protect the partnership process, the government simply ignored the thrust of the ASTI argument, and imposed the PPF. Paying secondary teachers the 8.5 per cent instalment due in October 2000, it justified its step by indicating that it did not wish to break with the established common basic scale for all teachers. For their part, secondary teachers had little choice but to regard the 8.5 per cent as a down-payment on their just claim. The concept of benchmarking remained anathema, however, and for many in the ASTI it came to represent all that was wrong with the PPF and with the partnership process generally.

Pending the result of the ASTI ballot on industrial action, standing committee responded by directing its members to withdraw immediately from the various government working parties, councils and commissions to which they had been nominated (including the National Council for Curriculum and Assessment) and not to participate in in-service training for new programmes or in school development planning.[42]

The result of the ballot was overwhelming. With 68 per cent of those eligible participating, there was a margin of eight to one in favour of industrial action to secure the 30 per cent – and to reject any idea of benchmarking. At its meeting of 19/20 October, standing committee agreed a programme of action, the main features of which were two one-day strikes on 14 November and 5 December (another would be arranged for 14 December) and a ban on the supervision of students outside of class and on voluntary cover for absent colleagues on six of the intervening days.[43] The 'supervision and cover' ban was devised as a creative means of closing schools without teachers having to sacrifice pay. Given the enormous mortgage commitments of younger teachers in particular, an all-out strike was not considered to be a realistic option, but the withdrawal of supervision might have an equal impact. The calculation was that schools would be unable to admit pupils who would not be supervised, while the department would be unable to financially penalise teachers who refused to undertake supervisory duties that they were not contracted to carry out. A strategy which combined occasional strike action with a 'work to rule' in the form of a supervision ban, together with non-co-operation with the department's programme of educational reform, was therefore considered to be the most appropriate in the circumstances.[44]

The first one-day strike, on 14 November 2000, was a complete success in that all the 600 or so schools targeted were obliged to close. For one observer, the strikers were 'unlikely radicals' and, to make his point, he cited guidelines issued by ASTI officials (in the light of industrial relations legislation in respect of picketing): 'Pathways should be kept clear, traffic should not be disrupted and no more than six teachers should picket the school gates at any one time.' One of the 'unlikely radicals', Jean Rogers, a Tipperary-based guidance counsellor, reflected in *The Irish Times* on the occasion of her first ever stint of picket duty:

During my twenty years in the education system, I saw these underpaid teachers take time out to help students, working from an ethos that is as much about inclusion as it is about performance. It is this point that seems to be missed by many of those commenting on the current industrial dispute ... Benchmarking means linking salaries of comparable jobs, and identifying specific measurable activities for these jobs. But it is not possible to benchmark the interventions so important in making a school day run smoothly. It is not possible to benchmark motivation, compassion, interest and care.[45]

Under the heading, 'Memories of 1969 Revived in Limerick', a journalist reported on the mood among teachers – some of them not even born in 1969 – on picket duty outside schools in the city. For John O'Kane at St Munchin's College, the issue was a straightforward one: 'It is a benchmark if you can buy your own home with the job you are in'; for John Hurley, a former ASTI president who taught at the Crescent Comprehensive College, the extent of support from the public was 'gratifying'.[46] A few days later, another journalist spoke to several of the fifty-three teachers at Coláiste Cholm Cille in Ballyshannon. One of them was Denise Horan, a teacher of PE and Irish and a member of the Mayo team that had recently won an All-Ireland football title, who coached school teams at lunch-time and in the evenings. Another was Mary Duggan, a member of standing committee, who reported that the mood in the school was 'very, very militant':[47]

Usually in these situations you might expect to find a 'doubting Thomas' or two, but there is absolute solidarity. People feel the time has come when a stand has to be made ... People are very angry and they may be less forthcoming in giving up their time for games, drama, debating, etc. in the future.[48]

The rights and wrongs of the dispute were a source of much public debate throughout the country, with, for example, the *Tuam Herald*, the *Anglo-Celt*, and the *Meath Chronicle* all editorialising on the subject on the weekend after the first one-day strike. Waterford county councillors also had an opportunity to discuss the issue when one of their number put down a motion deploring the 30 per cent claim. Indicating that the ASTI was not yet completely isolated, the motion was defeated on a vote of eleven to eight.[49]

Arguably, discussions about the dispute had more immediacy in the TUI than elsewhere, especially after the ASTI decided to place pickets on schools where members of both unions were employed. While TUI members observed the pickets on the ground, some of them were unhappy that they had to do so, and their union protested to the ASTI about the matter.[50]

Pay campaign: (ii) 'Another kick in the teeth!'
Towards the end of 2000, there was satisfaction that ASTI membership had passed 17,000, that during a very fractious year it had registered its largest ever numerical increase. Another source of satisfaction before the Christmas holidays was that support for the industrial actions taken had remained solid through November and December. And a breakthrough seemed possible, for ahead of a national one-day strike on 14 December there had been efforts to initiate direct negotiations between the ASTI and the government. These came to fruition during the weekend after the stoppage, with the intervention of the minister for education, Dr Michael Woods. Woods, a long-time TD for North Dublin, was an experienced government minister who served in Education between 2000 and 2002. At a private meeting with Charlie Lennon and President Don McCluskey, the minister agreed to the appointment of a special intermediary to devise a process for negotiations. The individual selected was Labour Relations Commission (LRC) official Tom Pomphrett, who had experience of the teachers' conciliation process.[51]

No sooner had a chink of light appeared, however, than it was extinguished, for in the days before Christmas the Department of Education made it known that it would be deducting teachers' pay, not only for the strike days but for the days when supervision had been withdrawn. It was a decision that had evidently been taken before the facilitation process had begun, but this knowledge did not lessen the irritation of the ASTI's leadership, who rejected as inadequate the government's offer to defer making further deductions, and to consider refunding those already made in the context of an overall settlement. Standing committee resolved to legally challenge the deduction, and to withdraw from talks until the government undertook to repay the deductions in respect of the withdrawal of supervision.[52]

Hostilities resumed with a series of regional one-day strikes in mid-January, prompting a public intervention by Taoiseach Bertie Ahern, who was critical of the ASTI's demand for a refund of the deducted pay in an article in *The Irish Times*:

Most people would regard it as fair that industrial action which inevitably results in the cancellation of classes, such that children could not go to school, should result in a sanction. It is not reasonable to expect that people should be paid as normal by the taxpayer when, in effect, they are failing to deliver any service.[53]

The taoiseach was also very critical of the ASTI action more generally:

So what is this strike about? We have been told that it is a 'crusade'. Against whom is this crusade being conducted? It seems it is partly about a power struggle within the ASTI, with the crusade designed to achieve dominance for particular groups. It seems to be partly a crusade against the rest of the public service and the whole social partnership process ... Ultimately perhaps this is a crusade against the government. If it is, it is certainly not because of any lack of willingness on the part of government to support education and the role of teachers ... So I repeat the question, why is this strike happening? What is certain is that children around the country are suffering unnecessarily. They see the action being taken as totally disproportionate to the facts of the situation. Their parents know that it is unnecessary and unreasonable.[54]

The article was criticised by opposition leader John Bruton, who thought it inappropriate for a taoiseach to speculate publicly about power struggles in trade unions. There was great indignation within the Association at Mr Ahern's intervention, and a public response followed from Bernadine O'Sullivan, who had been quoted as using the term 'crusade' in relation to the ASTI's demands. For her, the allegation of a power struggle was 'erroneous', being an 'example of a classic political ploy and distraction technique'.[55]

However, the taoiseach's interest signalled an end to what was characterised as 'the row within a row', and the facilitation process was resumed within a week. The agreement that emerged from that process was to refer the full claim 'on an ad hoc basis' to the Labour Court (not the usual forum for teachers' pay claims because they had their own conciliation and arbitration scheme). This procedure was accepted by the CEC on a margin of four to one, the facilitator having advised that 'in accordance with good industrial relations practice, while this process is operating, the union should suspend all forms of industrial and strike action'.[56]

When the Labour Court eventually issued its report on 9 March 2001 there was real disappointment, for an expectation had built up in the ranks of the Association that a way out of the impasse would be found. According to *Industrial Relations News,* however, the court came under great pressure, 'not only directly from the Government, but also indirectly from the public sector unions', to make no concession to the ASTI, so as 'to keep the PPF and benchmarking afloat'. The result, according to *The Irish Times* was a 'devastating critique' of the Association – 'The court employs honeyed words and nuanced phrases, but the message is clear: it is telling the ASTI to take a running jump.'[57] The recommendation was that the Association should enter the benchmarking process, a recommendation that was generally unacceptable and that was seen as boosting the position of so-called 'hardliners'. One such 'hardliner' was quoted as follows: 'These people had asked us to put our trust in the Labour Court, and what did we get? Another kick in the teeth!' At CEC, the court's recommendations were rejected by a margin of fifteen to one, and a resolution to resume industrial action was overwhelmingly carried. It was agreed that a ban on examination work would be implemented and that strike action would be taken on six days during the remainder of the month of March.[58] In response, Minister Woods declared that he was determined that the examinations would proceed. To give effect to this promise, the department placed advertisements for superintendents.[59]

It was the conclusion of one analyst that a key element of the government strategy in the dispute was to manoeuvre parents and their representatives into becoming active opponents of the secondary teachers.[60] Since its establishment, the National Parents' Council, Post Primary (NPCPP) had enjoyed a good relationship with the ASTI, and it was a relationship that was valued by the Association's officials.[61] The council had refrained from criticising the pay strategy pursued during 2000, but this position came under pressure as the effects of industrial action began to be felt. A government announcement that it would pay parents to act as supervisors in schools widened the gulf between parents and teachers – as was intended. Dissatisfaction among some of the NPCPP constituents at the alleged passivity of the council was reflected in implicitly critical public statements from Barbara Johnston, spokesperson for the Catholic Secondary School Parents' Association (CSSPA).[62] The breaking of ranks reflected deeper tensions within NPCPP and these came to a head early in 2001 when a new leadership took over. When the government announced its intention to recruit non-ASTI examination supervisors, Marie Danaswamy, the new NPCPP president, declared this was 'a good idea'. For the CSSPA, Johnston went further, suggesting there was an opportunity for 'taking exams out of the hands of the teachers on a permanent basis'. 'Something as important as exams,' she continued, 'should not be an arbitrary target for teachers.'[63]

Barbara Johnston followed with an intemperate attack on the ASTI in *The Irish Times*, and an appeal to parents to act as examination supervisors:

> You have kidnapped our children's future and are now holding that future to ransom. Instead of behaving like professionals, you are behaving like terrorists ... We would therefore ask parents to write to the ASTI union representative in their child's school. State unequivocally that you do not support the ASTI's action in using the exams to bring the dispute to a head. Finally we would urge all parents to respond positively to the advertisements in this week's papers and put themselves forward for the supervision of exams.[64]

By mid-March, therefore, parents' organisations were regarded as being in the government camp. Moreover, with the backing of the NPCPP and other groups, the Department of Education was inundated with applications for the examination supervisors' positions. There was encouragement from NPCPP sources for parents to mobilise at local level, and also tacit encouragement for school students to make their feelings known. School students responded – and their disposition was very different to that of their predecessors during previous teachers' disputes in 1969, 1971 and 1985. Student demonstrators in 2001 were, in general, far less disciplined than those of previous decades and, significantly, far more hostile towards their teachers. The change in attitude in this respect may, in part, reflect the broader change in attitudes to schools and teachers during these years, which is discussed in Chapter 10.

A student walk out on 15 March at Coláiste Dún Iascaigh in Cahir, County Tipperary, was followed by others in Cork, Monaghan, Wexford, Kilkenny and Donegal. Several of these became disorderly, notably a protest by 500 school students in Letterkenny, during which vehicles were damaged and, according to the *Irish Independent*, 'eggs, potatoes and other missiles were thrown at gardaí'. The NPCPP urged only that students 'protest peacefully'.

There were expectations that crowds of student protestors would join a 'national' demonstration called for 21 March outside Dáil Éireann, with a spokesperson for one national parents' association predicting that 15,000 school students 'from across the country' would attend. As things transpired, only a few hundred assembled at the Dáil. Disorderly protests continued to occur over the following days, however, and there was conflict between students and members of An Garda in Navan, County Meath, with arrests reported from demonstrations in Coolock, Ballyfermot, Bray and Waterford.[65]

A number of students from the Marian College in Ballsbridge and the Louis High School in Rathmines took the initiative in establishing a Union of School Students – for which they received assistance from the Union of Students in Ireland (USI). Their efforts were commended by columnist, Fintan O'Toole, a veteran of the earlier IUSS of the 1970s, who also made some observations on the circumstances that had generated them:

> As today's school students have learned to their cost in recent months, the other players in the education system have their own agendas ... The people who own the system – teachers, the State and, to a lesser extent, parents – are left to fight it out among themselves while the people for whom it is supposedly run are caught in the middle. As soon as they force their way into the headlines, as they did this week, the nature of the debate changes radically.[66]

The student walk outs and demonstrations certainly changed the 'nature of the debate' within the ASTI. There was shock and disillusionment at the extent of the hostility from students, as well as concern about the riotous character of some of the mobilisations, and fear that it might gather momentum. In several schools in the greater Dublin area, teachers' cars were vandalised on Monday 26 March. From at least one school in the capital, teachers required a Garda escort to leave the premises.[67]

Renewed contacts with the Labour Court provided an excuse for the cancellation by standing committee of the two remaining strike days before Easter, but the indications are that the alarm caused by the student protests was a significant factor in the decision.[68]

When Labour Court chairman Finbarr Flood issued a 'clarification' of the earlier report, there was no significant movement on the substantive issue – though there were inducements in the form of a suggested payment of £1,750 lump sum for teachers for ensuring that the school programme for 2000–01 was completed and of grants of up to £350 for individual teachers for the purchase of IT equipment. If the offer was not significantly different, circumstances were very different to what they had been three weeks earlier, and the CEC agreed to put it to members in a national ballot. Two issues were to be balloted upon: whether to accept the somewhat revised offer, and whether to persist with the ban on examination supervision. Before the ballot took place, however, convention intervened.

Coming soon in the aftermath of the abandoned strike action, it was to be expected that the 2001 convention would be an occasion of accusation and recrimination. Even so, observers were surprised by the depth of antagonisms. The public relations guru Tom Savage thought that the event was 'the mother of all PR disasters':

> I've watched open-mouthed as members of the ASTI have taken every public chance to blame politicians, media, parents, and students for the ASTI's problems ... Media was going to be there, and media was going to have a ready-made audience eager to view whatever way the teachers presented themselves to be viewed ... Going out of your way to abuse and barrack journalists has its rewards. You can go back to your mates and truthfully claim to have 'told that lot what you think of them'. It's just not a productive pleasure. If any of the teachers who berated re-

porters at the conference believe that their angry words will change the behaviour of those reporters or the editorial stance of the media outlets for which each reporter works, they're kidding themselves.[69]

Public relations was not the only concern of the ASTI delegates who gathered in Galway on 19, 20 and 21 April 2001; there were important decisions to be made in respect of strategy and leadership. But it must be acknowledged that the convention was a notably fractious one. And it was not only journalists that complained about their reception: so did parents' representatives, one of whom alleged he was assaulted; so also did Minister Woods, who asserted that delegates influenced by the Socialist Workers Party were responsible for leading a walk out during his speech; so also did Charlie Lennon, who drew public attention to the 'threats and abuse' that he endured. Indicative of the tetchiness of delegates was the passing of a resolution demanding that ICTU return the affiliation fee that the ASTI had paid before their separation more than a year previously.[70]

Important decisions were taken in relation to pay strategy. In regard to the first of three key motions from standing committee, it was decided to recommend rejection of the Labour Court offer, overturning a CEC decision that no recommendation should be made. In regard to the second, it was agreed that a ballot on the examination ban should proceed as planned. The third was a complex resolution to determine the form that action should take in the event of members rejecting the Labour Court offer. Twelve options were offered, eight of which were adopted. Significantly, a resumption of strike action in September was rejected by delegates, as were proposals to withdraw from parent–teacher meetings and from co-operation with organisations representing parents. Adopted were proposals to withdraw from voluntary supervision, substitution, and extra-curricular activities in schools, and from co-operation in a range of activities with the department.[71]

Not surprisingly, there was a high level of participation in the ballot, the result of which was announced on 3 May 2001. A record 13,200 members voted, 75 per cent of those eligible, ranging from 64 per cent in Cork North to 91 per cent in West Waterford. Overall, 57 per cent voted to reject the Labour Court recommendation, but there were variations from one branch to the next – 84 per cent in New Ross, and 76 per cent in Wexford favoured rejection, but only 33 per cent in East Cork and 23 per cent in West Limerick. There was a vote of more than 77 per cent against continuing with the ban on examination work, with not a single branch in favour, although there were wide divergences, ranging from 40 per cent in favour of the ban in Bray to 6 per cent in East Galway.[72]

In the aftermath of convention and ballot, the room for manoeuvre of ASTI pay strategists was severely limited. Two of the most effective weapons in the armoury of industrial action had been decommissioned: strikes, 'all-out' or intermittent, had been ruled out by convention, while an examination ban had been overwhelmingly rejected by the members. From the Department of Education's perspective, the threatened non-co-operation would be inconvenient, but it would be no more than that. The withdrawal of supervision presented a real problem for the department and for the school authorities – as events during 2000–01 had shown – but some attention was being given to finding a way of keeping schools open in this eventuality. George O'Callaghan, the representative of the school management bodies, indicated as much in a newspaper article published after the convention. Non-teachers, he advised the delegates, would be hired to do supervisory work if ASTI members would not do it.[73] And this in fact is what would happen.

Internal division

That the Association found itself in such an unenviable position as schools closed for the summer holidays of 2001 was due to a number of factors. It had faced formidable opposition, not just from the Department of Education and the government, but also from other trade unions and from the industrial relations apparatus of the state. And the perception among teachers that the media, from the start, treated their claim in an unsympathetic fashion also had a certain basis.[74] Given such adversaries, victory was never going to be easy to achieve, but internal division would make it almost impossible, and it would be no exaggeration to describe relationships within the Association as dysfunctional during the period of the dispute. While there is not unanimity on the question, there is considerable evidence that the breakdown in relations which had come to public notice at the time of the alleged leak to the *Irish Independent* early in 2000, and which manifested itself in walk outs and a work-to-rule in head office, was not successfully repaired and that the hostility between ASTI employees (and some members who empathised with them) and the grouping identified in the media as 'the militants' seemed to become stronger as time went on. In such an atmosphere, minor misunderstandings and differences of opinion became quarrels, quarrels led to official complaints, and complaints led to investigations. Inevitably, there was a tendency to judge differences, not on their merits, but on perceptions of the personalities involved – a symptom of a deeper malaise. Controversies of a storm-in-a-teacup character consequently consumed both time and energy.[75]

For one authority in industrial relations, the division was between 'the "professional" union negotiators or officials who are employed by the union and the passionate amateurs or officers',[76] and indeed there are indications of a tendency on the part of the full-timers to regard union activists as 'amateurs' in the worst sense of the word, as people prone to rushing into decisions without considering their longer-term implications. In the case of presidents, the fact that they had only one year to make their impact may help to explain the degree of impatience on their part. On the other side of the question, it should be borne in mind that criticism of the 'professionals' by certain elected officers and committee members found an echo in many sections of the Association.

Suspicions about the Association's full-time apparatus had several roots, some of them connected with the traditions of the teachers' unions themselves. Historically, these unions had few staff, and much of the day-to-day business, including negotiation, was conducted by executive members and officers. While developments in industrial relations in the post-war period had pressed craft and general unions into extending their professional apparatus,[77] the teachers' unions continued to rely on their own elected officers, partly because they had their own conciliation and arbitration bodies, and partly because, as educated people with responsible positions, teachers felt that they were capable of representing themselves. Hence, at the time of the ASTI's affiliation to ICTU in 1969, its workforce consisted, in the words of one senior member, of a 'highly efficient but over-worked office secretary and part-time staff'.[78] The great increase in the number of specialist professionals that came to work for the Association in the 1980s and 1990s in particular, together with the growing complexity of social partnership arrangements, was registered in the form of a reduction of the authority of the elected element in the ASTI. While it was broadly accepted that specialised communications, negotiations and technical skills were necessary if the greatly expanded Association was to flourish in the conditions of the late twentieth century, there was a sense of regret at the passing of what seemed like a more intimate and informal era.

Contributing also to division was a general disposition, often found among workers in the front line, to be sceptical of the contribution of officials and administrators. This disposition was reinforced during the dispute by material circulated by left-wing political groupings – the Socialist Party in particular – which, from an ideological perspective that was antagonistic towards what they characterised as 'trade union bureaucracy', made specific criticisms of leading ASTI officials.[79]

In the course of the dispute, a feeling took hold among some members that head office was completely 'out of touch' with the views and the needs of teachers – that the industrial relations professionals in the ASTI had made common cause with industrial relations professionals elsewhere in the trade union movement, in the state's arbitration bodies, and in government bodies. There was certainly a perception that Charlie Lennon was more considerate of his erstwhile colleagues on the ICTU executive and of the other 'partners' in the social partnership process than of ASTI members. That his brother was the government press secretary, and that he had a background in the INTO became symbols of Charlie Lennon's divided loyalties[80] – even though there is no evidence that he was ever less than completely committed to the ASTI.

For their part, the full-time employees, who were represented by SIPTU (mainly), but also by the National Union of Journalists (NUJ) and the Amalgamated Transport and General Workers' Union (ATGWU), used industrial relations procedures to defend their conditions of employment. One outcome of discussions was a 'Protocol' accepted by standing committee in October 2001, from which the following is excerpted:

In the interests of the members and the organisation generally, it is essential that there is full cooperation and mutual respect between the members, those elected to represent the membership and those who are employed by the ASTI. Those elected to represent members are entitled to the respect that the status of elected officer requires. Those who are employed by the ASTI are entitled to the respect that their status as employees requires ... Where there is a deviation from mutually acceptable standards in the course of an ASTI meeting, the presiding officer must make an appropriate intervention at the earliest opportunity ... Where an employee or an elected representative becomes aware of information that is directly relevant to the work or responsibility of another employee or elected representative, this should be communicated with due regard to the rights of all individuals involved to confidentiality.[81]

Whether matters like 'mutual respect' and 'full cooperation' may usefully be legislated for is questionable, however.

'Impossible demands ... cannot be conciliated'

As the dispute entered its third year, therefore (and the Public Service Benchmarking Body continued with its work), there was disillusionment and fractiousness in the ASTI – one sign of which was a High Court case taken by a standing committee member against the Association. Nonetheless, in a joint article in the first issue of *ASTIR* of the 2001–02 academic year, which was entitled 'Achievements of the Pay Campaign', Charlie Lennon and the new president, Catherine Fitzpatrick, who succeeded Don McCluskey, did their best to put a brave face on things. The 'achievements', it will be noted, were modest enough:

We have obtained formal statements from statutory bodies that teachers have a sustainable case for a substantial pay rise ... We have established a better public understanding of the complex and demanding role of the teacher. We have underlined the extent to which schools depend on the voluntary contribution of teachers to function ... We have demonstrated that the ASTI is a strong democratic trade union responsive to its members' interests and concerns. We have established that there is grave parental and student concern at any disruption of the education service in second-level schools and that threatening the state examinations provokes a hostile furore. We have established that the media is voracious in its appetite for controversy and conflict and often has more regard for sensationalism than for balance ...[82]

Following the roller-coaster of the previous year, 2001–02 was inevitably less eventful, though it was not without controversy. The year began with some positive news for ASTI members, when the data protection commissioner ruled in September that the Department of Education had broken the law by utilising information held for the purpose of deducting union contributions in order to withhold teachers' salaries for the days of the supervision ban in November–December 2000. However, a survey of members carried out soon afterwards by the Association indicated that there was little appetite for renewed militancy. At rank-and-file level, the preference was for lobbying politicians and persisting with the policy of non-co-operation with departmental initiatives rather than for strikes or boycotts. Significantly, the survey showed that there was support for submitting the document prepared earlier in the year for the Labour Court to the benchmarking body – a step that would have been at odds with official ASTI policy.[83]

Benchmarking, indeed, was one of the two issues that would dominate discussions during the year. The other was payment for supervision and substitution.

The question of payment for supervision had assumed prominence earlier in 2001 in the course of discussions between the INTO and the TUI and the Department of Education. The department had offered £12 an hour, an amount which was not acceptable to the unions. The ASTI joined the discussions on the issue in August, and by October the offer had been raised to £27 an hour (to a total of £1,000 p.a.). From the trade union perspective, there were two major problems – the amount was still too low, and it was not to be taken into account for pension purposes – but different approaches were taken. INTO members voted to accept the payment on a margin of two to one, with a view to having it improved in arbitration. Ballots in the TUI and the ASTI produced narrow margins against. The narrowness of the margin (55 per cent to 45 per cent), together with the relatively low participation of members, presented tactical problems for the ASTI, and action was postponed on several occasions. Eventually in February 2002, the CEC announced that supervision and substitution would be withdrawn, in pursuit of improvements in the scheme: that the minimum annual payment should be €2,500 (worth £1,970, the Euro currency having been introduced on 1 January 2002); that this should be pensionable; that existing pensioners should benefit; that duties involved should fall within the twenty-two hours maximum weekly teaching time.[84]

With no further progress achieved in relation to these demands by the deadline of 4 March 2002, the ASTI acted on its threat to withdraw supervision. This caused minimal disruption in schools at first, because part-time supervisors had been recruited. There was resentment in some quarters, however, at the introduction of newcomers. From the south of the country, there were reports of 'cold-shouldering by some teachers', and from the west of 'a frosty reception'.[85] Resentment was exacerbated by the fact that the non-teaching supervisors were being paid about 35 per cent more per hour than fully qualified part-time teachers.[85]

But the pursuit of the demands was not a straightforward matter, for the CEC voted also in February not to engage in discussions on the supervision claim until its pay claim was addressed. The weapon of supervision, therefore, was being deployed again in the pay campaign. However, the apparent folly of the sequence of decisions (which involved the Association in industrial action but prevented it from negotiating a solution) seemed to embolden opponents of the CEC majority, and a number of outspoken comments were made. For the INTO's Joe O'Toole, it was 'excruciating to watch [the ASTI] as it now publicly disembowels itself and see its influence diminished and the professionalism of its members demeaned as a consequence of the misguided decision of a dominant clique'.[86]

Charlie Lennon, who had heretofore been publicly reserved about his position, used a pre-convention newspaper interview to express his frustration with people whom he alleged were more 'interested in fomenting internal division than in working towards achieving policies', and who made their points 'by shouting and banging tables'. He continued:

They are trying to exploit the justifiable anger and frustration of members at the way in which the government has dealt with the pay claim for their own purposes ... The union's chance of getting a much-deserved general pay increase for teachers has now been reduced to zero. There are a small number of people who seem to spend most of their time targeting individuals and trying to undermine them. They have targeted the present and past presidents [Catherine Fitzpatrick and Don McCluskey] and myself in particular … They have given the impression that I determine strategies and policies, which I don't. I am a professional employee of the union and not a member of the executive bodies. I give my professional opinion and advise these bodies. I have a right to defend myself because my position has been misrepresented by these people.[87]

Lennon further argued for a change in the way that the Association conducted its ballots, arguing that the views of the 'moderate' majority of teachers were not fully reflected under the established system. This was the subject of a contentious resolution on the convention programme.

At the convention, the guest speaker was former general secretary Kieran Mulvey, who announced himself 'an advocate for the teaching profession' and one who retained 'a deep sense of concern for the Association, for its officers, its members, and the students they educate'. He was quite forthright in his criticism of a section of his audience:

Every dispute has to have a solution and preferably one which has been mutually agreed and over which the parties retain ownership. The nature of the business of industrial relations is compromise. Tactically, it is a question of having a sense of the potential, achieving the possible, avoiding the cul-de-sac, and knowing where and when to have an exit strategy … Parties in dispute must make it possible for each side to deal with each other. Impossible demands and terms for settlement cannot be conciliated if these become a precondition to negotiations themselves. Time and time again those of us who behind the scenes have attempted to establish the parameters of a settlement in the ASTI dispute have been thwarted by such decisions … If you forego the opportunity to influence the outcome of these processes, then the credibility of your arguments against the result will be diminishing among the public whose support you need and have to retain. It would appear that some have already prejudged the outcome of the benchmarking process – and by their continuing vocal opposition to the process are seeking to predetermine the outcome to match their expectations.[88]

The various critical comments did not have the desired effect on the convention delegates. Quite the opposite indeed, and *Industrial Relations News* judged the several interventions – and Charlie Lennon's in particular – to have 'back-fired badly'. Angry delegates rejected by large margins resolutions calling for the reopening of talks on supervision, and a change to school-based ballots. A resolution proposing reaffiliation to ICTU was withdrawn by its proposers, who concluded that it would be overwhelmingly rejected. Moreover, individuals identified with the anti-benchmarking position were elected to officer positions. In this regard, a particularly significant result was the very narrow victory of Patricia Wroe over Michael Ward. Ward had been treasurer for twenty-six years.[89]

In the general election campaign that followed soon afterwards, there were a few signs that the Association's intensive political lobbying had made some impact when, in response to a questionnaire, both Fine Gael and the PDs stated that they were willing to initiate talks with the ASTI outside the benchmarking process. In their responses to the same question, however, both Fianna Fáil and Labour were adamant that they would not make such a concession.[90]

The end of the pay dispute

The long-awaited report from the Public Service Benchmarking Body was eventually published at the end of June 2002. It recommended a wide spread of awards, ranging from 2.5 per cent to 25 per cent, but averaging 8.9 per cent. Teachers, who were awarded an above-average 13 per cent (with rather more for principals and deputy principals), were considered by one analyst to have been the only substantial group of workers to have got an award that was 'over the odds'. For some, this was no more than recognition of the fact that teachers had fallen behind other public servants during the previous years; for others, the 13 per cent indicated that the benchmarking body had been influenced by the militancy of the ASTI pay campaign. As Emmet Oliver, *The Irish Times* education correspondent, put it: 'A feeling, justified or not, that the bad boys and girls of the public service classroom are being rewarded may leave a bitter taste in the mouths of some union leaders.'[91]

The 13 per cent award may have been above average, but it was a long way from 30 per cent. The ASTI's attitude was complicated by the continuing supervision/substitution dispute, and by ongoing negotiations between the Department of Education and the other teachers' unions in respect of eligibility for pension purposes of supervision payments, so it was slow to react publicly. There was a special CEC meeting on the benchmarking report, which was followed by a meeting with the new minister for education, Noel Dempsey – a former ASTI member who had represented the Meath constituency since 1987. Dempsey was insistent that all claims would have to be pursued 'within the parameters of government pay policy'.[92]

By decision of standing committee, a series of regional information meetings was organised, followed by a special convention of 19 October 2002. A degree of battle-weariness, evidently, combined with the fact that significant tangible benefits had been brought within the reach of teachers, both from benchmarking and supervision payments (the department had offered the sought-for pension concession), had made the ASTI rank-and-file more amenable to a resolution, and this was reflected in the votes at the October convention.[93] One of the four resolutions adopted committed the Association to campaigning to 'bridge the gap between the pay of teachers and that of those in other comparable professions', but the result of the other votes indicated that attitudes were softening. Almost 70 per cent of the delegates voted to put the government's offer on supervision/substitution to a ballot of the members; 65 per cent of them voted in favour of holding a ballot on whether to co-operate with the introduction of new syllabi; 58 per cent of them voted in favour of requesting the CEC to consider the benchmarking award when full details became available. The outcome of the convention was regarded as a victory for Charlie Lennon and President P.J. Sheehy over those favouring the 'go it alone' strategy.[94]

The outcome of the membership ballots, as reported to standing committee in late November 2002 was sixty-three to thirty-seven in favour of accepting the offer on supervision/substitution, and fifty-eight to forty-two in favour of co-operating with the introduction of new syllabi. If this seemed to settle the supervision dispute, there were a few hurdles remaining, for the ASTI's interpretation of the scheme was rather different to that of the department and the school authorities. Accordingly, standing committee instructed members to withhold their co-operation in the matter 'until issues surrounding the implementation of the scheme have been clarified'.[95]

Clarification was forthcoming, but it was not to the satisfaction of the CEC, which recommended in January that members reject the department's proposals in another national ballot which was arranged for the month of March.[96] In the interval between the decision and the ballot, Minister Dempsey intervened with his own series of regional information meetings, in the course of which he stated that he intended to make the contingency plan permanent if the ASTI did not accept what was on the table. For the minister, the meetings represented an effort to provide full information, so that teachers might 'make an informed choice on the question of participation'. For the ASTI, the minister's action amounted to an 'extraordinary and unprecedented intervention by an employer in a union ballot'.[97] As the date of the supervision ballots approached the CEC convened a special meeting to discuss the benchmarking award – in line with the decision of the October special convention. Linked to the benchmarking issue by this point was the freshly negotiated social partnership agreement, Sustaining Progress, and the CEC decided by a substantial margin to put both to a ballot of members during early April.[98]

In the supervision ballot, members rejected the Association's official advice and accepted the deal by a margin of fifty-nine to forty-one. According to one commentator, the result was 'vindication of the decision by the Minister … to hold a series of meetings with ASTI members'.[99] Just two weeks later, members voted three to one to accept benchmarking and the new partnership agreement. Ironically, this outcome meant that the ASTI had become one of the strongest trade union supporters of Sustaining Progress.[100]

The two decisions brought a definitive end to a dispute that had gone on for more than three years. There was an expectation that delegates to an early April special convention might continue on the same moderate course and accept a change from branch-based to school-based ballots. Indeed, a small majority backed this proposal which had been strongly commended by Charlie Lennon, but it was a long way short of the two-thirds required for a rule change to come into effect.[101]

Aftershocks
With the pay dispute essentially resolved, it was anticipated by commentators that the 2003 annual convention, which took place a mere three weeks after the most recent special convention, would be a restrained affair that would usher in a period of 'normality'.[102] For *The*

Irish Times on the opening day, it was 'a very different kind of ASTI conference', one where there was much 'courtesy and plain good humour on display'. However, a few days later, a headline in the same paper conveyed the very different message: 'ASTI divisions dominate week.'[103] Rather than 'normality', the Association faced a number of aftershocks consequent on the great tumult of the previous few years.

Delegates in Limerick were startled by the resignation from the position of national organiser of Noel Buckley, who had supported the pay campaign but who now felt that it was time for the Association to move on and to change out of 'self-destruct mode'. Charlie Lennon had a similar message, but his call to delegates to 'engage in internal review, reflection and reform, and to re-evaluate and renew our relationships with our colleagues in other trade unions' was not received sympathetically. Rather, on the following day, an extraordinary petition signed by more than a quarter of the delegates demanded an emergency debate which would determine whether to initiate a review of the general secretary's performance.[104] President P.J. Sheehy ruled the demand out of order, citing legal advice to the effect that a review of the type proposed would breach the contractual arrangement between the Association and the general secretary. However, the president was over-ruled by a narrow majority of the CEC the next day, when a similar resolution was tabled.[105]

In another vote during convention week, a proposal to reaffiliate to ICTU was rejected, with incoming president Pat Cahill responding to Lennon's call for 'reform' with the argument that it was not the ASTI that needed to be reformed but ICTU, which he characterised as 'no better than IBEC'. Delegates also turned down a proposal to initiate merger talks with the TUI, because of lingering resentment that the other union had not supported the ASTI's pay campaign. Significantly, however, there was discontent about pay in the TUI and delegates to its Easter 2003 convention rejected an anti-benchmarking resolution by only a single vote.[106]

The developments during the closing days of the convention set the tone for the following year, during which internal struggles took centre stage. The battle between Charlie Lennon and his opponents would be fought to a conclusion before Christmas, but differences between the Association's leading bodies and its other employees would continue into the following year. There were some difficulties also in re-engaging with the social partnership process.

In this last respect, the Association came into conflict with the Department of Education and Science in September 2003, when it issued a directive to members not to co-operate with the new Junior Certificate Science syllabus until acknowledged deficiencies in the majority of school laboratories were addressed. The directive, it was found, was in breach of the social partnership agreement and the ASTI was forced to back down, so as to ensure that its members were not denied the increase due under the terms of Sustaining Progress.[107] Of this encounter, it was judged that the ASTI had 'provided the government with a perfect "target" in its bid to prove that benchmarking can deliver productivity changes'.[108] In a similar way during 2004, Sustaining Progress would hamper the Association in its efforts to win improvements in the supervision and substitution scheme.[109]

As the demands for a 'review' of the general secretary's performance indicated, mutual suspicion continued to characterise relations between the elected and professional leaderships of the Association. In the aftermath of the election of Patricia Wroe as treasurer in 2002, and in particular after the settlement of the pay dispute, the issues of contention increasingly became financial ones. Changes in procedure were introduced with regard to employee pensions and to the claiming of expenses, which staff regarded as unilateral and unreasonable, and these were among the issues that were referred to the Labour Court by SIPTU and the NUJ on behalf of their members employed at ASTI head office. On legal advice, however, the Association declined to attend Labour Relations Commission (LRC) talks on the complaint in June 2003 and a subsequent Labour Court hearing in October 2003. (The advice was given in the light of a separate dispute between the Association and its general secretary.) SIPTU's Patricia King strongly criticised the ASTI's stance, stating that it had been 'discourteous' to the Labour Court and that its members would be 'appalled' if they realised how head office staff had been treated by the 'management' (that is, the elected officers of the Association).[110] The Labour Court itself was equally critical of the ASTI, finding that 'proper attention to the welfare of the employees has not been in place for some time'. The court was sympathetic to the employees' complaint about the payment of expenses, and severe in its assessment of the working conditions of the ASTI staff, who, it stated, were entitled to 'operate in a workplace where they can get on with their job without the constant fear, or threat, from elected individuals who would appear to have no direct line responsibility'.[111] Controversially, standing committee rejected the Labour Court findings at a special two-day meeting – and was strongly criticised by other trade unions as a result. The dispute would rumble on for almost another year, until the Advisory Services Division of the LRC eventually brokered an agreement that was acceptable to the several parties.[112]

The new treasurer's scrutiny of financial records and procedures resulted in differences between the ASTI and its long-term auditors which would bring an end to that relationship. A substantial voluntary payment by the Association to the revenue commissioners was another consequence of these differences.[113]

The focus of the 'review' of Charlie Lennon's performance also shifted to financial issues in the months following the 2003 convention, and specifically to claims submitted in respect of day-to-day expenses incurred in the execution of his duties. In September 2003, Lennon won a High Court injunction blocking such inquiries on the grounds that the ASTI officers conducting them were biased against him. Subsequently, following negotiations at senior level, the CEC approved terms which would lead to the general secretary's departure from the Association. Lennon secured a substantial settlement, but, according to Seán Flynn of *The Irish Times*, it was hardly enough to 'compensate him for what has been the most difficult three years of his professional life'.[114]

After a further interval, there were signs of a return to the long-anticipated 'normality' in ASTI affairs. John White, former president, assistant general secretary at the time of deputy general secretary Charlie Lennon's departure and acting general secretary afterwards, was appointed general secretary in 2005. Also in 2005, convention voted to ballot members on whether to reaffiliate to ICTU. By a margin of almost four to one members voted to return to the fold in March 2006.[115] For his part, Charlie Lennon returned to work in the trade union movement, when he secured a senior position with Education International (EI) – Europe. In 1993, ASTI was one of the founder members of EI, the successor to the WCOTP, and Lennon had been prominently involved in its affairs during the following decade.[116]

*

As intimated earlier, any historical assessment of the pay campaign of 2000–03 and the related and consequent developments would be premature. That it placed great strain on the Association and, to varying extents, on relationships with the Department of Education, with parents, students, and employers, with other trade unions and with the industrial relations apparatus of the state will be readily agreed by all involved. That there was an adverse impact on morale in the profession will be conceded by most. And that the conduct of the struggle itself left much to be desired will also be acknowledged. The fact was that strategy – the efforts of a pay strategy committee notwithstanding – was devised in the heat of battle and was the fruit of compromises, of shifting alliances, of hasty responses to unexpected developments, and of the clashes of entrenched individuals. Even for Bernadine O'Sullivan, the person most publicly associated with the dispute, the battleground was poorly chosen. Writing in March 2002, she was critical of the strategy being then pursued – of the supervision ban, in particular, which she felt had 'distracted attention from the union's pay campaign'.[117] Unpredictability, of course, is inherent in conflict and it is rarely given to adversaries to choose the ideal circumstances for battle.

Half a decade on, there are many who strongly believe that benchmarking and supervision awards were pushed considerably upwards for all teachers by the combativeness of ASTI members. For others, the years of the pay campaign were years in the wilderness, during which injury was inflicted on relationships within the Association and on relationships between the Association and those on whom it depends. Sheila Parsons, president in 2005–06, contends however that key relationships, those between staff in the schools, those between teachers and students, and those between teachers and parents, returned to normal very soon after the dispute.[118]

12

The Association then and now
Conclusion

Not long after the establishment of the ASTI, journalist Sydney Brooks remarked as follows: 'More than any country I am acquainted with ... Ireland is a network of "organisations", leagues, factions and cliques. Almost every department of life seems to be on a committee basis ... A genius for combination penetrates to the lowest strata.'[1] The English visitor's impression is supported by other sources, in pointing to the intensity of democratic (and conspiratorial) activity at all levels of society at that time.

In such circumstances, it was to be expected that the assistant masters and assistant mistresses employed in the Irish intermediate education system should have wished to emulate tenant farmers, town tenants, national teachers, transport workers, drapers' assistants and others in establishing an association to assert their own rights. But if it seemed natural in 1909 to seek redress for grievances through collective action, to choose to do so brought consequences. The families of the Dublin transport workers who founded the ITGWU in the same year that the ASTI was founded paid a high price for their fortitude a few years later. Although the attrition rate was lower, there were also secondary teachers who were dismissed for standing by their Association. Among a number who lost their positions during 1911–12, for example, was the editor of its *Journal*, P.F. Condon. And later, in 1920, secondary teachers in Limerick were obliged – just as ITGWU members had been in 1913 – to choose between their union and their jobs. The choice was not usually as stark as that, but, as the recollections of Joe O'Connor and others show, individual ASTI members, scattered in ones and twos in schools throughout the island, had to confront or petition 'superiors' in order to secure basic entitlements.

Circumstances during its first decade pressed the Association into allying itself with the state in its clash with the school authorities – if not overtly so. The British state saw the necessity of improving Irish intermediate education and was prepared to invest in it, but insisted on a greater degree of state regulation in return. For teachers, state intervention promised common professional standards, with consequent improvements in pay and other conditions. There was undoubted progress on several fronts between 1909 and 1919, and it was during these years that secondary teachers first acquired a paymaster, the state, which was not their legal employer.

The ASTI successfully negotiated the transition to Saorstát Éireann – even if its character was changed somewhat by the loss of many of its Protestant members. And in reforming the secondary education system in the mid-1920s, the architects of the new state accepted the validity of much of the case made by teachers' representatives. While there were financial constraints, the reform programme initiated under the old regime was taken on board (though with the position of the Irish language strengthened). The more objectionable features of intermediate education were discarded, the recently-introduced teacher registration scheme was maintained, a new pension scheme was introduced, and the principle that the state should supplement the salaries of the privately employed secondary teachers of Ireland was accepted and applied in a more satisfactory fashion than it had been in the dog days of the old administration.

That, in relation to these issues, ASTI officers found themselves making representations to personal acquaintances, including old comrades in the national revolutionary movement and in the Association itself, undoubtedly gave advantages to secondary teachers, but there were limits to their influence. The architects of the new state in the 1920s and 1930s were disposed to accepting, in large measure, religious control in secondary education, and the ASTI's aspiration for a more democratic system, which would give a voice to teachers and local communities, could not be realised. Indeed, in the 1930s, due partly to the efforts of that wily and determined cleric John Charles McQuaid, even the aspiration was relinquished. The Association might be able to represent its members in a narrowly vocational sense, but it would be denied influence in relation to the system of education.

It was a judgement of the *FIRE* report, commissioned by the Catholic school management bodies and completed in 1973, that the ASTI had been largely 'ineffective' between the foundation of the state and the 1960s. Arguably, however, if the authors of the report were not Marxists, they were applying Marxist criteria in their assessment of the Association, evidently regarding a commitment to class warfare as the hallmark of the 'progressive' teacher representative, and indeed as the 'essence of trade unionism'.[2] It was certainly true, as they pointed out, that the ASTI had not 'adopted a militant attitude' between 1920 and 1969, but did that mean it had been ineffective? If one was to look at conditions and relative pay, it clearly did not. From being the Cinderellas of the profession in 1909, secondary teachers had been able to secure professional conditions during the following two decades, had been able to maintain and improve these conditions, and had been able to gain a salary advantage over other teachers. To charge the representative of the teachers concerned with being 'ineffective' is not justified therefore. The ASTI was insular between the 1920s and the 1960s – disconnected from the Irish trade union movement and having minimal contact with teachers' organisations elsewhere – but it was by and large alert to what was achievable for its members. It was a small organisation representing a small profession. Concessions were not that expensive therefore, from the state's perspective, provided they were confined to secondary teachers. So a policy of 'going it alone', combined with the cultivation of contacts in civil service and government, was understandable in the circumstances, even if it was not exactly 'progressive'. In pursuit of its claims from the school management bodies during this period, however, the ASTI was very careful, mainly because its members felt that in any struggle that pitted them against the Catholic Church, they would lose.

A great change came about in the 1960s. In an expanding and rapidly changing educational system, maintaining sectional privilege was problematic, but the ASTI was slow to adapt to the changed circumstances. Following the publication of the report of the Ryan Tribunal in 1968, it found itself in a protracted dispute, not just with the state, but with unions representing other teachers. The Catholic management bodies, themselves feeling threatened by the pace and direction of developments, gave some support to their employees, but it was lukewarm support and it was conditional. The last ditch effort to maintain the superior conditions of secondary teachers did not succeed – although the ASTI's militancy in 1969–71 may have won benefits for teachers generally. During the period of unrest, moreover, the Association had re-engaged with the broader Irish trade union movement, and during the 1970s, there was more of a co-ordinated response from the teachers' unions to the challenges posed by the expanding post-primary system and the decline in the number of teaching religious. During that decade, lay secondary teachers gained positions of authority in the schools and began to secure rights to representation in the management boards of their schools. Elements of the democratic education system envisaged by the ASTI's early leaders were finally being implemented.

The expansion of the system increased the size of the profession, and the ASTI grew at an unprecedented rate during the 1970s – some growth was inevitable, but the trebling of membership in that decade was due to the careful attention paid to the recruitment and retention of members. If the Association was not unique among teaching and other public service unions in organising almost all who were eligible to join, it was by no means inevitable that it should have done so.

Success in this respect was attributable to extraordinary commitment on the part of school stewards, of branch officers, and of those elected onto the leading bodies of the Association. In the testimony of many of those interviewed for this study, there were details of personal sacrifice and of risks taken in the course of representing teachers. One striking illustration was in the account of future president Tommy Francis of driving through the night from committee meetings in Dublin during the 1970s and 1980s, on a route that took him through bomb-torn Northern Ireland, so as to be in time for morning classes in his school in Falcarragh, County Donegal.[3]

While membership has grown steadily since the end of the 1970s, the professional apparatus of the Association has been completely transformed. It was necessary to employ specialists in negotiations, in education, in communications and other fields for a variety of reasons: the administrative requirements of a much larger organisation; the increasing demand among members for professional services; the difficulty of obtaining voluntary commitment on the necessary scale; the increasing complexity of post-primary education and industrial relations; the fresh opportunities that arose to influence educational policy. There were changes in the culture of the Association as a result of the influx, and a reordering of power relationships. That the adjustment would give rise to some tensions was inevitable, and some of these were seen starkly during the pay dispute that began in 2000. While this was a major dispute, which was intensely fought, historians will see it as but one of a number of significant episodes in the Association's story, during which its representatives, voluntary and professional, did their utmost to champion the cause of the secondary teacher in the understanding that 'a system of education that ignores the teacher is radically unsound', in the words of the first ASTI president, P.J. Kennedy.

*

Since the end of the most recent pay dispute, the Association has continued to deal with issues as they arise and to develop. In 2005, John White was appointed general secretary, having been acting general secretary for a period before that. A member of the Association since the early 1970s, who taught in the De La Salle College in Dundalk, he is the first former president since T.J. Burke to have assumed the senior administrative role. In a 2009 profile in *The Irish Times*, he was described as an 'unperturbable' and 'soft-spoken' individual, who had provided the 'measured leadership' that was so much required by the ASTI in the aftermath of the disputes of 2000–03.[4]

Acknowledging that he took over a 'battered organisation', White says that he was determined that it should 'look to the future rather than dwelling on the past'. Reviewing developments in the years between the pay dispute and the Association's centenary, he identified two areas in which he considers that important advances were made. The first was the achievement of security for many part-time and temporary teachers; the second was the restoration of the relationship with the broader teacher movement and the broader trade union movement.[5]

After a period as an observer immediately after the ASTI's reaffiliation, White was elected onto ICTU's executive council, like his two immediate predecessors. In that role, he feels that he has been able to influence national negotiations in the interests of his members. The agreement in relation to the part-timers was prompted by a European directive on contract working, but White argues that the very satisfactory way in which it was implemented in the education sector was attributable to the effective joint intervention of the teachers' unions. Education was the first sector for which an agreement was concluded, and a large number of teachers secured contracts of indefinite duration as a result. These were, in essence, permanent contracts.

In other respects, White contends that the role of the ASTI has been largely defensive since 2004. Social partnership agreements and 'benchmarking' have demanded 'modernisation' in the public sector, requiring the Association to make concessions with regard to the working conditions of teachers. He believes that changes in the arrangements governing parent–teacher meetings and staff meetings have been introduced in a way that does not 'place an excessive burden on teachers', and that a new scheme for addressing the issue of under-performing teachers has adequate safeguards. The ASTI has also been required to compromise in regard to its long-standing view that seniority be a central criterion in the promotion of teachers, but the phasing in of the new arrangements over a six-year period has allowed people time to adapt.

There have been challenges also from a 'marketisation' impulse affecting education, which has been felt in the publication of league tables and, until recently at least, in the proliferation of grind schools. The ASTI has been supported by parents' organisations in opposing league tables, which both agree are reductive and misleading. The Association also continues to oppose grind schools, as White explains:

> We have nailed our colours to the mast of a broad and holistic education … We have always argued that you can get a much better education than the force-feeding that you get in the grind schools, the so-called fifth-form colleges. As you go through life, it will serve you so much better if you've been given the opportunity to play hurling for your school, or to participate in debating, or to become involved in a school play …[6]

This is the philosophy that also informs the Association policy in relation to curriculum, and it seeks to persuade school authorities to offer programmes like transition year, Leaving Certificate Applied, and Leaving Certificate Vocational. It remains the ASTI's policy, according to White, that 'the best schools are those that educate students from all social backgrounds and of all levels of ability'. Selection, therefore, it regards as neither 'educationally valid nor socially defensible'.

In 2008–09, fresh challenges presented themselves when the government responded to the crisis in the public finances by cutting back in public services generally, and in public service pay in particular. Wage increases negotiated in the most recent social partnership agreement were frozen, levies were imposed on public servants and a recruitment embargo was announced (although teaching vacancies were exempted). For the first time since the early 1990s, ASTI members face a real decline in their standard of living. In the schools, at the same time, they will also have to address the consequences of government 'savings' in the supervision and substitution scheme.

In a challenging period for teachers' trade unions, White believes that deepening co-operation between them is vital – in order to defend education, and to defend the conditions of teachers.

> There has been good co-operation between ourselves, the TUI, the INTO and IFUT, and some discussion recently on the creation of a federal structure ... The important thing there is that we have a structure that we can all live with, that maximises our power and authority, but equally that doesn't destroy our individuality. We all have different histories. In any structure, we have to respect the fact that there are different terms of employment, different arrangements in several respects, different management structures, in the various sectors. In other words, we have to maximise what unites us, without diminishing too much our own sense of where we came from ...[7]

As the ASTI reaches its centenary, there are reasons for satisfaction and for optimism. Due largely to an increase in the number of special needs teachers in the system in recent years, it has over 18,000 members, the largest number in its history. Moreover, as White points out, teaching itself remains a worthwhile occupation, one with a moral dimension, one that provides job satisfaction, one in which the working conditions are generally good. And, as the hollowness of much of what was esteemed in the 'Celtic Tiger' era is being recognised, teaching as a career is again proving attractive to a new generation of younger people.

Appendix I
Presidents 1909–2009

Mr. W.S. Cooney, 1909–10 (chairman)
Mr. P.J. Kennedy, 1910–12
Mr. W. Johnston, 1912–13
Mr. G.A. Watson, 1913–17
Mr. W.J. Williams, 1917–18
Mr. G.A. Watson, 1918–19
Mr. T.J. Burke, 1919–20
Mr. L.C. Murray, 1920–21
Mr. B. Gillespie, 1921–23
Mr. M. Kinsella, 1923–24
Mr. A. Ruttledge, 1923–24
Mr. J.H. Kane, 1924–25
Mr. T.P. Waller, 1925–26
Miss A.J. Mulligan, 1926–27
Mr. J.J. Murphy, 1927–28
Mr. G.P. Duggan, 1928–29
Mr. J.H. Kane, 1929–30
Mr. T. O'Beirne, 1930–32
Mr. T. O'Donoghue, 1932–33
Mr. C.L. Dillon, 1933–34
Mr. G.D. Daly, 1934–35
Mr. J.H. Kane, 1935–37
Mr. F. Kennedy, 1937–38
Mr. T.P. Waller, 1938–40
Mr. T.J. Boylan, 1940–42
Mr. T. O'Donoghue, 1942–43
Mr. C.L. Dillon, 1943–45
Mr. T. Walsh, 1945–46

Mr. D. Buckley, 1946–47
Mr. O. P. War,d 1947–49
Mr. W.G. Kirkpatrick, 1949–50
Mr. S. Ó Mathúna, 1950–51
Mr. D. Ó Conalláin, 1951–52
Mr. T.C. Coppinger, 1952–53
Mr. W. Meyler, 1953–54
Mr. P.J. O'Reilly, 1954–55
Mr. G. Ó Maoilmhichíl, 1955–56
Mr. P.J. Hardiman, 1956–57
Mr. L.A. Comerford, 1957–58
Miss N. Kelleher, 1958–59
Mr. C.L. Dillon, 1959–60
Mr. J. Wilson, 1959–60
Mr. T. Murphy, 1960–61
Mr. P.S. Gillman, 1961–62
Mr. G. Lyons, 1962–63
Mr. D. Ó Murchú, 1963–64
Mr. P. Finnegan, 1964–65
Mr. D. Buckley, 1965–66
Mr. J.A. Bromell, 1966–68
Mr. H. Duffy, 1968–69
Mr. M. Sheedy, 1969–70
Mr. T. O'Dea, 1970–71
Padraig Ó Riordáin, 1971–72
Kevin Meehan, 1972–73
Pierce Purcell, 1973–74
Liam Hogan, 1974–75
Alf Sheehy, 1975–76
Macartan MacCormack, 1976–77
Derek Nolan, 1977–79
Mary MacCarthy, 1979–80
David Barry, 1980–81
Tony Boland, 1981–82
Margaret Walsh, 1982–83
Ray Kennedy, 1983–84
Henry Collins, 1984–85
Louis O'Flaherty, 1985–86
John White, 1986–87

Dermot Quish, 1987–88
Kathleen O'Sullivan, 1988–89
Éamon Ó hAllmhuráin, 1989–90
Joe Costello, 1990–91
Willie Ruane, 1991–92
Joe Whyte, 1992–93
Mary Dowling Maher, 1993–94
Sean Higgins, 1994–95
Tommy Francis, 1995–96
John Mulcahy, 1996–97
John Hurley, 1997–98
Michael Corley, 1998–99
Bernadine O'Sullivan, 1999–2000
Don McCluskey, 2000–01
Catherine Fitzpatrick, 2001–02
P.J. Sheehy, 2002–03
Pat Cahill, 2003–04
Susie Hall, 2004–05
Sheila Parsons, 2005–06
Michael Freeley, 2006–07
Patricia Wroe, 2007–08
Pat Hurley, 2008–09
Joe Moran, 2009–2010

Appendix II
General Secretaries

The terms 'general secretary' was in use at least from 1914. Some gaps exist for the early years.

Mr. P.F. Condon 1909–11
Mr. G. Dempsey 1912–13
Mr. Gallagher 1913–14
Mr. Mellett 1914–15
Mr. W.J. Williams 1916–17
Miss A. McHugh 1917–18
Mr. T.J. Burke August 1920–August 1937 (first full-time general
    secretary; worked as part-time general secretary from home 1926-37)
Mr. J. Carey September 1937–January 1938 (acting general secretary)
Mr. Liam Glynn January 1938–May 1938
Miss F.E. Quirke May 1938–July 1957 (full-time general secretary)
Messrs D. Buckley and C. O'Gara, August 1957–May 1958
Miss Máire MacDonagh June 1958–March 1983
Mr. Kieran Mulvey 1983–91
Mr. Charlie Lennon 1991–2003
Mr. John White acting General Secretary 2003–05; General Secretary
    2005–present

Endnotes

Chapter 1: *An 'outcast pedagogue'*

1. H. Sheehy-Skeffington, 'Irish secondary teachers', *Irish Review*, October 1912, p. 396. See also L. Levenson, and J.H. Naterstad, *Hanna Sheehy Skeffington: Irish feminist*, Syracuse, 1986, pp. 1–32.
2. Sheehy Skeffington, 'Irish secondary teachers', p. 369.
3. ibid.
4. *Intermediate Education (Ireland) Commission,* 1899, xxiii, minutes of evidence, p. 651.
5. ibid; S. Chuinneagáin, *Catherine Mahon: first woman president of the INTO*, Dublin, 1998, pp. 24–7.
6. P. Pearse, 'The murder machine', *Political writings and speeches*, Dublin, 1962, p. 42.
7. The first chair of education at an Irish university was established at Trinity in 1905; UCG (Queen's College Galway until 1908) did not acquire its own chair until 1915.
8. M. Breathnach, *Cuimhne an tseanpháiste*, Dublin, 1966, pp. 150–56; R. Butler (ed.), *St Flannan's College, 1881–1981*, Ennis, 1981, p. 73; J. Cunningham, *St Jarlath's College, Tuam: 1800–2000*, Tuam, 1999, pp. 153–60.
9. J. O'Connor, 'Disillusioned', *The School & College Yearbook*, 1954, pp. 17–18.
10. *Irish Times*, 16 October 1911.
11. S. O'Faolain, *Vive moi! An autobiography*, London, 1965, p. 183–84.
12. J. Coolahan, *The ASTI and post-primary education in Ireland, 1909–1984*, Dublin, 1984, p. 10; O'Connor, 'Disillusioned', pp. 17–18.
13. T.J. O'Connell, *History of the Irish National Teachers' Organisation, 1868–1968*, Dublin, 1969, p. 152.
14. M. Hearn, *Below stairs: domestic service remembered in Dublin and be-*

yond, 1880–1922, Dublin, 1993, p. 48; F.A. Darcy, 'Wages of labourers in the Dublin building industry, 1667–1918', *Saothar*, vol. 14, 1989, pp. 17–32, and 'Wages of skilled workers in the Dublin building industry, 1667-1918', *Saothar*, vol. 15, 1990, pp. 21–37; D.J. O'Sullivan, *The Irish constabularies, 1822–1922: a century of policing in Ireland*, Dingle, 1999, pp. 232–33.

15. J. O'Connor, '"Old, unhappy, far-off things": a personal reminiscence', *The School & College Yearbook*, 1956.

16. ibid.

17. Cited in E.G. West, 'The political economy of alienation: Karl Marx and Adam Smith', in J. Cunningham Wood (ed.), *Karl Marx's economics: critical assessments*, vol. 1, Beckenham, 1988, pp. 140–41.

18. J.H. Murphy, *Nos autem: Castleknock College and its contribution*, Dublin, *c.*1996, p. 90.

19. T.J. McElligott, *Secondary education in Ireland, 1870–1921*, Dublin, 1981, pp. 1–29; J. Coolahan, *Irish education: history and structure*, Dublin, 1981, pp. 52–81.

20. ibid. Of course, students in second-level schools were prepared for matriculation examinations in the universities and, after 1870, for civil service examinations.

21. S. Farragher, *Pere Leman: educator and missionary, founder of Blackrock College*, Dublin, 1988, pp. 388–416; Cunningham, *St Jarlath's College*, pp. 132–34.

22. Coolahan, *Irish education,* pp. 56–65; McElligott, *Secondary education,* pp. 41–78; D. Raftery, S.M. Parkes, *Female education in Ireland, 1700–1900: Minerva or Madonna*, Dublin, 2007, pp. 76–81.

23. *Irish Times*, 16 October 1911.

24. E.B. Titley, *Church, state, and the control of schooling in Ireland, 1900–1944*, Montreal, 1983, pp. 37–38; McElligott, *Secondary education,* pp. 61–63.

25. Pearse, 'Murder machine' p. 35.

26. Coolahan, *ASTI*, p. 10; T. Foley and F. Bateman, 'English, History, and Philosophy', in Foley (ed.), *From Queen's College to National University: essays on the academic history of QCG/UCG/NUI Galway*, Dublin, 1999, pp. 395–96.

27. F.H. O'Donnell, *The ruin of education in Ireland: and the Irish Fanar*, London, 1903 (cited in Titley, *Control of Schooling*). See also A. Ní Chonghaile, *F.H O'Donnell: a shaol agus a shaothar*, Dublin, 1992, *passim*.

28. C. Clear, *Nuns in nineteenth-century Ireland*, Dublin, 1997, pp. 120–22.

29. Alice Oldham in Bourke et al, *The Field Day Anthology of Irish Writing, vol.5, Irish Women's Writing and Tradition,* Cork, 2002, pp. 665–66.

30. E. Larkin, 'Church, state, and nation in modern Ireland', *American Historical Review,* vol. 80, no. 5, 1980, p. 1260.

31. ibid., pp. 1261–66.

32. Titley, *Control of schooling,* pp. 7–10, 71–80, 130–35: Coolahan, *ASTI, passim.*

33. Titley, *Control of schooling,* p. 14.

34. ibid., pp. 13–22; 43–48.

35. *Report of Messrs F.H. Dale and T.A. Stephens on intermediate education in Ireland,* 1905, xxviii, p. 42; S. Pašeta, *Before the revolution: nationalism, social change, and Ireland's Catholic elite, 1879–1922,* Cork, 1999, p. 31.

36. Coolahan, *ASTI,* pp. 23, 35.

37. Breathnach, *Cuimhne,* p. 159; *Report of Dale and Stephens,* p. 43; Sheehy-Skeffington, 'Irish secondary teachers', p. 397.

38. *Report of Dale and Stephens,* pp. 39–40; Pašeta, *Before the revolution,* p. 30.

39. Pašeta, *Before the revolution,* p. 37; C.C. O'Brien, *States of Ireland,* London, 1971, p. 61. F. Campbell, *The Irish establishment, 1879–1914,* Oxford 2009, pp. 312–18.

40. *Report of Dale and Stephens,* p. 40–41.

41. J. O'Connor, *Hostage to fortune,* Dublin, 1951, p. 133; Breathnach, *Cuimhne,* p. 184.

42. Cunningham, *St Jarlath's College,* pp. 168–70; G.K. White, *A history of St Columba's College, 1843–1974,* Dublin, 1981, pp. 128–29; E. Sisson, *Pearse's patriots: St Enda's and the cult of boyhood,* Cork, 2004, p. 32.

43. C. Clear, *Social change and everyday life in Ireland, 1850–1922,* Manchester, 2007, p. 50.

44. Breathnach, *Cuimhne,* p. 187. M. Ní Mhurchú and D. Breathnach, 'Micheál Breathnach', *1983–2003, Beathaisnéis,* Dublin 2003.

45. O'Connor, *Hostage,* pp. 163-64.

46. D. Rudd, *Rochelle: the history of a school in Cork,* Cork, 1979, pp. 72–74; A. Jordan, *Margaret Byers: pioneer of women's education and founder of Victoria College, Belfast,* Belfast, 1987, pp. 43–44.

47. A.V. O'Connor and S.M. Parkes, *Gladly learn and gladly teach: a history of Alexandra College and School, 1866–1966,* Dublin, 1983, p. 130.

Chapter 2: *'Dissatisfaction with the present condition of things'*

1. *Irish Independent,* 15 January 1907; *Irish Times,* 15 September 1915;

ASTI, register for 1913.

2. *Irish Independent*, 15 January 1907.

3. *Irish School Weekly*, 24 November 1934, 28 March 1936.

4. O'Connor, 'Far-off things', p. 19.

5. Coolahan, *ASTI*, pp. 14–15; J. O'Connor, 'Far-off things', p. 19; *Southern Star*, 17 July 1909.

6. Coolahan, *ASTI*, p. 6.

7. ibid., pp. 6–7.

8. Coolahan, *ASTI*, p.13; cf. M. Coleman, *IFUT, a history: the Irish Federation of University Teachers, 1963–1999*, Dublin, 2000, p. 3; *Intermediate Education (Ireland) Commission, 1899, Appendix ix: persons to whom schedules were issued*, pp. liii–liv. A.E. Dowds BA and Douglas Scott BA, both employed at Trinity College, were among the AIUT members consulted by the Intermediate Education Commissioners.

9. *Freeman's Journal*, 8 January 1898.

10. ibid., 10 January 1898.

11. Coolahan, *ASTI*, p. 8.

12. Chuinneagáin, *Catherine Mahon*, pp. 49–51.

13. Coolahan, *ASTI*, p. 9; *Freeman's Journal*, 10 January 1898.

14. AIUT, *Secondary education in Ireland: a plea for reform*, Dublin, 1904, pp. 2–3, 7; *Irish Times*, 31 March 1904; Coolahan, *ASTI* p. 14, *passim*.

15. Titley, *Control of Schooling*, pp. 22-25.

16. ibid.

17. AIUT, *Secondary education*, p. 5; *Freeman's Journal*, 29 January, 3 November 1908.

18. *Irish Times*, 25 June 1907; *Irish Independent*, 15 January 1907.

19. *Intermediate Education (Ireland) Commission,* 1899, xxiii, minutes of evidence, par. 9480–81, Appendix ix, pp.liii-liv, Appendix xi, p. 8; *Irish Times,* 1 August 1905.

20. J.A. Norstedt, *Thomas MacDonagh, a critical biography*, Charlottesville, 1980, p. 24–27, 37–38; E.W. and A.W. Parks, *Thomas MacDonagh: the man; the patriot; the writer*, Athens, Georgia 1967, pp. 8-14

21. Earl of Longford and T.P. O'Neill, *Eamon de Valera*, Dublin 1970, pp. 12–14; S. Farragher, 'Éamon de Valera and Blackrock, 1898–1921', in G. Doherty and D. Keogh, *De Valera's Irelands*, Cork, 2003, pp. 2944.

22. C.F. Fallon, *Soul of fire: a biography of Mary MacSwiney,* Cork, 1986, pp. 32–34; UCD Archives, Mary MacSwiney papers, P48a/7: Correspondence between Sister M Elizabetts, Ursuline convent, Blackrock, Cork, and Cork branch of ASTI, relating to Mary MacSwiney's loss of

her teaching post at St Angela's.

23. C.D. Greaves, *The Irish Transport and General Workers Union: the formative years* Dublin 1982, pp. 11–50.

24. Coolahan, *ASTI*, p. 13–15; Norstedt, *Thomas MacDonagh*, pp. 37–38.

25. Cited in Parks and Parks, *Thomas MacDonagh*, p. 9.

26. *Cork Examiner*, 16 November 1910. I am grateful to John Mulcahy, ASTI president 1996–97, for drawing my attention to this item.

27. ibid.

28. *Irish Journal of Education*, January 1914; J. Fleming and S. O'Grady, *St Munchin's College Limerick, 1796-1996*, Limerick, 1996, pp. 147–54.

29. P.J.N. Riordan, 'The Association of Secondary Teachers, Ireland, 1909-1968: some aspects of its growth and development', unpublished MA thesis, UCC, 1975, p. 28.

30. P.F. Sexton, 'The lay teachers' struggle for status in Catholic secondary schools in Ireland between 1878 and 1937', unpublished MEd. thesis, University of Birmingham, 1972, pp. 61–62; *Irish Journal of Education*, September 1912.

31. *Irish Journal of Education*, September 1912, February 1913; *Irish Times*, 1 October 1912.

32. *Irish Journal of Education*, September 1912.

33. O'Connor, 'Far-off things', p. 19. In this context, *cadhain aonair* might be translated as 'scattered geese'.

34. *Irish Journal of Education*, March 1910, December 1911.

35. ibid., March 1910.

36. ibid, April, November 1910, April 1912.

37. ibid., June 1913, March 1914, January 1915; *Southern Star*, 15 July 1909.

38. *Report of Dale and Stephens*, pp. 19–20, appendix vi.

39. ASTI, Dublin membership and attendance register, 1912-16.

40. *Irish Journal of Education*, April 1910, March, April, September 1911.

41. Titley, *Control of schooling*, pp. 37–38, 47–48; *Irish Journal of Education*, October 1912; J.A. Gaughan, *A political odyssey: Thomas O'Donnell, M.P. for West Kerry, 1900–1918*, Dublin, 1983, pp. 54–65, 13-31.

42. *Irish Journal of Education*, June 1915.

43. Ibid., October, November 1915, February 1916; *Report of Dale & Stephens*, appendix vi; *Southern Star*, 15 September 1909.

44. M. Ó hÓgartaigh, 'Female teachers and professional trade unionism in early 20th century Ireland', *Saothar*, vol. 29, 2004 pp. 33–41; M. Luddy, 'Working women, trade unionism and politics in Ireland, 1830-

1945', in Lane and Ó Drisceoil (eds) *Politics and the Irish working class, 1830–1945*, Houndmills, 2005, pp. 46-51, 53-54.

45. *Irish Journal of Education*, April 1914.

46. ibid., September 1916; H. Kean, 'Teachers and the state, 1900–30', *British Journal of Sociology of Education*, vol. 10, no. 2, 1989.

47. M. Ward, *Unmanageable revolutionaries: women and Irish nationalism* Dingle, 1983, pp. 40-41.

48. Chuinneagáin, *Catherine Mahon*, pp. 13–14; M. Jones, *'These obstreperous lassies': a history of the Irish Women Workers' Union*, Dublin, 1988, pp. 1–31; T. Moriarty, 'Mary Galway', in Cullen and Luddy (eds), *Female activists: Irish women and change, 1900–1960*, Dublin 2001.

49. *Irish Journal of Education*, January 1911, March 1912, December 1914; O'Connor and Parkes, *Alexandra College and School*, pp. 50, 53.

50. *Irish Journal of Education*, May 1912.

51. *Irish Journal of Education*, May 1912, December 1913; T.W. Moody, *Queen's, Belfast: the history of a university*, London, 1959, pp. 450–51, 503–04.

52. *Irish Journal of Education*, January 1915; Chuinneagáin, *Catherine Mahon*, pp. 61–69.

53. *Irish Journal of Education*, April 1914.

54. Cited in Coolahan, *ASTI*, p. 22.

55. ibid., pp. 22–25; Titley, *Control of schooling*, pp. 20, 32.

56. Titley, *Control of Schooling*, pp. 13-17.

57. Riordan, 'Association of Secondary Teachers, Ireland', p. 31.

58. *Irish Journal of Education*, October 1912.

59. Riordan, 'Association of Secondary Teachers, Ireland', pp. 33–34; Coolahan, *ASTI* pp. 25–29.

60. Titley, *Control of schooling*, p. 41–43, 46.

61. ibid.

62. *Irish Journal of Education*, September, October, December 1912; Coolahan, *ASTI*, pp. 28–29; G. Fitzpatrick, *St Andrew's College: ardens sed virens*, Dublin, 1994, pp. 23, 41, 98, 166.

63. Coolahan, *ASTI*, pp. 29-30; Riordan, 'Association of Secondary Teachers, Ireland', pp. 34–39.

64. Riordan, 'Association of Secondary Teachers, Ireland', pp. 44–45.

65. Coolahan, ASTI, pp. 34–35

66. O'Connor, 'Far-off things', p. 23

67. ibid.

68. *Irish Journal of Education*, April 1916.

69. R. Tubridy, 'The origins and development of the Registration Council for Secondary Teachers in Ireland, 1914–1960', unpublished MEd. thesis, UCD 1984, pp. 44-59.

70. ibid., pp. 60–77, Coolohan, *ASTI*, pp. 35–38.

71. Sexton, 'Lay teachers' struggle', pp. 84–93; T.J. O'Connell, *History of the INTO*, pp. 180–82, 289-91; Raftery and Parkes, *Minerva or Madonna*, pp. 98-101.

72. Cited in Sexton, 'Lay teacher's struggle,' p. 85.

73. ibid., pp. 87–88.

74. Cited in McElligott, *Secondary education*, p. 134.

75. ibid.

76. ASTI: General meeting, 5 July 1919; standing committee, 15 October 1919; CEC, 2 January 1920.

77. *Irish Journal of Education*, March, September 1912.

78. ibid., March 1914.

79. ibid., September 1916, January 1917.

80. E. O'Connor, *Syndicalism in Ireland, 1917–23,* Cork, 1988, *passim*; E. O'Connor, *A labour history of Ireland, 1824–1960*, pp. 94-108; C. Kostick, 'Labour militancy during the War of Independence', in Lane and Ó Drisceoil (eds), *Politics and the Irish working class*, pp. 187–206.

81. G. McMullan, 'The Irish bank "strike"', 1920, *Saothar,* vol. 5, 1979, pp. 39–49; E. O'Connor, 'Dawn chorus: the origins of trade unionism in vocational education', in Logan (ed) *Teachers' Union: the TUI and its forerunners, 1899–1994,* Dublin, 1999, pp. 47–48; O'Connell, *Irish National Teachers' Organisation*, pp. 466–67.

82. Cited R.H. Mapstone, 'Trade union and government relations: a case study of influence on the Stormont government', *Saothar*, vol. 12, 1987, p. 36. See also Mapstone, *The Ulster Teachers' Union: an historical perspective*, Coleraine, 1986, pp. 35–41.

83. Coolahan, *ASTI*, pp. 55–58

84. ibid.; Riordan, 'Association of Secondary Teachers, Ireland', p. 61.

85. Sexton, 'Lay teachers' struggle', pp. 93–94; John Coolahan, 'The ASTI and the secondary teachers' strike of 1920', *Saothar*, vol. 10, 1985, pp. 43–59; Riordan, 'Association of Secondary Teachers, Ireland', pp. 60–63.

86. Coolahan, *ASTI* p. 51.

87. Riordan, 'ASTI', pp. 62-63. 'Scavengers' were street cleaners.

88. As reported by *Irish Times,* 14 September 1920.

89. Coolahan, 'Strike of 1920', p.49.

90. ibid., pp. 43–59.

91. Fr Corboy, Mungret College, Limerick, to CHA secretary, cited in Sexton, 'Lay teachers' struggle', p. 116.

92. Coolahan, 'Strike of 1920', pp. 50–51.

93. Sexton, 'Lay teachers' struggle', p. 118.

94. Riordan, 'Association of Secondary Teachers, Ireland', pp. 64–65; Coolahan, 'Strike of 1920', pp. 50–51; Sexton, 'Lay teachers' struggle', pp. 115-18.

95. Riordan, 'Association of Secondary Teachers, Ireland', pp. 62–63; Coolahan, 'Strike of 1920, pp. 51–52.

96. Cited in Sexton, 'Lay teachers' struggle', p. 113.

97. *Irish Independent*, 1 June 1920.

98. *Freeman's Journal*, 2, 7 June 1920.

99. Sexton, 'Lay teachers' struggle', p. 118; Coolahan, *ASTI*, p. 55.

100. *Irish School Weekly*, 3 August 1920.

Chapter 3: *'Patient effort to effect an improvement'*

1. *Irish School Weekly*, 1 December 1934.

2. ibid., 22 December 1934.

3. P. O'Mahony and G. Delanty, *Rethinking Irish history: nationalism, identity, and ideology*, Houndmills, 1998, pp. 75–78.

4. D. O'Leary, *Vocationalism and social Catholicism in twentieth-century Ireland*, Dublin, 2000, p. 50.

5. *Irish Independent*, 10 December 1934.

6. *Irish School Weekly*, 22 December 1934.

7. *Irish Times*, 10 December, 1934.

8. J.J. Lee, *Ireland, 1912–1985: politics and society*, Cambridge, 1989, p. 42.

9. S. Farren, *The politics of Irish education, 1920–65*, Belfast, 1995, pp. 15–20

10. ibid., 52–54.

11. ibid., 56-58; Coolahan, *ASTI*, pp. 70–71.

12. B.P. Murphy, *The* Catholic Bulletin *and republican Ireland, 1898–1926, with special reference to J.J. O'Kelly* Belfast 2005, *passim*.

13. J.M. Regan, *The Irish counter-revolution, 1921–1936* Dublin 1999, pp. 93–94, 198–224; Farren, *Irish education*, pp. 106–13; Titley, *Control of Schooling*, pp. 101-06.

14. *Irish Times*, 10 January, 14 April 1923.

15. D.H. Akenson, *A mirror to Kathleen's face: education in independent*

Ireland, Montreal, 1975, pp. 26–33; Lee, *Ireland*, p. 105; P. Bew, *Ireland: the politics of enmity, 1798–2006* Oxford, 2007, p. 445. See also biographical studies of MacNeill: F.X. Martin, *The scholarly revolutionary: Eoin MacNeill, 1867–1945, and the making of the new Ireland*, Shannon 1973; Tierney, M. Eoin MacNeill: scholar and man of action, 1867–1945, Oxford, 1980.

16. Cited in Titley, *Control of schooling*, p. 91.

17. S. Ó Buachalla, *Education policy in twentieth-century Ireland*, Dublin 1988, pp. 253-56.

18. Cited in Coolahan, *ASTI*, p. 65.

19. *Irish Times*, 16 December 1924.

20. Ó Buachalla, *Education policy*, pp. 257–59; Regan, *Counter-revolution*, p. 252; J. O'Connor, 'The teaching of Irish: testament of a pioneer', *Capuchin Annual*, 1949, p. 212.

21. Titley, *Control of schooling*, pp. 94–100, Akenson, pp. 44–47; Coolahan, *ASTI*, pp. 36, 45.

22. O'Connor, 'The teaching of Irish', p. 209.

23. Cited in Titley, *Control of schooling*, p. 94.

24. ibid, p. 100.

25. O'Connor, 'The teaching of Irish', p. 210.

26. D. MacFhionnlaoich, 'Comments on the article', *Capuchin Annual*, 1949, pp. 237–40.

27. Department of Education, *Report of the Council of Education on the Curriculum of the Secondary School*, 1960, pp. 70–76.

28. ibid., pp. 72, 88.

29. Coolahan, *ASTI*, pp. 131–32; O'Connell, *Irish National Teachers' Organisation*, pp. 466–68; N. Puirséil, *The Irish Labour Party, 1922–73*, Dublin, 2007, pp. 8–30.

30. Coolahan, *ASTI*, p. 67.

31. ASTI, Dublin branch minutes, 30 January 1926, 27 March 1926.

32. ibid., 17 April 1926. *Infra dignitatem*: beneath (our) dignity.

33. Coolahan, *ASTI*, pp. 131–32.

34. O'Connor, *A labour history*, pp. 120–24; E. McKay., 'Changing with the tide: the Irish Labour Party, 1927–33, *Saothar*, vol. 11, 1986, pp. 27–38; Puirséil, *Labour Party*, pp. 30–33.

35. Coolahan, *ASTI*, p. 97.

36. Coolahan, *ASTI*, pp. 88–89; *Intermediate Education (Ireland) Commission* 1899, p. liv.

37. Coolahan, *ASTI*, pp. 6 9–71.

38. ibid., pp. 74–75.

39. O'Faolain, *Vive moi!*, p. 187.

40. Coolahan, *ASTI*, pp. 79–80; E. De Blaghd, *Gaeil á múscailt*, Dublin, 1973, pp. 119–21.

41. Riordan, 'Association of Secondary Teachers, Ireland', pp. 87–88, 159–60; Coolahan, *ASTI*, pp. 79–80.

42. Coolahan, *ASTI*, pp. 86–87, 98–101.

43. *Cork Examiner,* 16 November 1910.

44. ASTI, *Security of tenure*, Dublin, 1934, p. 23.

45. ibid., p. 19.

46. Sexton, 'Lay teachers' struggle', pp. 115–18; Coolahan, 'Strike of 1920', pp. 50–51, and *ASTI*, pp. 50, 83–84.

47. Coolahan, *ASTI*, pp. 81-83, 111-12; Riordan, 'Association of Secondary Teachers, Ireland', pp. 80-92.

48. Coolahan, *ASTI*, pp. 113–16.

49. Cited in O'Leary, *Vocationalism and Social Catholicism,* p. 51.

50. ibid.

51. Dublin Diocesan Archive, Archbishop Byrne papers, McQuaid to Byrne, 15 June 1934.

52. ibid., 1 October 1934.

53. ibid., 5 October 1934.

54. ibid., 1 October 1934.

55. Riordan, 'Association of Secondary Teachers, Ireland', p. 94.

56. ibid., p. 99.

57. ibid., pp. 99–106; Sexton, 'Lay teachers' struggle', pp. 101–2.

58. ASTI, *Official report of 15th annual convention* 1937, p. 24.

59. ibid.

60. ibid., p. 23.

61. Coolahan, *ASTI*, pp. 118–20.

62. Cited in Coolahan, *ASTI,* p. 114.

63. ASTI, Minutes of the 1935 convention.

64. Coolahan, *ASTI*, pp. 135–37.

65. 'Thomas Joseph Burke' (obituary), *Blackrock Annual*, 1970, pp. 228–29.

Chapter 4: *'Diligence and enthusiasm in the interests of secondary teachers'*

1. Coolahan, *ASTI*, pp. 137, 174; ASTI, *Official programme of the 16th annual convention*, 1938, p. 15; M.J. Wigham, *Newtown School, Waterford, 1798–1998: a history*, Waterford, 1998, pp. 176–79.

2. ASTI, Quirke file.

3. Coolahan, *ASTI*, p. 174; *Irish Independent*, 21 April 1938; W.G.K., 'An appreciation of the ex-General Secretary', *School & College Yearbook*, 1958, p. 37.

4. ASTI, *Official programme of the 15th annual conference*, 1938, pp. 8-9, 34–35.

5. Coolahan, *ASTI*, pp. 176–77; ASTI, *Official programme of the 24th annual conference*, 1946, pp. 9–10, 22–23.

6. Coolahan, *ASTI*, p. 97.

7. ASTI, Quirke file.

8. B. Girvin, 'The state and vocational education, 1922–1960', pp. 62–92, and Á. Hyland, 'The curriculum of Vocational Education, 1930–1966', both in Logan (ed.), *Teachers' Union* pp. 131–56.

9. Coolahan, *ASTI*, pp. 142–46.

10. J. Cooney, *John Charles McQuaid: ruler of Catholic Ireland*, Dublin 1999, p. 112.

11. ibid, pp. 59–93; Coolahan, *ASTI*, pp. 95–96; O'Leary, *Social Catholicism*, pp. 38–64.

12. Tubridy, 'Registration Council', pp. 83–95, 147–65.

13. ASTI, *Official programme of the 24th annual convention*, 1946, p. 29.

14. Tubridy, 'Registration Council', pp. 156–67.

15. Coolahan, *ASTI*, pp.110, 162–63.

16. ASTI, *Official programme of the 24th annual convention*, 1946, pp. 27–28.

17. A graduate teacher, 'The position of secondary teachers', and 'Secondary education in Ireland', *Cork University Record*, no. 6, 1946, pp. 37–42, and no. 8, 1946, pp. 24–26; A lay teacher, 'The stop-gap profession', *Cork University Record*, no. 15, 1949, pp. 21–23.

18. *Cork University Record*, no. 8, , 1946, p. 25.

19. ibid., no. 6, 1946 pp. 39–40.

20. ibid., no. 15, 1949, p. 23.

21. ibid., pp. 22, 23.

22. ibid, no. 15, p. 21, no. 17, 1949, p. 23.

23. Cunningham, *St Jarlath's College*, pp. 5–6.

24. Coolahan, *ASTI*, pp. 157–58. J.A. Gaughan, *Alfred O'Rahilly, vol. 3, controversialist: part 1, social reformer* pp. 126–65; part. 2, *controversialist*, Dublin 1992, pp. 46–47, Puirséil, *Labour Party*, pp. 84–85, 104–05.

25. Rev. T. Foy, 'The stop-gap profession', *Cork University Record*, no. 19,

1949, pp. 30-34.

26. ibid.

27. *Cork University Record*, no. 8, 1946, pp. 24–26.

28. Coolahan, *ASTI*, pp. 150, 167–69.

29. D. Ó Drisceoil, '"Whose emergency is it?":": wartime politics and the Irish working class, 1939–45', in Lane and Ó Drisceoil (eds), *Politics and the Irish working class*, pp. 262–80.

30. Ó Buachalla, *Education policy*, pp. 261–68: B. Arnold, *The Irish Gulag: how the state betrayed its innocent children*, Dublin 2009, pp. 31–42.

31. Riordan, 'Associaton of Secondary Teachers, Ireland', p. 159–61.

32. ibid., pp.160–62; Coolahan, *ASTI*, pp. 153.

33. E. McCormick, *The INTO and the 1946 Teachers' Strike*, Dublin 1996, pp. 13–23.

34. ibid., pp. 36–48; E. MacDermott, *Clann na Poblachta*, Cork, 1998, pp. 34–37.

35. ASTI, Dublin branch minutes, March–November 1946.

36. National Archives, TAOIS/6341 A 10.

37. Coolahan, *ASTI*, pp. 153–55; Riordan, 'Associaton of Secondary Teachers, Ireland', pp. 140–41.

38. D. McCullagh, *A makeshift majority: the first inter-party government, 1948–51* Dublin 1998, *passim*; MacDermott, *Clann na Poblachta*, pp. 66–80; D. Keogh, *Twentieth-century Ireland: nation and state,* Dublin, 1994, pp. 182–86.

39. Coolahan, *ASTI*, p.159.

40. National Archives, TAOIS/6341 A 10; Coolahan, *ASTI*, p. 160.

41. Coolahan, *ASTI*, pp. 164–65, 187–89.

42. ibid., pp. 198–205.

43. *Irish Times,* 13 October 1954, 15 March 1957, 24 October 1959, 22 August 1973.

44. Coolahan, *ASTI*, p. 175; ASTI/34, Minutes of the Dublin branch, 16 January, 6 February, 6 March 1943.

45. ASTI/32, Buckley file.

46. Minutes of ASTI Kilmallock/Desmond branch, 4 December 1948, 17 November 1951, 14 October 1959.

47. ibid., 15 October 1949, 14 October 1959.

48. ibid., postscript to minutes for 13 October 1958; 31 January 1962.

49. ibid., 20 January 1958, 28 April 1959.

50. ibid., 17 October 1962.

51. ibid., 8 September 1955, 17 October 1955.

52. ibid., 30, 24 January 1953, 29 May, 16 October 1954, 22 January 1955.

53. ibid., 4 December 1948.

54. ibid., 14 October 1957.

55. ibid., 13 October 1958, 14 October 1959.

56. Desmond minutes, *passim*.

57. ASTI, Convention minutes, 1931–36.

58. ASTI, *Official programme of the 15th annual convention*, 1937; *25th* 1947; *35th* 1957, *passim*.

59. ibid., Coolahan, *ASTI*, pp. 89–90.

60. ASTI/51, File relating to the annual convention of 1957.

61. ibid.

62. ASTI *Official programme of the 35th annual convention*, 1957, pp. 8–9; *Irish Independent*, 25 April 1957.

63. ASTI, *Official programme of the 35th annual convention*, 1957.

64. *Irish Independent*, 25 April 1957; *Irish Times*, 25 April 1957; *Connacht Tribune*, 27 April 1957; J. Cooney, 'The bishops ... and the Spanish dictator', *Irish Independent*, 21 March 2006.

65. *Irish Independent*, 25 April 1957.

66. ibid.

67. Farren, *Politics of Irish education*, pp. 217–19.

68. 'An Iubhaile Órga', *School & Colleges Yearbook*, 1959, pp. 7–9; ASTI, *Official programme of the 35th annual convention*, 1957, p. 12; *37th*, 1959, pp. 7–9.

69. ASTI, *Official programme of the 37th annual convention*, 1959, p. 48.

70. ASTI/181–182a, MacDonagh application, 14 March 1958; Coolahan, *ASTI*, pp. 223–24.

71. ASTI, *Official programme of the 37th annual convention*, 1959, pp. 17, 30; Amendment of agreement (employment) between the General Secretary and ASTI, 1964: 'Teacher organises teachers', *Irish Independent*, 6 April 1964.

72. Coolahan, *ASTI*, p. 198; *Irish Independent*, 3 October 1968.

73. Miss N. Kelleher, 'Presidential Address', *School & College Yearbook*, 1960, pp. 17–25.

74. ibid.

75. 'Address of Dr P.J. Hillery, Minister for Education', ibid., pp. 5–8.

76. Lee, *Ireland*, pp. 341–59, 371–409.

77. 'Address of P.J Hillery', p. 5.

Chapter 5: '*And look at us now!*'

1. F. Tobin, *The best of decades: Ireland in the 1960s,* Dublin, 1984; C. Mc-Carthy, *The decade of upheaval: Irish trade unions in the 1960s,* Dublin, 1973.
2. *Irish Times,* 1 January 1962.
3. Sister E. Randles, *Post-primary education in Ireland, 1957–1970,* Dublin, 1975, p. 160.
4. S. Mac Réamoinn, *Vatacáin II agus an réabhlóid chultúrtha,* Dublin 1987, pp. 40–43; Tobin, *Best of decades,* pp. 81–83.
5. Tobin, *Best of decades,* pp. 182–84, 194–98, 219–24.
6. D. McCartney, *UCD: a national idea: the history of University College, Dublin,* Dublin, 1999, pp. 345–88; J.A. Murphy, *The College: a history of Queen's/University College Cork, 1845-1995,* Cork, 1995, pp. 315–18; P. Pettit, *The gentle revolution: crisis in the universities,* Dublin, 1969, *passim.*
7. T. O'Dea, 'The true, the good, and the beatnik', *School & College Yearbook,* 1960, pp. 57–59.
8. ibid.
9. Sparsely Populated Areas Commission of the Church of Ireland, *Careers in Ireland,* Dublin, 1959, pp. 135–36.
10. Coolahan, *ASTI,* p. 209.
11. Coolahan, *ASTI,* p. 196; G. Allen, *The Garda Síochána: policing independent Ireland, 1922–82,* Dublin, 1999, pp. 166–78.
12. P. Purcell, 'Church influence on the working conditions of secondary teachers in Ireland, 1960–2000', MA thesis, UCD, 2001, p. 24.
13. G. Fitzgerald, 'The murder machine', *Secondary Teacher* vol.1, no. 4, April 1966, pp. 21–23.
14. P. Duffy, *The lay teacher: a study of the position of the lay teacher in an Irish Catholic environment,* Dublin, *c.*1966, pp.49–50, 65–66.
15. ibid., pp. 52, 58, 63.
16. ibid., pp.51–63; K. Waldron, *Out of the shadows: emerging secondary schools in the archdiocese of Tuam, 1940–69,*Tuam, 2002, pp. 98–102.
17. Cunningham, *St Jarlath's College,* pp. 5–6.
18. OECD/Department of Education, *Investment in education: report of the survey team,* 1965, pp. 276–79.
19. Duffy, *Lay teacher,* pp. xiii–xviii, 89–94.
20. Purcell, 'Church influence', p. 26.
21. ibid., p. 24.
22. P. Clancy, 'Education in the Republic of Ireland: the project of modernity', in Clancy et al, *Irish society: Sociological Perspectives,* Dublin, 1995,

pp. 467–94; J. Walsh, *The politics of expansion: the transformation of education in the Republic of Ireland, 1957–72*, Manchester, 2009, pp. 74–101.

23. See Ó Buachalla, *Education policy*, pp. 278–86, for an assessment of the contributions of these ministers.

24. Randles, *Post-primary education* pp.41-43; Farren, *Politics of Irish education*, pp. 236–38; Walsh, *Politics of expansion*, p. 40.

25. Dáil Report, 28 October 1959.

26. *Irish Times*, 22 October 1959.

27. Dáil Report, 28 October 1959.

28. Randles, *Post-primary education*, p. 305; Walsh, *Politics of expansion*, pp. 62–104.

29. Randles, pp. 65–67, 105–08, 159.

30. Randles, pp. 305–06.

31. Randles, pp. 112–13; J. Walsh, *Politics of expansion*, pp. 322–23.; D. Ó Conalláin, 'Education – free for all', *Secondary Teacher*, September 1966, p. 6.

32. Randles, *Post-primary education*, pp. 109–118.

33. *Irish Times*, 21 May 1963.

34. ibid.

35. *Farmers' Journal*, 25 May 1963.

36. Coolahan, *Irish education*, p. 165.

37. S. O'Connor, *A troubled sky: reflections on the Irish educational scene, 1957–68* Dublin 1986, pp. 110-11.

38. ibid., p.112.

39. Cited in ibid., p. 121.

40. ibid., pp. 100–2; 109-10, 124–28, 134–36; 'Letter from the Minister re post-primary education', ASTI, *Official programme of the 44th annual convention*, 1966, pp. 26–29.

41. P.J. Browne, *Unfulfilled promise: memories of Donogh O'Malley*, Dublin, 2008, pp. 21–46.

42. Randles, *Post-primary education* pp. 216–17.

43. J. Horgan, *Seán Lemass: the enigmatic patriot*, Dublin 1999, pp. 297–98.

44. ibid., p.298.

45. *Irish Times*, 12 September 1966.

46. ibid., 22 September 1966.

47. *Secondary Teacher*, September 1966, p. 1; November 1966, p. 1.

48. Ó Conalláin, 'Education', p. 7.

49. ibid.

50. See, for example, *Sunday Independent*, 1 July 1962.

Chapter 6: *'It could mean Mountjoy or hunger strike'*

1. McCarthy, *Decade of upheaval,* pp. 198–216; J. Logan, 'The making of a modern union: the Vocational Teachers' Association, 1954–1973' in Logan, *Teachers' Union*, pp. 171–79; M. Moroney, *National teachers' salaries and pensions, 1831–2000*, Dublin, 2007, pp. 165–90; Riordan, 'Association of Secondary Teachers, Ireland', pp. 147–59; Coolahan, *ASTI*, pp. 198–205, 228–308.

2. There are accounts of both episodes in Coolahan, *ASTI,* pp.198–205, 215–16, 235–38.

3. Tubridy, 'Registration Council', p. 199–200; Coolahan, *ASTI,* pp. 215–16.

4. Louis O'Flaherty interview, 11 April 2007.

5. Coolahan, *ASTI,* pp. 215–16.

6. *Irish Times*, 10 March 1961.

7. ibid.

8. O'Flaherty interview; Coolahan, *ASTI,* pp. 215–16.

9. Coolahan, *ASTI,* pp. 198–205.

10. Michael O'Meara interview.

11. Coolahan, *ASTI*, pp. 235–38; E. Doyle, *Leading the way: managing voluntary secondary schools*, Dublin 2000, pp. 118–20.

12. Logan, 'The making of a modern union', p. 172; Moroney, *National teachers' salaries*, pp. 168–69.

13. O'Flaherty interview.

14. Moroney, *National teachers' salaries,* pp. 160–61; Coolahan, *ASTI,* p. 193.

15. Cited in Riordan, 'Association of Secondary Teachers, Ireland', p. 147.

16. Coolahan, *ASTI,* p. 191.

17. Cited in Riordan, 'Association of Secondary Teachers, Ireland', p. 150.

18. ibid., pp. 150–52; Moroney, *National teachers' salaries,* pp. 166–67.

19. O'Meara interview; Desmond branch minutes, 13 April 1964; Mc-Carthy, *Decade of upheaval,* pp. 58–71.

20. *Irish Times*, 9 April 1964; Coolahan, *ASTI,* p. 245.

21. Coolahan, *ASTI,* p. 245.

22. *Sunday Independent*, 26 April 1964.

23. Coolahan, *ASTI* pp. 245–46.

24. INTO, *Reports of the Central Executive Committee for the year 1964–65,*

pp. 16–17. See also *Sunday Independent,* 10 May 1964.

25. Desmond branch minutes, 13 April 1964; O'Meara interview.

26. Coolahan, *ASTI,* pp. 247–48.

27. ibid., pp. 248–49.

28. Doyle, *Leading the way,* pp. 171–73; McCarthy, *Decade of upheaval,* p. 207, Moroney, *National Teachers' salaries,* pp. 181–83.

29. Logan, 'Modern union', pp. 173-75; *Irish Times,* 25 April 1968.

30. Riordan, 'Association of Secondary Teachers, Ireland', pp. 155–56.

31. *Irish Times,* 24 May 1968.

32. *Secondary Teacher,* October 1968, p. 6.

33. ASTI, Dublin North minutes, 27 May 1968.

34. ibid.

35. ibid.

36. *Secondary Teacher,* October 1968.

37. ibid., November 1968.

38. ibid.

39. ASTI/182/b, 'Report of the special convention, 30 July 1968'.

40. ibid.

41. ibid. The INTO strike referred to was, quite possibly, one that occurred in 1962 in Ballina, County Mayo. The strike was in response to the bishop of Killala's attempt to introduce a religious order to a national school in the town, thereby depriving lay teachers of promotional opportunities (O'Connell, *Irish National Teachers' Organisation,* pp. 93–120).

42. ASTI/182b, 'Report of the special convention, 30 July 1968'.

43. ibid.

44. Coolahan, *ASTI,* pp. 279–82.

45. ASTI/182b, Minutes of special convention, 19 October 1968.

46. Desmond branch minutes, 11 November 1968.

47. Minutes of special convention, 23 November 1968.

48. *Secondary Teacher,* September 1969; interview with Éamon Ó hAllmhuráin, 11 April 2007; W. Roy, 'Membership participation in the National Union of Teachers', in R. Kimber and J.J. Richardson (eds), *Pressure groups in Britain: a reader,* London, 1974, pp. 86, 106; R.A. Manzer, *Teachers and politics: the role of the National Union of Teachers in the making of national education policy in England and Wales since 1944,* Manchester, 1970, pp. 20–21.

49. O'Connor, *Labour history,* pp. 123–24, 155–58; M. O'Riordan, *The voice of a thinking intelligent movement: James Larkin Junior and the ide-*

ological modernisation of Irish trade unionism, Dublin, 2001, pp. 17–27; O'Connell, Irish National Teachers' Organisation, pp. 466–68; M. Jones, "For the youth of the common people": the Vocational Education Officers' Association, 1930-1954', in Logan (ed.), *Teachers' Union,* pp. 94–95.

50. Coolahan, *ASTI,* pp. 179–80, 219; Jones, 'Vocational Education Officers', p. 199; ASTI, *Official programme of the 35th annual convention,* 1957, p. 13.

51. McCarthy, *Decade of upheaval,* p. 20–21; A. Kelly, 'White collar trade unionism', in D. Nevin (ed.), *Trade unions and change in Irish society* Cork 1980, pp. 65–81; W.K. Roche, 'Industrial relations', in D. Nevin (ed.), *Trade union century,* Cork, 1994, pp. 133–46; F. Devine and E. O'Connor, 'Congress? Congress!', *Saothar* vol. 19, 1994, pp. 3–6.

52. *Secondary Teacher,* September 1969, pp. 7–8.

53. ibid.

54. ibid.

55. Doyle, *Leading the way* pp. 118–32, 151–52; Ó Buachalla, *Education policy* pp. 158–69.

56. Coolahan, *ASTI,* pp. 282–83.

57. ASTI/182/b, Sample ballot paper.

58. ibid.

59. *Irish Times,* 1, 3 February 1969.

60. Coolahan, *ASTI,* 282–84.

61. *Irish Times,* 1 February 1969.

62. ibid., 5 February 1969.

63. S. O'Connor, 'Post-primary education: now and in the future', *Studies,* Autum 1968, pp. 223–49; Doyle, *Leading the way* pp. 136–41.

64. Interview with Pierce Purcell, 19 May 2007; interview with Tommy Francis, 11 April 2007; interview with John White, 10 September 2008; interview with Michael Corley, 19 May 2007.

65. *Irish Times,* 3 February 1969.

66. ibid.

67. *Sunday Independent,* 2 February 1969.

68. *Irish Times,* 4 February 1969.

69. ibid., 6 February 1969; CHA, Minutes of half-yearly meeting, 6 May 1969.

70. *Secondary Teacher,* September 1969.

71. ibid., October 1969.

72. *Irish Times* 1 May 1969, 18 February 1971, 8 January 1973; *Irish In-*

dependent, 22 February 1971. ASTI/115, Correspondence with Irish School Students' Union.

73. *Connacht Sentinel,* 11 February 1969; *Irish Times,* 18 February 1969.

74. CHA, Minutes of half-yearly meeting, 6 May 1970.

75. CHA, ibid., 6 May 1969, 8 October 1969, 6 May 1970, circular from John Hughes, SJ, 15 April 1970.

76. Coolahan, *ASTI,* pp. 284–85; McCarthy, *Decade of Upheaval,* pp. 210–13.

77. Coolahan, *ASTI,* pp. 283–86.

78. Ibid.; *Irish Times,* 25 February 1969.

79. ASTI/182b, Letters to general secretary; Corley interview.

80. Wigham, *Newtown School,* pp. 213–14.

81. White, *St Columba's College,* pp. 179–80.

82. ASTI/182b, CDF to M. MacDonagh, 15 January 1969.

83. CDF to M. MacDonagh, 4 February 1969.

84. ibid., 21 July 1969.

85. ASTI/182b, FF to general secretary, 26 February 1969.

86. Coolahan, *ASTI,* p. 287.

87. *Irish Times,* 9 April 1969; Logan, 'The making of a modern union', pp. 176-78.

88. *Irish Times,* 8, 11 April 1969.

89. ibid., 27, 28 May 1969; Logan, 'Modern union', p. 178.

90. Coolahan, *ASTI,* pp. 286–91.

91. *Secondary Teacher,* December 1970.

92. Coolahan, *ASTI,* pp. 289–91.

93. ibid.

94. ASTI, standing committee minutes, 31 January 1970.

95. ASTI, Dublin North minutes, 27 January, 18 February 1970.

96. ibid., Desmond branch minutes, 26 February 1970; Coolahan, *ASTI,* pp. 292–93.

97. *Irish Times,* 4 June 1970. There are discussions of circumstances surrounding the boycott in Coolahan, *ASTI,* pp. 294–95, and Randles, *Post-primary education,* pp. 298–99.

98. *Irish Times,* 16 June 1970; ASTI standing committee minutes, 6 June 1970; ASTI, CEC minutes, 13 June 1970.

99. ASTI, standing committee minutes, 20 June 1970.

100. *Irish Times,* 3 July 1970.

101. ASTI, standing committee minutes, 20 July 1970.

102. ibid., 20 July, 8 September 1970; Coolahan, *ASTI,* p. 294.

103. Coolahan, *ASTI,* pp.289–95.

104. *Secondary Teacher,* November 1970, p. 3.

105. Coolahan, *ASTI,* pp. 295–97.

106. ibid., p. 296.

107. National Archives, TAOIS/2003/16/397.

108. Coolahan, *ASTI,* pp. 297–98; ASTI, CEC minutes, 16 January 1971.

109. Mapstone, *Ulster Teachers' Union,* pp. 96–97.

110. Desmond branch minutes, 19 January 1970.

111. Coolahan, *ASTI,* p. 298.

112. ibid., p. 302; O'Flaherty interview; Ó hAllmhuráin interview.

113. CHA, Circular to members from John Hughes, SJ, undated.

114. Suppressed statement in National Archives, TAOIS/2003/16/397.

115. Doyle, *Leading the way,* p. 172; Corley interview; *Irish Independent,* 6 April 1964.

116. Coolahan, *ASTI,* p. 300; ASTI, standing committee minutes, 15 February 1971; *Irish Independent,* 15, 16 February 1971.

117. Michael Ward interview, 10 September 2008; *Irish Times,* 16, 17 February 1971; *Irish Independent,* 17, 18, 19 February 1971.

118. *Irish Times,* 16 February 1971.

119. *Irish Independent,* 17 February 1971.

120. *Irish Times,* 17 February 1971.

121. *Irish Times,* 17 February 1971; John Mulcahy interview, 11 April 2007.

122. *Connacht Tribune,* 19 February 1971; *Connacht Sentinel,* 23 February 1971.

123. *Irish Independent,* 19 February 1971.

124. *Irish Independent,* 18 February 1971; Ó hAllmhuráin interview.

125. O'Flaherty interview; *Connacht Tribune,* 19 February 1971.

126. Mulcahy interview; Coolahan, *ASTI,* pp. 301–03.

127. *Irish Times,* 29 March 1971.

128. *Irish Times,* 1 March 1971.

129. Ward interview; Coolahan, *ASTI,* pp. 305–06.

130. Coolahan, *ASTI,* pp. 308–12; Moroney, *National teachers' salaries,* pp. 190–91.

Chapter 7: *'Properly and fully organised'*

1. Ó Buachalla, *Education policy,* p. 132.

2. Desmond branch minutes, 1953, 1954; Corley interview; Sheila Parsons, pers. comm.

3. Coolahan, *ASTI,* pp. 351–54.

4. ibid., p. 354; T. Bromell., *Rian mo chos ar ghaineamh an tsaoil,* Indreabhán, 2006, pp. 97–118.

5. Coolahan, *ASTI,* p. 354; *ASTIR* December 1992.

6. ASTI, *Official programme of the 51st annual convention,* 1973, pp. 79–80.

7. ibid.

8. ibid., *54th annual convention,* 1976, pp. 116-17.

9. Coolahan, *ASTI,* p. 388; ASTI, *Official programme of the 53st annual convention,* 1975, pp. 133–34; *58th,* 1980, p. 192; *62nd,* 1984, pp. 128–29; *63rd,* 1985, p. 161.

10. ASTI, *Official programmes of the 51st annual convention,* 1973, pp. 79–80; *52nd,* 1974, p. 108; *53rd,* 1975, pp. 133–34; *54th,* 1976, pp. 115–17; *55th,* 1977, p. 96; *56th,* 1978, pp. 90–91; *57th,* 1979, pp. 90–91; D. Barry, 'The involvement and impact of a professional interest group', in D.G. Mulcahy and D. O'Sullivan (eds), *Irish educational policy: process and substance,* Dublin, 1989, pp. 147–48.

11. M.P. McCann, 'Teaching at second level: a case study of the role and job satisfaction of second level teachers in Galway city schools', unpublished M.Ed thesis (minor), UCG, 1980, pp.81–82.

12. P.H. Purcell, 'Church influence of the working conditions of secondary teachers in Ireland, 1960–2000', unpublished MA thesis, UCD, 2001, pp. 48–49.

13. ASTI, Minutes of Carrickmacross branch, May 1964–November 1971; ASTI, Minutes of Clare branch, October, 1973–February 1994.

14. ASTI, Minutes of Carrickmacross branch, 24 May 1971.

15. ibid., 19 January 1971.

16. ibid., 26 February 1971.

17. ibid., 24 May, 27 November 1971.

18. O'Meara interview; Clare branch minutes, October 1973–December 1979, *passim*; ASTI/47, Minutes of the 1936 convention.

19. Clare branch minutes, *passim.*

20. ibid., 2 November 1973, 30 May 1974, 27 October 1976, 5 April, 10 September, 3 October, 17 December 1979.

21. ibid., 20 March, 11 April 1974, 4 June 1975, 13 March 1978, *passim.*

22. ibid., 5 December 1974.

23. Interview with P.J. Sheehy, 11 April 2007.

24. Interview with Christina Heneghan, 11 April 2007.

25. Interview with Paddy Daly, 11 April 2007.

26. Interview with Lily Cronin.

27. ibid.

28. Coolahan, *ASTI,* pp. 358–59; ASTI, 'Report on branch rationalisation', *Official programme of 57th convention,* 1979, pp. 91–93.

29. Doyle, *Leading the way,* pp. 142–45.

30. Coolahan, *ASTI,* pp. 358–59.

31. ASTI, 'School stewards courses', *Official programme of the 60th annual convention,* 1982, pp. 145–46; *59th,* 1981, p. 126; Coolahan, *ASTI,* p. 387; O'Flaherty interview; Ó hAllmhuráin interview.

32. ASTI, *Official programme of the 61st annual convention,* 1983, pp. 142–43.

33. ibid., *51st annual convention,* 1973, p. 56.

34. Rev. Dr James Good, cited in Purcell, 'Church influence', p. 56.

35. L. O'Flaherty, *Management and control in Irish education,* Dublin, 1992, pp. 93–96.

35. Working party on the future involvement of religious in education, *FIRE Report,* February 1973, Appendix 1, pp. 31–34.

35. ibid., pp. 31–32.

36. ibid., p. 34.

37. ibid.

38. ibid.

39. O'Flaherty, *Management and Control,* pp. 94–95.

40. Coolahan, *ASTI,* pp. 317–24; Purcell, 'Church influence', pp. 45–47.

41. Coolahan, *ASTI,* pp. 317–24, 368–69.

42. Barry, 'Impact of interest group', pp. 145-57; O'Flaherty, *Management and control* pp. 42–74.

43. O'Flaherty, *Management and control,* p. 45.

44. ibid., pp.42–49.

45. Fr James Gerrard, cited in ibid., p. 51.

46. Barry, 'Impact of interest group', pp. 145–46.

47. ibid.; ASTI, *Official programme of the 49th annual convention* 1971, p. 23.

48. ASTI, *Official programme of the 50th annual convention,* 1972, pp. 82–84.

49. ibid., p.83. In this regard, Pierce Purcell recalls: 'A rumour, which I heard repeatedly, was circulating that the community schools would be funded by money from the World Bank, an organisation that was "infiltrated by Communists".' ('Church influence', p. 54.)

50. Cited in Barry, 'Impact of interest group', p. 149.

51. O'Flaherty, *Control and management,* pp .54–58.

52. ibid., p. 58.

53. ibid., p. 56.

54. ibid., pp. 58–62; Barry, 'Impact of interest group', pp. 150–51; M. McGinley and F. Donoghue, 'The modern union: the Teachers' Union of Ireland, 1973-1994, Logan, *Teachers' Union*, pp. 257–58.

55. O'Flaherty, *Management and control*, pp. 58–62.

56. ibid., pp. 65–66; *Irish Times,* 14 July 2007.

57. ASTI, *Official programme of the 59th annual convention,* 1979, pp. 114–38.

58. ibid.

59. O'Flaherty, *Management and Control,* pp. 68–71; Barry, 'Impact of interest group', pp. 150–52; S.E. Murphy, 'The growth of influence of the teachers' unions on educational policy and practice in Ireland, 1968–82', MEd. (minor) thesis, UCC 1983, pp. 159–62.

60. *Irish Times* 8 December 1983.

61. ibid.

62. ibid.

63. J.A. Murphy, 'Association to trade union: the organising of secondary teachers', *Saothar,* vol. 11, 1986, pp. 63–66.

64. ASTI, *Official programme of the 78th annual convention* 1978, p. 64; *59th,* 1981, p. 97; *60th,* 1982, p. 75; *61st,* 1983, p. 108.

65. ibid., *67th,* 1989, p. 199.

66. ASTI, *Official programme of the 63rd annual convention,* 1985, p. 88; *64th,* 1986, pp. 63, 109; *65th,* 1987, p. 88.

67. ibid., *59th,* 1981, p.125; *67th,* 1989, p. 235.

68. Roche, 'Industrial relations', pp. 133–46; McGinley and Donoghue, 'The modern union', pp. 240–41; G. Sweeney, *In public service: a history of the Public Service Executive Union, 1890–1990,* Dublin, 1990, pp. 233–35.

69. McCann, 'Galway city schools', pp. 80–81.

70. ASTI, *Official programme of the 59th annual convention,* 1981, p. 68.

71. ibid., *58th,* 1980, p. 73.

72. ibid.; *49th* convention, 1971, pp. 36–40; *60th,* 1982, pp. 155; K. Lynch, *The hidden curriculum: reproduction in education, an appraisal.* London, 1989, pp. 40–42.

73. Coolahan, *ASTI* pp. 384–85; Doyle, *Leading the way,* pp. 58–59, 65; White interview, 2008.

74. O'Flaherty, *Management and control* pp. 108.

75. ibid., pp. 93–112; Coolahan, *ASTI,* pp. 363-67; Murphy, 'Influence of

teachers' unions', pp. 111–23, 159–62.

76. Purcell, 'Church influence', pp. 60–61.

77. ASTI, *Official programme of the 64th annual convention*, 1986, pp. 209-10; *65th*, 1987, pp. 187–88; *Members' handbook*, 1990, pp.91–92.

78. Interview with Kieran Mulvey, 10 September 2008; J. Walshe, 'Smiling socialist who delivered if he said he would', *Irish Times*, 22 December 1990.

79. Mulvey interview.

80. ibid., John White interview; Louis O'Flaherty interview; Tommy Francis interview; Michael Ward interview.

81. Mulvey interview; ASTI, standing committee minutes, 7 February 1981; *Official programme of the 61st annual convention*, 1983, p. 142; *62nd*, 1984, p. 125; *64th*, 1986, p. 87.

82. Mulvey interview.

83. *Irish Times* 26 May 1966, 18 February 1969, 26 May 1976, 31 January 1984: Doyle, *Leading the way*, p. 58.

84. Coolahan, *ASTI*, p. 266, 269; ASTI, *Official programme of the 59th annual convention*, 1985, pp. 158–61.

85. Mulvey interview.

Chapter 8: *'We are the gentle angry teachers'*

1. Cited in Moroney, *National teachers' salaries*, p. 259.

2. ibid.

3. ibid., pp. 259–62; McGinley and Donoghue, 'The modern union', pp. 249–50.

4. *Irish Times*, 6 December 1985.

5. ibid., *Irish Independent*, 6 December 1985; Mary Glynn, pers. comm.

6. *Irish Times*, 6 December 1985.

7. O'Meara interview; Purcell, 'Church influence', p. 37.

8. Logan, 'Modern union', pp. 166-67, Purcell, 'Church influence', pp. 39–40.

9. McGinley and Donoghue, 'The modern union', pp. 266–68; Coolahan, *ASTI*, p. 390.

10. See T.R. Dwyer, *Short fellow: a biography of Charles J. Haughey*, Dublin 1994; R. Smith, *Garret the enigma: Dr Garret Fitzgerald*, Dublin, 1985. The acronym GUBU was coined by Conor Cruise O'Brien after Haughey characterised the capture of a murderer in the apartment of his government's attorney general as being 'grotesque, unbelievable, bizarre and unprecedented'.

11. Moroney, *National teachers' salaries* p. 205.

12. 'Obituary: Gerry Quigley', *Belfast Telegraph,* 23 December 2003.

13. Mulvey interview.

14. R. O'Donnell and C. O'Reardon, 'Ireland: recasting social partnership in a new context', in P. Pochet (ed.), *Wages policy in Europe,* Brussels, 2002.

15. *Irish Times,* 2 May 1979.

16. John Carroll, quoted in ibid., 26 July 1979.

17. Gerry Quigley, quoted in *Irish Times,* 24 May 1979.

18. Moroney, *National teachers' salaries,* p. 219.

19. ibid., pp. 206–07.

20. ASTI, standing committee minutes, 19 August 1980.

21. *Irish Times,* 9 October 1980.

22. ASTI, Clare branch minutes, 9 October 1980.

23. Moroney, *National teachers' salaries,* pp. 213–15; Coolahan, *ASTI,* pp. 372–73. Posts of responsibility were introduced by agreement in 1971, reflecting special responsibility allowances. The A post allowance was set at more than twice the level of the B allowance.

24. ibid., pp. 216–17; McGinley and Donoghue, 'The modern union', pp. 248-68.

25. ASTI, standing committee minutes, 8 October, 15 November 1980; ASTI, Clare branch minutes, 11 November 1980; Moroney, *National teachers' salaries,* pp. 215–16.

26. Coolahan, *ASTI,* pp. 371–73: Moroney, *National teachers' salaries,* pp. 246–48.

27. ASTI pp. 370–73, standing committee minutes, 10 February 1982; Coolahan, *ASTI*; Moroney, *National teachers' salaries,* pp. 272–73.

28. Coolahan, *ASTI,* pp. 373–74.

29. *Irish Independent,* 31 July 1982.

30. ibid., 27 January 1983.

31. Moroney, *National teachers' salaries,* pp. 249–51.

32. *Irish Independent,* 25 January 1983.

33. ibid., 27 January 1983.

34. Moroney, *National teachers' salaries,* pp. 252–53.

35. ibid.

36. *Irish Independent,* 17 November 1984.

37. ASTI, Minutes of CEC, 1–2 February 1985; Moroney, *National teachers' salaries,* pp. 254–55.

38. See introduction to present chapter.

39. McGinley and O'Donoghue, 'The modern union', pp. 268–69.

40. ASTI, Minutes of CEC, 18 January 1986; Moroney, *National teachers' salaries*, pp. 263–64.

41. Mulvey interview.

42. G. Fitzgerald, *All in a life: an autobiography*, Dublin, 1991, p. 620.

43. *Farmers' Journal*, 18 January 1986.

44. G. Hussey, *At the cutting edge: cabinet diaries, 1982–1987*, Dublin, 1990, pp. 188, 192, 211.

45. *Irish Times*, 14 February 1986.

46. Hussey, *Cabinet diaries*, p. 197.

47. Fitzgerald, *All in a life*, p. 622; Lee, *Ireland, 1912–1984: politics and society*, pp. 480, 484.

48. *Sunday Independent*, 13 April 1986.

49. *Irish Times*, 12, 15 April 1986.

50. ibid., 17 April 1986.

51. *Sunday Independent*, 20 April 1986.

52. Moroney, *National teachers' salaries* pp. 266–68.

53. *Irish Independent*, 6, 10, 12 May 1986.

54. ASTI, Minutes of CEC, 4 April, 10 May 1986; Moroney, *National teachers' salaries*, pp. 269-71; McGinley and Donoghue, 'The modern union', p. 250.

55. Tony McKernan interview, 11 April 2007.

56. *Irish Times*, 5 December 1990; Moroney, *National teachers' salaries*, pp. 269–70.

57. Mulvey interview; Ó hAllmhuráin interview; ASTI, CEC minutes, 15-16 January 1993; Moroney, *National teachers' salaries*, p. 290.

58. ASTI, standing committee minutes, 13 March 1992, 6 June 1992, 1 July 1992.

59. ibid., 11 December 1992.

60. ibid., 21 May 1993; Moroney, *National teachers' salaries*, pp. 294–97; McGinley and Donoghue, 'The modern union', p. 270.

61. ASTI, standing committee minutes, 11 March, 13 May, 25–26 August 25–26 November, 16–17 December 1994; *Irish Times*, 21 April 1995.

62. *Irish Times*, 21 April 1995.

63. ASTI, standing committee minutes, 5–6 May 1995, 12 January 1996.

Chapter 9: *'Highlighting the imbalance'*

1. *Irish Independent*, 9 March 1985.

2. ASTI/148, copy of 'Report of Employment Appeals Tribunal,

UD235/1983'.

3. ibid., letter from O'Connor, solrs, to J. O'Dowd, 15 December 1983.

4, ibid.; *Irish Times,* 10 February 1984.

5. Cited in N. McCafferty, 'School days', *The best of Nell: a selection of writings over fourteen years,* Dublin, 1993, pp. 55–57.

6. ibid.

7. ibid.; *Irish Times,* 3 April 1985. C. Hug, *The politics of sexual morality in Ireland,* Houndmills 1999, pp. 121–22; G. Kerrigan, 'The moral civil war', *Magill,* September 1983.

8. *Sunday Independent,* 12 February 1984.

9. *Irish Times,* 27 April 1984, ASTI, *Official programme of the 63rd annual convention,* 1985, p. 68.

10. Michael Waddell interview, 2 December 2008.

11. *Irish Times,* 20 February, 27 April 1984.

12. ASTI, standing committee minutes, 15 February 1984.

13. *Irish Independent,* 14 January 1985; *Irish Times,* 9 March 1985; McCafferty, 'School days', pp. 55–56.

14. *Irish Times,* 6 July 1984.

15. ASTI/148, press cuttings.

16. ASTI/150, C.F. to Kieran Mulvey, 17 July 1984.

17. ASTI/150, E. Flynn to K.Mulvey, 9 November 1984; standing committee minutes, 16–17 November 1984.

18. ASTI, Clare branch minutes, 24 January 1985.

19. *Irish Times,* 9 March 1985.

20. *Sunday Press,* 10 March 1985.

21. *Irish Times,* 7 February 1997, 30 November 1999, 20 September 2008.

22. Purcell, 'Church influence', p. 28.

23. Chuinneagáin, *Catherine Mahon, passim*; R. Cullen Owens, *A social history of women in Ireland, 1870–1970,* Gill & Macmillan, Dublin, 2005, p. 205.

24. See Chapter 4 above.

25. Coolahan, *ASTI,* pp. 81, 160.

26. D. Lloyd, *Ireland after history,* Cork 1999, pp. 85–88; C. Clear, *Women of the house: women's household work in Ireland, 1922–1961,* Dublin, 2000, pp. 27–45; C. Bolt, *The women's movement in the United States and Britain from the 1790s to the 1920s,* London 1993, pp. 236–76.

27. Cullen Owen, *Women in Ireland,* pp. 190–247 (Bennett quote, p. 202); Jones, *Obstreperous lassies,* pp.113–49; M. Daly, *Women and work in Ireland,* Dundalk, 1997, pp. 41-54.

28. ASTI, *Official programmes of the 15th, 25th, 35th, and 45th annual conventions.*

29. ibid., *37th annual convention*, 1959, pp. 52–61.

30. K. Ryder, 'Into the limelight for married secondary teachers through the gallantry of the ASTI', *Issues in Education*, vol. 5., 2000, pp. 193-97.

31. *Irish Independent*, 22 April 1960.

32. ASTI/47, Minutes of 10th annual conference, 1932; *Official programme of the 24th annual convention*, 1946, p. 16; *25th*, convention, 1947, p. 17; *16th*, 1938, p. 19.

33. S. Parsons, 'Engendering an agenda: a union's relation to feminist issues', unpublished MA thesis, DCU, 1994, pp. 50–51; S.G. Kelly, *Teaching in the city*, Dublin, 1970, pp. 90-91; McCann, 'Teaching at second level, Tables 4.6 and 4.8.

34. Ryder, 'Into the limelight. pp. 196–97.

35. ibid., Kathleen Ryder, pers. comm.

36. *ASTIR*, March 2009.

37. ASTI, *Official programme of the 49th annual convention*, 1971, pp. 86–91, *51st*, 1973, p. 24.

38. Commission on the Status of Women, *Report to Minister for Finance*, December 1972, par. 270; Coolahan, *ASTI*, pp. 326–27; L. Connolly, *The Irish women's movement: from revolution to devolution*, Dublin, 2003, pp. 105–6.

39. ASTI, *Official programme for the 49th annual convention*, 1971, pp. 78–79.

40. ibid.

41. Connolly, *Irish women's movement*, pp. 97–99; F. Gardiner, 'Political Interest and participation of Irish women, 1922–1992: the unfinished revolution', in A. Smyth, *Irish women's studies reader*, Dublin, 1993, pp. 5153.

42. J. Beale, *Women in Ireland: voices of change*, Dublin, 1986, pp. 139–63; Connolly, *Irish women's movement*, pp. 89–110.

43. McGinley and Donoghue, 'The modern union', pp. 254–55.

44. *Irish Independent*, 22 April 1976.

45. ibid., 22 April 1976. See also 29 April 1976.

46. Commission of the Status of Women, *Report*, par. 536–37.

47. Connolly, *Irish women's movement*, p. 260; *Irish Times*, 24 October 1979.

48. Beale, *Women in Ireland*, pp. 156–57.

49. ICTU, *Fourth equality programme: delivering gender equality, 1999-2004*, Dublin, 1999, pp. 1–3.

50. Interview with Catherine Fitzpatrick, 11 April 2007.
51. Cited in Parsons, 'Engendering an agenda', pp. 48–49.
52. ibid., pp. 50–53.
53. ASTI, *Official programme of the 65th annual convention*, 1987, pp. 52–59; *66th*, 1988, p. 76; Parsons, 'Engendering an agenda', pp. 65–66.
54. ASTI, *Official programme of the 66th annual convention*, 1988, pp. 81–87.
55. ASTI, *Official programme of the 67th annual convention*, 1989, pp.106–22; ASTI, *Reports of annual convention, 2000*, Resolution 57.
56. Parsons, 'Engendering an agenda', *passim*; Council of Teachers' Unions, 'Report from workshop', *Equality conference, 9 May 1992*, Dublin, 1992, pp. 30–32,
57. Parsons, 'Engendering an agenda', pp. 88–96.
58. ibid.; A. McBride, *Gender democracy in trade unions*, Aldershot, 2001, pp. 9–33; Beale, *Women in Ireland*, pp. 156–61; ASTI, *Official programme of the 67th annual convention*, 1989, pp. 222–23.
59. Parsons, 'Engendering an agenda', pp. 99–101; A. McElduff, 'Participation of women in the teachers' unions', Council of Teachers' Unions, *Equality conference, 9 May 1992*, Dublin, 1992, pp. 19–29.
60. Council of Teachers' Unions, *Equality conference, 9 May 1992*, pp. 30–32.
61. McElduff, 'Participation', p. 20.
62. John White interview; Kieran Mulvey interview.
63. Catherine Fitzpatrick interview.
64. ASTI, *Convention handbook*, 1988, p. 21.
65. ASTI, *Convention handbook*, 1994, pp. 174–95.
66. *Irish Times*, 4 April 1997.

Chapter 10: *'As if education was a commodity'*
1. *ASTIR*, March 1994.
2. Mulvey interview; Ward interview.
3. *Irish Times*, 15 April 1991.
4. ibid.
5. ibid., 20 April 1993.
6. R. Wynne, N. Clarkin, and C. Dolphin, *The experience of stress among Irish school teachers; a report on a survey of ASTI, TUI and INTO members: summary report*, Dublin, 1991, *passim*.
7. *Irish Times*, 18 April 1995.
8. ibid.

9. ibid., 13 April 1993.

10. ibid.

11. A.E. Murphy, *The 'Celtic Tiger': an analysis of Ireland's economic growth performance,* European University Institute Working Paper, RSC no. 2000/16, p. 5.

12. J. Fitzgerald, 'The way we are: education and the Celtic Tiger', *Issues in Education,* vol. 3, 1998, pp. 35–44.

13. P. Fortin, *The Irish economic boom: facts, causes, and lessons,* Industry Canada Discussion Paper, no. 12, Ottawa, 2002, p. 10.

14. *ASTIR,* September 1996, p. 12.

15. Fortin, *Irish economic boom,* pp. 3–5; R.F. Foster, *Luck and the Irish: a brief history of change, 1970-2000,* London, 2007, pp. 1–6, 147–83.

16. P. Sweeney, *The Celtic Tiger: Ireland's continuing economic miracle* 1999 edn, Dublin, pp. 92–94.

17. T. Hastings, B. Sheehan and P. Yeates, *Saving the future: how social partnership shaped Ireland's economic success,* Dublin, 2007, *passim*; Sweeney, *Celtic Tiger,* pp. 99–105. For a contrary view, see K. Allen, *The Celtic tiger: the myth of social partnership in Ireland,* Manchester, 2000, *passim.*

18. W.K. Roche and J.F. Geary, '"Collaborative production" and the Irish boom: work organisation, partnership and direct involvement in Irish workplaces', in D'Art and Turner (eds), *Irish employment relations in the new economy,* Dublin, 2002, pp. 58–92; Hastings, Sheehan and Yeates, *Saving the future, passim*; P. Fairbrother, and P. Stewart, 'The dilemmas of social partnership and union organisation: questions for British trade unions, Fairbrother and Yates (eds), *Trade unions in renewal: a comparative study,* Abingdon, 2003, pp. 158-79.

19. *Irish Times,* 22 July 2000.

20. ibid.

21. D. Harvey, *A brief history of neoliberalism,* Oxford, 2005, pp. 39–86; N. Klein, *The shock doctrine: the rise of disaster capitalism,* London, 2007, pp. 116–41; R.M. Abrams, *America transformed: sixty years of revolutionary change, 1941–2001,* Cambridge, 2008, pp. 290–311; P. Bourdieu, 'Utopia of endless exploitation: the essence of neoliberalism', *Le Monde Diplomatique* (English edition), December 1998; P.M. Garrett, *'Transforming'* children's services? Social work, neoliberalism and the *'modern' world',* Maidenhead 2009, pp. 12–28.

22. A.T. Kearney Inc., 'Measuring globalization: who's up; who's down?' *Foreign policy,* no. 134, January–February 2003, pp. 60–72.

23. P. Gunnigle, G. McMahon and G. Fitzgerald, *Industrial relations in Ireland: theory and practice*, 1999 edn, Dublin, pp. 437–39; Hastings, *Saving the future*, pp. 92–93; White interview, 2008.

24. Hug, *Sexual morality*, pp. 49–75; M. Raftery and E. O'Sullivan, *Suffer the little children: the inside story of Ireland's industrial schools*, Dublin 1999, *passim*; D. Keogh, *Twentieth-century Ireland: revolution and state building* Dublin 2005, pp. 431–44; I. Bacik, *Kicking and screaming: dragging Ireland into the 21st century*, Dublin, 2004, pp. 29–58.

25. Doyle, *Leading the way*, p. 272; N. Keating, 'The changing role of the principal today', *Secondary Teacher*, vol. 17, no. 4, 1988, pp. 2–7; M.J. Mullarkey, 'Women in educational leadership: secular female principals in Irish post-primary schools', unpublished MEd. thesis (minor), UCG, 1994, pp. 10, 92–93.

26. *ASTIR*, December 1990.

27. Mullarkey, 'Secular female principals', p. 10; ASTI, *The promotional expectations and achievements of teachers*, Dublin, 1991, *passim*; K. Lynch, 'Women teach and men manage: why men dominate senior posts in Irish education', *Education commission of CORI*, Dublin, 1994, pp. 1–36.

28. S. Drudy, and K. Lynch, *Schools and society in Ireland*, Dublin, 1993, pp. 11, 92; M.C. Clegg, 'Trusteeship: a model in progress', in N. Prendergast and L. Monahan (eds), *Reimagining the Catholic school*, Dublin, 2003, pp. 189-94.

29. Purcell, 'Church influence', p.68.

30. ASTI, *Education – invest in our children's future: the ASTI response to the Education Green Paper, 1992, Education for a changing world* Dublin 1992; *Response to the White Paper on education*, Dublin, 1996; Doyle, *Leading the way*, pp. 218–20.

31. Dáil Debates, 16 October 1992.

32. ASTI, *Invest in our children's future*, pp. 8–10, 49, 62-63, *passim*; *ASTIR*, December 1992.

33. *Irish Times*, 13 April 1995.

34. ibid., 13, 14 April 1995; *ASTIR*, September 1992.

35. *Irish Times*, 22 April 1992, 20 April 1995.

36. *Irish Independent*, 6 April 1994; C.E. Kennedy, 'A comparison of the Irish and Japanese education systems with particular reference to grind schools and private fee-paying education in both countries', unpublished MEd. thesis (minor), NUI Galway, 1999. pp. 83–87.

37. *Irish Times*, 21 October 1997.

38. *ASTIR*, February 1996.

39. ibid., March 1996.
40. ASTI, *Guidelines on sexual harassment,* 1992; *Work Studies in the transition year,* 1994; *Technology in the Junior Certificate,* 1994; *School discipline: advice for teachers and school authorities,* 1995; *Model policy on the promotion of gender equity in schools,* 1996; *Issues in Education,* vol. 1, 1996.
41. ASTI, *Official programme for the 57th annual convention,* 1979, p. 58; *Irish Times,* 23, 24 April 1987; Cunningham, *St Jarlath's College,* pp. 261–62.
42. *Irish Times,* 1 April 1997.
43. K. Lynch and A. Lodge, *Equality and power in schools: redistribution, recognition and representation,* London, 2002, pp. 151–65.
44. ibid., p. 157.
45. M. Moroney, *National teachers' salaries,* pp. 311–14.
46. *Irish Times,* 25 May 1995.
47. ibid., December 1995.
48. ibid., 9 April 1999.
49. ibid.
50. L. Quinn, 'What business expects from the education system', *Issues in Education,* vol. 4, pp. 23–27; L.E. Lynn, *Public management: old and new,* New York, 2006, pp. 1–17, 104-32; M. Minogue, 'Changing the state: concepts and practice in the reform of the public sector', in Minogue et al, *Beyond new public management: changing ideas and practices in governance,* Cheltenham, 1998, pp. 17–37
51. *ASTIR,* May 1995.
52. ibid.

Chapter 11: *'Singing from different hymn sheets'*

1. *Irish Independent,* 6 December 2000.
2. *Irish Times,* 5 December 2000.
3. ibid.
4. See Hastings, *Saving the future, passim.*
5. ASTI, Minutes of CEC special meeting, 3 April 1996; *ASTIR,* April 1996, March 1997.
6. Charlie Lennon interview, 28 February 2009.
7. ibid.; ASTI, *Nuacht,* January, November 1997.
8. Bernadine O'Sullivan interview, 28 February 2009; ASTI, Minutes of CEC, 11 January 1987; Moroney, *National teachers' salaries,* pp. 329–33.
9. ASTI, Minutes of CEC, 11 January, 4 April 1997; *ASTIR,* January,

March 1997.

10. *Industrial Relations News,* 10 April 1997; *ASTIR,* February 1997.

11. ASTI, *Reports of Annual Convention,* 1999, pp. 1–2.

12. *ASTIR,* September 1999.

13. O'Sullivan interview; ASTI, *Reports of annual convention,* 1998, 1999; *Irish Times,* 21 March 2000.

14. See Hastings, pp. 84–86.

15. *Irish Times,* 26 April 2000; *Industrial Relations News,* 30 January 2000.

16. ASTI, Minutes of standing committee, 21 January 2000.

17. *Irish Times,* 18, 20 January 2000.

18. ASTI, Minutes of CEC, 22 January 2000; O'Sullivan interview; Ward interview, Francis interview.

19. ibid.

20. *Industrial Relations News,* 10 February 2000.

21. ibid., 10 February, 16 March 2000; *Irish Times,* 29 February 2000; *Irish Independent,* 17 March 2000; *TUI News,* February, April 2000.

22. *Industrial Relations News,* 16, 30 March 2000; *In Touch* (INTO), March 2000.

23. Hastings, Sheehan and Yeates, *Saving the future,* pp. 29, 48–49; D. D'Art and T. Turner, 'Corporatism in Ireland: a comparative perspective', in D'Art and Turner (eds), *Irish employment relations,* pp. 275–300.

24. ASTI, *Reports of annual convention,* 1998, Cassells address, pp.20-21.

25. See, for example, *Reports of annual convention,* 1998, par. 17, 1999 par. 13 and 14.

26. *Industrial Relations News,* 30 March 2000, 4 May 2000; *Irish Independent,* 29 April 2000.

27. ASTI, Minutes of standing committee, 14, 30 March 2000; *Industrial Relations News,* 4 April 2000.

28. ASTI, SIPTU file; Minutes of CEC, 20 May 2000; *Industrial Relations News,* 4 April 2000.

29. *Irish Independent,* 26 April 2000.

30. *Industrial Relations News,* 4 May 2000.

31. See Hastings, Sheehan and Yeates, pp. 84–85 and Sweeney, *Celtic Tiger,* pp. 121–23.

32. *Irish Times,* 21 October 2000.

33. ibid., 17 June 2000; ASTI, Minutes of standing committee, 31 May, 1, 16 June 2000.

34. ASTI, Minutes of CEC, 20 May 2000.

35. *Irish Times,* 29 August 2000; *ASTIR,* September 2000; Lennon interview; O'Sullivan interview.
36. *Irish Times,* 13 December 2000.
37. *ASTIR,* April 1991; Ward interview; pers. comms with ASTI staff.
38. *ASTIR,* April 1991; Lennon interview.
39. *Irish Times,* 4 November 2000.
40. ibid., 6 September 2000; ASTI, Minutes of standing committee, 21-22 September 2000 Minutes of CEC special meetings, 9, 30 September 2000.
41. *Irish Times,* 24 October 2000.
42. ASTI, Minutes of standing committee, 29 September 2000.
43. ibid., 19–20 October 2000; *Irish Independent,* 15 December 2000.
44. ASTI, Minutes of CEC special meeting, 30 September 2000; Minutes of standing committee, 19–20 October 2000; Coppinger interview, 30 October 2008.
45. *Irish Times,* 28 November 2000.
46. ibid., 15 November 2000.
47. ibid., 17 November 2000.
48. ibid.
49. *Tuam Herald,* 18 November; *Meath Chronicle,* 18 November 2000; *Munster Express,* 17 November, 2000; *Anglo-Celt,* 16 November 2000.
50. ASTI, Minutes of Standing Committee, 8 December 2000.
51. *ASTIR,* January 2001
52. ibid.; ASTI, Minutes of Standing Committee, 20 December 2000.
53. *Irish Times,* 16 January 2001.
54. ibid.
55. ibid., 17, 18 January 2001; Sheila Parsons interview, 1 June 2009.
56. ASTI, Minutes of standing committee, 5–6, 18–19, 2 February 2001.
57. *Industrial Relations News,* 15 March 2001; *Irish Times,* 12 March 2001.
58. *Irish Times* 12 March 2001; ASTI, Minutes of CEC special meeting, 10 March 2001, Minutes of standing committee, 2 March 2001.
59. *Industrial Relations News,* 15 March 2001.
60. *Irish Times,* 13 March 2001.
61. Mulvey interview; White interview.
62. *Irish Times,* 13 March 2001.
63. *Irish Independent,* 12 March 2001.
64. *Irish Times,* 12 March 2001.
65. *Donegal News,* 23 March 2001; *Irish Independent,* 24 March 2001.
66. *Irish Times* 24 March 2001.

67. ibid., 27 March 2001; Coppinger interview.

68. ASTI, Minutes of standing committee, 27 March 2001; Coppinger interview.

69. *Irish Independent,* 20 April 2001.

70. ibid., 18, 19, 20 April 2001.

71. ASTI, Minutes of standing committee, 16 April 2001; *ASTIR* May 2001.

72. *ASTIR,* May 2001.

73. *Irish Times,* 1 May 2001.

74. See Allen, K., *The corporate takeover of Ireland,* Dublin, 2007, p. 57.

75. ASTI, SIPTU (ii) file; Bernadine O'Sullivan, however, maintains that her relationship with ASTI employees were generally good during her term of office.

76. *Industrial Relations News,* 26 April 2001.

77. O'Connor, *A labour history of Ireland,* pp. 156–58.

78. *Secondary Teacher* September 1969, pp.7–8.

79. ASTI, SIPTU (ii) file.

80. The Lennon family relationship was frequently mentioned in the press – see for example, *Irish Times,* 18 November 2000, 23 January 2001, 14 June 2003, and *Sunday Independent,* 21 January 2001.

81. ASTI, SIPTU (ii) file.

82. *ASTIR,* September 2001.

83. ibid., December 2001,

84. ASTI, Minutes of standing committee, 14–15 February 2002.

85. *Irish Times,* 5 March 2002.

86. ASTI, Minutes of standing committee, 14–15 February 2002; *Industrial Relations News,* 7 March 2002.

87. *Irish Times,* 2 April 2002.

88. *ASTIR,* April/May 2002.

89. ASTI, *Reports of annual convention,* 2002; *Industrial Relations News,* 11 April 2002.

90. *Industrial Relations News,* 16 May 2002.

91. *Irish Times,* 29 June 2002.

92. ASTI, Minutes of standing committee, 19–20 September 2002.

93. ibid.; *ASTIR* September, October 2002; *Industrial Relations News,* 10 October 2002.

94. *Industrial Relations News,* 24 October 2002

95. ASTI, Minutes of standing committee, 21–22 November, 12–13 December 2002.

96. *Industrial Relations News,* 30 January 2003.

97. *Industrial Relations News,* 20 February 2003.
98. ASTI, Minutes of CEC, 7 March 2003.
99. *Industrial Relations News,* 20 March 2003.
100. ibid., 10 April 2003.
101. ibid.; Lennon interview.
102. *Irish Times,* 20 April 2003; *Industrial Relations News,* 10 April 2003.
103. *Irish Times,* 20, 23 April 2003.
104. *Industrial Relations News,* 1 May 2003.
105. ASTI, Minutes of CEC, 25 April 2003; *Irish Times,* 26, 28 April 2003.
106. *Industrial Relations News,* 1 May 2003.
107. ASTI, Minutes of standing committee, 6 September, 21 October 2003; *Industrial Relations News,* 4, 11 September 2003.
108. *Industrial Relations News,* 30 October 2003.
109. ibid., 23 September 2004.
110. ibid., 30 October 2003.
111. ibid., 27 November 2003.
112. ibid., 27 November 2003, 7 October 2004; ASTI, Minutes of standing committee, 14–15 October 2004.
113. ASTI, Minutes of CEC, 17 April 2003.
114. *Irish Times,* 27 November 2003.
115. *Industrial Relations News,* 16 March 2006.
116. ASTI, Minutes of standing committee, 12–13 February 1993, *Convention handbook,* 1997–98, pp. 298-314; Lennon interview.
117. *Irish Times,* 28 March 2002.
118. Parsons interview.

Conclusion
1. Cited by M. Wheatley, *Nationalism and the Irish Party: provincial Ireland, 1910–1916,* Oxford 2005, p. 33.
2. *FIRE,* pp. 31–34. See Chapter 7 above.
3. Francis interview.
4. *Irish Times,* 14 April 2009.
5. White interview.
6. ibid.
7. ibid.

Bibliography

A. ARCHIVAL MATERIAL

I) ASTI ARCHIVES
i) *ASTI headquarters, Winetavern Street, Dublin*
Minutes of annual conventions and special conventions
Minutes of Central Executive Committee, 1920–22 and 1928–2007
Minutes of standing committee, 1922–60, 1965–2007
ii) *Irish Labour History Society Museum and Archive, Haddington Road, Dublin*
This very substantial deposit includes material from the early years of the Association, such as the Dublin membership and attendance register, 1912–16, minutes of meetings of the Dublin branch, 1923–65, and some of its successor branches. There are also minute books of the Kilmallock (Desmond) branch, 1948–62; and of the Carrickmacross branch 1964–71, as well as reports of dismissal cases, post-1935, documentation relating to school contracts and conciliation and arbitration, and files of press cuttings in respect of controversies and commemorations. There is material on virtually every aspect of ASTI activity from *c.*1969, including significant files relating to the disputes of 1969–71, to the Eileen Flynn case, to the 'Teachers' United' campaign, and to the pay campaign of 2000–02.

OTHER ARCHIVAL MATERIALS CONSULTED
i) *National Archive of Ireland*
Reports and correspondence in Department of An Taoiseach relating to relationships with ASTI, 1939–73
ii) *UCD Archives*
Mary MacSwiney papers, P48a/7: Correspondence between Sister M. Elizabetts, Ursuline Convent, Blackrock, Cork, and Cork branch of ASTI,

relating to Mary MacSwiney's loss of her teaching post at St Angela's.

iii) *Clare branch, ASTI*

Minute book, 1973–79

iv) *Dublin Diocesan Archives*

Archbishop Byrne papers: correspondence with J.C. McQuaid relating to Catholic Headmasters, Association, 1930s

v) *Tuam Diocesan Archive*

Archbishop Gilmartin papers: correspondence relating to dismissal/reinstatement of teacher, 1930s

vi) *St Jarlath's College, Tuam Archive*

Catholic Headmasters' Association, minutes and correspondence, 1964–71

B. INTERVIEWS WITH ASTI MEMBERS AND OFFICIALS

Lily Cronin, 11 April 2007

Paddy Daly, 11 April 2007

Catherine Fitzpatrick, 11 April 2007

Tommy Francis, 11 April 2007

Christina Heneghan, 11 April 2007

John Mulcahy, 11 April 2007

Tony McKernan, 11 April 2007

Louis O'Flaherty, 11 April 2007

Éamon Ó hAllmhuráin, 11 April 2007

P.J. Sheehy, 11 April 2007

Michael Corley, 19 May 2007

Pierce Purcell, 19 May 2007

Michael O'Meara, 26 May 2007

Kieran Mulvey, 10 September 2008

Michael Ward, 10 September 2008

John White, 10 September 2008

Ruth Coppinger, 30 October 2008

Michael Waddell, 2 December 2008

Charlie Lennon, 28 February 2009

Bernadine O'Sullivan, 28 February 2009

John White, 19 May 2009

Sheila Parsons, 1 June 2009

C. PUBLISHED MATERIAL

i) PERIODICALS – ASTI

Irish Journal of Education (in National Library of Ireland), 1910–17

'ASTI notes', *Irish School Weekly*, 1920–37

The School & College Yearbook, 1936–65. (Title varied in early issues, 1936–39).

The Secondary Teacher, 1966–91

ASTIR, 1970–2009

Nuacht, 1988–2007

Issues in Education, 1996–2001

II) SELECTED OTHER ASTI PUBLICATIONS

Programmes of annual conventions, 1923–2007

Security of tenure, 1909–34, 1934

Education: what future? ASTI action plan to defend and expand the education service, 1983

Wynne, R., *Second-level teachers' working hours*, 1992

Education – invest in our children's future: the ASTI response to the Education Green Paper, 1992, 1992

Education – invest in our children's future: supplementary response of ASTI to the Green Paper on Education, 1993

Guidelines on Sexual Harassment, 1992

School Discipline: advice for teachers and school authorities, 1995

Technology in the Junior Certificate, 1994

Model policy on promotion of gender equity in Schools, 1996

Response to the White Paper on Education: the White Paper, charting our education future, 1996

ASTI survey on the implementation of codes of discipline in schools, 1996.

Purcell, E., *A short history of Winetavern Street and its environs*, 1996.

Staffing, funding and facilities in Irish second level education: survey commissioned by ASTI, 1996

Equality and education: proceedings of the joint Equality Authority/ASTI conference for second level teachers, 2001, 2002

III) OFFICIAL PUBLICATIONS

Report, minutes of evidence, and appendices, Intermediate Education (Ireland) Commission, 1899, vol. xxiii

Report of Messrs F.H. Dale and T.A. Stephens on intermediate education in Ireland, 1905, vol. xxviii

Correspondence between the Chief Secretary for Ireland and the Catholic Headmasters' Association on the proposed grants of £40,000 for secondary teachers in Ireland, 1913, vol. I

Report of the Vice-Regal committee on the conditions of service and remuner-
ation on teachers in Intermediate schools, and on the distribution of grants
from public funds for Intermediate education in Ireland, 1919, vol. xxi

Dáil Éireann debates and Seanad Éireann debates, 1919–2002

Report of the Commission on Vocational Organisation, 1944

Teachers' Salaries Committee: reports and appendices, 1960

Department of Education, *Report of the Council of Education on the cur-*
riculum of the secondary school, 1960

Investment in Education: report of the survey team, 1965

Report of Tribunal on Teachers' Salaries, 1968

Commission on the Status of Women, *Report to Minister for Finance*, 1972

Department of Education, *White Paper on educational development*, 1980

Department of Education, *A plan for education, 1984–87*, 1984

Department of Education, *Education for a changing world*, 1992

Department of Education, *Charting our education future: White Paper on*
education, 1995

IV) NEWSPAPERS AND PERIODICALS – GENERAL

Extensive use was made of digitised newspapers, in particular the *Irish In-*
dependent, The Irish Times, and, for the earlier period, the *Freeman's Jour-*
nal. There was occasional reference to other publications, in particular to
those regional papers that are available digitally via the Irish Newspaper
Archive, and to INTO and TUI periodicals. *Industrial Relations News* was
consulted for the period 1997–2009.

V) BOOKS AND PAMPHLETS

Abrams, R.M., *America transformed: sixty years of revolutionary change,*
1941–2001, Cambridge: Cambridge University Press, 2008

Akenson, D.H., *A mirror to Kathleen's face: education in independent Ireland*,
Montreal and London: McGill-Queen's University Press, 1975

Allen, G., *The Garda Síochána: policing independent Ireland, 1922–82*,
Dublin: Gill & Macmillan, 1999

Allen, K., *The Celtic Tiger: the myth of social partnership in Ireland*, Manchester: Manchester University Press, 2000

Arnold, B., *The Irish Gulag: how the state betrayed its innocent children*,
Dublin: Gill & Macmillan, 2009.

Association of Intermediate and University Teachers, *Secondary education*
in Ireland: a plea for reform, Dublin: AIUT, 1904

Bacik, I., *Kicking and screaming: dragging Ireland into the 21st century*,

Dublin: O'Brien, 2004

Beale, J., *Women in Ireland: voices of change*, Dublin: Gill & Macmillan, 1986

Bew, P., *Ireland: the politics of enmity, 1798–2006*, Oxford: Oxford University Press, 2007

Bolt, C. *The women's movements in the United States and Britain from the 1790s to the 1920s*, London: Harvester Wheatsheaf, 1993

Breathnach, M., *Cuimhne an tseanpháiste*, Dublin: Oifig an tSotháthar, 1966

Bromell, T., *Rian mo chos ar ghaineamh an tsaoil*, Indreabhán: Cló Iar-Chonnachta, 2006

Brown, T., *Ireland: a social and cultural history, 1922–2002*, London: Harper Perennial, 2004 edn

Browne, P.J., *Unfulfilled promise: memories of Donogh O'Malley*, Dublin: Currach Press, 2008

Butler, R. (ed.), *St Flannan's College, 1881–1981*, Ennis: St Flannan's College, 1981

Campbell, F., *The Irish Establishment 1879–1914*, Oxford: Oxford University Press, 2009.

Chuinneagáin, S., *Catherine Mahon: first woman president of the INTO*, Dublin: INTO, 1998

Clear, C., *Nuns in nineteenth-century Ireland*, Dublin: Gill & Macmillan, 1997.

Clear, C., *Women of the house: women's household work in Ireland, 1922–1961*, Dublin: Irish Academic Press, 2000

Clear, C., *Social change and everyday life in Ireland, 1850–1922*, Manchester: Manchester University Press, 2007

Coleman, M., *IFUT, a history: the Irish Federation of University Teachers, 1963–1999*, Dublin: IFUT, 2000

Connolly, L., *The Irish women's movement: from revolution to devolution*, Dublin: Lilliput Press, 2003

Coolahan, J., *Irish education: history and structure*, Dublin: Institute of Public Administration, 1981.

Coolahan, J., *The ASTI and post-primary education, 1909–1984*, Dublin: ASTI, 1984

Cooney, J., *John Charles McQuaid: ruler of Catholic Ireland*, Dublin: O'Brien Press, 1999

Council of Teachers' Unions, *Equality conference, 9 May 1992*, Dublin: CTU, 1992

353

Cullen, M., *Girls don't do honours: Irish women in education in the nineteenth and twentieth centuries*, Dublin: Women's Education Bureau, 1987

Cullen Owens, R., *A social history of women in Ireland, 1870–1970*, Dublin: Gill & Macmillan, 2005

Cunningham. J., *Labour in the west of Ireland: working life and struggle, 1890-1914*, Belfast: Athol Books, 1995

Cunningham, J., *St Jarlath's College, Tuam: 1800–2000*, Tuam: SJC, 1999

Cunningham, J., '*A town tormented by the sea': Galway, 1790–1914*, Dublin: Geography Publications, 2004

Daly, M., *Women and work in Ireland*, Dundalk: Economic and Social History Society of Ireland, 1997

De Blaghd, E., *Gaeil á múscailt*, Dublin: Sáirséil agus Dill, 1973

Devine, F., Lane, F., and Puirséil, N. (eds) *Essays in Irish Labour history: a festschrift for Elizabeth and John W. Boyle*, Dublin 2008

Doyle, E., *Leading the way: managing voluntary secondary schools*, Dublin: Secretariat of Secondary Schools, 2000

Drudy, S., and Lynch, K., *Schools and society in Ireland*, Dublin: Gill & Macmillan, 1993

Duffy, P., *The lay teacher: a study of the position of the lay teacher in an Irish Catholic environment*, Dublin: Fallons, c.1966.

Dwyer, T.R., *Short fellow: a biography of Charles J. Haughey*, Dublin: Marino, 1999

Fallon, C.F., *Soul of fire: a biography of Mary MacSwiney*, Cork: Mercier Press, 1986

Farragher, S., *Pere Leman: educator and missionary, founder of Blackrock College*, Dublin: Paraclete Press, 1988

Farren, S., *The politics of Irish education, 1920–65*, Belfast: Institute of Irish Studies, 1995

Fitzgerald, G., *All in a life: an autobiography*, Dublin: Gill & Macmillan, 1991

Fitzpatrick, G., *St Andrew's College:* ardens sed virens, Dublin: St Andrew's College, 1994

Fleming, J., and O'Grady, S., *St Munchin's College Limerick, 1796–1996*, Limerick: The College, 1996

Fortin, P., *The Irish economic boom: facts, causes, and lessons*, Ottawa: Industry Canada Discussion Paper, no. 12, 2002

Foster, R.F., *Modern Ireland, 1600-1972*, London: Penguin, 1988

Foster, R.F., *Luck and the Irish: a brief history of change, 1970–2000*, London: Penguin, 2007

Fuller, L., *Irish Catholicism since 1950: the undoing of a culture*, Dublin: Gill & Macmillan, 2004

Garrett, P.M., *'Transforming' Children's Services? Social work, neoliberalism and the 'modern' world*, Maidenhead: Open University Press, 2009

Gaughan, J.A., *A political odyssey: Thomas O'Donnell, M.P. for West Kerry, 1900-1918*, Dublin 1983.

Gaughan, J.A., *Alfred O'Rahilly, vol. 3 controversialist: part 1, social reformer; part.2, controversialist*, Dublin: Kingdom Books, 1992

Greaves, C.D., *The Irish Transport and General Workers Union: the formative years*, Dublin: Gill & Macmillan, 1982

Gunnigle, P., McMahon, G., and Fitzgerald, G., *Industrial relations in Ireland: theory and practice*, Dublin: Gill & Macmillan, 1999 edn

Harvey, D., *A brief history of neoliberalism*, Oxford: Oxford University Press, 2005

Hastings, T., Sheehan, B., and Yeates, P., *Saving the future: how social partnership shaped Ireland's economic success*, Dublin: Blackhall Publishing, 2007

Hearn, M., *Below stairs: domestic service remembered in Dublin and beyond, 1880–1922*, Dublin: Lilliput Press, 1993

Horgan, J., *Seán Lemass: the enigmatic patriot*, Dublin: Gill & Macmillan, 1999

Hug, C., *The politics of sexual morality in Ireland*, Houndmills: Macmillan, 1999

Hussey, G., *At the cutting edge: cabinet diaries, 1982–1987*, Dublin: Gill & Macmillan, 1990

Inglis, T., *Moral monopoly: the Catholic church in modern Irish society*, Dublin: UCD Press, 1998 edn

Irish Congress of Trade Unions, *Fourth equality programme: delivering gender equality, 1999–2004*, Dublin: ICTU, 1999

Jones, M., *'These obstreperous lassies': a history of the Irish Women Workers Union*, Dublin: Gill & Macmillan, 1988

Jordan, A., *Margaret Byers: pioneer of women's education and founder of Victoria College, Belfast*, Belfast: Institute of Irish studies, 1987

Kavanagh, A.J., *Secondary education in Ireland: aspects of a changing paradigm*, Tullow: Patrician Brothers, 1993

Kelly, S.G., *Teaching in the city*, Dublin: Gill & Macmillan, 1970

Klein, N., *The shock doctrine: the rise of disaster capitalism*, London: Allen Lane, 2007

Keogh, D., *Twentieth-century Ireland: revolution and state building*, Dublin: Gill & Macmillan, 2005

Laffan, M., *The resurrection of Ireland: the Sinn Féin party, 1916–1923*, Cambridge: Cambridge University Press, 1999

Lane, F., and Ó Drisceoil, D. (eds), *Politics and the Irish working class, 1830–1945*, Houndmills: Palgrave Macmillan, 2005

Lee, J.J., *Ireland, 1912–1985: politics and society*, Cambridge: Cambridge University Press, 1989

Levenson, L., and Naterstad, J.H., *Hanna Sheehy-Skeffington: Irish feminist*, Syracuse: Syracuse University Press, 1986

Lloyd, D., *Ireland after history*, Cork: Cork University Press; Field Day, 1999

Logan, J. (ed.), *Teachers' Union: the TUI and its forerunners, 1899–1994*, Dublin: A. & A. Farmer, 1999

Longford, Earl of, and O'Neill, T.P., *Eamon de Valera*, Dublin 1970

Lynch, K., *The hidden curriculum: reproduction in education, an appraisal*, London: Falmer Press, 1989

Lynch, K., and Lodge, A., *Equality and power in schools: redistribution, recognition and representation*, London: Falmer Press, 2002

Lynn, L.E., *Public management: old and new*, New York: Routledge, 2006

McBride, A., *Gender democracy in trade unions*, Aldershot: Ashgate, 2001

McCarthy, C., *The decade of upheaval: Irish trade unions in the 1960s*, Dublin: Institute of Public Administration, 1973

McCartney, D., *UCD: a national idea: the history of University College, Dublin*, Dublin: Gill & Macmillan, 1999

McCormick, E., *The INTO and the 1946 Teachers' Strike*, Dublin: INTO, 1996

McCullagh, D., *A makeshift majority: the first inter-party government, 1948–51*, Dublin: Institute of Public Administration, 1998

MacDermott, E., *Clann na Poblachta*, Cork: Cork University Press, 1998

McElligott, T.J., *Secondary education in Ireland, 1870–1921*, Dublin: Irish Academic Press, 1981

MacRéamoinn, S., *Vatacáin II agus an réabhlóid chultúrtha*, Dublin: Preas Cholmcille, 1987

Manzer, R.A., *Teachers and politics: the role of the National Union of Teachers in the making of national education policy in England and Wales since 1944*, Manchester: Manchester University Press, 1970

Mapstone, R.H.., *The Ulster Teachers' Union: an historical perspective*, Coleraine: University of Ulster, 1986

Martin, F.X., *The scholar revolutionary: Eoin MacNeill, 1867–1945, and the making of the new Ireland*, Shannon: Irish University Press, 1973

Moody, T.W., *Queen's, Belfast: the history of a university*, London: Faber & Faber, 1959

Moroney, M., *National teachers' salaries and pensions, 1831–2000*, Dublin: Institute of Public Administration, 2007

Murphy, A.E., *The 'Celtic Tiger': an analysis of Ireland's economic growth performance*, Florence: European University Institute Working Paper, RSC no. 2000/16

Murphy, B.P., The Catholic Bulletin *and republican Ireland, 1898–1926, with special reference to J.J. O'Kelly*, Belfast: Athol Books, 2005

Murphy, J.A., *Ireland in the 20th century*, Dublin: Gill & Macmillan, 1989 edn

Murphy, J.A., *The College: a history of Queen's/University College Cork, 1845–1995*, Cork: Cork University Press, 1995

Murphy, J.H., Nos autem*: Castleknock College and its contribution*, Dublin: Gill & Macmillan, c.1996

Ní Chonghaile, Á., *F.H. O'Donnell: a shaol agus a shaothar*, Dublin: Coiscéim, 1992

Ní Mhurchú, M., and Breathnach, D., *1983–2002, Beathaisnéis*, Dublin: An Clóchomhar, 2003

Norstedt, J.A., *Thomas MacDonagh, a critical biography*, Charlottesville: University Press of Virginia, 1980

O'Brien, C.C., *States of Ireland*, London: Hutchinson, 1971

Ó Buachalla, S., *Education policy in twentieth-century Ireland*, Dublin: Wolfhound, 1988

O'Connell, T.J., *History of the Irish National Teachers' Organisation, 1868–1968*, Dublin: INTO, 1968

O'Connor, A.V., and Parkes, S.M., *Gladly learn and gladly teach: a history of Alexandra College and School 1866–1966*, Dublin: Blackwater Press, 1983

O'Connor, E., *Syndicalism in Ireland, 1917–23*, Cork: Cork University Press, 1988

O'Connor, E., *A labour history of Ireland, 1824-1960*, Dublin: Gill & Macmillan, 1992

O'Connor, J., *Hostage to fortune*, Dublin: M.F. Moynihan, 1951

O'Connor, S., *A troubled sky: reflections on the Irish educational scene, 1957–68*, Dublin: St Patrick's College, 1986

Ó Faoláin, S., *Vive Moi!: an autobiography*, London: R. Hart-Davis, 1965

O'Flaherty, L., *Management and control in Irish Education*, Dublin: Drumcondra Teachers' Centre, 1992

Ó Gráda, C., *A new economic history of Ireland, 1780–1939*, Oxford: Oxford University Press, 1994

Ó Gráda, C., *The rocky road: the Irish economy since the 1920s*, Manchester: Manchester University Press, 1997

O'Leary, D., *Vocationalism and social Catholicism in twentieth-century Ireland*, Dublin: Irish Academic Press, 2000

O'Mahony, P., and Delanty, G., *Rethinking Irish history: nationalism, identity, and ideology*, Houndmills: Macmillan, 1998

O'Riordan, M., *The voice of a thinking intelligent movement: James Larkin Junior and the ideological modernisation of Irish trade unionism*, Dublin: Irish Labour History Society, 2001

O'Sullivan, D.J., *The Irish constabularies, 1822-1922: a century of policing in Ireland*, Dingle: Brandon, 1999

Parks, E.W. and A.W., *Thomas MacDonagh: the man; the patriot; the writer*, Athens: University of Georgia Press, 1967

Pettit, P., *The gentle revolution: crisis in the universities*, Dublin: Scepter Books, 1969

Raftery, D., and Parkes, S.M., *Female education in Ireland, 1700–1900: Minerva or Madonna*, Dublin: Irish Academic Press, 2007

Raftery, M., and O'Sullivan, E., *Suffer the little children: the inside story of Ireland's industrial schools*, Dublin: New Island, 1999

Randles, Sister E., *Post-primary education in Ireland, 1957–1970*, Dublin: Veritas Publications, 1975

Regan, J.M., *The Irish counter-revolution, 1921–1936*, Dublin: Gill & Macmillan, 1999

Rudd, D., *Rochelle: the history of a school in Cork*, Cork: Rochelle, 1979

Share, P., Tovey, H., and Corcoran, M.P., *A sociology of Ireland*, Dublin: Gill & Macmillan, 2007 edn

Sisson, E., *Pearse's patriots: St Enda's and the cult of boyhood*, Cork: Cork University Press, 2004

Smith, R., *Garret the enigma: Dr Garret Fitzgerald*, Dublin: Aherlow, 1985

Sparsely Populated Areas Commission of the Church of Ireland, *Careers in Ireland*, Dublin: Church of Ireland, 1959

Sweeney, G., *In public service: a history of the Public Service Executive Union, 1890–1990*, Dublin: Institute of Public Administration, 1990

Sweeney, P., *The Celtic Tiger: Ireland's continuing economic miracle*, Dublin: Oak Tree, 1999 edn

Tierney, M., *Eoin MacNeill: scholar and man of action, 1867–1945*, Oxford: Oxford University Press, 1980

Titley, E.B., *Church, state, and the control of schooling in Ireland, 1900–1944*, Montreal: McGill-Queen's University Press, 1983

Tobin, F., *The best of decades: Ireland in the 1960s*, Dublin: Gill & Macmillan, 1984 edn

Waldron, K., *Out of the shadows: emerging secondary schools in the archdiocese of Tuam, 1940-69*, Tuam: Nordlaw Books, 2002.

Walsh, J., *The politics of expansion: the transformation of education in the Republic of Ireland, 1957-72*, Manchester: Manchester University Press, 2009

Ward, M., *Unmanageable revolutionaries: women and Irish nationalism*, Dingle: Brandon, 1983

Wheatley, M., *Nationalism and the Irish Party: provincial Ireland, 1910–1916*, Oxford: Oxford University Press, 2005

White, G.K., *A history of St Columba's College, 1843–1974*, Dublin: Old Columban Society, 1981

Whyte, J.H., *Church and state in modern Ireland, 1923–1979*, Dublin: Gill & Macmillan, 1984

Wigham, M.J., *Newtown School, Waterford, 1798–1998: a history*, Waterford: Newtown School, 1998

Working Party on the Future Involvement of Religious in Education, *FIRE Report*, Dublin, February 1973

Wynne, R., Clarkin, N., and Dolphin, C., *The experience of stress among Irish school teachers: a report on a survey of ASTI, TUI and INTO members: summary report*, Dublin: Council of Teachers' Unions, 1991

VI) ARTICLES

A graduate teacher, 'The position of secondary teachers', *Cork University Record*, no. 6, 1946

A graduate teacher, 'Secondary education in Ireland', *Cork University Record*, no. 8, 1946

A lay teacher, 'The stop-gap profession', *Cork University Record*, no. 15, 1949

Anon., 'An Iubhaile Órga', *School & Colleges Yearbook*, 1959

Anon., 'Thomas Joseph Burke' (obituary), *Blackrock Annual*, 1970

A.T. Kearney Inc., 'Measuring globalization: who's up; who's down?', *Foreign policy*, no. 134, January–February 2003

Barry, D., 'The involvement and impact of a professional interest group',

Mulcahy, D.G., and O'Sullivan, D. (eds), *Irish educational policy: process and substance*, Dublin: Institute of Public Administration, 1989

Bourdieu, P., 'Utopia of endless exploitation: the essence of neoliberalism', *Le Monde Diplomatique* (English edition), December 1998

Clegg, M.C., 'Trusteeship: a model in progress', in Prendergast, N., and Monahan, L. (eds), *Reimagining the Catholic school*, Dublin: Veritas, 2003

Clancy, M., 'Working lives, women's lives: some research sources and possibilities', *Saothar*, vol. 32, 2007

Clancy, P., 'Education in the Republic of Ireland: the project of modernity', in Clancy et al, *Irish society: sociological perspectives*, Dublin: Institute of Public Administration, 1995

Clear, C., '"The red ink of emotion": Maura Laverty, women's work and Irish society in the 1940s', *Saothar*, vol. 28, 2003

Coolahan, J., 'The ASTI and the secondary teachers' strike of 1920', *Saothar*, vol. 10, 1985

Cooney, J., 'The bishops ... and the Spanish dictator', *Irish Independent*, 21 March 2006

Cunningham, J., 'Politics and the Irish working class', *Saothar*, vol. 31, 2006.

Daly, M.E., 'Women in the Irish workforce from pre-industrial to modern times,' *Saothar* vol. 7, 1981

Darcy, F.A., 'Wages of labourers in the Dublin building industry, 1667–1918', *Saothar*, vol. 14, 1989

Darcy, F.A., 'Wages of skilled workers in the Dublin building industry, 1667–1918', *Saothar* vol. 15, 1990

D'Art, D., and Turner, T., 'Corporatism in Ireland: a comparative perspective', in D'Art D., and Turner, T., (eds), *Irish employment relations in the new economy*, Dublin: Blackhall, 2002

Devine, F., and O'Connor, E., 'Congress? Congress!,' *Saothar*, vol. 19, 1994

Fairbrother, P., and Stewart, P., 'The dilemmas of social partnership and union organisation: questions for British trade unions, in Fairbrother, P., and Yates, C.A.B. (eds), *Trade unions in renewal: a comparative study*, Abingdon: Continuum, 2003.

Farragher, S., 'Eamon de Valera and Blackrock, 1898–1921', Doherty, G., and Keogh, D., *De Valera's Irelands*, Cork: Mercier, 2003

Fitzgerald, G., 'The murder machine', *Secondary Teacher*, vol. 1, no. 4, April 1966

Fitzgerald, J., 'The way we are: education and the Celtic Tiger', *Issues in Education*, vol. 3, 1998

Fitzpatrick, D., 'Strikes in Ireland, 1914-21', *Saothar,* vol. 6, 1980

Foley, T., and Bateman, F., 'English, History, and Philosophy', in Foley, T., (ed), *From Queen's College to National University: essays on the academic history of QCG/UCG/NUI Galway*, Dublin: Four Courts, 1999

Foy, Rev. T., 'The stop-gap profession', *Cork University Record,* no. 19, 1949

Gardiner, F., 'Political interest and participation of Irish women, 1922-1992: the unfinished revolution', in Smyth, A., *Irish women's studies reader*, Dublin: Attic Press, 1993

Girvin, B., 'The state and vocational education, 1922–1960, Logan, J. (ed), *Teachers' Union: the TUI and its forerunners, 1899–1994*: Dublin: A. & A. Farmer, 1999

Holloway, P., and Cradden, T., ' The Irish Trade Union Congress and working women, 1894–1914', *Saothar,* vol. 23, 1998

Hyland, Á., 'The curriculum of vocational education, 1930–1966', in Logan, J. (ed.), *Teachers' Union: the TUI and its forerunners, 1899–1994*, Dublin: A. & A. Farmer, 1999

Jones, M., '"For the youth of the common people": the Vocational Education Officers' Association, 1930–1954', Logan, J. (ed.), *Teachers' Union: the TUI and its forerunners, 1899–1994*, Dublin: A. & A. Farmer, 1999

Kean, H., 'Teachers and the state, 1900–30', *British Journal of Sociology of Education*, vol. 10, no. 2, 1989

Keating, N., 'The changing role of the principal today', *Secondary Teacher*, vol. 17, no. 4, 1988

Kelleher, N., 'Presidential Address', *School & College Yearbook*, 1960

Kelly, A., 'White collar trade unionism', in Nevin, D. (ed.), *Trade unions and change in Irish society*, Cork: Mercier, 1980

Kerrigan, G., 'The moral civil war', *Magill*, September 1983

Kirkpatrick, W.G., 'An appreciation of the ex-general secretary', *School & College Yearbook*, 1959

Kostick, C., 'Labour militancy during the War of Independence', in Lane, F., and Ó Drisceoil, D., *Politics and the Irish working class, 1830–1945*, Houndmills: Palgrave Macmillan, 2005

Larkin, E. 'Church, state, and nation in modern Ireland', *American Historical Review*, vol. 80, no. 5, 1980

Logan, J., 'The making of a modern union: the Vocational Teachers' Association, 1954–1973', in Logan, J. (ed), *Teachers' Union: the TUI and its forerunners, 1899–1994*, Dublin: A. & A. Farmer, 1999

Luddy, M., 'Working women, trade unionism and politics in Ireland, 1830–1945', Lane, F., and Ó Drisceoil, D., *Politics and the Irish working class, 1830–1945*, Houndmills: Palgrave Macmillan, 2005

McCafferty, N., 'School days', *The best of Nell: a selection of writings over fourteen years*, Dublin: Attic Press, 1993 edn

McElduff, A., 'Participation of women in the teachers' unions', in Council of Teachers' Unions, *Equality conference, 9 May 1992*, Dublin: Council of Teachers' Unions, 1992

McKay, E., 'Changing with the tide: the Irish Labour Party, 1927–33, *Saothar,* vol. 11, 1986

McMullan, G., 'The Irish bank "strike"', 1920, *Saothar,* vol. 5, 1979

Mapstone, R.H., 'Trade union and government relations: a case study of influence on the Stormont government', *Saothar* vol. 12, 1987

Minogue, M., 'Changing the state: concepts and practice in the reform of the public sector', in Minogue et al, *Beyond new public management: changing ideas and practices in governanc*e, Cheltenham: Edward Elgar, 1998

Moriarty, T., 'Mary Galway', in Cullen, M., and Luddy, M. (eds), *Female activists: Irish women and change, 1900–1960*, Dublin: Woodfield Press, 2001

Mullarkey, M.J., 'Women in educational leadership: secular female principals in Irish post-primary schools', M.Ed thesis (minor), UCG 1994

Murphy, J.A., 'Association to trade union: the organising of secondary teachers', *Saothar,* vol. 11, 1986

Ó Conalláin, D., 'Education – free for all', *Secondary Teacher*, September 1966

O'Connor, E., 'Dawn chorus: the origins of trade unionism in vocational education', in Logan, J. (ed.), *Teachers' Union: the TUI and its forerunners, 1899–1994*, Dublin: A. & A. Farmer, 1999

Logan J., '"All the children": the vocational school and education reform, 1930–1990', in Logan, J. (ed.), *Teachers' Union: the TUI and its forerunners, 1899–1994*, Dublin: A. & A. Farmer, 1999

O'Connor, J., 'The teaching of Irish: testament of a pioneer', *Capuchin Annual*, 1949

O'Connor, J., 'Disillusioned', *School & College Yearbook*, 1954

O'Connor, J., '"Old, unhappy, far-off things": a personal reminiscence', *School & College Yearbook*, 1956

O'Connor, S., 'Post-primary education: now and in the future', *Studies*, Autumn 1968

O'Dea, T., 'The true, the good, and the beatnik', *School & College Yearbook*,

1960

O'Donnell, R., and O'Reardon, C., 'Ireland: recasting social partnership in a new context', in Pochet, P., (ed), *Wages policy in Europe*, Brussels: Peter Lang, 2002

Ó Drisceoil, D., '"Whose emergency is it?": wartime politics and the Irish working class, 1939–5', Lane and Ó Drisceoil (eds), *Politics and the Irish working class, 1830–1945*, Houndmills: Palgrave Macmillan, 2005

Ó hÓgartaigh, M., 'Female teachers and professional trade unionism in early 20th century Ireland', *Saothar*, vol. 29, 2004

Oldham, A., in Bourke, A., et al, *The Field Day Anthology of Irish Writing, vol. 5, Irish Women's Writing and Tradition*, Cork: Cork University Press, 2002

O'Leary, E., 'The Irish National Teachers' Organisation and the marriage ban for women teachers, 1933–1958, *Saothar*, vol. 12, 1987

Pearse, P., 'The murder machine', *Political writings and speeches*, Dublin: Phoenix, 1962

Puirséil, N., 'Labour and coalition: the impact of the first inter-party government, 1948–51, *Saothar*, vol. 27, 2002

Quinn, L., 'What business expects from the education system', *Issues in Education*, vol. 4, 1999

Roche, W.K., 'Industrial relations', Nevin, D., (ed.), *Trade union century*, Cork: Mercier, 1994

Roche, W.K., and Geary, J.F., '"Collaborative production" and the Irish boom: work organisation, partnership and direct involvement in Irish workplaces', in D'Art, D., and Turner, T., (eds), *Irish employment relations in the new economy*, Dublin: Blackhall, 2002

Roy, W., 'Membership participation in the National Union of Teachers', Kimber, R., and Richardson, J.J., (eds), *Pressure groups in Britain: a reader*, London: Dent, 1974

Ryder, K., 'Into the limelight for married secondary teachers through the gallantry of the ASTI', *Issues in Education*, vol. 5

Sheehy-Skeffington, H, 'Irish secondary teachers', *Irish Review*, October 1912

Swift, J., 'Report of Commission on Vocational Organisation and its times, 1930s–40s', *Saothar*, vol. 1, 1975.

Walshe, J., 'Smiling socialist who delivered if he said he would', *Irish Times*, 22 December 1990

Ward, E., '"Clergy, politicians, and mutual friends": the Vocational Committee, 1930–1992, Logan, J. (ed.), *Teachers' Union: the TUI and its forerunners, 1899–1994*, Dublin: A. & A. Farmer, 1999

West, E.G., 'The political economy of alienation: Karl Marx and Adam Smith', in Cunningham Wood, J., (ed.), *Karl Marx's economics: critical assessments*, vol.1, Beckenham: Croom Helm, 1988

White, J., 'Enhancing professionalism – the role of the Teaching Council, *Issues in Education*, vol. 5, 2000

vii) UNPUBLISHED ACADEMIC THESES

Kennedy, C.E., 'A comparison of the Irish and Japanese education systems with particular reference to grind schools and private fee-paying education in both countries', unpublished MEd. thesis (minor), NUI Galway, 1999

McCann, M.P., 'Teaching at second level: a case study of the role and job satisfaction of second level teachers in Galway city schools', unpublished MEd (minor) thesis, UCG, 1980

Mullarkey, M.J., 'Women in educational leadership: secular female principals in Irish post-primary schools', unpublished MEd. thesis (minor), UCG, 1994.

Murphy, S.E., 'The growth of influence of the teachers' unions on educational policy and practice in Ireland, 1968–82, unpublished MEd. (minor) thesis, UCC, 1983

Parsons, S., 'Engendering an agenda: a union's relation to feminist issues', unpublished MA thesis, DCU, 1994.

Purcell, P.H., 'Church influence on the working conditions of secondary teachers in Ireland, 1960–2000', unpublished MA thesis, UCD, 2001.

Riordan, P.J.N., 'The Association of Secondary Teachers, Ireland, 1909-1968: some aspects of its growth and development', unpublished MA thesis, UCC, 1975

Sexton, P.F., 'The lay teachers' struggle for status in Catholic secondary schools in Ireland between 1878 and 1937', unpublished MEd. thesis, University of Birmingham, 1972

Tubridy, R.,'The origins and development of the Registration Council for Secondary Teachers in Ireland, 1914–1960', unpublished MEd. thesis, UCD, 1984

Index